PEARSON CUSTOM LIBRARY

ENGLISH
MERCURY READER

Technical Writing
WR 227

Cover Art: "Gigantia Mountains & Sea of Cortes," by R.G.K. Photography, Copyright © Tony Stone Images; "Dime," courtesy of the Shaw Collection; "Open Book On Table Edge w/Pencil," courtesy of PhotoAlto Photography/Veer Incorporated; "Open Book On Table Near Table's Corner," courtesy of Fancy Photography/Veer Incorporated; "Scrabble Pieces and a Die," by G. Herbst, courtesy of PlainPicture Photography/Veer Incorporated; "Binary codes in bowls," by John Still, courtesy of Photographer's Choice/Getty Images; "Close-up of an open book," courtesy of Glowimages/Getty Images; "College Students Sitting At Tables," courtesy of Blend/PunchStock; "Red and blue circles," courtesy of Corbis Images; "Laptop screen showing photograph of landscape," courtesy of Martin Holtcamp/ Getty Images; "Apples flying," courtesy of Arne Morgenstern/Getty Images; "Light Globe Idea," courtesy of iStockphoto; "Sky is the Limit," courtesy of iStockphoto; "Riverdance," by Angela Sciaraffa; "Stone path leading through a garden" and "Book pages" courtesy of Getty Images, Inc; "Chicago" by Kristen Kiley. Additional images courtesy of Photodisc/Getty Images and Pearson Learning Solutions.

Please visit our website at *www.pearsonlearningsolutions.com.*

Attention bookstores: For permission to return any unsold stock, contact
us at *pe-uscustomreturns@pearson.com*.

Pearson Learning Solutions, 501 Boylston Street, Suite 900, Boston, MA 02116
A Pearson Education Company
www.pearsoned.com

Printed in the United States of America.

32 17

ISBN 10: 1-269-25868-0
ISBN 13: 978-1-269-25868-5

General Editors

Janice Neuleib
Illinois State University

Kathleen Shine Cain
Merrimack College

Stephen Ruffus
Salt Lake Community College

Table of Contents

Introduction to Technical Communication

Introduction to Technical Communication

SuperStock

"Writing is essential to my work. Everything we do at my company results in a written product of some kind—a formal technical report, a summary of key findings, recommendations and submissions to academic journals or professional associations. We also write proposals to help secure new contracts. Writing is the most important skill we seek in potential employees and nurture and reward in current employees. It is very hard to find people with strong writing skills, regardless of their academic background."

—Paul Harder, President, mid-sized consulting firm

LEARNING OBJECTIVES FOR THIS CHAPTER

- Define technical communication
- Understand that technical communication has a global reach
- Appreciate the role of technical communication in most careers
- Identify the main features and aims of technical communication
- Recognize a typical technical document
- Observe the challenges facing one communicator at work

WHAT IS TECHNICAL COMMUNICATION?

Technical communication is the exchange of information that helps people interact with technology and solve complex problems. Almost every day, we make decisions or take actions that depend on technical information. When we install any new device, from a microwave oven to a new printer, it's the setup information that we look for as soon as we open the box. Before we opt for the latest high-tech medical treatment, we learn all we can about its benefits and risks. From banking systems to online courses to business negotiations, countless aspects of daily life are affected by technology. To interact with technology in so many ways, we need information that is not only technically accurate but also easy to understand and use.

Technical communication helps us interact with technology in our daily lives

Chapter overview
(Go to *Student Resources>Chapter 1*)

Technical communication serves various needs in various settings. People may need to perform a task (say, assemble a new exercise machine), answer a question (say, about the safety of a flu shot), or make a decision (say, about suspending offshore oil drilling). In the workplace, we are not only consumers of technical communication, but producers as well. Any document or presentation we prepare (memo, letter, report, Web page, PowerPoint) must advance the goals of our readers, viewers, or listeners.

Technical communication helps us solve complex problems

Figure 1 shows a sampling of the kinds of technical communication you might encounter or prepare, either on the job or in the community.

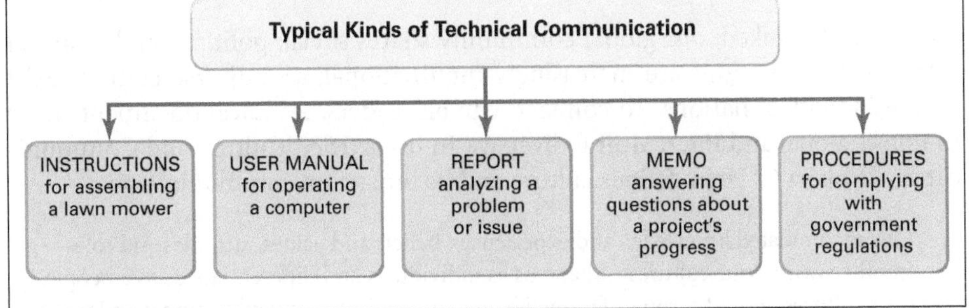

FIGURE 1 **Technical Communication Serves Various Needs**

TECHNICAL COMMUNICATION IS A DIGITAL *AND* A HUMAN ACTIVITY

In today's world of digital tools, we write and communicate more than ever: texting, emailing, using social networking sites, looking up research and news information on the Web, video conferencing with colleagues, and so forth. We do all this with such speed that we often forget to pay attention to basic professional standards for workplace communication.

Digital communication requires attention to style and tone

For instance, we sometimes use an informal, chatty tone—appropriate for friends but not for the office—when sending a workplace email. Or we might be in a hurry and fail to notice our use of humor, which may be welcomed in person but could be misunderstood in an email. An unclear or inaccurate email could easily cause a legal conflict or a safety error; a tone that seems inappropriate could result in wasted hours spent resolving the interpersonal situation instead of working on the project.

Digital technology is no substitute for human interaction

Despite the power of digital technology, only humans can give meaning to all the information that we convey and receive. Information technology is no substitute for human interaction. People make information meaningful by thinking critically and addressing questions that no computer can answer:

Questions that only a person can answer

- Which information is relevant to this situation?
- Can I verify the accuracy of this source?
- What does this information mean?
- What action does it suggest?
- How does this information affect me or my colleagues?
- With whom should I share it?
- How might others interpret this information?

With so much information available via the Web and other sources, no one can afford to "let the data speak for themselves."

TECHNICAL COMMUNICATION REACHES A GLOBAL AUDIENCE

Write to a diverse audience

Electronically linked, our global community shares social, political, and financial interests. Corporations are increasingly multinational, and diverse cultures exist within individual nations. To connect with all readers, technical documents need to reflect global and intercultural diversity. In his article, "Culture and Communication," Robert G. Hein defines culture and its impact on communication:

How cultures shape communication styles

> Our accumulated knowledge and experiences, beliefs and values, attitudes and roles—in other words, our cultures—shape us as individuals and differentiate us as a people. Our cultures, inbred through family life, religious training, and educational and work

> experiences . . . manifest themselves . . . in our thoughts and feelings, our actions and reactions, and our views of the world.
>
> Most important for communicators, our cultures manifest themselves in our information needs and our styles of communication . . . our expectations as to how information should be organized, what should be included in its content, and how it should be expressed. (125)

Cultures differ over which behaviors seem appropriate for social interaction, business relationships, contract negotiation, and communication practices. An effective communication style in one culture may be offensive elsewhere. For example, one survey of top international executives reveals the following attitudes toward U.S. communication style (Wandycz 22–23):

How various cultures view U.S. communication style

- Latin America: "Americans are too straightforward, too direct."
- Eastern Europe: "An imperial tone . . . It's always about how [Americans] know best."
- Southeast Asia: "To get my respect, American business [people] should know something about [our culture]. But they don't."
- Western Europe: "Americans miss the small points."
- Central Europe: "Americans tend to oversell themselves."

In addition to being broadly accessible, any document prepared for a global audience must reflect sensitivity to cultural differences.

TECHNICAL COMMUNICATION IS PART OF MOST CAREERS

Whatever your job description, expect to be evaluated, at least in part, on your communication skills. At one IBM subsidiary, for example, 25 percent of an employee's evaluation is based on how effectively that person shares information (Davenport 99). Even if you don't anticipate a "writing" career, expect to be a part-time technical communicator, who will routinely face situations such as these:

Most professionals serve as part-time technical communicators

- As a medical professional, psychologist, social worker, or accountant, you will keep precise records that are, increasingly, a basis for legal action.
- As a scientist, you will report on your research and explain its significance.
- As a manager, you will write memos, personnel evaluations, inspection reports, and give oral presentations.
- As a lab or service technician, you will keep daily activity records and help train coworkers in installing, using, or servicing equipment.
- As an attorney, you will research and interpret the law for clients.

- As an engineer or architect, you will collaborate with colleagues as well as experts in related fields before presenting a proposal to your client. (For example, an architect's plans are reviewed by a structural engineer who certifies that the design is sound.)
- As an employee or intern in the nonprofit sector (an environmental group or a government agency), you will research important topics and write brochures, press releases, or handbooks for clients.

The more you advance in your field, the more you will need to share information and establish contacts. Managers and executives spend much of their time negotiating, setting policies, and promoting their ideas—often among diverse cultures around the globe.

In addition, most people can expect to work for multiple different employers throughout their career. Each employer will have questions such as the following:

Employers seek portable skills

- Can you write and speak effectively?
- Can you research information, verify its accuracy, figure out what it means, and shape it for the reader's specific purposes?
- Can you work on a team, with people from diverse backgrounds?
- Can you get along with, listen to, and motivate others?
- Are you flexible enough to adapt to rapid changes in business conditions and technology?
- Can you market yourself and your ideas persuasively?
- Are you ready to pursue lifelong learning and constant improvement?

These are among the portable skills employers seek in today's college graduates—skills all related to communication.

TECHNICAL COMMUNICATORS PLAY MANY ROLES

What technical communicators do

Full-time technical communicators serve many roles. Trade and professional organizations employ technical communicators to produce newsletters, pamphlets, journals, and public relations material. Many work in business and industry, preparing instructional material, reports, proposals, and scripts for industrial films. They also prepare sales literature, publicity releases, handbooks, catalogs, brochures, Web pages, intranet content, articles, speeches, and oral and multimedia presentations.

Related career paths

Technical communicators also do other work. For example, they edit reports for punctuation, grammar, style, and logical organization. They may also oversee publishing projects, coordinating the efforts of writers, visual artists, graphic designers, content experts, and lawyers to produce a complex manual or proposal. Given their broad range of skills, technical communicators often enter related fields such as publishing, magazine editing, Web site management, television, and college teaching.

MAIN FEATURES OF TECHNICAL COMMUNICATION

Almost any form of technical communication displays certain shared features: The communication is reader-centered, accessible, and efficient, often produced by teams, and delivered in both paper and digital versions.

Reader-Centered

Focus on the reader, not the writer

Unlike poetry, fiction, or college essays, a technical document rarely focuses on the writer's personal thoughts and feelings. This doesn't mean that your document should have no personality (or voice), but it does mean that the needs of your readers come first.

What readers expect

Workplace readers typically are interested in "who you are" only to the extent that they want to know what you have done, what you recommend, or how you speak for your company. Reader-centered documents focus on what people need to learn, do, or decide.

Accessible and Efficient

Make documents easy to navigate and understand

Readers expect to find the information they need and to get questions answered clearly. For instance, the document shown in Figure 2 is written and designed so that a nontechnical audience can find and follow the information. Instead of long technical passages, the content is presented in short chunks, in the form of questions that readers might ask.

An accessible and efficient technical document includes elements such as those displayed in Figure 2 and listed below.

Elements that make an accessible and efficient document

- **worthwhile content**—includes all (and only) the information readers need
- **sensible organization**—guides the reader and emphasizes important material
- **readable style**—promotes fluid reading and accurate understanding
- **effective visuals**—clarify concepts and relationships, and substitute for words whenever possible
- **effective page design**—provides heads, lists, type styles, white space, and other aids to navigation
- **supplements (abstract, appendix, glossary, linked pages, and so on)**—allow readers to focus on the specific parts of a long document that are relevant to their purpose

Recognize your legal accountability

Accessible, efficient communication is no mere abstract notion: In the event of a lawsuit, faulty writing is treated like any other faulty product. If your inaccurate, unclear, or incomplete information leads to injury, damage, or loss, you and your company or organization can be held responsible.

NOTE *Make sure your message is clear and straightforward—but do not oversimplify. Information designer Nathan Shedroff reminds us that, while clarity makes information easier to understand, simplicity is "often responsible for the 'dumbing down' of information rather than the illumination of it" (280). The "sound bytes" that often masquerade as network news reports serve as a good case in point.*

Often Produced by Teams

Prepare for teamwork

Technical documents are often complex. Instead of being produced by a lone writer, complex documents usually are created by teams composed of writers, Web designers, engineers or scientists, managers, legal experts, and other professionals. The teams might be situated at one site or location or distributed across different job sites, time zones, and countries.

Delivered in Paper and Digital Versions

Select the appropriate medium or combination of media

Technical documents can be delivered in a variety of media such as print (hard copy), CDs, Web pages, PDF documents, ebooks, podcasts, and online videos. In fact, distinctions between print and digital communication are becoming blurred. Figure 2 is a good example: The document is in PDF format and can be read on the Web, downloaded to your own computer for future reading, or printed on paper. Technical communicators must write well but must also be able to think about page design and media choices.

NOTE *In many cases, print documents are still the basis for much of a company's communication. Despite continued advances in electronic communication, paper is not going away.*

PURPOSES OF TECHNICAL COMMUNICATION

What purpose or combination of purposes will your document serve?

Most forms of technical communication address one of three primary purposes: (1) to anticipate and answer questions (inform your readers); (2) to enable people to perform a task or follow a procedure (instruct your readers); or (3) to influence people's thinking (persuade your readers). Often, as in Figure 2, these purposes will overlap.

Documents That Inform

Anticipate and answer your readers' questions

Informational documents are designed to inform—to provide information that answers readers' questions clearly and efficiently. Figure 2 is primarily informational. It is designed for a wide audience of readers who may know little about the topic.

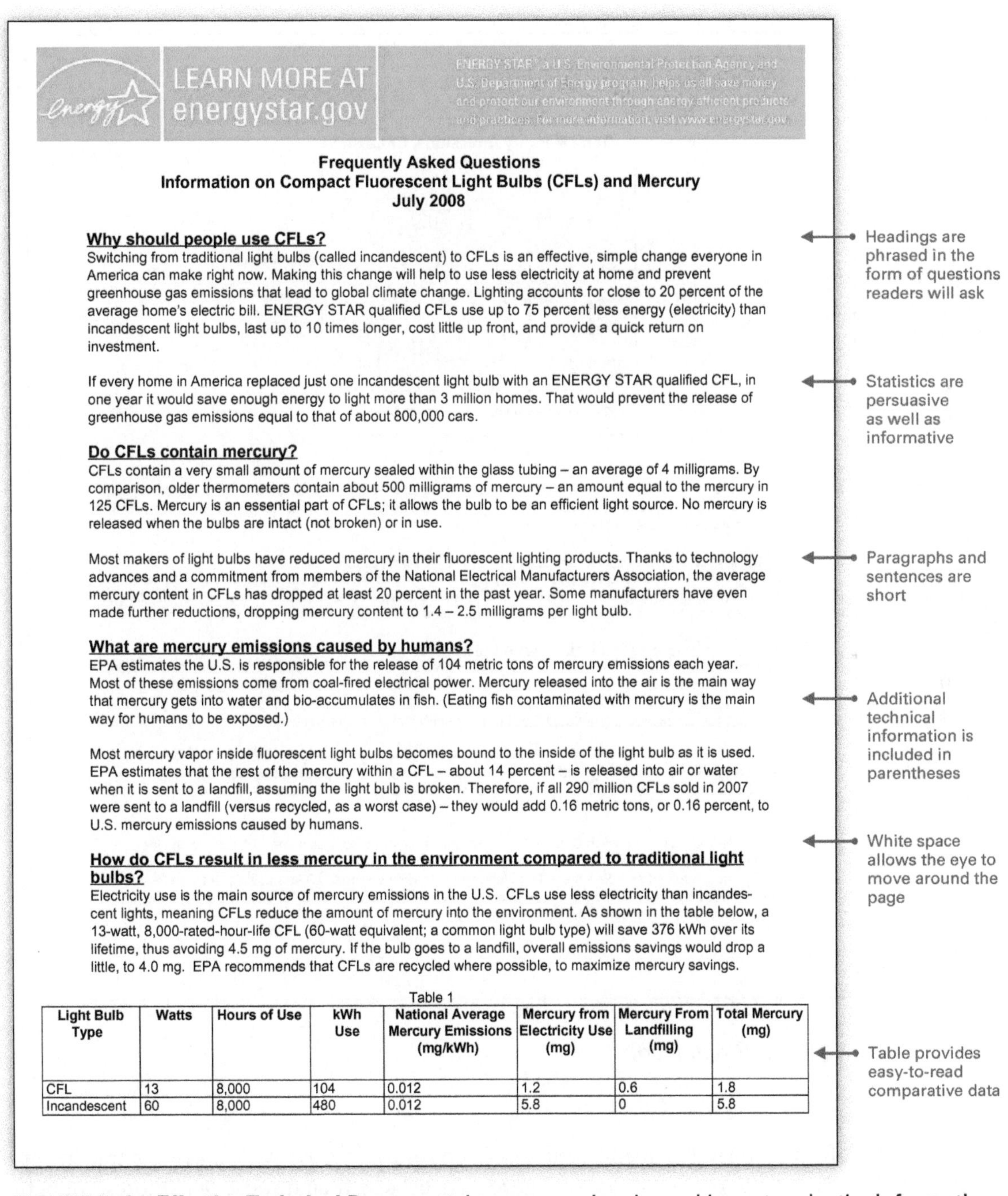

LEARN MORE AT energystar.gov

ENERGY STAR® a U.S. Environmental Protection Agency and U.S. Department of Energy program, helps us all save money and protect our environment through energy efficient products and practices. For more information, visit www.energystar.gov

Frequently Asked Questions
Information on Compact Fluorescent Light Bulbs (CFLs) and Mercury
July 2008

Why should people use CFLs?
Switching from traditional light bulbs (called incandescent) to CFLs is an effective, simple change everyone in America can make right now. Making this change will help to use less electricity at home and prevent greenhouse gas emissions that lead to global climate change. Lighting accounts for close to 20 percent of the average home's electric bill. ENERGY STAR qualified CFLs use up to 75 percent less energy (electricity) than incandescent light bulbs, last up to 10 times longer, cost little up front, and provide a quick return on investment.

If every home in America replaced just one incandescent light bulb with an ENERGY STAR qualified CFL, in one year it would save enough energy to light more than 3 million homes. That would prevent the release of greenhouse gas emissions equal to that of about 800,000 cars.

Do CFLs contain mercury?
CFLs contain a very small amount of mercury sealed within the glass tubing – an average of 4 milligrams. By comparison, older thermometers contain about 500 milligrams of mercury – an amount equal to the mercury in 125 CFLs. Mercury is an essential part of CFLs; it allows the bulb to be an efficient light source. No mercury is released when the bulbs are intact (not broken) or in use.

Most makers of light bulbs have reduced mercury in their fluorescent lighting products. Thanks to technology advances and a commitment from members of the National Electrical Manufacturers Association, the average mercury content in CFLs has dropped at least 20 percent in the past year. Some manufacturers have even made further reductions, dropping mercury content to 1.4 – 2.5 milligrams per light bulb.

What are mercury emissions caused by humans?
EPA estimates the U.S. is responsible for the release of 104 metric tons of mercury emissions each year. Most of these emissions come from coal-fired electrical power. Mercury released into the air is the main way that mercury gets into water and bio-accumulates in fish. (Eating fish contaminated with mercury is the main way for humans to be exposed.)

Most mercury vapor inside fluorescent light bulbs becomes bound to the inside of the light bulb as it is used. EPA estimates that the rest of the mercury within a CFL – about 14 percent – is released into air or water when it is sent to a landfill, assuming the light bulb is broken. Therefore, if all 290 million CFLs sold in 2007 were sent to a landfill (versus recycled, as a worst case) – they would add 0.16 metric tons, or 0.16 percent, to U.S. mercury emissions caused by humans.

How do CFLs result in less mercury in the environment compared to traditional light bulbs?
Electricity use is the main source of mercury emissions in the U.S. CFLs use less electricity than incandescent lights, meaning CFLs reduce the amount of mercury into the environment. As shown in the table below, a 13-watt, 8,000-rated-hour-life CFL (60-watt equivalent; a common light bulb type) will save 376 kWh over its lifetime, thus avoiding 4.5 mg of mercury. If the bulb goes to a landfill, overall emissions savings would drop a little, to 4.0 mg. EPA recommends that CFLs are recycled where possible, to maximize mercury savings.

Table 1

Light Bulb Type	Watts	Hours of Use	kWh Use	National Average Mercury Emissions (mg/kWh)	Mercury from Electricity Use (mg)	Mercury From Landfilling (mg)	Total Mercury (mg)
CFL	13	8,000	104	0.012	1.2	0.6	1.8
Incandescent	60	8,000	480	0.012	5.8	0	5.8

FIGURE 2 **An Effective Technical Document** Language, visuals, and layout make the information easy for everyday readers to understand.

Source: U.S. Environmental Protection Agency <www.energystar.gov/ia/partners/promotions/change_light/downloads/Fact_Sheet_Mercury.pdf> Energy Star, a joint program of the U.S. Environmental Protection Agency and the U.S. Department of Energy.

Bar graph provides an informative and persuasive function

Instructions are easy to follow

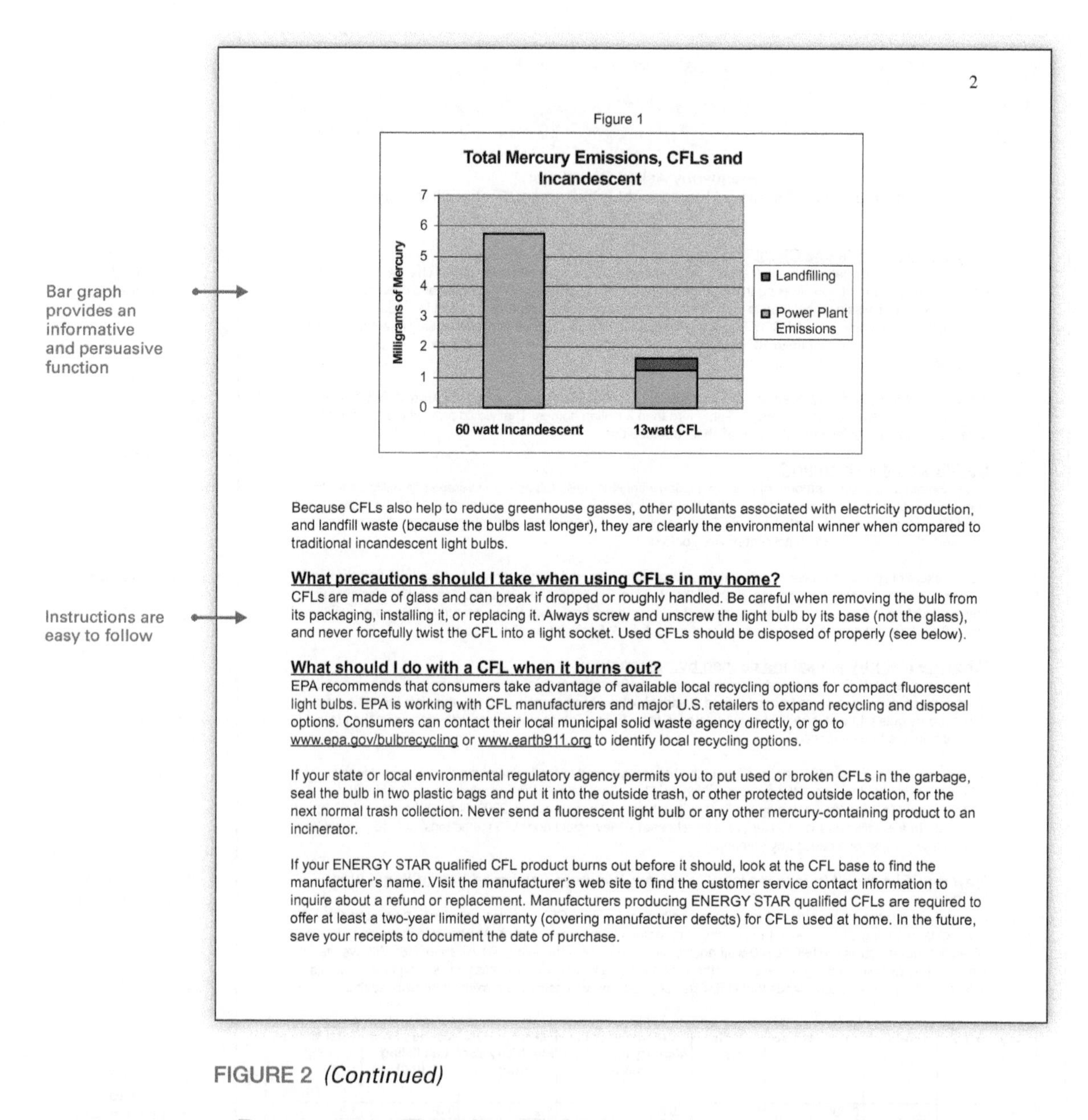

FIGURE 2 *(Continued)*

Documents That Instruct

Enable your readers to perform certain tasks

Instructional documents help people do something: assemble a new computer, perform CPR, or, in the case of Figure 2, install and then dispose of a fluorescent light bulb safely. On page 2 of that document the steps are grouped under specific headings and written using action verbs ("unscrew the light bulb by its base"; "seal the bulb in two plastic bags"). Cautions about what *not* to do appear as needed ("Never send a fluorescent light bulb . . . to an incinerator.").

Documents That Persuade

Persuasion encourages people to take a desired action. While some documents (such as a sales letter) are explicitly persuasive, even the most technical of documents can have an implicitly persuasive purpose. The bar graph in Figure 2, for example, encourages readers to use compact fluorescent bulbs by showing their low amount of mercury emissions relative to traditional light bulbs.

Motivate your readers

PREPARING EFFECTIVE TECHNICAL DOCUMENTS

Whether you are a full-time communication professional or an engineer, nurse, scientist, technician, legal expert, or anyone whose job requires writing and communicating, the main question you face is this: "How do I prepare the right document for this group of readers and this particular situation?"

A main question you must answer

Regardless of the type, producing an effective document typically requires that you complete the four basic tasks depicted in Figure 3 and described below.

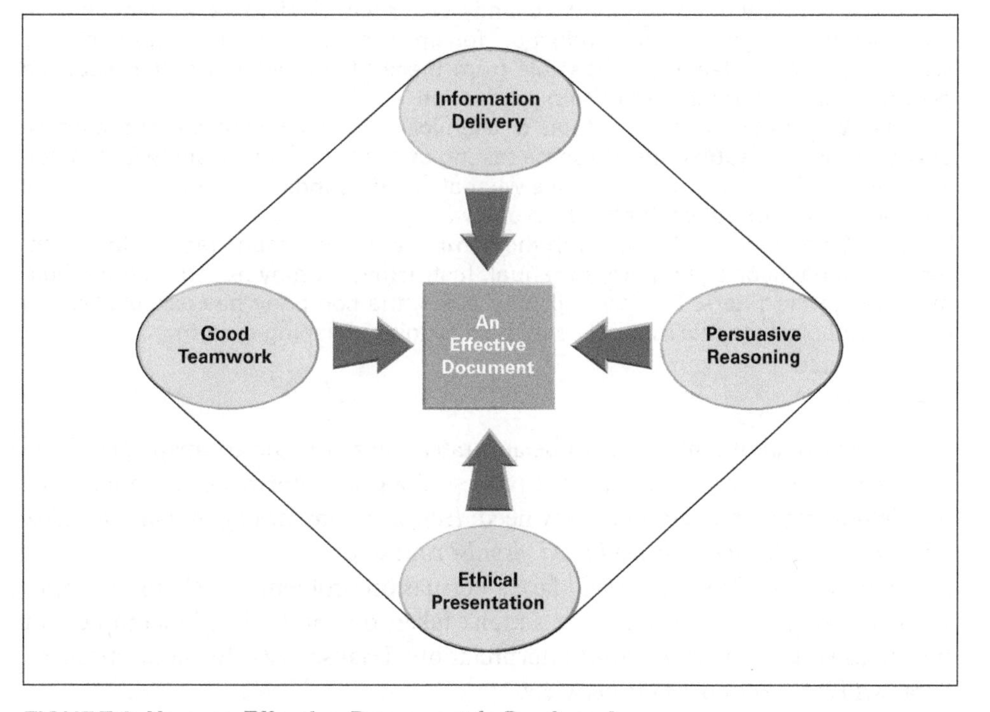

FIGURE 3 **How an Effective Document Is Produced**

A workplace communicator's four basic tasks

- **Deliver information readers can use**—because different people in different situations have different information needs.
- **Use persuasive reasoning**—because people often disagree about what the information means and what action should be taken.
- **Weigh the ethical issues**—because unethical communication lacks credibility and could alienate readers.
- **Practice good teamwork**—because working in teams is how roughly 90 percent of U.S. workers spend some part of their day ("People" 57).

The short cases that follow illustrate how a typical professional confronts these tasks in her own day-to-day communication on the job.

CASE Providing Information Readers Can Use

"Can I provide exactly what readers need?"

Sarah Burnes was hired two months ago as a chemical engineer for Millisun, a leading maker of cameras, multipurpose film, and photographic equipment. Sarah's first major assignment is to evaluate the plant's incoming and outgoing water. (Waterborne contaminants can taint film during production, and the production process itself can pollute outgoing water.) Management wants an answer to this question: How often should we change water filters? The filters are expensive and hard to change, halting production for up to a day at a time. The company wants as much "mileage" as possible from these filters, without either incurring government fines or tainting its film production.

Sarah will study endless printouts of chemical analysis, review current research and government regulations, do some testing of her own, and consult with her colleagues. When she finally determines what all the data indicate, Sarah will prepare a recommendation report for her bosses.

Later, Sarah will collaborate with the company training manager and the maintenance supervisor to prepare a manual, instructing employees on how to check and change the filters. To cut publishing costs, the company has asked Sarah to design and produce this manual using its desktop publishing system.

Sarah's report, above all, needs to be accurate; otherwise, the company gets fined or lowers production. Once she has processed all the information, she faces the problem of giving readers what they need: *How much explaining should I do? How will I organize the manual? Do I need visuals?* And so on.

In other situations, Sarah will face a persuasion problem as well, for example, when decisions must be made or actions taken on the basis of incomplete or inconclusive facts or conflicting interpretations (Hauser 72). In these instances, Sarah will seek consensus for *her* view.

CASE Being Persuasive

"Can I influence people to see things my way?"

Millisun and other electronics producers are located on the shores of a small harbor, the port for a major fishing fleet. For twenty years, these companies have discharged effluents containing metal compounds, PCBs, and other toxins directly into the harbor. Sarah is on a multicompany team, assigned to work with the Environmental Protection Agency to clean up the harbor. Much of the team's collaboration occurs via email.

Enraged local citizens are demanding immediate action, and the companies themselves are anxious to end this public relations nightmare. But the team's analysis reveals that any type of cleanup would stir up harbor sediment, possibly dispersing the solution into surrounding waters and the atmosphere. (Many of the contaminants can be airborne.) Premature action might actually increase danger, but team members disagree on the degree of risk and on how to proceed.

Sarah's communication here takes on a persuasive dimension: She and her team members first have to resolve their own disagreements and produce an environmental impact report that reflects the team's consensus. If the report recommends further study, Sarah will have to justify the delays to her bosses and the public relations office. She will have to make other people understand the dangers as well as she does.

In the preceding case, the facts are neither complete nor conclusive, and views differ about what these facts mean. Sarah will have to balance the various political pressures and make a case for her interpretation. Also, as company spokesperson, Sarah will be expected to protect her company's interests. Some elements of Sarah's persuasion problem: *Are other interpretations possible? Is there a better way? Can I expect political or legal fallout?*

CASE Considering the Ethical Issues

"Can I be honest and still keep my job?"

To ensure compliance with OSHA[1] standards for worker safety, Sarah is assigned to test the air purification system in Millisun's chemical division. After finding the filters hopelessly clogged, she decides to test the air quality and discovers dangerous levels of benzene (a potent carcinogen). She reports these findings in a memo to the production manager, with an urgent recommendation that all employees be tested for benzene poisoning. The manager phones and tells Sarah to "have the filters replaced," but says nothing at all about her recommendation to test for benzene poisoning. Now Sarah has to decide what to do about this lack of response: Assume the test is being handled, and bury the memo in some file cabinet? Raise the issue again, and risk alienating her boss? Send copies of her original memo to someone else who might take action?

[1] Occupational Safety and Health Administration.

As the preceding case illustrates, Sarah also will have to reckon with the ethical implications of her writing, with the question of "doing the right thing." For instance, Sarah might feel pressured to overlook, sugarcoat, or suppress facts that would be costly or embarrassing to her company.

Situations that compromise truth and fairness present the hardest choices of all: remain silent and look the other way, or speak out and risk being fired. Some elements of Sarah's ethics problem: *Is this fair? Who might benefit or suffer? What other consequences could this have?*

In addition to solving these various problems, Sarah has to work in a team setting: Much of her writing will be produced in collaboration with others (editors, managers, graphic artists), and her audience will extend beyond readers from her own culture.

CASE Working on a Team and Thinking Globally

"Can I connect with all these different colleagues?"

Recent mergers have transformed Millisun into a multinational corporation with branches in eleven countries, all connected by an intranet. Sarah can expect to collaborate with coworkers from diverse cultures on research and development and with government agencies of the host countries on safety issues, patents and licensing rights, product liability laws, and environmental concerns. Also, she can expect to confront the challenges of addressing the unique needs and expectations of people from various cultures across the globe. She will need to be careful about how she writes her daily email status reports, for example, so that these reports convey respect for cultural differences.

In order to standardize the sensitive management of the toxic, volatile, and even explosive chemicals used in film production, Millisun is developing automated procedures for quality control, troubleshooting, and emergency response to chemical leakage. Sarah has been assigned to a team that is preparing computer-based training packages and instructional videos for all personnel involved in Millisun's chemical management worldwide.

As a further complication, Sarah will have to develop working relationships with people she has never met face-to-face, people from other cultures, and people she knows only via an electronic medium.

Chapter quiz, Exercises, Web links, and Flashcards (Go to *Student Resources>Chapter 1)*

For Sarah Burnes, or any of us, writing is a process of discovering what we want to say, "a way to end up thinking something [we] couldn't have started out thinking" (Elbow 15). Throughout this process in the workplace, we rarely work alone but instead collaborate with others for information, help in writing, and feedback.

Projects

GENERAL

1. Write a memo to your boss, justifying reimbursement for this course. Explain how the course will help you become more effective on the job.
2. Locate a Web site for an organization that hires graduates in your major. In addition to technical knowledge, what writing and communication skills does this organization seek in job candidates? Discuss your findings in class and write a short memo to other students, explaining what communication skills they require in order to find a job in this or a similar organization.

TEAM

Introducing a Classmate

Class members will work together often this semester. To help everyone become acquainted, your task is to introduce to the class the person seated next to you. (That person, in turn, will introduce you.) Follow this procedure:

a. Exchange with your neighbor whatever personal information you think the class needs: background, major, career plans, communication needs of your intended profession, and so on. Each person gets five minutes to tell her or his story.

b. Take careful notes; ask questions if you need to.

c. Take your notes home and select only the information you think the class will find useful.

d. Prepare a one-page memo telling your classmates who this person is.

e. Ask your neighbor to review the memo for accuracy; revise as needed.

f. Present the class with a two-minute oral paraphrase of your memo, and submit a copy of the memo to your instructor.

DIGITAL

With a team of 2–3 other students, visit a government Web site, such as the Food and Drug Administration <www.fda.gov>, the Centers for Disease Control <www. cdc.gov>, the U.S. Department of Agriculture <www. usda.gov>, or the Environmental Protection Agency <www.epa.gov>. Locate documents that are similar in purpose to Figure 1 in this chapter. Analyze these documents, noting whether they are available in PDF and whether they conform to one of the three purposes (informative, instructional, persuasive) described in this chapter or whether they are a blend of these purposes. Note how long it took your team to find information on these individual Web sites: Are some easier to use than others? What questions did different team members have about the content and type of documents that you located?

GLOBAL

Look back at the Sarah Burnes case in this chapter. Assume that you are about to join a team at work, a team that has members from Ireland, India, China, and the United States. Use the Internet to learn what you can about patterns of communication; issues to look for include politeness, turn-taking, use of first names or titles, and gender roles. Describe your findings in a short memo to your instructor.

For more support in mastering the objectives of this chapter, go to **www.mytechcommlab.com**

Designing Pages and Documents

Designing Pages and Documents

"Sometimes, even if a book I'm working on only needs a light revision, I end up designing the document, too. I have a coworker who designs documents professionally though, so if I need something fancy, he designs it and I follow the specs. If an email is long and complex, sometimes I try to impose some structure to it. If you are giving someone a written correspondence more than a page long, you probably should be worrying about the design of it. If you don't make things easy to follow, sometimes people panic and won't read what you've written."

—Lorraine Patsco, Director of Prepress and Multimedia Production

LEARNING OBJECTIVES FOR THIS CHAPTER

- Understand why document design is important
- Learn design skills that are needed in today's workplace
- Know how to use white space and margins
- Know how to choose typefaces and type sizes
- Know how to use color, shading, and other highlighting elements
- Know how to use headings, subheads, and running heads
- Understand that on-screen documents have special design requirements

Page design, the layout of words and graphics, determines the look of a document. Well-designed pages invite readers into the document, guide them through the material, and help them understand and remember the information.

Chapter overview
(Go to *Student Resources>Chapter 13*)

In this electronic age the term "page" takes on broad meanings: On the computer screen, a page can scroll on endlessly. Also, *page* might mean a page of a report, but it can also mean one panel of a brochure or part of a reference card for installing printer software. The following discussion focuses mainly on traditional paper (printed) pages. See Designing Digital Documents later in this chapter for a discussion of pages in electronic documents.

PEARSON mtcl

Document design/ visuals tutorial
(Go to *Document Design and Graphics>Tutorial*)

PAGE DESIGN IN WORKPLACE DOCUMENTS

Technical documents rarely get undivided attention

People read work-related documents only because they have to. If there are easier ways of getting the information, people will use them. In fact, busy readers often only skim a document, or they refer to certain sections during a meeting or presentation. Amid frequent distractions, readers want to be able to leave the document and then return and locate what they need easily.

> **NOTE** *Although many documents are available in both print and digital forms, the "paperless office" is largely a myth. People often prefer to read print copies of reports, proposals, and other longer documents. In some ways, information technology has produced more paper than ever.*

Readers are attracted by documents that appear inviting and accessible

In an age where visual information—on computer screens, televisions, and cell phones—surrounds us, a printed document competes for audience attention with these highly visual forms. Therefore, print documents need a clean, clear, attractive page design. Before actually reading a document, people usually scan it for a sense of what it's about and how it's organized. An audience's first impression tends to involve a purely visual, aesthetic judgment: "Does this look like something I want to read, or like too much work?" Instead of an unbroken sequence of paragraphs, users look for charts, diagrams, lists, various type sizes and fonts, different levels of headings, and other aids to navigation. Having decided at a glance whether your document is visually appealing, logically organized, and easy to navigate, readers will draw conclusions about the value of your information, the quality of your work, and your overall credibility.

HOW PAGE DESIGN TRANSFORMS A DOCUMENT

To appreciate the impact of page design, consider Figures 1 and 2: Notice how the information in Figure 1 resists interpretation. Without design cues, we have no way of chunking that information into organized units of meaning. Figure 2 shows the same information after a design overhaul.

DESIGN SKILLS NEEDED IN TODAY'S WORKPLACE

As the number of page layout and design programs increases, you will likely be asked to prepare actual publications as part of your job—often without the help of clerical staff, print shops, and graphic artists. In such cases, you will need to master a variety of technologies and to observe specific guidelines.

Desktop Publishing

Desktop publishing helps you produce professional looking pages

Desktop publishing (DTP) systems such as *Adobe InDesign*, *Adobe Framemaker*, or *Quark* combine word processing, typesetting, and graphics. Using this software along with scanners and laser printers, one person, or a group working collaboratively, controls the entire production cycle: designing, illustrating, laying out, and printing the final document. Documents or parts of documents used repeatedly (*boilerplate*) can be retrieved when needed, or modified or inserted in some other document. With *groupware* (group authoring systems), writers from different locations can produce and distribute drafts online, incorporate reviewers' comments into their drafts, and publish documents collaboratively.

Electronic Publishing

Electronic publishing works well for large, complex documents

Your work may involve electronic publishing, in which you use programs such as *Adobe RoboHelp* or *Adobe Dreamweaver* to create documents in digital format for the Web, the company intranet, or as online help screens. You also might produce Portable Document Files, PDF versions of a document, using software such as *Adobe Acrobat* or *Apple Preview*.

The Centers for Disease Control and Prevention (CDC) offer the following information on Chronic obstructive pulmonary disease, or COPD. COPD refers to a group of diseases that cause airflow blockage and breathing-related problems. It includes emphysema, chronic bronchitis, and in some cases asthma.

COPD is a leading cause of death, illness, and disability in the United States. In 2000, 11,900 deaths, 726,000 hospitalizations, and 1.5 million hospital emergency department visits were caused by COPD. An additional 8 million cases of hospital outpatient treatment or treatment by personal physicians were linked to COPD in 2000.

COPD has various causes. In the United States, tobacco use is a key factor in the development and progression of COPD, but asthma, exposure to air pollutants in the home and workplace, genetic factors, and respiratory infections also play a role. In the developing world, indoor air quality is thought to play a larger role in the development and progression of COPD than it does in the United States.

In the United States, an estimated 10 million adults had a diagnosis of COPD in 2000, but data from a national health survey suggest that as many as 24 million Americans are affected.

From 1980 to 2000, the COPD death rate for women grew much faster than the rate for men. For U.S. women, the rate rose from 20.1 deaths per 100,000 women to 56.7 deaths per 100,000 women over that 20-year span, while for men, the rate grew from 73.0 deaths per 100,000 men to 82.6 deaths per 100,000 men.

U.S. women also had more COPD hospitalizations (400,000) than men (322,000) and more emergency department visits (898,000) than men (551,000) in 2000. Additionally, 2000 marked the first year in which more women (59,936) than men (59,118) died from COPD.

However, the proportion of the U.S. population aged 25–54, both male and female, with mild or moderate COPD has declined over the past quarter century, suggesting that increases in hospitalizations and deaths might not continue.

The fact that women's COPD rates are rising so much faster than men's probably reflects the increase in smoking by women, relative to men, since the 1940s. In the United States, a history of currently or formerly smoking is the risk factor most often linked to COPD, and the increase in the number of women smoking in the past half-century is mirrored in the increase in COPD rates among women. The decreases in rates in both men and women aged 25–54 in the past quarter century reflect the decrease in overall smoking rates in the United States since the 1960s.

Document is untitled and provides no visual hierarchy: everything looks equal

Small margins make the document look crowded

Inadequate white space makes this version hard to read

Paragraphs look dense and intimidating

FIGURE 1 **Ineffective Page Design** This design provides no visual cues to indicate how the information is structured, what main ideas are being conveyed, or where readers should focus.

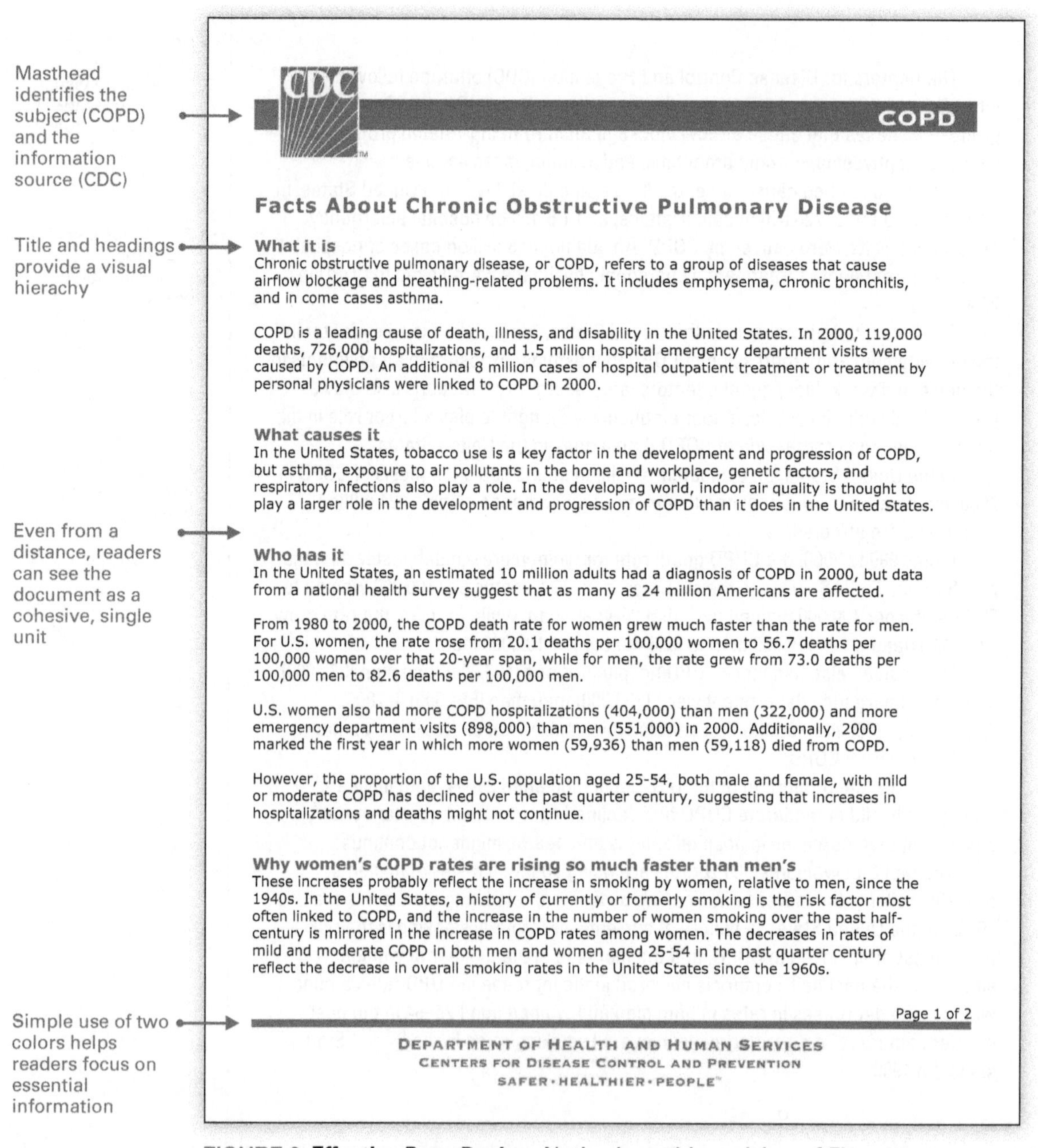

CDC

COPD

Facts About Chronic Obstructive Pulmonary Disease

What it is
Chronic obstructive pulmonary disease, or COPD, refers to a group of diseases that cause airflow blockage and breathing-related problems. It includes emphysema, chronic bronchitis, and in come cases asthma.

COPD is a leading cause of death, illness, and disability in the United States. In 2000, 119,000 deaths, 726,000 hospitalizations, and 1.5 million hospital emergency department visits were caused by COPD. An additional 8 million cases of hospital outpatient treatment or treatment by personal physicians were linked to COPD in 2000.

What causes it
In the United States, tobacco use is a key factor in the development and progression of COPD, but asthma, exposure to air pollutants in the home and workplace, genetic factors, and respiratory infections also play a role. In the developing world, indoor air quality is thought to play a larger role in the development and progression of COPD than it does in the United States.

Who has it
In the United States, an estimated 10 million adults had a diagnosis of COPD in 2000, but data from a national health survey suggest that as many as 24 million Americans are affected.

From 1980 to 2000, the COPD death rate for women grew much faster than the rate for men. For U.S. women, the rate rose from 20.1 deaths per 100,000 women to 56.7 deaths per 100,000 women over that 20-year span, while for men, the rate grew from 73.0 deaths per 100,000 men to 82.6 deaths per 100,000 men.

U.S. women also had more COPD hospitalizations (404,000) than men (322,000) and more emergency department visits (898,000) than men (551,000) in 2000. Additionally, 2000 marked the first year in which more women (59,936) than men (59,118) died from COPD.

However, the proportion of the U.S. population aged 25-54, both male and female, with mild or moderate COPD has declined over the past quarter century, suggesting that increases in hospitalizations and deaths might not continue.

Why women's COPD rates are rising so much faster than men's
These increases probably reflect the increase in smoking by women, relative to men, since the 1940s. In the United States, a history of currently or formerly smoking is the risk factor most often linked to COPD, and the increase in the number of women smoking over the past half-century is mirrored in the increase in COPD rates among women. The decreases in rates of mild and moderate COPD in both men and women aged 25-54 in the past quarter century reflect the decrease in overall smoking rates in the United States since the 1960s.

Page 1 of 2

DEPARTMENT OF HEALTH AND HUMAN SERVICES
CENTERS FOR DISEASE CONTROL AND PREVENTION
SAFER • HEALTHIER • PEOPLE™

FIGURE 2 **Effective Page Design** Notice how this revision of Figure 1 uses a title, white space, headings, and color to help readers.

Source: Centers for Disease Control and Prevention <www.cdc.gov/nceh/airpollution/copd/pdfs/copdfaq.pdf>.

Using Style Sheets and Style Guides

Style sheets provide design consistency

Style sheets are specifications that ensure consistency across a single document or among a set of documents. If you are working as part of a team, each writer needs to be using the same typefaces, fonts, headings, and other elements in identical fashion. Here are two examples of what you might find in a style sheet:

Possible style sheet entries

- The first time you use or define a specialized term, highlight it with *italics* or **boldface.**
- In headings, capitalize prepositions of five or more letters ("Between," "Versus").

The more complex the document, the more specific the style sheet should be. All writers and editors should have a copy. Consider keeping the style sheet on a Web page for easy access and efficient updating.

In addition to style sheets for specific documents, some organizations produce style guides containing rules for proper use of trade names, appropriate punctuation, preferred formats for correspondence, and so on. Style guides help ensure a consistent look across a company's various documents and publications.

CREATING A DESIGN THAT WORKS FOR YOUR READERS

Approach your design decisions to achieve a consistent look, to highlight certain material, and to aid navigation. First, consider the overall look of your pages, and then consider the following three design categories (as shown in Figure 3): styling the words and letters, adding emphasis, and using headings for access and orientation.

NOTE *All design considerations are influenced by the budget for a publication. For instance, adding a single color (say, to major heads) can double the printing cost.*

If your organization prescribes no specific guidelines, the general design principles that follow should serve in most situations.

Shaping the Page

In shaping a page, consider its look, feel, and overall layout. The following suggestions will help you shape appealing and usable pages.

Use the Right Paper. For routine documents (memos, letters, in-house reports) print in black, on low-gloss, white paper. Use rag-bond paper (20 pound or heavier) with a high fiber content (25 percent minimum).

For documents that will be published (manuals, marketing literature), consider the paper's grade and quality. Paper varies in weight, grain, and finish—from low-cost newsprint to specially coated paper with custom finishes. Choice of paper

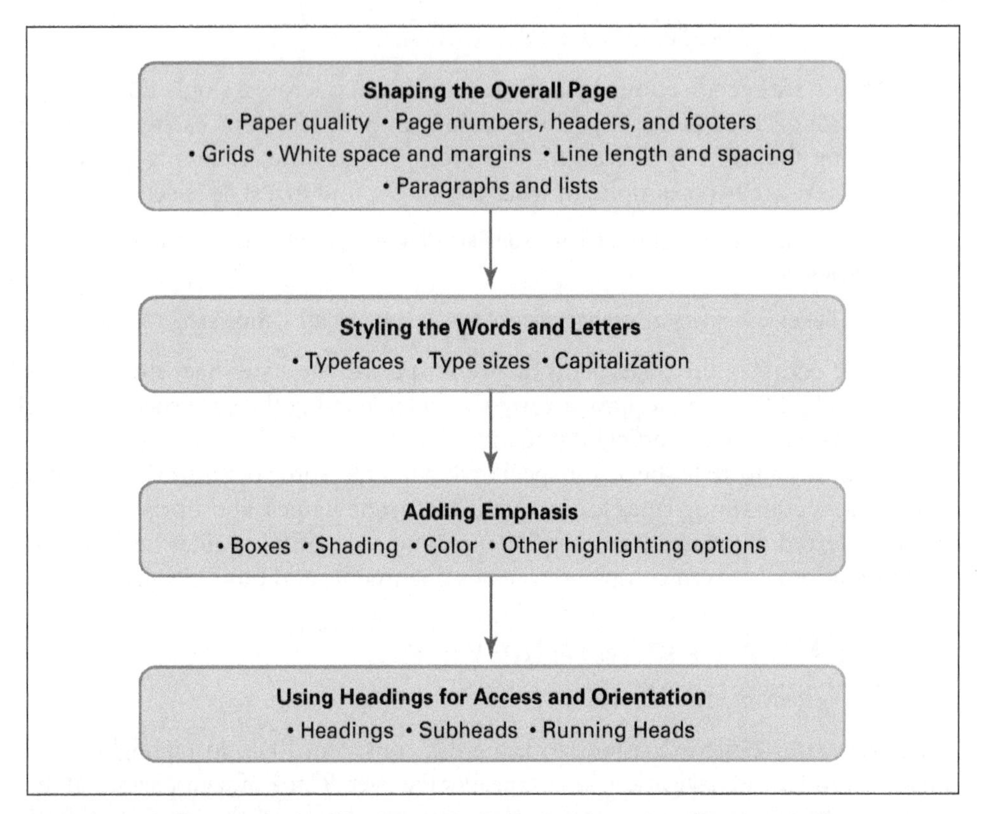

FIGURE 3 **A Flowchart for Decisions in Page Design** An effective design strategy requires a series of informed choices.

depends on the artwork to be included, the type of printing, and the intended aesthetic effect: For example, you might choose specially coated, heavyweight, glossy paper for an elegant effect in an annual report (Cotton 73).

Provide Page Numbers, Headers, and Footers. For a long document, count your title page as page i, without numbering it, and number all front matter pages, including the table of contents and abstract, with lowercase roman numerals (ii, iii, iv). Number the first text page and subsequent pages with arabic numerals (1, 2, 3). Along with page numbers, *headers* or *footers* (or *running heads* and *feet*) appear in the top or bottom page margins, respectively. These provide chapter or article titles, authors' names, dates, or other publication information.

Use a Grid. Readers make sense of a page by looking for a consistent underlying structure, with the various elements located where they expect them. With a view of a page's Big Picture, you can plan the size and placement of your visuals and calculate the number of lines available for written text. Most important, you can rearrange text and visuals repeatedly to achieve a balanced and consistent design (White, *Editing* 58). Figure 4 shows a sampling of grid patterns. A two-column grid is commonly used in manuals. (See also the *Consider This* boxes in this text.) Brochures and newsletters typically employ a two- or three-column grid. Web pages often use a combined vertical/horizontal grid. Figure 2 uses a single-column grid, as do most memos, letters, and reports. (Grids are also used in storyboarding.)

Figure 5 illustrates how a horizontal grid can transform the design of important medical information for consumers.

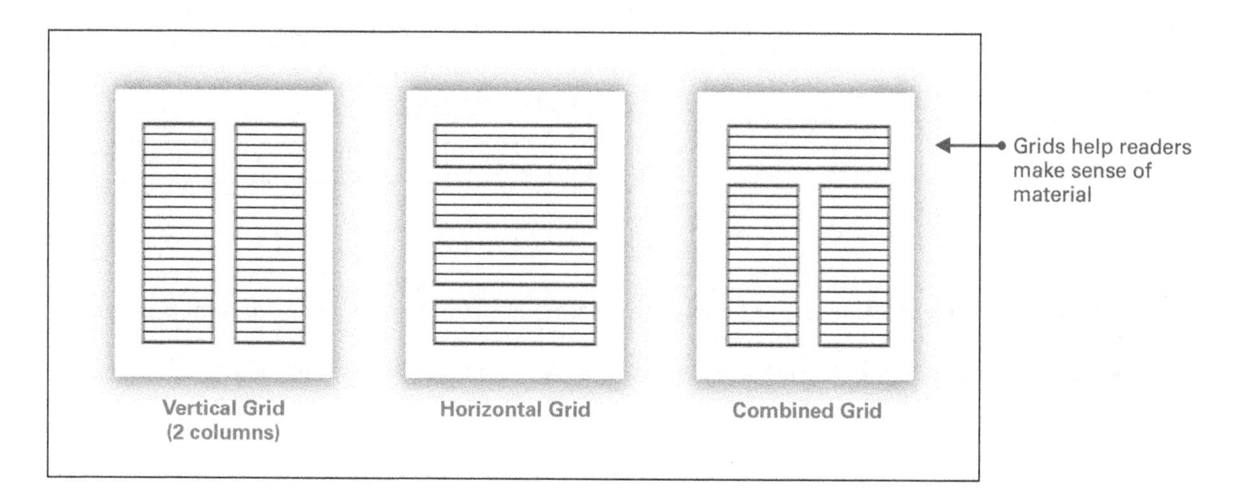

FIGURE 4 **Grid Patterns** By subdividing a page into modules, grids provide a blueprint for your page design as well as a coherent visual theme for the document's audience.

Use White Space to Create Areas of Emphasis. Sometimes, what is *not* on the page can make a big difference. Areas of text surrounded by white space draw the reader's eye to those areas.

Well-designed white space imparts a shape to the whole document, a shape that orients readers and lends a distinctive visual form to the printed matter by keeping related elements together, by isolating and emphasizing important elements, and by providing breathing room between blocks of information.

In the examples in Figure 6, notice how the white space pulls your eye toward the pages in different ways. Each example causes the reader to look at a different place on the page first. White space can keep a page from seeming too

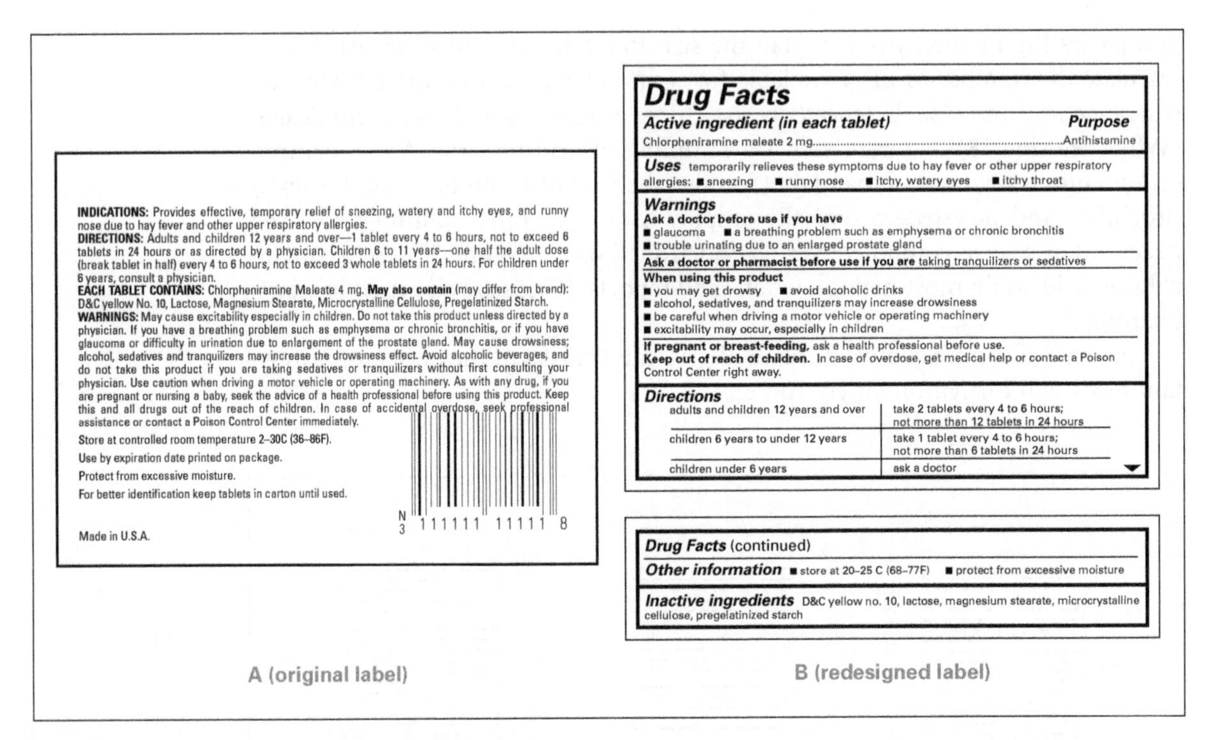

FIGURE 5 **Two Versions of a Consumer Label** The discrete horizontal modules in version B provide an underlying structure that is easy to navigate.

Source: Nordenberg, Tamar. "*New Drug Label Spells It Out Simply.*" *FDA Consumer* (Reprint) July 1999.

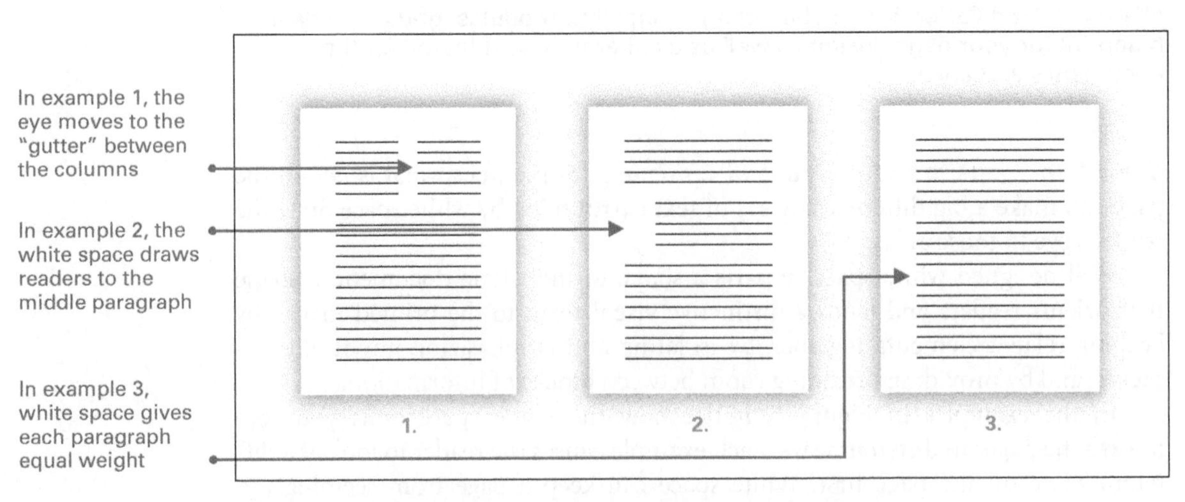

FIGURE 6 **White Space** White space creates areas of emphasis.

cluttered, and pages that look uncluttered, inviting, and easy to follow convey an immediate sense of user-friendliness.

Provide Ample Margins. Small margins crowd the page and make the material look difficult. On your $8^1/_2$-by-11-inch page, leave margins of at least 1 or $1^1/_2$ inches. If the manuscript is to be bound in some kind of cover, widen the inside margin to two inches.

Headings, lines of text, or visuals that abut the right or left margin, without indentation, are designated as *flush right* or *flush left.*

Choose between *unjustified* text (uneven or "ragged" right margins) and *justified* text (even right margins). Each arrangement creates its own "feel."

> To make the right margin even in justified text, the spaces vary between words and letters on a line, sometimes creating channels or rivers of white space. The eyes are then forced to adjust continually to these space variations within a line or paragraph. Because each line ends at an identical vertical space, the eyes must work hard to differentiate one line from another (Felker 85). Moreover, in order to preserve the even margin, words at line's end are often hyphenated, and frequently hyphenated line endings can be distracting.

Justified lines are set flush left and right

> Unjustified text, on the other hand, uses equal spacing between letters and words on a line, and an uneven right margin (as traditionally produced by a typewriter). For some readers, a ragged right margin makes reading easier. These differing line lengths can prompt the eye to move from one line to another (Pinelli 77). In contrast to justified text, an unjustified page looks less formal, less distant, and less official.

Unjustified lines are set flush left only

Justified text is preferable for books, annual reports, and other formal materials. Unjustified text is preferable for more personal forms of communication such as letters, memos, and in-house reports.

Keep Line Length Reasonable. Long lines tire the eyes. The longer the line, the harder it is for the reader to return to the left margin and locate the beginning of the next line (White, *Visual Design* 25).

Notice how your eye labors to follow this apparently endless message that seems to stretch in lines that continue long after your eye was prepared to move down to the next line. After reading more than a few of these lines, you begin to feel tired and bored and annoyed, without hope of ever reaching the end.

Short lines force the eyes back and forth (Felker 79). "Too-short lines disrupt the normal horizontal rhythm of reading" (White, *Visual Design* 25).

> Lines that are too
> short cause your eye
> to stumble from one

fragment to another
at a pace that too
soon becomes
annoying, if not
nauseating.

A reasonable line length is sixty to seventy characters (or nine to twelve words) per line for an $8^1/_2$-by-11-inch single-column page. The number of characters will depend on print size. Longer lines call for larger type and wider spacing between lines (White, *Great Pages* 70).

Line length, of course, is affected by the number of columns (vertical blocks of print) on your page. Two-column pages often appear in newsletters and brochures, but research indicates that single-column pages work best for complex, specialized information (Hartley 148).

Keep Line Spacing Consistent. For any document likely to be read completely (letters, memos, instructions), single-space within paragraphs and double-space between paragraphs. Instead of indenting the first line of single-spaced paragraphs, separate them with one line of space. For longer documents likely to be read selectively (proposals, formal reports), increase line spacing within paragraphs by one-half space. Indent these paragraphs or separate them with one extra line of space.

NOTE *Although academic papers generally call for double spacing, most workplace documents do not.*

Tailor Each Paragraph to Its Purpose. Readers often skim a long document to find what they want. Most paragraphs, therefore, begin with a topic sentence forecasting the content. As you shape each paragraph, follow these suggestions:

Shape each paragraph

- Use a long paragraph (no more than fifteen lines) for clustering material that is closely related (such as history and background, or any information best understood in one block).
- Use short paragraphs for making complex material more digestible, for giving step-by-step instructions, or for emphasizing vital information.
- Instead of indenting a series of short paragraphs, separate them by inserting an extra line of space.
- Avoid "orphans," leaving a paragraph's opening line at the bottom of a page, and "widows," leaving a paragraph's closing line at the top of the page.

Make Lists for Easy Reading. Whenever you find yourself writing a series of related items within a paragraph, consider using a list instead, especially if you are describing a series of tasks or trying to make certain items easy to locate. Types of items you might list: advice or examples, conclusions and recommendations, criteria for evaluation, errors to avoid, materials and equipment for a procedure, parts of a mechanism, or steps or events in a sequence. Notice how the items just mentioned, integrated into the previous sentence as an *embedded list*, become easier to grasp and remember when displayed below as a *vertical list.*

An embedded list is part of the running text

Types of items you might display in a vertical list:

- advice or examples
- conclusions and recommendations
- criteria for evaluation
- errors to avoid
- materials and equipment for a procedure
- parts of a mechanism
- steps or events in a sequence

A vertical list draws readers' attention to the content of the list

A list of brief items usually needs no punctuation at the end of each line. A list of full sentences or questions requires appropriate punctuation after each item. For more on punctuating embedded and vertical lists, see pages 734–35 or consult your organization's style guide.

Depending on the list's contents, set off each item with some kind of visual or verbal signal, as in Figure 7: If the items follow a strict sequence or chronology (say, parts of a mechanism or a set of steps), use arabic numbers (*1, 2, 3*) or the words *First, Second, Third.* If the items require no strict sequence (as in the sample vertical list above), use dashes, asterisks, or bullets. For a checklist, use open boxes.

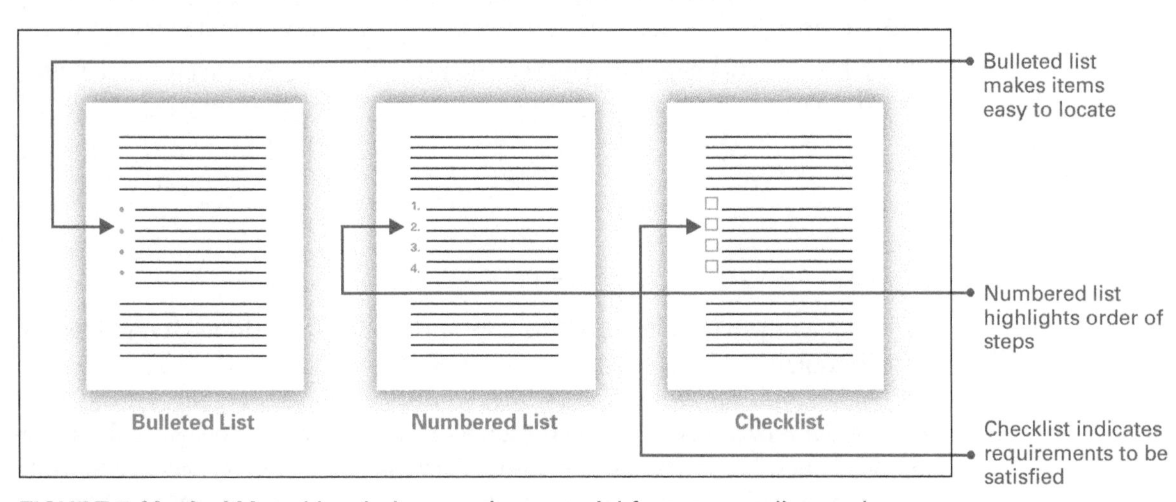

FIGURE 7 **Vertical Lists** Lists help organize material for easy reading and comprehension.

Introduce your list with a forecasting phrase ("Topics to review for the exam:") or with a sentence ("To prepare for the exam, review the following topics:").

Phrase all listed items in parallel grammatical form. When items suggest no strict sequence, try to impose some logical ranking (most to least important, alphabetical, or some such). Set off the list with extra white space above and below.

> **NOTE** *A document with too many vertical lists appears busy, disconnected, and splintered (Felker 55). And long lists could be used by unethical writers to camouflage bad or embarrassing news.*

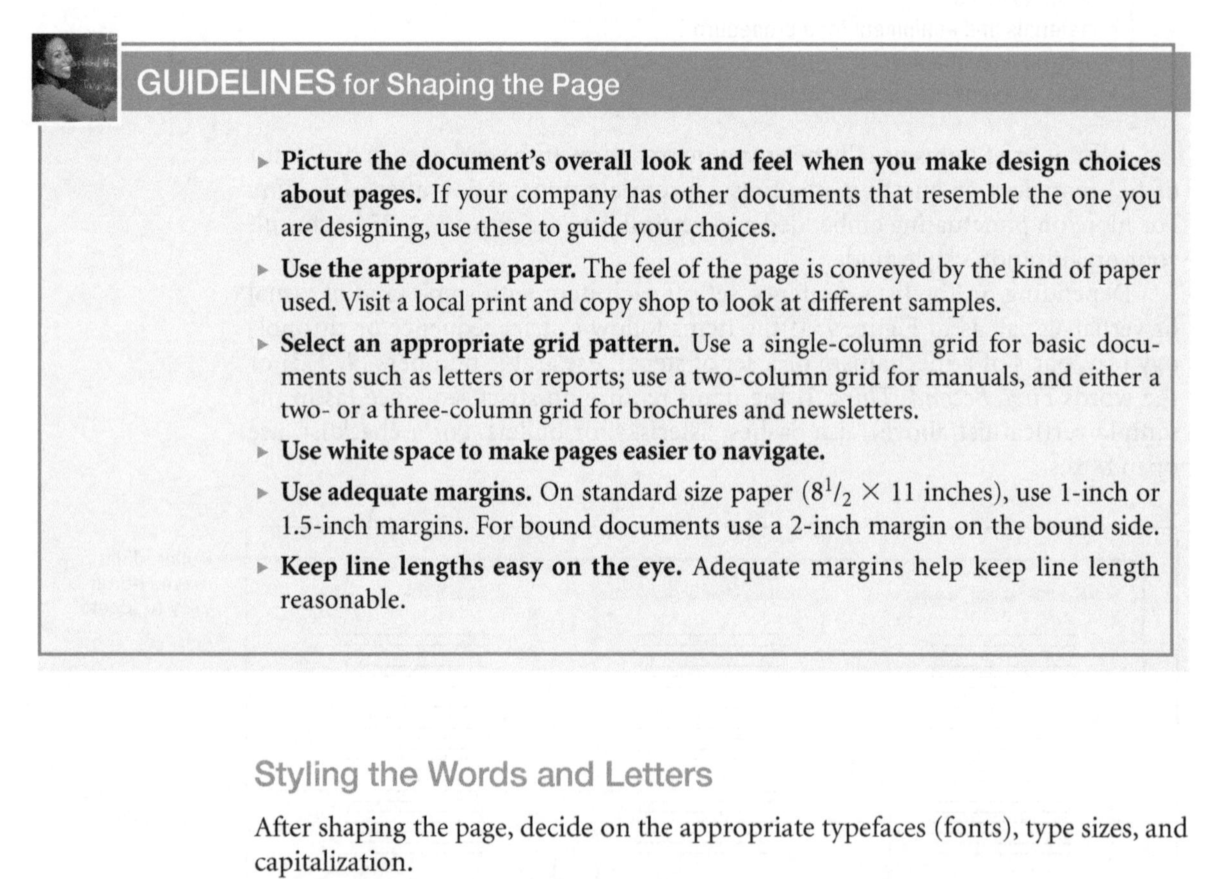

GUIDELINES for Shaping the Page

- **Picture the document's overall look and feel when you make design choices about pages.** If your company has other documents that resemble the one you are designing, use these to guide your choices.
- **Use the appropriate paper.** The feel of the page is conveyed by the kind of paper used. Visit a local print and copy shop to look at different samples.
- **Select an appropriate grid pattern.** Use a single-column grid for basic documents such as letters or reports; use a two-column grid for manuals, and either a two- or a three-column grid for brochures and newsletters.
- **Use white space to make pages easier to navigate.**
- **Use adequate margins.** On standard size paper ($8^1/_2 \times 11$ inches), use 1-inch or 1.5-inch margins. For bound documents use a 2-inch margin on the bound side.
- **Keep line lengths easy on the eye.** Adequate margins help keep line length reasonable.

Styling the Words and Letters

After shaping the page, decide on the appropriate typefaces (fonts), type sizes, and capitalization.

Typography, the art of type styling, consists of choices among various typefaces. *Typeface*, or *font*, refers to all the letters and characters in one particular family such as Times, Helvetica, or New York. Each typeface has its own personality: Some convey seriousness; others convey humor; still others convey a technical or businesslike quality. Choice of typeface can influence reading speed by as much as 30 percent (Chauncey 36).

All typefaces divide into two broad categories: *serif* and *sans serif* (Figure 8). Serifs are the fine lines that extend horizontally from the main strokes of a letter:

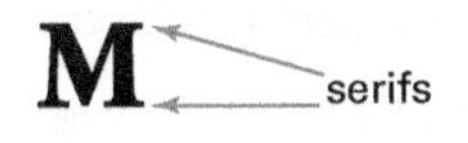

Serif type makes printed body copy more readable because the horizontal lines "bind the individual letters" and thereby guide the reader's eyes from letter to letter (White, *Visual Design* 14). Serif fonts look traditional, the sort you see in newspapers and formal reports.

Sans serif type is purely vertical. Clean looking and "businesslike," sans (French for "without") serif is ideal for technical material (numbers, equations, etc.), marginal comments, headings, examples, tables, and captions, and any other material set off from the body copy (White, *Visual Design* 16). Sans serif is also more readable in *projected* environments such as overhead transparencies and PowerPoint slides.

Serif type

Sans serif type

FIGURE 8 **Serif Versus Sans Serif Typefaces** Each version makes its own visual statement.

Readers from various cultures generally have their own font preferences. Learn all you can about the design conventions of the culture you are addressing.

Select an Appropriate Typeface. In selecting a typeface, consider the document's purpose. If the purpose is to help patients relax, choose a combination that conveys ease; fonts that imitate handwriting are often a good choice, but they can be hard to read if used in lengthy passages. If the purpose is to help engineers find technical data in a table or chart, use Helvetica or some other sans serif typeface—not only because numbers in sans serif type are easy to see but also because engineers will be more comfortable with fonts that look precise. Figure 9 offers a sampling of typeface choices.

For visual unity, use different sizes and versions (**bold,** *italic,* SMALL CAPS) of the same typeface throughout your document. For example, you might decide

Times New Roman is a standard serif typeface.

Palatino is a slightly less formal serif alternative.

Helvetica is a standard sans serif typeface.

Arial seems a bit more readable than Helvetica.

Chicago makes a bold statement.

A font that imitates handwriting can be hard to read in long passages.

Ornate or whimsical fonts should generally be avoided.

FIGURE 9 **Sample Typefaces** Except for special emphasis, choose traditional typefaces (Times Roman, Helvetica). Decorative typefaces are hard to read and inappropriate for most workplace documents.

on Times for an audience of financial planners, investors, and others who expect a traditional font. In this case, use Times 14 point bold for the headings, 12 point regular (roman) for the body copy, and 12 point italic, sparingly, for emphasis.

If the document contains illustrations, charts, or numbers, use Helvetica 10 point for these; use a smaller size for captions (brief explanation of a visual) or sidebars (marginal comments). You can also use one typeface (say, Helvetica) for headings and another (say, Times) for body copy. In any case, use no more than two different typeface families in a single document—and use them consistently.

Use Type Sizes That Are Easy to Read. To map out a page, designers measure the size of type and other page elements (such as visuals and line length) in picas and points (Figure 10).

The height of a typeface, the distance from the top of the *ascender* to the base of the *descender*, is measured in points.

Select the appropriate point size

Standard type sizes for body copy run from 10 to 12 point, depending on the typeface. Use different sizes for other elements: headings, titles, captions, sidebars, or special emphasis. Whatever the element, use a consistent type size throughout your document. For overhead transparencies or computer projection in oral presentations, use 18 or 20 point type for body text and 20 or greater for headings.

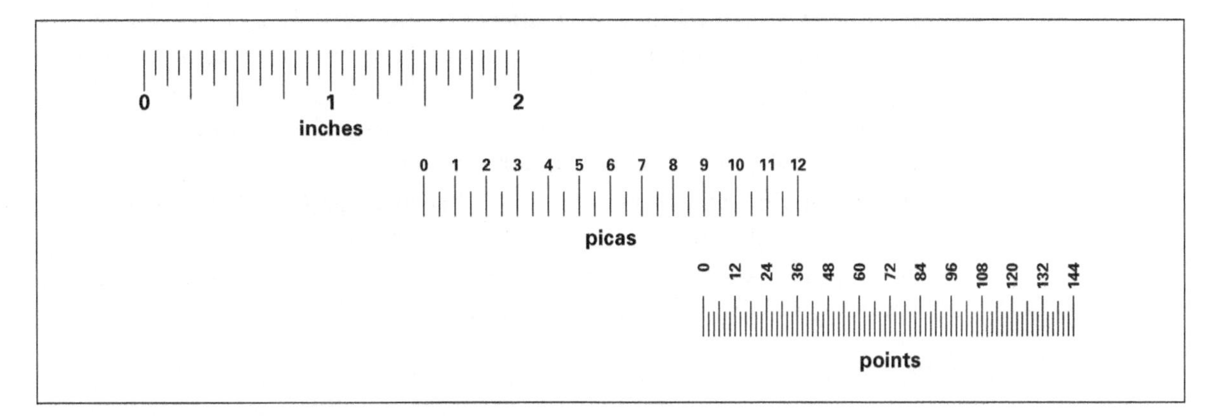

FIGURE 10 **Sizing the Page Elements** One pica equals roughly 1/6 of an inch and one point equals 1/12 of a pica (or 1/72 of an inch).

Use Full Caps Sparingly. Long passages in full capitals (uppercase letters) are hard to recognize and remember because uppercase letters lack ascenders and descenders, and so all words in uppercase have the same visual outline (Felker 87). The longer the passage, the harder readers work to grasp your emphasis.

Use full caps as section headings (INTRODUCTION) or to highlight a word or phrase (WARNING: NEVER TEASE THE ALLIGATOR). As with other highlighting options discussed below, use them sparingly.

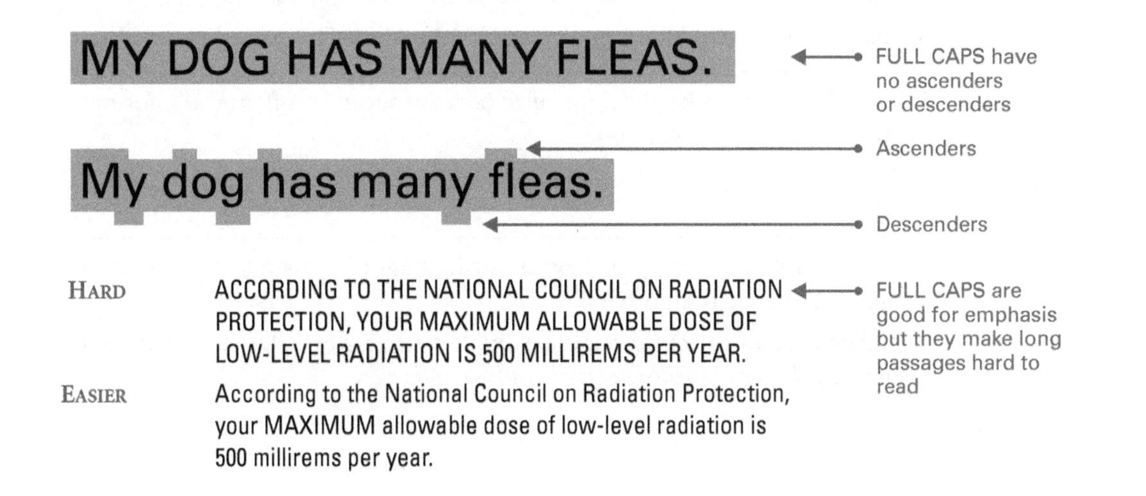

GUIDELINES for Styling the Words and Letters

- **Use a serif font (such as Times New Roman) for formal documents such as reports, legal communication, and letters.** Also use serif fonts for newspapers, magazines, and other documents where readers' eyes will need to move across long lines of text.
- **Use a sans serif font (such as Helvetica) for captions, most visuals (charts, graphs, and tables), and engineering specifications.**
- **Create visual unity by using the same typeface throughout.** Different sizes and versions (bold, italic) are fine within the same typeface.
- **Keep fonts at sizes that people can read.** Standard body copy should be between 10 and 12 points. Use different sizes for headings, titles, captions, and so on.

Adding Emphasis

Once you have selected the appropriate font, you can use different features, such as boldface or italics, to highlight important elements such as headings, special terms, key points, or warnings. The following guidelines offer some basic highlighting options.

GUIDELINES for Adding Emphasis

- You can indent (and use a smaller or a different type) to set off examples, explanations, or any material that should be differentiated from body copy.
- Using ruled horizontal lines, you can separate sections in a long document:

- Using ruled lines, broken lines, or ruled boxes, you can set off crucial information such as a warning or a caution.

Caution: Excessive highlights make a document look too busy.

When using typographic devices for highlighting, keep in mind that some options are better than others:

- **Boldface is good for emphasizing a single sentence or brief statement, and is seen by readers as "authoritative"** (*Aldus Guide* 42).

- *More subtle than boldface, italics can highlight words, phrases, book titles, or anything else one might otherwise underline. But long passages of italic type can be hard to read.*
- Small type sizes (usually sans serif) work well for captions and credit lines and as labels for visuals or to set off other material from the body copy.
- ***Avoid large type sizes and dramatic typefaces—unless you really need to convey forcefulness.***
- Color is appropriate in some documents, but only when used sparingly. Color can influence audience perception and interpretation of a message.

Whichever options you select, be consistent: Highlight all headings at one given level identically; set off all warnings and cautions identically. And never mix too many highlights.

Using Headings for Access and Orientation

Readers of a long document often look back or jump ahead to sections that interest them most. Headings announce how a document is organized, point readers to what they need, and divide the document into accessible blocks or "chunks." An informative heading can help a person decide whether a section is worth reading. Besides cutting down on reading and retrieval time, headings help readers remember information.

Lay Out Headings by Level. Like a good road map, your headings should clearly announce the large and small segments in your document. When you write your material, think of it in chunks and subchunks. In preparing any long document, you most likely have developed a formal outline (page 195). Use the logical divisions from your outline as a model for laying out the headings in your final draft.

Figure 11 shows how headings vary in their position and highlighting, depending on their rank. However, because of space considerations, Figure 11 does not show that each higher-level heading yields at least two lower-level headings.

Many variations of the heading format in Figure 11 are possible. For example, one such variation using decimal notation is shown in Figure 12.

Decide How to Phrase Your Headings. Depending on your purpose, you can phrase your headings in various ways (*Writing User-Friendly Documents* 17):

When to use which type of heading

HEADING TYPE	EXAMPLE	WHEN TO USE
Topic headings use a word or short phrase.	**Usable Page Design**	When you have lots of headings and want to keep them brief. Or to sound somewhat formal. Frequent drawback: too vague.
Statement headings use a sentence or explicit phrase.	**How to Create a Usable Page Design**	To assert something specific about the topic. Occasional drawback: wordy and cumbersome.
Question headings pose the questions in the same way readers are likely to ask them.	**How Do I Create a Usable Page Design?**	To invite readers in and to personalize the message, making people feel directly involved. Occasional drawbacks: too "chatty" for formal reports or proposals; overuse can be annoying.

To avoid verbal clutter, brief *topic headings* can be useful in documents that have numerous subheads (as in a textbook or complex report)—as long as readers understand the context for each brief heading. *Statement headings* work well for explaining how something happens or operates (say, "How the Fulbright Scholarship Program Works"). *Question headings* are most useful for explaining how to do something because they address the actual questions users will have (say, "How Do I Apply for a Fulbright Scholarship?").

Phrase your headings to summarize the content as concisely as possible. But remember that a vague or overly general heading can be more misleading or confusing than no heading at all (Redish et al. 144). Compare, for example, a heading titled "Evaluation" versus "How the Fulbright Commission Evaluates a Scholarship Application"; the second version announces exactly what to expect.

Make Headings Visually Consistent and Grammatically Parallel. Feel free to vary the formats shown in Figures 11 and 12—as long as you are consistent. When drafting your document, you can use the marks *h1*, *h2*, *h3*, and *h4* to indicate heading levels. All *h1* headings would then be set identically, as would each lower level of heading. For example, on a word-processed page, level one headings might use 14 point, bold upper case type, and be centered on the page; level two headings would then be 12 point, bold in upper and lower case and set flush left with the margin (or extended into the margin); level three headings would be 11 point bold, set flush left; level four would be 10 point bold, flush left, with the text run in (as in Figure 11).

SECTION HEADING

In a formal report, center each section heading on the page. Use full caps and a type size roughly 4 points larger than body copy (say, 16 point section heads for 12 point body copy), in boldface. Avoid overly large heads, and use no other highlights, except possibly a second color.

Major Topic Heading

Place major topic headings at the left margin (flush left), and begin each important word with an uppercase letter. Use a type size roughly 2 points larger than body copy, in boldface. Start the copy immediately below the heading, or leave one space below the heading.

Minor Topic Heading

Set minor topic headings flush left. Use boldface, italics (optional), and a slightly larger type size than in the body copy. Begin each important word with an uppercase letter. Start the copy immediately below the heading, or leave one space below the heading.

Subtopic Heading. Incorporate subtopic headings into the body copy they head. Place them flush left and set them off with a period. Use boldface and roughly the same type size as in the body copy.

FIGURE 11 **One Recommended Format for Headings** Note that each head is set one extra line space below any preceding text. Also, different type sizes reflect different levels of heads.

1.0 SECTION HEADING

xxxxxxxxxxxxxxxxxxxxxxxxxxxxxxxxxxxxxxxxxxxxxxxxxxxxxxxx
xxxxxxxxxxxxxxxxxxxxxxxxxxxxxxxxxxxxxxxxxxxxxxxxxxxxxxxx
xxxxxxxxxxxxxxxxxxxxxxxxxxxxxxxxxxxxxxxxxxxxxxxxxxxxxxxx
xxxxxxxxxxxxxxxxxxxxxxxxxxxxxxxx

1.1 Major Topic Heading

xxxxxxxxxxxxxxxxxxxxxxxxxxxxxxxxxxxxxxxxxxxxxxxxxxxxxxxx
xxxxxxxxxxxxxxxxxxxxxxxxxxxxxxxxxxxxxxxxxxxxxxxxxxxxxxxx
xxxxxxxxxxxxxxxxxxxxxxxxxxxxxxxxxxxxxxxxxxxxxxxxxxxxxxxx
xxxxxxxxxxxxxxxxxxxxxxxxx

1.1.1 Minor Topic Heading

xxxxxxxxxxxxxxxxxxxxxxxxxxxxxxxxxxxxxxxxxxxxxxxxxxxxxxxx
xxxxxxxxxxxxxxxxxxxxxxxxxxxxxxxxxxxxxxxxxxxxxxxxxxxxxxxx
xxxxxxxxxxxxxxxxxxxxxxxxxxxxxx

1.1.1.1. Subtopic Heading. xxxxxxxxxxxxxxxxxxxxxxxxxxxxxxx
xxxxxxxxxxxxxxxxxxxxxxxxxxxxxxxxxxxxxxxxxxxxxxxxxxxxxxxx
xxxxxxx

FIGURE 12 **One Alternative Format for Headings**

Along with being visually consistent, headings of the same level should also be grammatically parallel. For example, if you phrase headings in the form of reader questions, make sure all are phrased in this way at that level. Or if you are providing instructions, begin each heading with the verb (shown in italics) that names the required action: "To avoid damaging your CDs: (1) *Clean* the CD drive heads. (2) *Store* CDs in appropriate containers—and so on.

GUIDELINES for Using Headings

- **Ordinarily, use no more than four levels of headings (section, major topic, minor topic, subtopic).** Excessive heads and subheads make a document seem cluttered or fragmented.
- **Divide logically.** Be sure that beneath each higher-level heading you have at least two headings at the next-lower level.
- **Insert one additional line of space above each heading.** For double-spaced text, triple-space before the heading and double-space after; for single-spaced text, double-space before the heading and single-space after.
- **Never begin the sentence right after the heading with "this," "it," or some other pronoun referring to the heading.** Make the sentence's meaning independent of the heading.
- **Never leave a heading floating as the final line of a page.** If at least two lines of text cannot fit below the heading, carry it over to the top of the next page.
- **Use running heads (headers) or feet (footers) in long documents.** Include a chapter or section heading across the top or bottom of each page (see Figure 13). In a document with single-sided pages, running heads or feet should always be placed consistently, typically flush right. In a document with double-sided pages, such as a book, the running heads or feet should appear flush left on left-hand pages and flush right on right-hand pages.

AUDIENCE CONSIDERATIONS IN PAGE DESIGN

In deciding on a format, work from a detailed audience and use profile. Know your audience and their intended use of your information. Create a design to meet their particular needs and expectations (Wight 11):

How readers' needs determine page design

- If people will use your document for reference only (as in a repair manual), make sure you have plenty of headings.
- If readers will follow a sequence of steps, show that sequence in a numbered list.

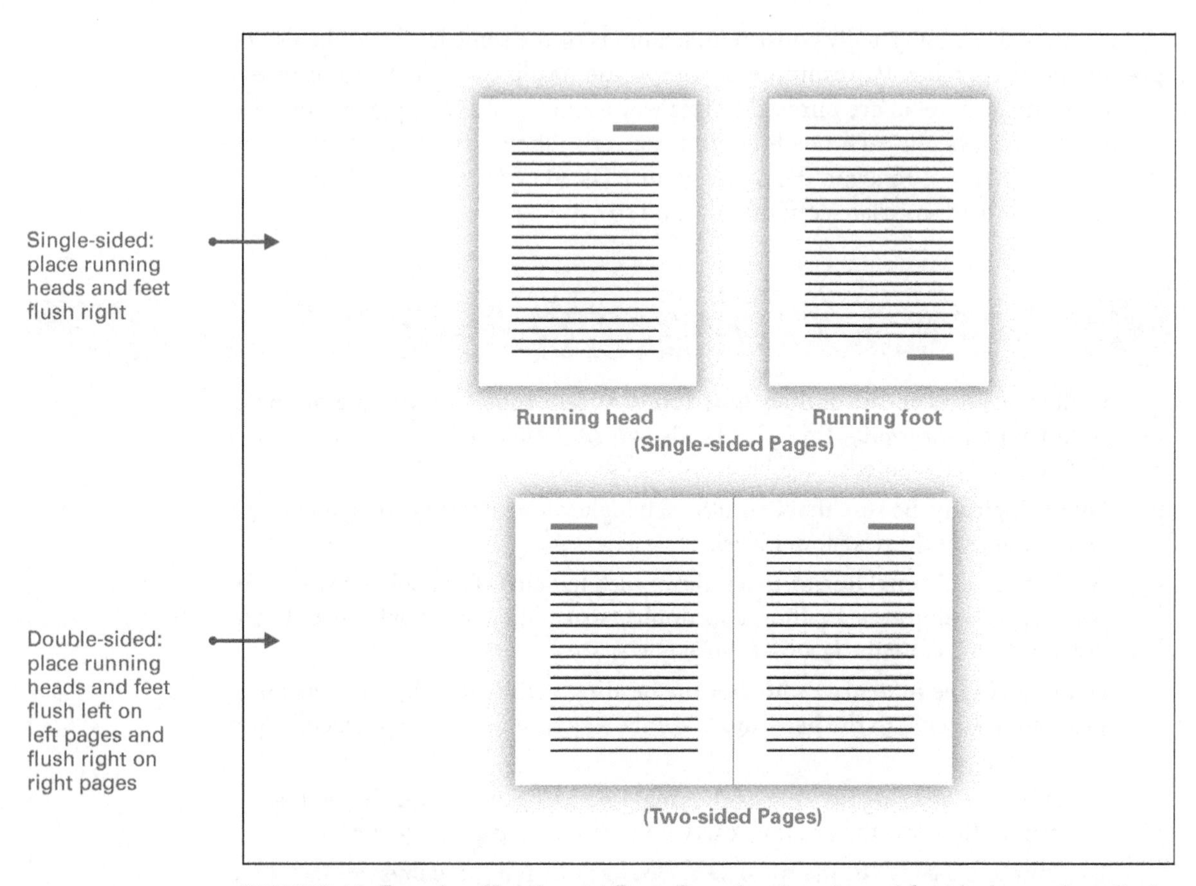

FIGURE 13 **Running Heads and Feet** Running heads and feet help readers find material and stay oriented

- If readers need to evaluate something, give them a checklist of criteria (as in this chapter).
- If readers need a warning, highlight the warning so that it cannot possibly be overlooked.
- If readers have asked for a one-page report or résumé, save space by using a 10 point type size.
- If readers will be encountering complex information or difficult steps, widen the margins, increase all white space, and shorten the paragraphs.

Regardless of the audience, never make the document look "too intellectually intimidating" (White, *Visual Design* 4).

Consider also your audience's cultural expectations. For instance, Arabic and Persian text is written from right to left instead of left to right (Leki 149). In other cultures, readers move up and down the page, instead of across. A particular culture might be offended by certain colors or by a typeface that seems too plain or too fancy (Weymouth 144). Ignoring a culture's design conventions can be interpreted as disrespect.

> **NOTE** *Even the most brilliant page design cannot redeem a document with worthless content, chaotic organization, or unreadable style. The value of any document ultimately depends on elements beneath the visual surface.*

DESIGNING DIGITAL DOCUMENTS

Print versus digital formats

Most of the techniques in this chapter are appropriate for both print and digital documents. In fact, many documents are designed for use in multiple formats. For instance, a manufacturer of lawn and gardening equipment might create a printed User Guide that accompanies its lawnmowers. But, because people often lose or misplace the User Guide, the company might also post the Guide to its Web site, in PDF format. Similarly, a company that makes medical devices (such as heart pacemakers) might supply a small print manual with each device, but might also provide a CD so that medical staff can download the manual onto their computers for future reference.

Whether you are designing for print or digital documents, follow the earlier guidelines in this chapter. For digital documents, pay special attention to the additional features discussed below.

Web Pages

Each "page" of a Web document typically stands alone as a discrete module (like a single page in a print document). But instead of the traditional introduction-body-conclusion sequence of pages, Web content is displayed in screen-sized chunks, with material often linked to other pages. Links can serve the same function as headings (discussed earlier) by providing visual cues and by guiding readers to new information.

The shape of Web pages

Because they are on a computer screen, Web pages need to be designed to accommodate small screen sizes, reduced resolution, and reader resistance to scrolling. Also, the shape of a typical computer screen is more "landscape" than "portrait" —wider than it is high. So, pages must provide for plenty of marginal width, and lines of text can't be too long.

Tools for creating Web pages

Regular word-processing software (such as *Microsoft Word* or *Apple Pages*) offers features that let you save documents as Web pages. This approach works well for simple Web pages. But most Web designers use more sophisticated tools, such as *Adobe Dreamweaver*, to create Web pages. Even with these tools, Web designers need to tinker with the margins, headings, fonts, and page makeup in order to achieve an accessible design.

NOTE *Because Web page design is complicated, you may want to take a class on this topic. Many organizations have Webmasters or Web designers on staff who could work with you on designing your Web page.*

Online Help

Like Web design, designing online help screens is a specialty. Many organizations, especially those that produce software, hire technical communicators who know how to produce online help screens. As with all page design, paper or electronic, producing online help screens requires consistency.

Adobe Acrobat™ and PDF Files

Unlike normal Web pages, which may display differently on different computers or browsers, PDF (Portable Document Format) documents retain their formatting and appear exactly as they were designed, both on the screen and when printed out (see Figure 14). Also, unlike normal Web pages, PDF files typically cannot be altered or manipulated by other users, thus protecting the integrity of your document. Created with *Adobe Acrobat* software, PDF files can be placed on the Web. Users link to these just as they would to any Web site, using *Adobe Acrobat Reader* software, which usually can be downloaded free. PDF files also can be sent as email attachments. PDF technology enables companies to make their user documentation and product manuals available to anyone with a Web connection without having to reproduce and distribute the actual manuals in hard-copy form. For more information about PDF, go to <www.adobe.com/products/acrobat>.

CDs and Other Media

You can't predict the types of media that will be used to deliver your documents. You may design an instruction manual or a customer information brochure with the intent of printing it, but the document may eventually be delivered and read on the Web, on a hand-held device or a CD. For most media types, you can use *Adobe Acrobat's* PDF format to ensure that documents will look the same on the CD as they do in print. If designing for an iPod or smart phone, work within the current specifications and software required for these devices. In short, the best you can do is identify as early as possible the media in which your document might be delivered, and work with your organization's design team to ensure that your intended audience will be able to access the information.

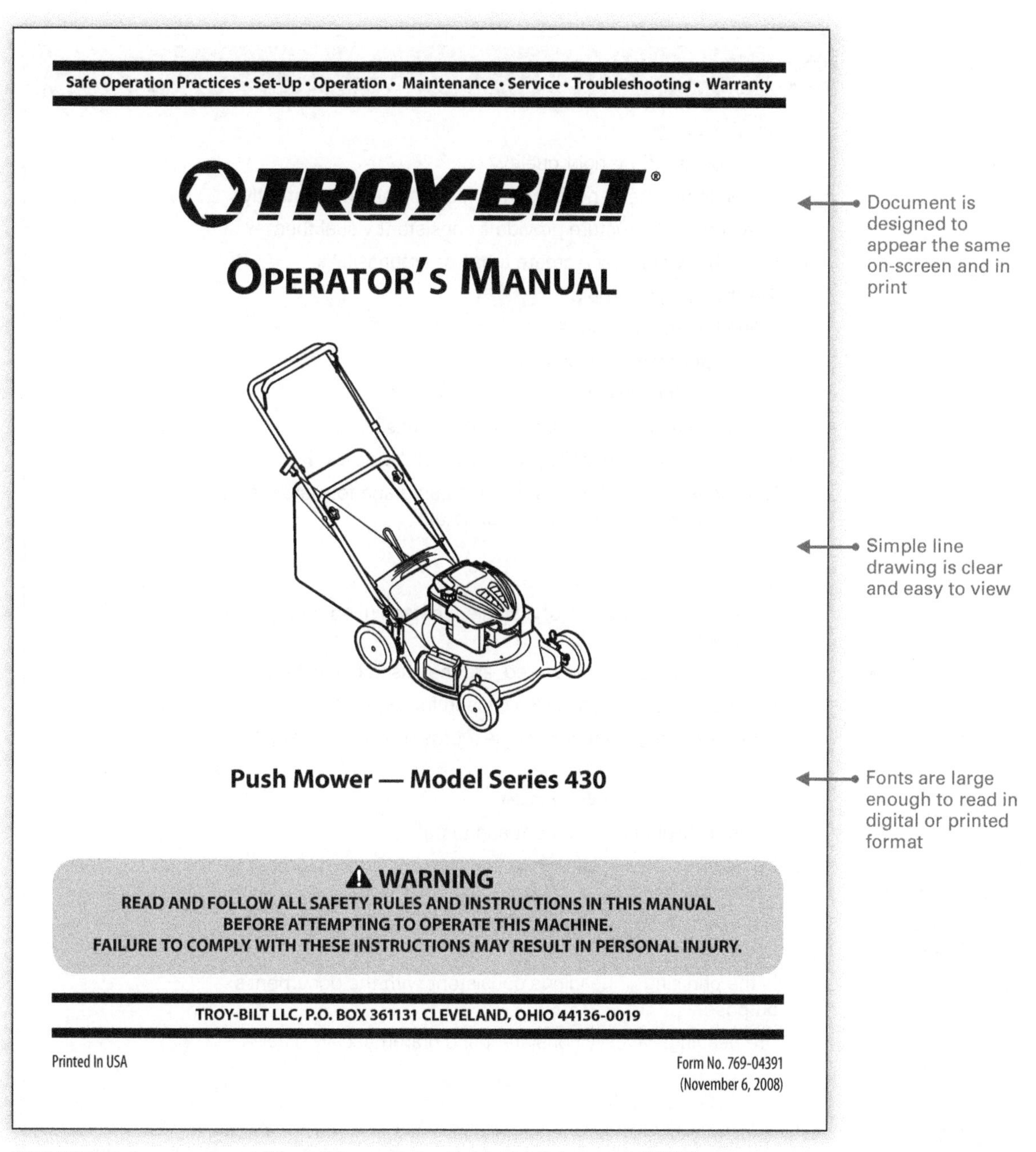

FIGURE 14 **Lawnmower User Manual, Available in Print and PDF Formats**
Source: Cover of Troy-Bilt® Operator's Manual for Push Mower - Model Series 430. Used with permission from MTD Products.
<http://lawnandgarden.manualsonline.com/manuals/mft/troybilt/>

CHECKLIST: Page Design

Shape of the Page

- ☐ Is the paper of the right quality?
- ☐ Are page numbers, headers, and footers used consistently?
- ☐ Does the grid structure provide a consistent visual theme?
- ☐ Does the white space create areas of emphasis?
- ☐ Are the margins ample?
- ☐ Is line length reasonable?
- ☐ Is the right margin unjustified?
- ☐ Is line spacing appropriate and consistent?
- ☐ Is each paragraph tailored to suit its purpose?
- ☐ Are paragraphs free of "orphan" lines or "widows"?
- ☐ Is a series of parallel items within a paragraph formatted as a list (numbered or bulleted, as appropriate)?

Style of Words and Letters

- ☐ In general, are versions of a single typeface used throughout the document?
- ☐ If different typefaces *are* used, are they used consistently?
- ☐ Are typefaces and type sizes chosen for readability?
- ☐ Do full caps highlight only single words or short phrases?

Emphasis, Access, and Orientation

- ☐ Is the highlighting consistent and tasteful?
- ☐ Do headings clearly announce the large and small segments in the document?
- ☐ Are headings formatted to reflect their specific level in the document?
- ☐ Is the phrasing of headings consistent with the document's purpose?
- ☐ Are headings visually consistent and grammatically parallel?

Audience Considerations

- ☐ Does this design meet the audience's needs and expectations?
- ☐ Does this design respect the cultural conventions of the audience?

Chapter quiz, Exercises, Web links, and Flashcards
(Go to *Student Resources>Chapter 13*)

Document design/visuals Activities, Case studies, and Quizzes
(Go to *Document Design and Graphics*)

Projects

GENERAL

1. Find an example of effective page design. Photocopy a selection (two or three pages), and attach a memo explaining to your instructor and classmates why this design is effective. Be specific in your evaluation. Now do the same for an example of ineffective page design, making specific suggestions for improvement. Bring your examples and explanations to class, and be prepared to discuss them.

   As an alternative assignment, imagine that you are a technical communication consultant, and address each memo to the manager of the organization that produced each document.

2. The following are headings from a set of instructions for listening. Rewrite the headings to make them parallel.

   - You Must Focus on the Message
   - Paying Attention to Nonverbal Communication
   - Your Biases Should Be Suppressed
   - Listen Critically
   - Listen for Main Ideas
   - Distractions Should Be Avoided
   - Provide Verbal and Nonverbal Feedback
   - Making Use of Silent Periods
   - Are You Allowing the Speaker Time to Make His or Her Point?
   - Keeping an Open Mind Is Important

3. Using the checklist on page design, redesign an earlier assignment or a document you've prepared on the job. Submit to your instructor the revision and the original, along with a memo explaining your improvements. Be prepared to discuss your design in class.

4. On campus or at work, locate a document with a design that needs revision. Candidates include career counseling handbooks, financial aid handbooks, student or faculty handbooks, software or computer manuals, medical information, newsletters, or registration procedures. Redesign the whole document or a two- to five-page selection from it. Submit to your instructor a copy of the original, along with a memo explaining your improvements. Be prepared to discuss your revision in class.

TEAM

Working in small groups, redesign a document you select or your instructor provides. Prepare a detailed explanation of your group's revision. Appoint a group member to present your revision to the class.

DIGITAL

Many of today's technical documents are designed so they can be displayed on the computer and also printed and used in hard copy. The best choice for this approach is to create the document in PDF format. Find a government Web site, such as the Centers for Disease Control <www.cdc.gov> or the Environmental Protection Agency <www.epa.gov> and compare documents that are created as Web pages versus documents that are created as PDFs. Write a short memo to your instructor analyzing each document and explaining why you think the choice was made to use a Web versus a PDF format.

GLOBAL

Find a document that presents the same information in several languages (assembly instructions for various products are often written in two or three languages, for example). Evaluate the design decisions made in these documents. For example, are the different languages presented side by side or in different sections? Write a memo to classmates and your instructor evaluating the document and making recommendations for improvement.

For more support in mastering the objectives of this chapter, go to **www.mytechcommlab.com**

Designing Visual Information

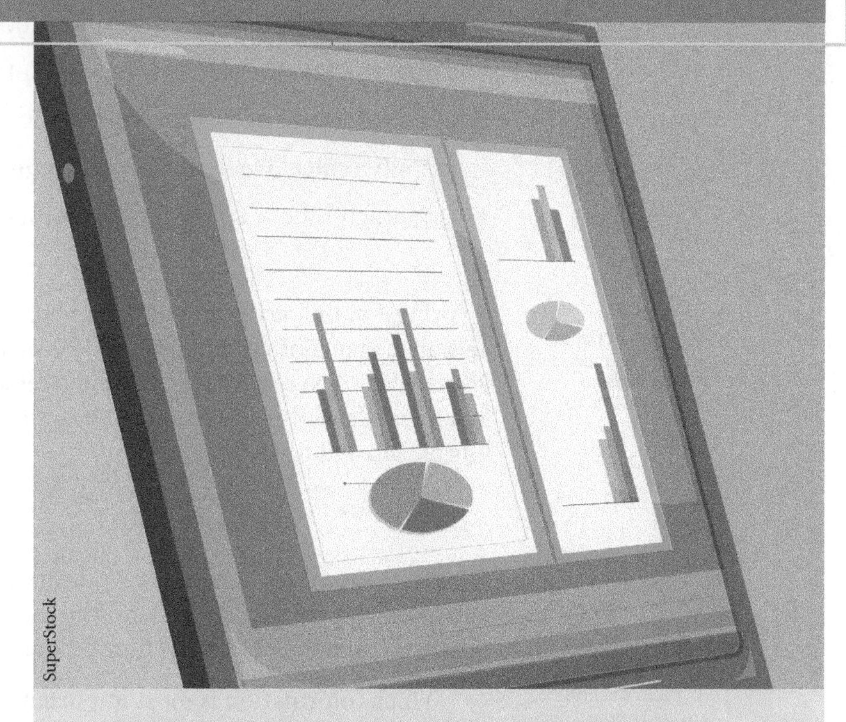

SuperStock

"Every presentation, report, or specification I create is heavily dependent on visuals. Among my fellow scientists, charts and graphs help condense large sets of data into patterns and trends that we can grasp quickly. And even when I write a document for lawyers or other non-scientists at the company, I use visuals to make complicated scientific information easy for them to understand. Managers, for example, appreciate charts that illustrate the various pieces of the puzzle that go into researching a new product. Presentation and spreadsheet software make it easy to create professional looking visuals—but I always check the visual carefully before using it in my presentation or document because, as we all know, computers don't catch everything."

—Nanette Bauer,
Research Scientist at a large biotechnology company

LEARNING OBJECTIVES FORTHIS CHAPTER

- Understand the role of visuals in technical communication
- Determine when to use visuals
- Select the right visuals for your readers
- Create tables, graphs, charts, illustrations, photographs, and videos
- Increase visual appeal by using color appropriately
- Identify ethical issues when using visuals
- Understand how cultural considerations affect your choice of visuals

Chapter overview
(Go to *Student Resources>Chapter 12*)

In printed or online documents, in oral presentations or multimedia programs, visuals are a staple of communication. Because they focus and organize information, visuals make data easier to interpret and remember. By offering powerful new ways of looking at data, visuals also reveal meanings that might otherwise remain buried in lists of facts and figures.

WHY VISUALS MATTER

Readers want more than just raw information; they want this material shaped and enhanced so they can understand the message at a glance. Visuals help us answer questions posed by readers as they process information:

Typical audience questions in processing information

- Which information is most important?
- Where, exactly, should I focus?
- What do these numbers mean?
- What should I be thinking or doing?
- What should I remember about this?
- What does it look like?
- How is it organized?
- How is it done?
- How does it work?

Document design/ visuals tutorial
(Go to *Document Design and Graphics>Tutorial*)

When people look at a visual pattern, such as a graph, they see it as one large pattern—the Big Picture that conveys information quickly and efficiently. For instance, the following line graph has no verbal information. The axes are not labeled, nor is the topic identified. But one quick glance, without the help of any words or numbers, tells you that the trend, after a period of gradual rise, has risen sharply. The graph conveys information in a way plain text never could.

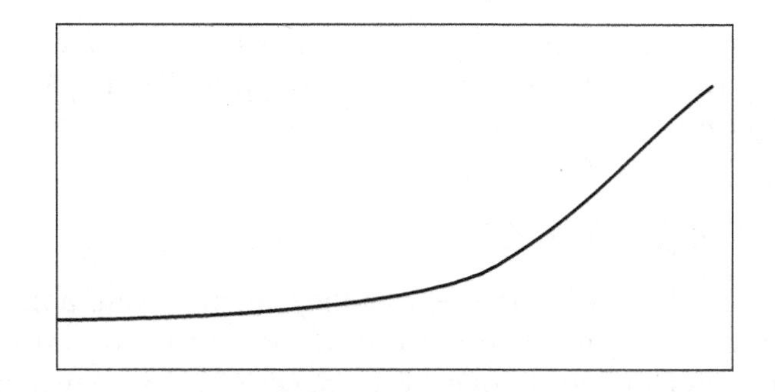

Surveys provide multiple, fresh viewpoints on a topic

The trend depicted in the above graph would be hard for readers to visualize by just reading the long list of numbers in the following passage:

> The time required for global population to grow from 5 to 6 billion was shorter than the interval between any of the previous billions. It took just 12 years for this to occur, just slightly less than the 13 years between the fourth and fifth billion, but much less time than the 118 years between the first and second billion. . . .

Technical data in prose form can be hard to interpret

When all this information is added to the original graph, as in Figure 1, the numbers become much easier to comprehend and compare.

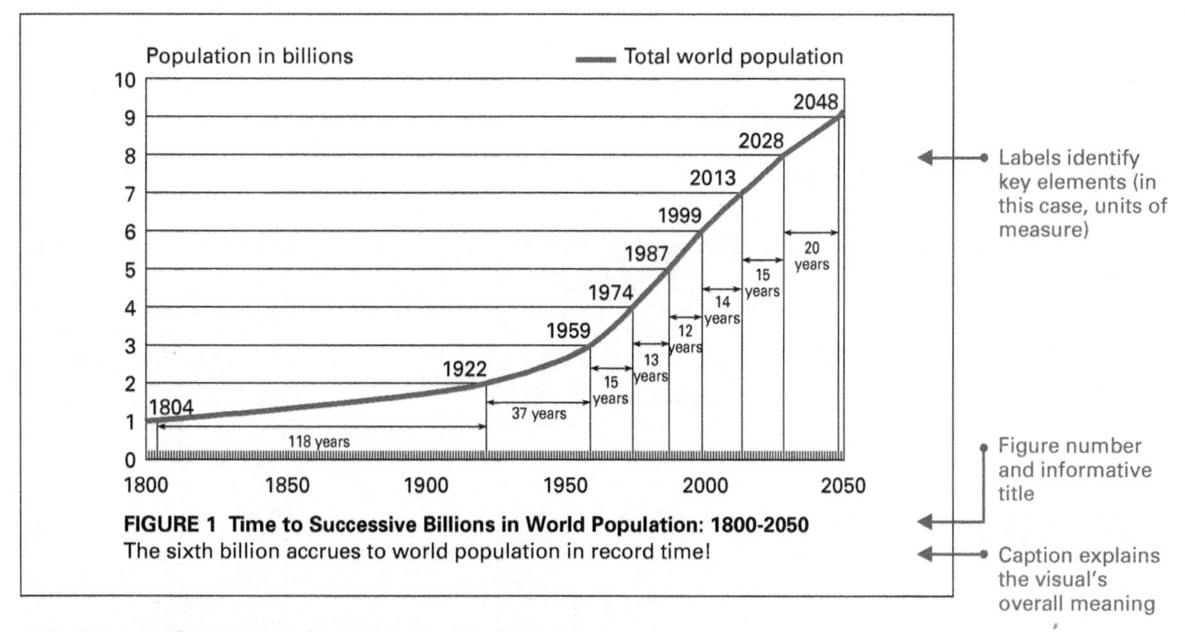

FIGURE 1 A Graph that Conveys the Big Picture
Source: United Nations (1995b); U.S. Census Bureau, International Programs Center, International Database and Unpublished Tables.

NOTE *Visuals enhance—but do not replace—essential discussion in your written text. In your document refer to the visual by number ("see Figure 1") and explain what to look for and what it means.*

WHEN TO USE VISUALS

Use visuals in situations like these

In general, you should use visuals whenever they can make your point more clearly than text or when they can enhance your text. Use visuals to clarify and support your discussion, not just to decorate your document. Use visuals to direct the audience's focus or help them remember something. There may be organizational reasons for using visuals; for example, some companies may always expect a chart or graph as part of their annual report. Certain industries, such as the financial sector, routinely use graphs and charts (such as the graph of the daily Dow Jones Industrial Average).

TYPES OF VISUALS TO CONSIDER

The following overview sorts visual displays into four categories: tables, graphs, charts, and graphic illustrations. Common examples within each category are shown in the table below. Note how each type of visual offers a unique way of seeing, a different perspective for understanding and processing the information.

Types of Visuals and Their Uses

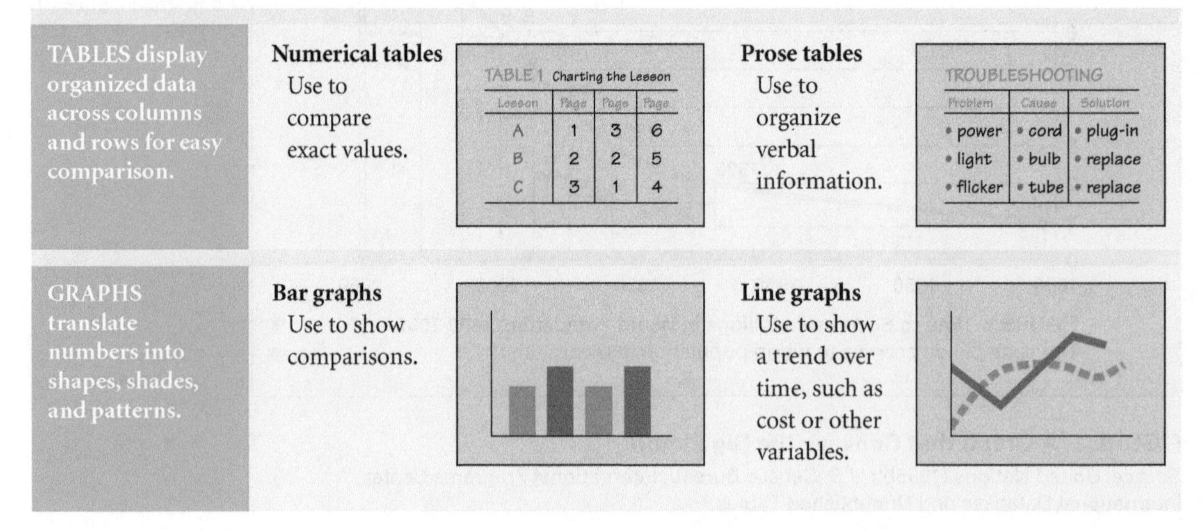

CHARTS depict relationships via geometric, arrows, lines, and other design elements.

Pie charts
Use to relate parts or percentages to the whole.

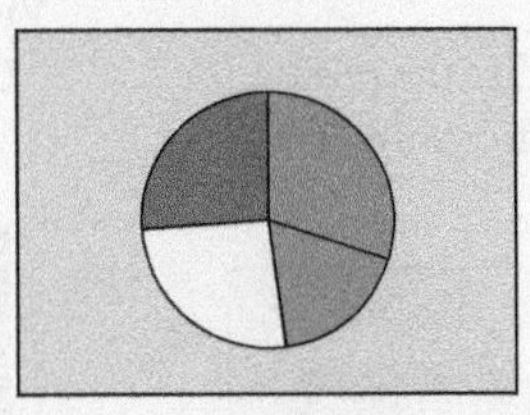

Organization charts
Use to show the hierarchy in a company.

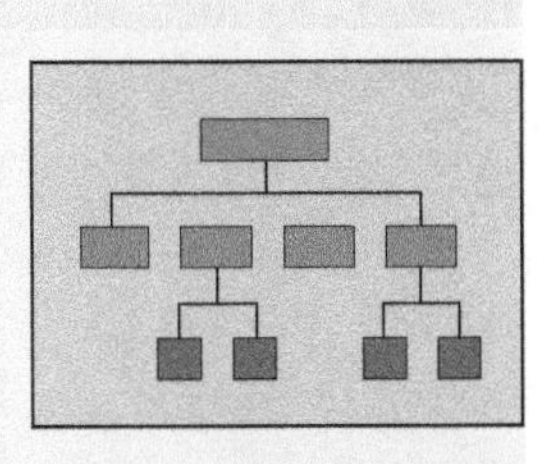

Flowcharts
Use to trace the steps (or decisions) in a procedure or process.

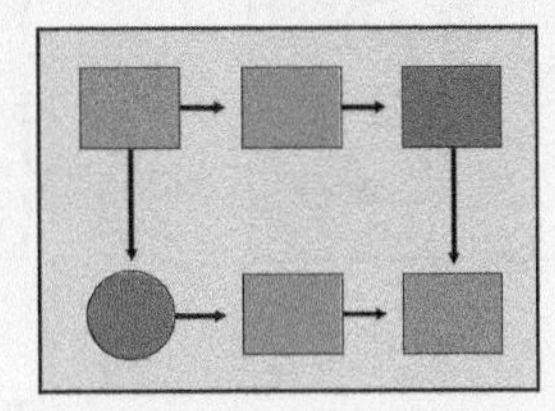

Gantt and PERT charts
Use to depict how the phases of a project relate.

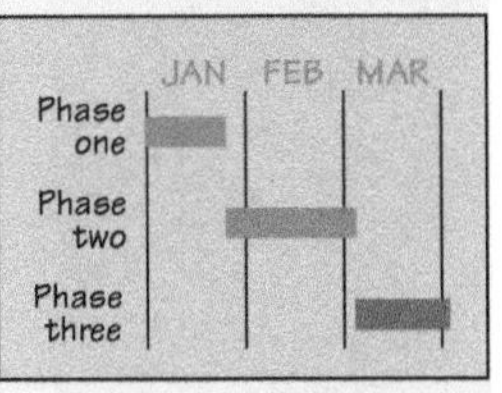

Tree charts
Use to show how the parts of an idea or concept relate.

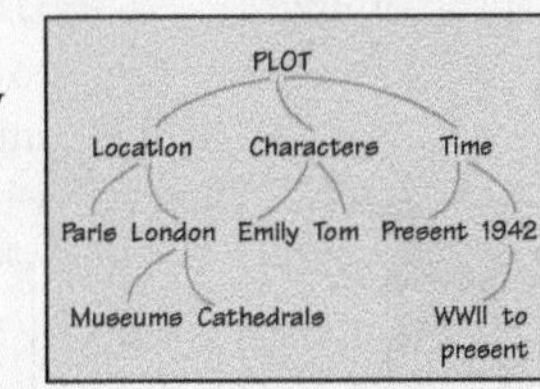

Pictograms
Use icons or other graphic devices that represent the displayed items.

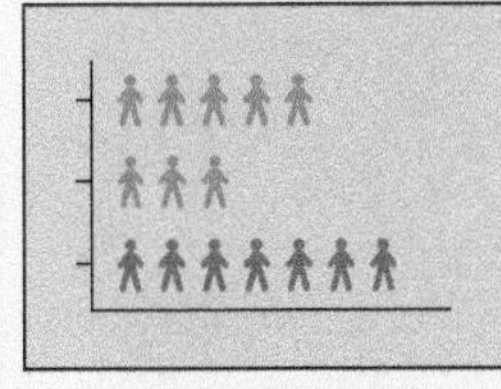

GRAPHIC ILLUSTRATIONS rely on pictures rather than on data or words.

Illustrations
Use to present a realistic but simplified view.

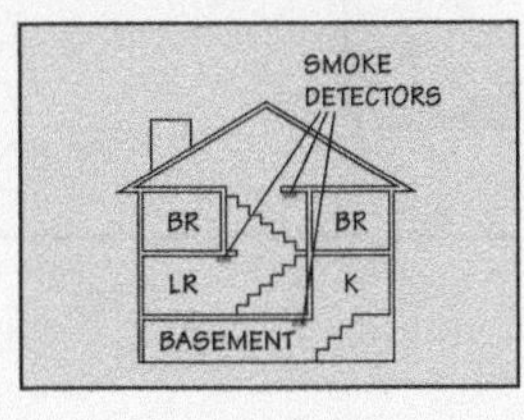

Cutaway diagrams
Use to show what is inside of a device or to help explain how a device works.

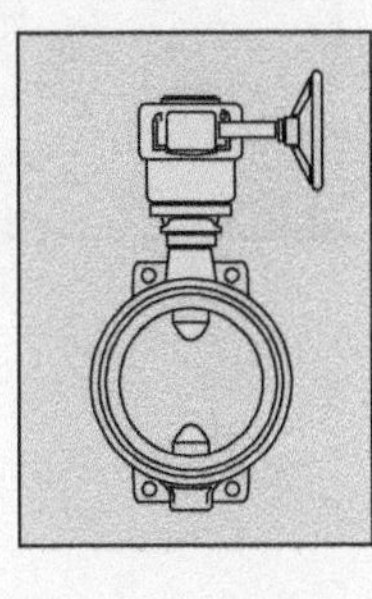

Exploded diagrams
Use to explain how an item is put together or how a user should assemble a product.

Block diagrams
Use to present the conceptual elements of a process or system—in depicting function instead of appearance.

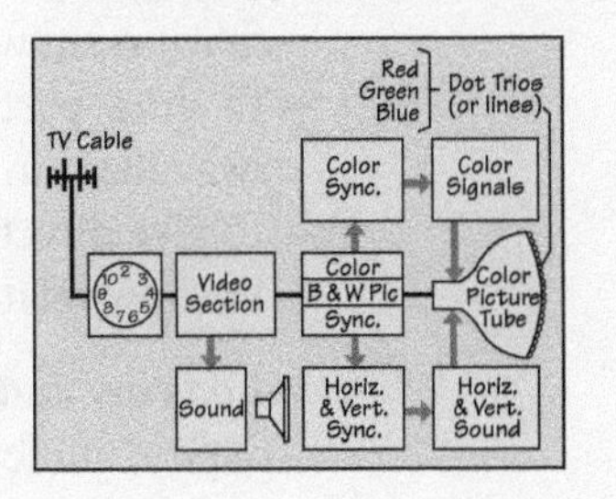

Maps
Use to help users visualize the position, location, and interrelationship of various data.

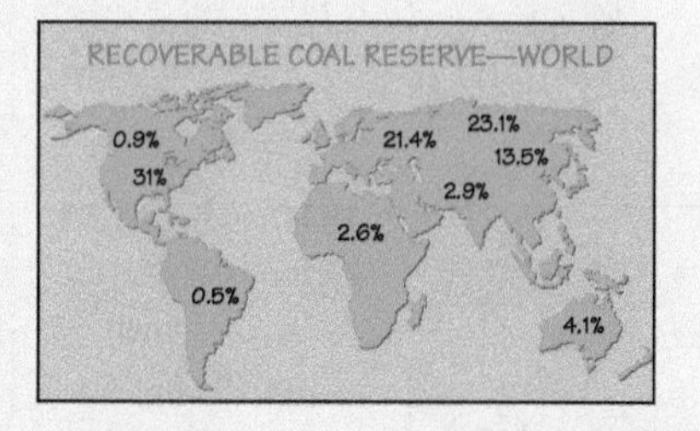

Videos
Use to show a procedure.

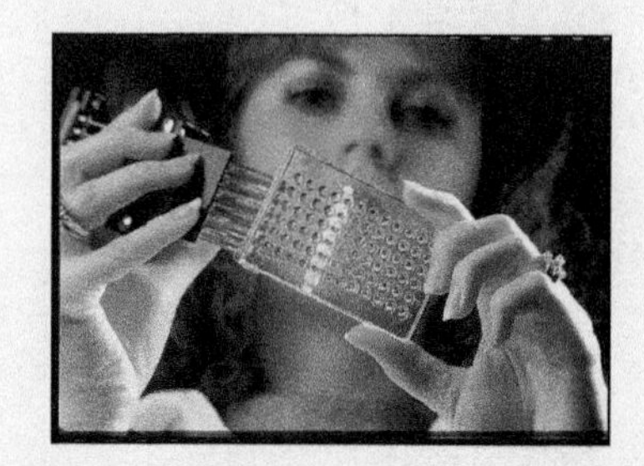

Photographs
Use to show exactly what something looks like.

Symbols and icons
Use to make concepts understandable to broad audiences, including international audiences and people who may have difficulty reading.

HOW TO CHOOSE THE RIGHT VISUALS

To select the most effective display, answer these questions:

Questions about a visual's purpose and audience

- **What is the purpose for using this visual?**
  - To convey facts and figures alone, a table may be the best choice. But if I want my audience to draw conclusions from that data, I may use a graph or chart to show comparisons.
  - To show parts of a mechanism, I probably want to use an exploded or cutaway diagram, perhaps together with a labeled photograph.
  - To give directions, I may want to use a diagram.
  - To show relationships, my best choice may be a flowchart or graph.
- **Who is my audience for these visuals?**
  - Expert audiences tend to prefer numerical tables, flowcharts, schematics, and complex graphs or diagrams that they can interpret for themselves.

  - General audiences tend to prefer basic tables, graphs, diagrams, and other visuals that direct their focus and interpret key points extracted from the data.
  - Cultural differences might come into play in the selection of appropriate visuals.

NOTE *Although visual communication has global appeal, certain displays might be inappropriate in certain cultures.*

- **What form of information will best achieve my purpose for this audience?**
  - Is my message best conveyed by numbers, shapes, words, pictures, or symbols?
  - Will my audience most readily understand a particular type of display?

Although several alternatives might work, one particular type of visual (or a combination) usually is superior. The best option, however, may not be available. Your audience or organization may express its own preferences, or choices may be limited by lack of equipment (software, scanners, digitizers), insufficient personnel (graphic designers, technical illustrators), or budget. Regardless of the limitations, your basic task is to enable the audience to interpret the visual correctly.

The many kinds of visuals you can use in your documents are described throughout this chapter. Regardless of type, certain requirements apply to all visuals. These requirements include

Features required in any visual

- using a title and number for each visual
- keeping the design of the visual clean and easy to read
- labeling all parts of the visual and providing legends as needed.
- placing the visual near the text it is helping to describe
- citing the sources of your visual material (both the source of the data and, when appropriate, the source of the actual visual—for instance, the creator of the bar chart or the person who took the photograph)

See the Guidelines boxes throughout this chapter for more information about using specific types of visuals.

NOTE *If you fail to cite the source or creator of a visual, you may be plagiarizing.*

TABLES

A table is a powerful way to display dense textual information such as specifications or comparisons. Numerical tables such as Table 1 present *quantitative information* (data that can be measured). Prose tables present *qualitative information* (prose

Title explains the table's purpose

Each column has a clear heading

Numbers are aligned properly for ease of reading

Where helpful, data are tallied

Caption explains the numeric relationships

Death Rates for Heart Disease and Cancer 1970–2006

	Number of Deaths (per 100,000)			
	Heart Disease		Cancer	
Year	Male	Female	Male	Female
1970	419	309	248	163
1980	369	305	272	167
1990	298	282	280	176
2000	256	260	257	206
2010	235	236	233	161
% change, 1970–2010	–43.9	–23.6	–6.0	–1.2

Both male and female death rates from heart disease decreased between 1970 to 2010, but males had nearly twice the rate of decrease. After increasing between 1970 and 1990, cancer death rates for both groups decreased to slightly below their 1970 levels.

TABLE 1 **Data Displayed in a Table** Organizes data into columns and rows for easy comparison.

Source: Adapted from *Statistical Abstract of the United States: 2010 (129th ed.).* Washington: GPO. Tables 113, 115.

Column headings lead into the information

Phrases are brief and aligned for ease of reading

Numbers enhance the verbal information

Note provides more detail

Radon Risk if You Smoke

Radon level	If 1,000 people who smoked were exposed to this level over a lifetime . . .	The risk of cancer from radon exposure compares to . . .	WHAT TO DO: Stop smoking and . . .
20 pCi/L[a]	About 135 people could get lung cancer	←100 times the risk of drowning	Fix your home
10 pCi/L	About 71 people could get lung cancer	←100 times the risk of dying in a home fire	Fix your home
8 pCi/L	About 57 people could get lung cancer		Fix your home
4 pCi/L	About 29 people could get lung cancer	←100 times the risk of dying in an airplane crash	Fix your home
2 pCi/L	About 15 people could get lung cancer	←2 times the risk of dying in a car crash	Consider fixing between 2 and 4 pCi/L
1.3 pCi/L	About 9 people could get lung cancer	(Average indoor radon level)	(Reducing radon levels below 2 pCi/L is difficult)
0.4 pCi/L	About 3 people could get lung cancer	(Average outdoor radon level)	

Note: If you are a former smoker, your risk may be lower.

[a]picocuries per liter

TABLE 2 **A Prose Table** Displays numerical and verbal information.

Source: Home Buyer's and Seller's Guide to Radon. Washington: GPO, 1993.

descriptions, explanations, or instructions). Table 2 combines numerical data, probability estimates, comparisons, and instructions.

NOTE *Including a caption with your visual enables you to analyze or interpret the trends or key points you want readers to recognize (as in Table 1).*

No table should be overly complex for its audience. Table 3, designed for expert readers, is hard for nonspecialists to interpret because it presents too much

Can cause information overload for nontechnical audiences

Toxic Chemical Releases by Industry: 2010

[In millions of pounds (4,438.7 represents 4,438,700,000), except as indicated.]

Industry	2010 SIC[1] code	Total on- and off-site releases	On-site release			Off-site releases/ transfers to disposal
			Total[2]	Point source air emissions	Surface water discharges	
Total[3]	**(X)**	**4,438.7**	**3,920.7**	**1,381.3**	**222.6**	**518.0**
Metal mining	10	1,245.7	1,244.7	1.8	0.7	1.0
Coal mining	12	12.9	12.9	0.1	0.2	-
Food and kindred products	20	153.2	145.8	35.1	83.1	7.3
Tobacco products	21	3.2	2.8	2.4	0.1	0.4
Textile mill products	22	7.4	6.5	4.8	0.3	0.9
Apparel and other textile products	23	0.7	0.5	0.4	-	0.2
Lumber and wood products	24	33.0	31.0	27.0	0.1	2.0
Furniture and fixtures	25	6.2	6.1	5.4	0.0	0.1
Paper and allied products	26	215.0	209.6	146.2	18.7	5.3
Printing and publishing	27	15.0	14.7	7.4	-	0.3
Chemical and allied products	28	544.7	500.3	168.6	44.5	44.4
Petroleum and coal products	29	75.0	71.9	34.6	17.1	3.1
Rubber and misc. plastic products	30	75.3	65.8	51.3	0.1	9.5
Leather and leather products	31	2.1	1.0	0.7	0.0	1.1
Stone, clay, glass products	32	51.2	45.8	38.1	2.1	5.5
Primary metal industries	33	477.5	198.1	35.9	39.4	279.4
Fabricated metals products	34	58.6	38.8	23.7	2.3	19.8
Industrial machinery and equipment	35	14.3	10.7	4.1	0.2	3.6
Electronic, electric equipment	36	20.3	13.8	6.5	3.6	6.4
Transportation equipment	37	74.8	63.5	51.1	0.2	11.2
Instruments and related products	38	8.7	7.9	5.1	1.0	0.8
Miscellaneous	39	7.1	4.9	3.9	0.1	2.2

X Not applicable. [1]Standard Industrial Classification, see text, Section 12. Labor Force. [2]Includes on-site disposal to underground injection for Class I wells, Class II to V wells, other surface impoundments, land releases, and other releases, not shown separately. [3]Includes industries with no specific industry identified, not shown separately.

TABLE 3 **A Complex Table Causes Information Overload** This table is too complex for anyone but experts.

Source: Environmental Protection Agency, *Annual Toxics Release Inventory.*

information at once. An unethical writer might use a complex table to bury numbers that are questionable or embarrassing (Williams 12). For laypersons, use fewer tables and keep them as simple as possible.

Audience and purpose

Like all other parts of a document, visuals are designed with audience and purpose in mind (Journet 3). An accountant doing an audit might need a table listing exact amounts, whereas the average public stockholder reading an annual report would prefer the "big picture" in an easily grasped bar graph or pie chart (Van Pelt 1). Similarly, scientists might find the complexity of data shown in Table 3 perfectly appropriate, but a nonexpert audience (say, environmental groups) might prefer the clarity and simplicity of a chart.

Tables work well for displaying exact values, but often graphs or charts are easier to interpret. Geometric shapes (bars, curves, circles) are generally easier to remember than lists of numbers (Cochran et al. 25).

For specific information about creating tables, see How to Construct a Table later in this chapter.

NOTE *Any visual other than a table is usually categorized as a figure, and so titled ("Figure 1 Aerial View of the Panhandle Mine Site").*

GRAPHS

Graphs show comparisons and trends

Graphs translate numbers into shapes, shades, and patterns. Graphs display, at a glance, the approximate values, the point being made about those values, and the relationship being emphasized. Graphs are especially useful for depicting comparisons, changes over time, patterns, or trends.

A graph's horizontal axis shows categories (the independent variables) to be compared, such as years within a period (1990, 2000, 2010). The vertical axis shows the range of values (the dependent variables) for comparing the categories, such as the number of deaths from heart failure in a given year. A dependent variable changes according to activity in the independent variable (say, a decrease in quantity over a set time, as in Figure 2).

Bar Graphs

Generally easy to understand, bar graphs show discrete comparisons, such as year-by-year or month-by-month. Each bar represents a specific quantity. You can use bar graphs to focus on one value or to compare values over time.

Simple Bar Graph A simple bar graph displays one trend or theme. The graph in Figure 2 shows one trend extracted from Table 1, male deaths from heart disease. If the audience needs exact numbers, you can record exact values above each bar.

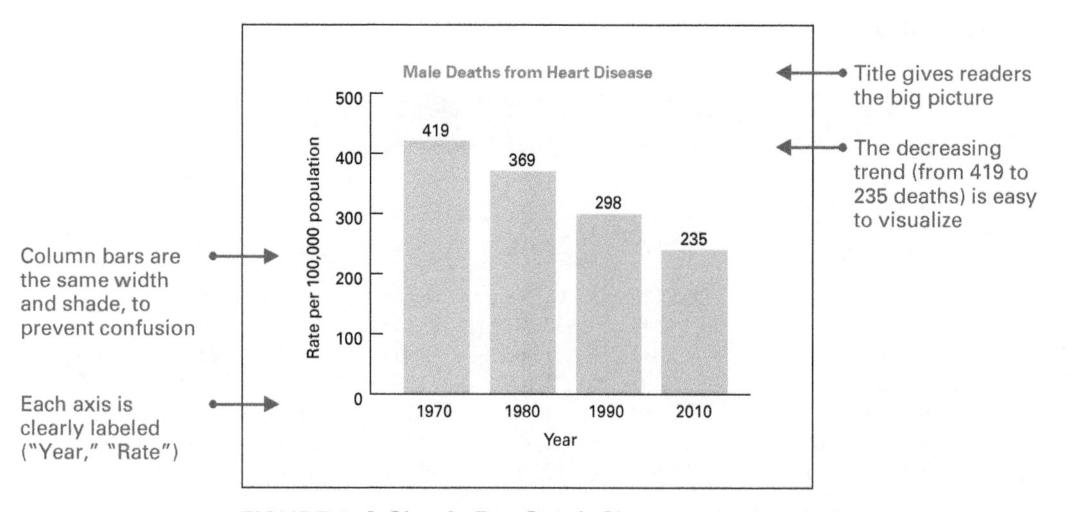

FIGURE 2 **A Simple Bar Graph** Shows a single relationship in the data.

Multiple-Bar Graph A bar graph can display two or three relationships simultaneously. Figure 3 contrasts two sets of data, to show comparative trends. Be sure to use a different pattern or color for each data set, and include a key (or *legend*) so that viewers will know which color or pattern corresponds with which data set. The more relationships you include, the more complex the graph becomes, so try to include no more than three on any one graph.

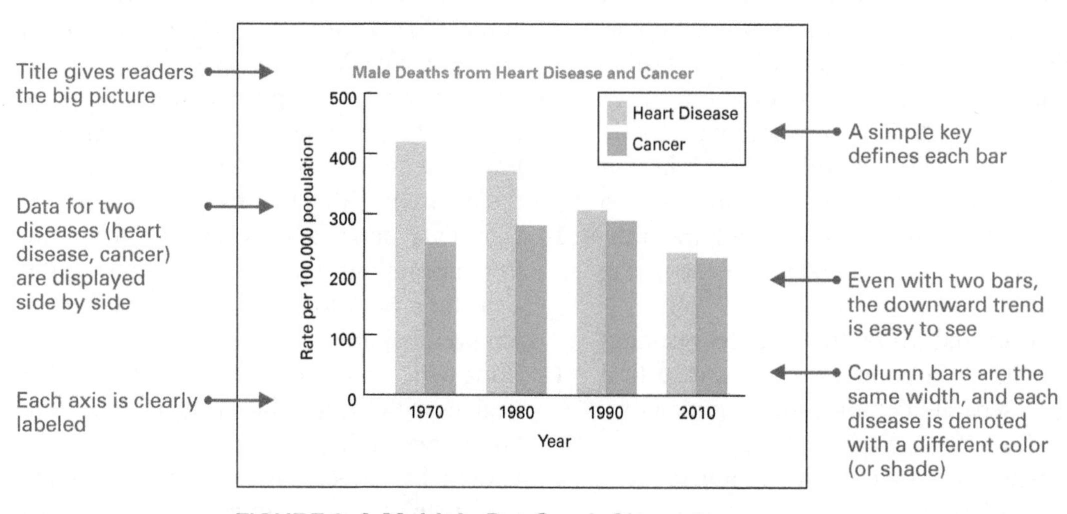

FIGURE 3 **A Multiple-Bar Graph** Shows two or more relationships.

How to Construct a Table

TABLE 14.4 ■ Federal Student Financial Assistance: 2002 – 2006

STUB HEAD Number of Awards (1000)[a]	2002	2003	2004	2005	2006[b]
Total	**55,525**	**62,249**	**68,629**	**73,020**	**76,604**
Pell Grant	11,640	12,681	13,091	12,901	12,745
Opportunity Grant	1,033	1,064	975	985	(X)
Work-Study	1,097	1,106	1,194	1,184	1,172
Perkins Loan	1,460	1,638	1,263	1,137	1,135
Direct Student Loan	11,689	11,969	12,840	13,860	13,874
Family Educ. Loan	28,606	33,791	39,266	42,953	46,703

(COLUMN HEADS; ROW HEADS; NOTE; SRC)

[a]As of June 30. [b]Estimate. (X) Not available.

Source: U.S. Department of Education, Office of Postsecondary Education, unpublished data. *Statistical Abstract of the United States: 2007* (126th Edition). Washington: GPO. Table 279.

1. Number the table in its order of appearance and provide a title that describes exactly what is being measured.
2. Label stub, column, and row heads (*Number of Awards*; *2006*; *Pell Grant*) to orient readers.
3. Specify units of measurement or use familiar symbols and abbreviations (*$, hr.*). Define specialized symbols or abbreviations (*Å = angstrom, db = decibel*) in a footnote.
4. Compare data vertically (in columns) instead of horizontally (rows). Columns are easier to compare. Try to include row or column averages or totals, as reference points for comparing individual values.
5. Use horizontal rules to separate headings from data. In a complex table, use vertical rules to separate columns. In a simple table, use as few rules as clarity allows.
6. List items in a logical order (alphabetical, chronological, decreasing cost). Space listed items for easy comparison. Keep prose entries as brief as clarity allows.
7. Convert fractions to decimals. Align decimals and all numbers vertically. Keep decimal places for all numbers equal. Round insignificant decimals to whole numbers.
8. Use *x*, *NA*, or a dash to signify any omitted entry, and explain the omission in a footnote (*Not available, Not applicable*).
9. Use footnotes to explain entries, abbreviations, or omissions. Label footnotes with lowercase letters so readers do not confuse the notation with the numerical data.
10. Cite data sources beneath any footnotes. When adapting or reproducing a copyrighted table for a work to be published, obtain written permission.
11. If the table is too wide for the page, turn it 90 degrees with the left side facing page bottom. Or use two tables.
12. If the table exceeds one page, write "continues" at the bottom and begin the next page with the full title, "continued," and the original column headings.

Horizontal-Bar Graph Horizontal-bar graphs are good for displaying a large series of bars arranged in order of increasing or decreasing value, as in Figure 4. This format leaves room for labeling the categories horizontally (*Doctorate,* and so on).

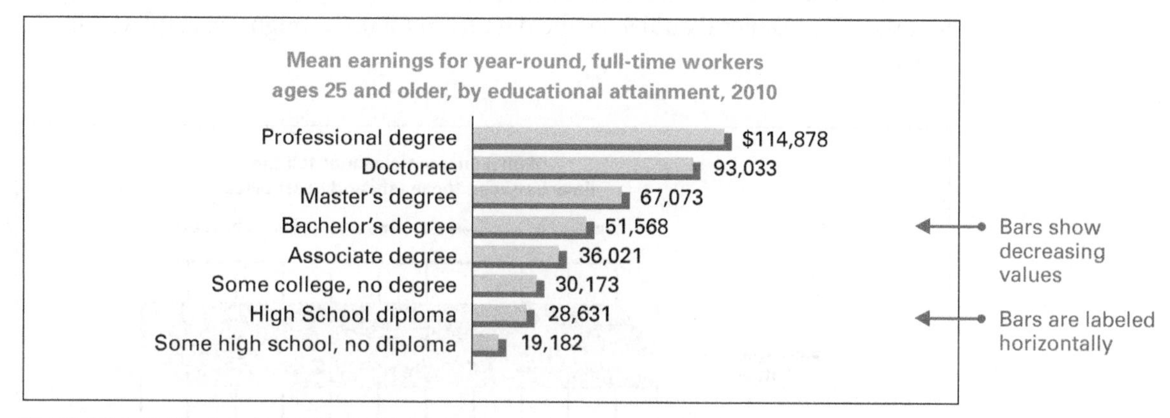

FIGURE 4 **A Horizontal-Bar Graph** Accommodates lengthy labels.
Source: Bureau of Labor Statistics.

Stacked-Bar Graph Instead of displaying bars side-by-side, you can stack them. Stacked-bar graphs show how much each data set contributes to the whole.

Figure 5 displays other comparisons from Table 1. To avoid confusion, don't display more than four or five sets of data in a single bar.

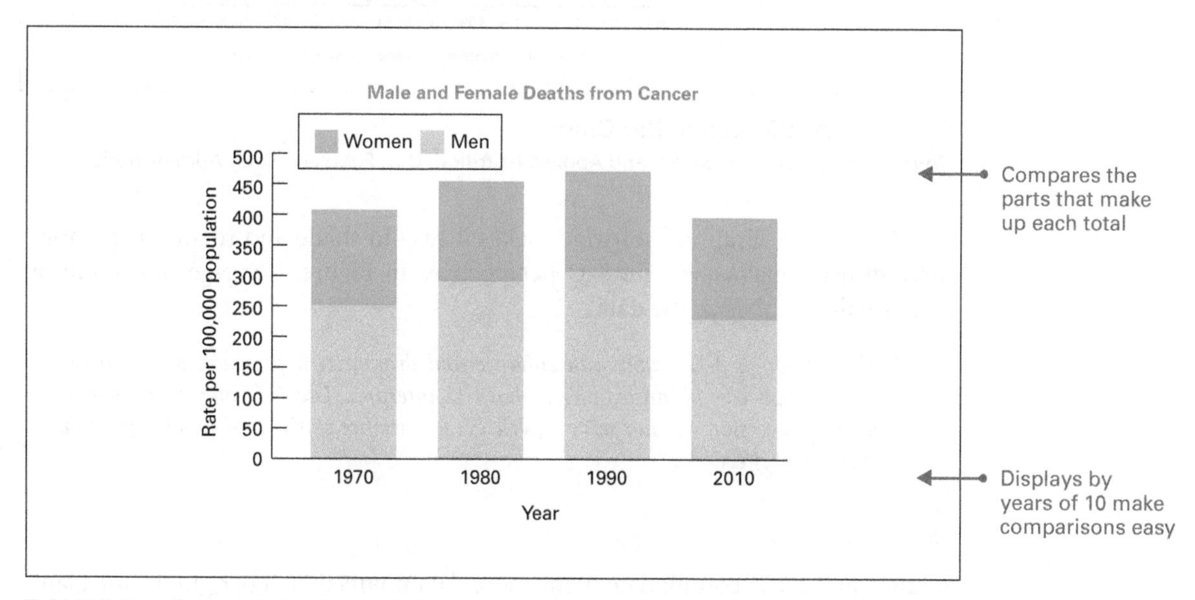

FIGURE 5 **A Stacked-Bar Graph** Displays of 10 make comparisons easy.

100-Percent Bar Graph A type of stacked-bar graph, the 100-percent bar graph shows the value of each part that makes up the 100-percent value, as in Figure 6. Like any bar graph, the 100-percent graph can have either horizontal or vertical bars.

Notice how bar graphs become harder to interpret as bars and patterns increase. For a general audience, the data from Figure 6 might be displayed in pie charts.

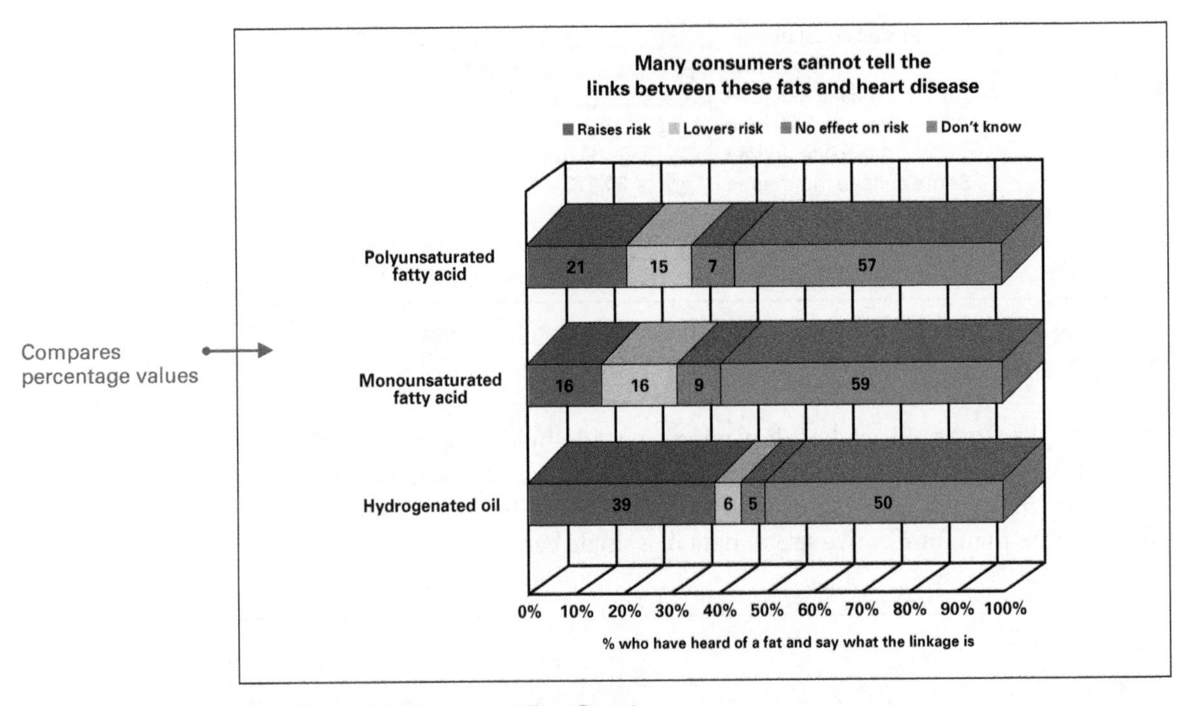

FIGURE 6 **A 100-percent Bar Graph**

Source: Center for Food Safety and Applied Nutrition, U.S. Food and Drug Administration.

3-D Bar Graph Graphics software makes it easy to shade and rotate images for a three-dimensional view. The 3-D perspectives in Figure 7 engage our attention and visually emphasize the data.

> **NOTE** *Although 3-D graphs can enhance and dramatize a presentation, an overly complex graph can be misleading or hard to interpret. Use 3-D only when a two-dimensional version will not serve as well. Never sacrifice clarity and simplicity for the sake of visual effect.*

Line Graphs

A line graph can accommodate many more data points than a bar graph (for example, a twelve-month trend, measured monthly). Line graphs help readers synthesize large bodies of information in which exact quantities don't need to be emphasized.

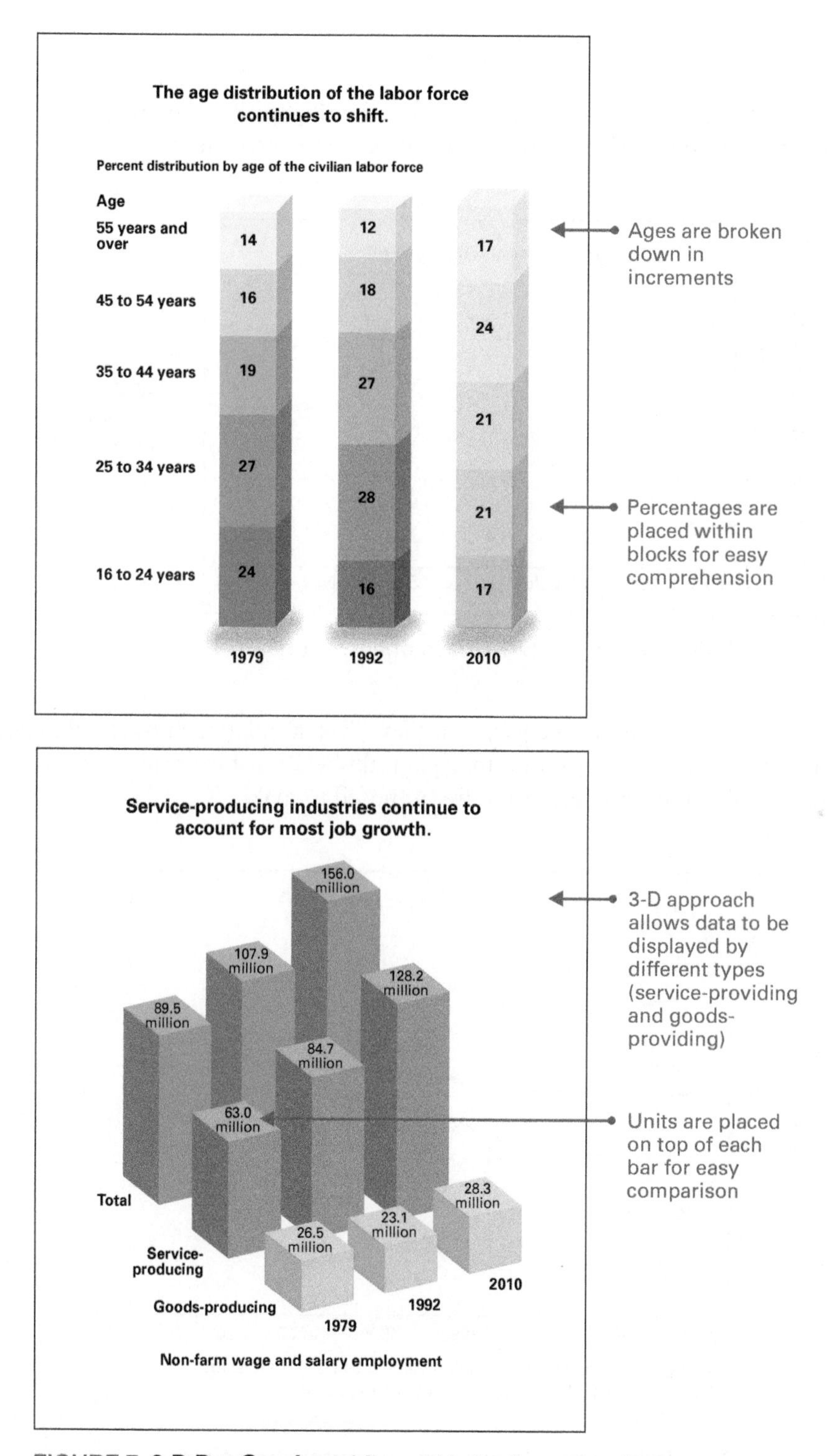

FIGURE 7 **3-D Bar Graphs** Adding a third axis creates the appearance of depth.

Source: Bureau of Labor Statistics.

Simple Line Graph A simple line graph, as in Figure 8, plots time intervals (or categories) on the horizontal scale and values on the vertical scale.

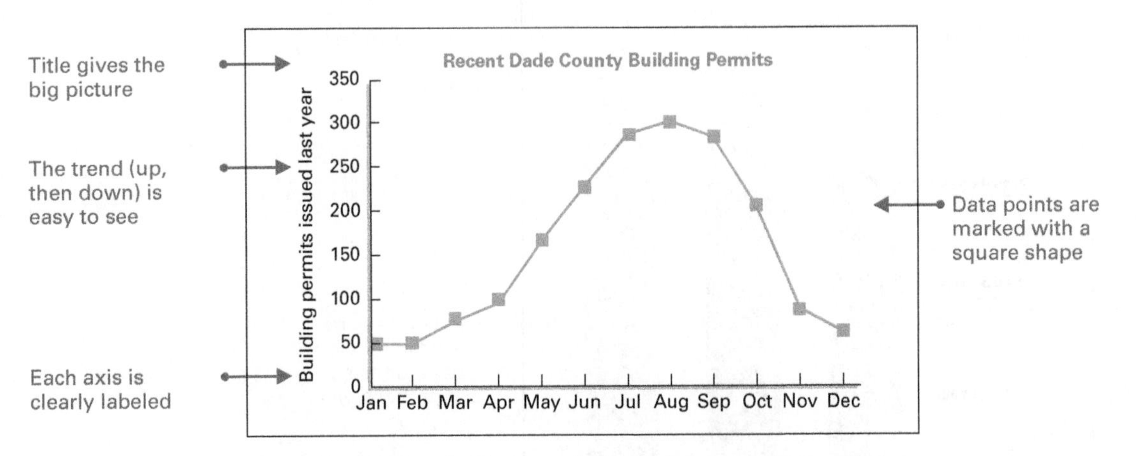

FIGURE 8 **A simple line graph** Displays one relationship.

Multiline Graph A multiline graph displays several relationships simultaneously, as in Figure 9. Include a caption to explain the relationships readers are supposed to see and the interpretations they are supposed to make.

FIGURE 9 **A Multiline graph** Displays multiple relationships.
Source: Bureau of Labor Statistics.

Deviation Line Graph Extend your vertical scale below the zero baseline to display positive and negative values in one graph, as in Figure 10. Mark values below the baseline in intervals parallel to those above it.

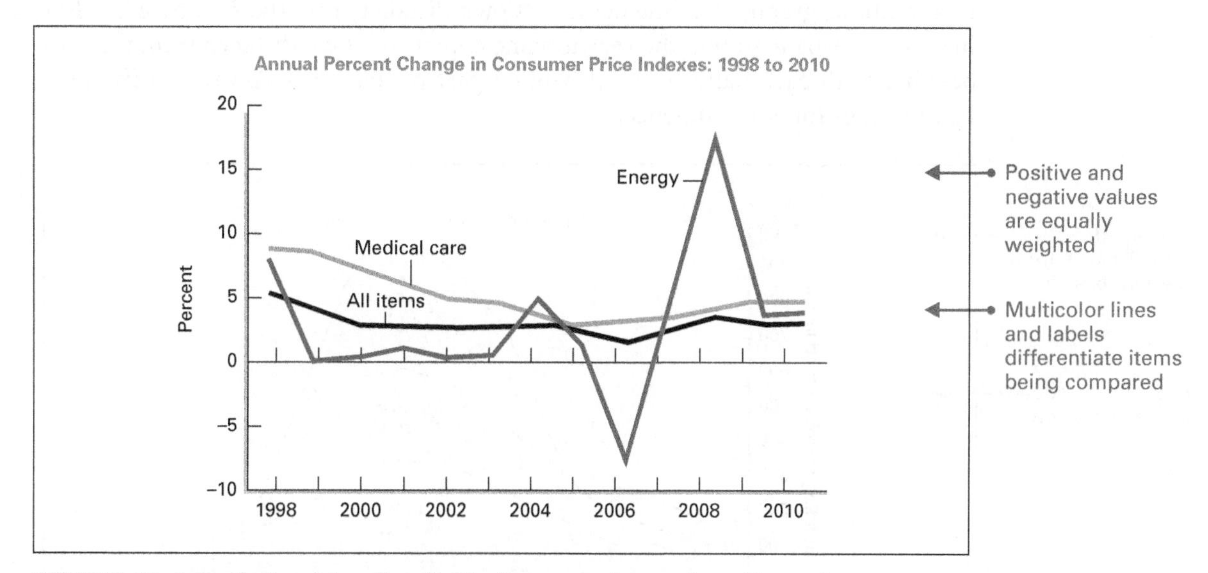

FIGURE 10 **A Deviation Line Graph** Displays negative and positive values.
Source: Chart prepared by U.S. Bureau of the Census.

Band or Area Graph By shading in the area beneath the main plot lines, you can highlight specific information. Figure 11 is another version of the Figure 8 line graph.

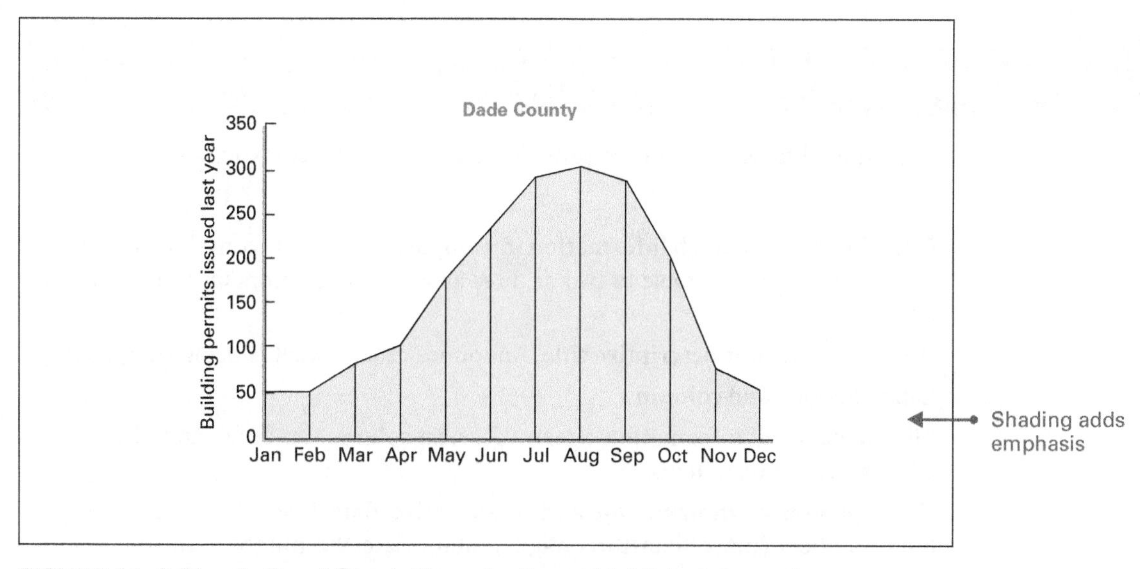

FIGURE 11 **A Simple Band Graph** Uses shading to highlight information.

Multiple-Band Graph The multiple bands in Figure 12 depict relationships among sums instead of the direct comparisons depicted in the Figure 9 multiline graph. Despite their visual appeal, multiple-band graphs are easy to misinterpret: In a multiline graph, each line depicts its own distance from the zero baseline. But in a multiple-band graph, the very top line depicts the *total* distance from the zero baseline, with each band below it being a part of that total. Always clarify these relationships for your audience.

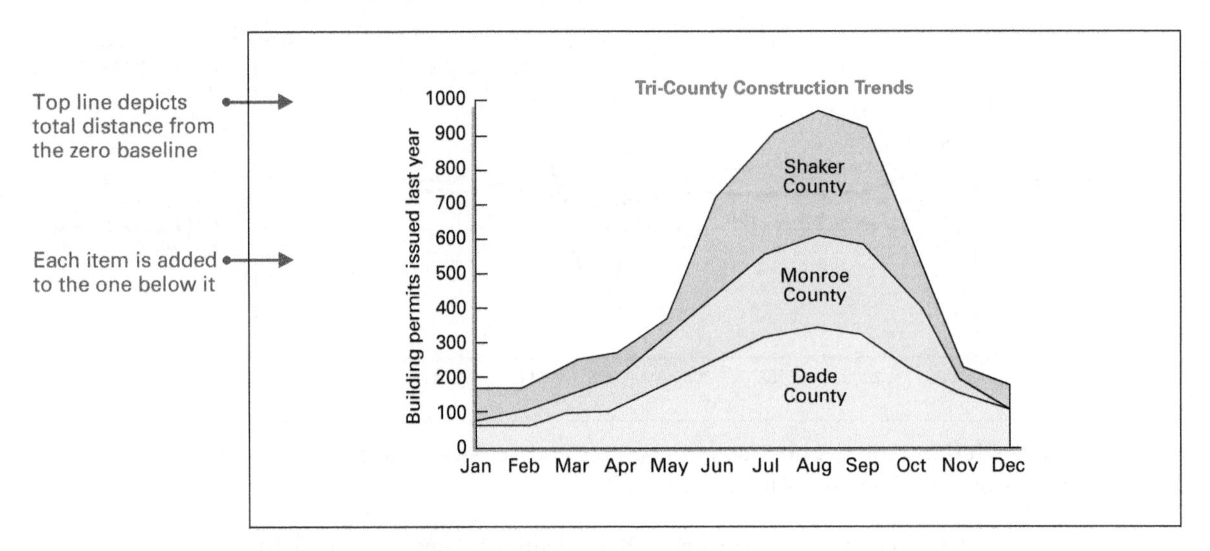

FIGURE 12 **A Multiple-Band Graph** Depicts relationships among sums instead of direct comparisons.

GUIDELINES for Creating Tables and Graphs

For all types of tables and graphs, provide a clear title and credit your sources.

Tables

- **Don't include too much information in a single table.** Overly complex tables are confusing. Limit your table to two or three areas of comparison. Or use multiple tables.
- **Provide a brief but descriptive title.** Announce exactly what is being compared.
- **Label the rows and columns.**
- **Line up data and information clearly.** Use neat columns and rows and plenty of white space between items.
- **Keep qualitative information and quantitative data brief.** When including high numbers (more than three digits), abbreviate the numbers and indicate

"in thousands," "in millions," and so on. When using text in a table, limit the number of words.

- **Provide additional information, if necessary.** Add footnotes or a caption at the bottom of the table to explain anything readers may not understand at first glance.

Bar Graphs

- **Use a bar graph only to compare values that are noticeably different.** Small value differences will yield bars that look too similar to compare.
- **Keep the graph simple and easy-to-read.** Don't plot more than three types of bars in each cluster. Avoid needless visual details.
- **Number your scales in units familiar to the audience.** Units of 1 or multiples of 2, 5, or 10 are best.
- **Label both scales to show what is being measured or compared.** If space allows, keep all labels horizontal for easier reading.
- **Use tick marks to show the points of division on your scale.** If the graph has many bars, extend the tick marks into *grid lines* to help readers relate bars to values.

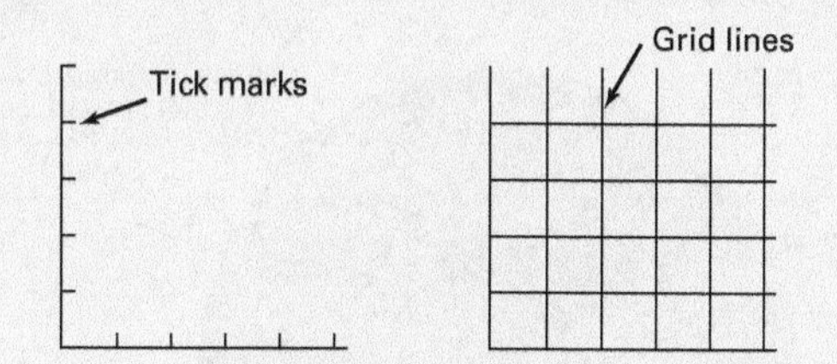

- **Make all bars the same width** (unless you are overlapping them).
- **In a multiple-bar graph, use a different pattern, color, or shade for each bar in a cluster.** Provide a key, or legend, identifying each pattern, color, or shade.
- **Refer to the graph by number ("Figure 1") in your text, and explain what the reader should look for.** Or include a prose caption with the graph.

Line Graphs

Follow the guidelines above for bar graphs, with these additions:

- **Display no more than three or four lines on one graph.**
- **Mark each individual data point used in plotting each line.**
- **Make each line visually distinct (using color, symbols, and so on).**
- **Label each line so readers know what the given line represents.**
- **Avoid grid lines that readers could mistake for plotted lines.**

and GANTT chart models
(Go to *Student Resources>Chapter 12> Models and Templates*)

CHARTS

The terms *chart* and *graph* often are used interchangeably. Technically, a chart displays relationships (quantitative or cause-and-effect) that are *not* plotted on a coordinate system (*x* and *y* axes).

Pie Charts

Easy for most people to understand, a pie chart displays the relationship of parts or percentages to the whole. Readers can compare the parts to each other as well as to the whole (to show how much was spent on what, how much income comes from which sources, and so on). Figure 13 shows a simple pie chart. Figure 14 is an exploded pie chart. Exploded pie charts highlight various pieces of the pie.

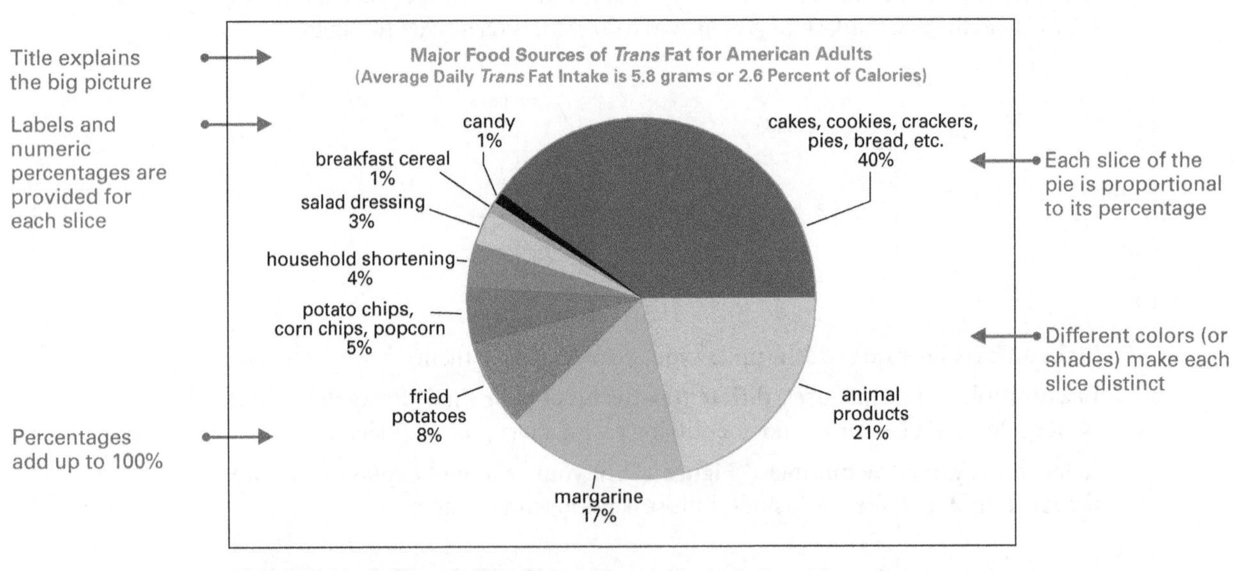

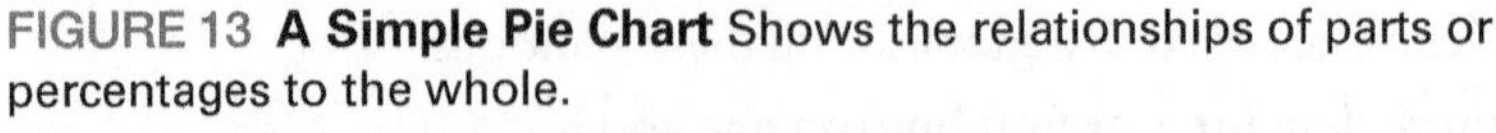

FIGURE 13 **A Simple Pie Chart** Shows the relationships of parts or percentages to the whole.
Source: U.S. Food and Drug Administration.

Organization Charts

An organization chart shows the hierarchy and relationships between different departments and other units in an organization, as in Figure 15.

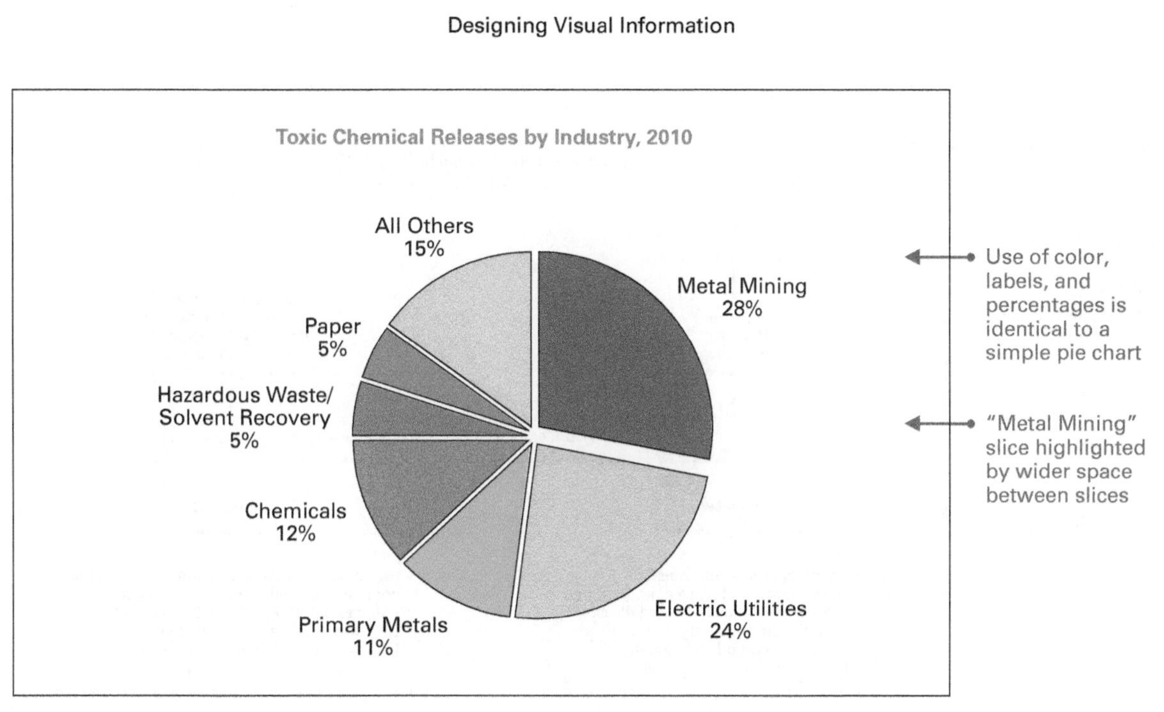

FIGURE 14 **An Exploded Pie Chart** Highlights various slices.
Source: U.S. Environmental Protection Agency. (See Table 3 earlier page, for data.)

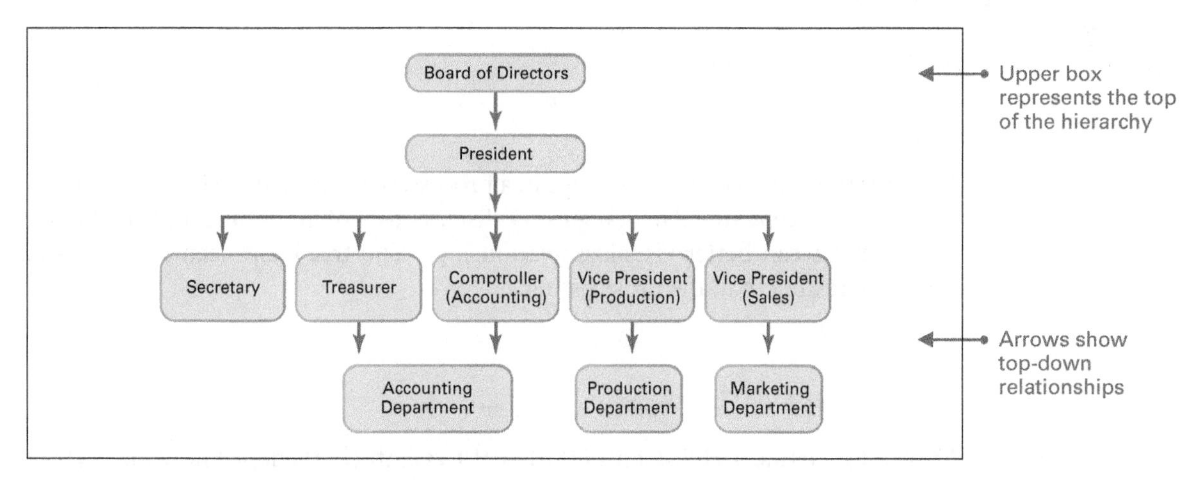

FIGURE 15 **An Organization Chart** Shows how different people or departments are ranked and related.

Flowcharts

A flowchart traces a procedure or process from beginning to end. Figure 16 illustrates the procedure for helping an adult choking victim.

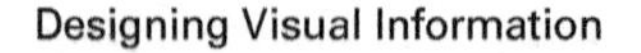

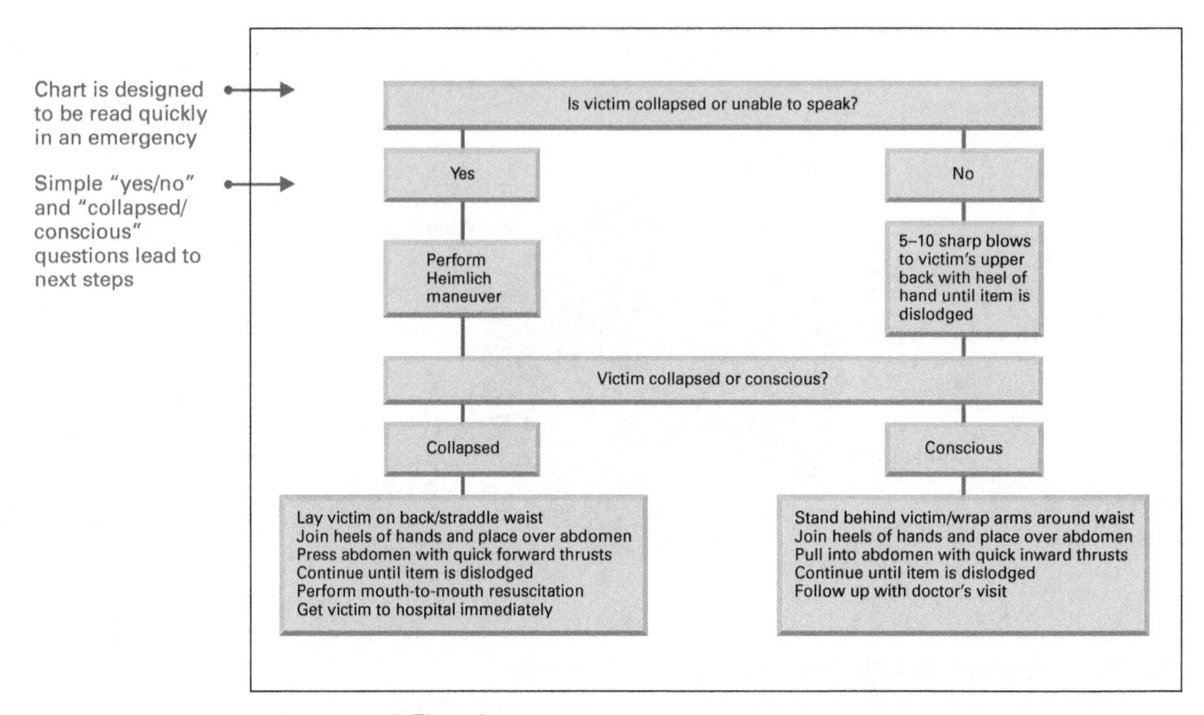

FIGURE 16 **A Flowchart** Depicts a sequence of events, activities, steps, or decisions.

Tree Charts

Whereas flowcharts display the steps in a process, tree charts show how the parts of an idea or concept are related. Figure 17 displays part of an outline for this chapter so that users can better visualize relationships. The tree chart seems clearer and more interesting than the prose listing.

Gantt and PERT Charts

Gantt and PERT charts are useful for project planning

Named for engineer H. L. Gantt (1861–1919), Gantt charts depict how the parts of an idea or concept relate. A series of bars or lines (time lines) indicates start-up and completion dates for each phase or task in a project. Gantt charts are useful for planning and tracking a project. The Gantt chart in Figure 18 illustrates the schedule for a manufacturing project. A PERT (Program Evaluation and Review Technique) chart uses shapes and arrows to outline a project's main activities and events (Figure 19). Both types of charts can be created with project management software such as *Microsoft Project*.

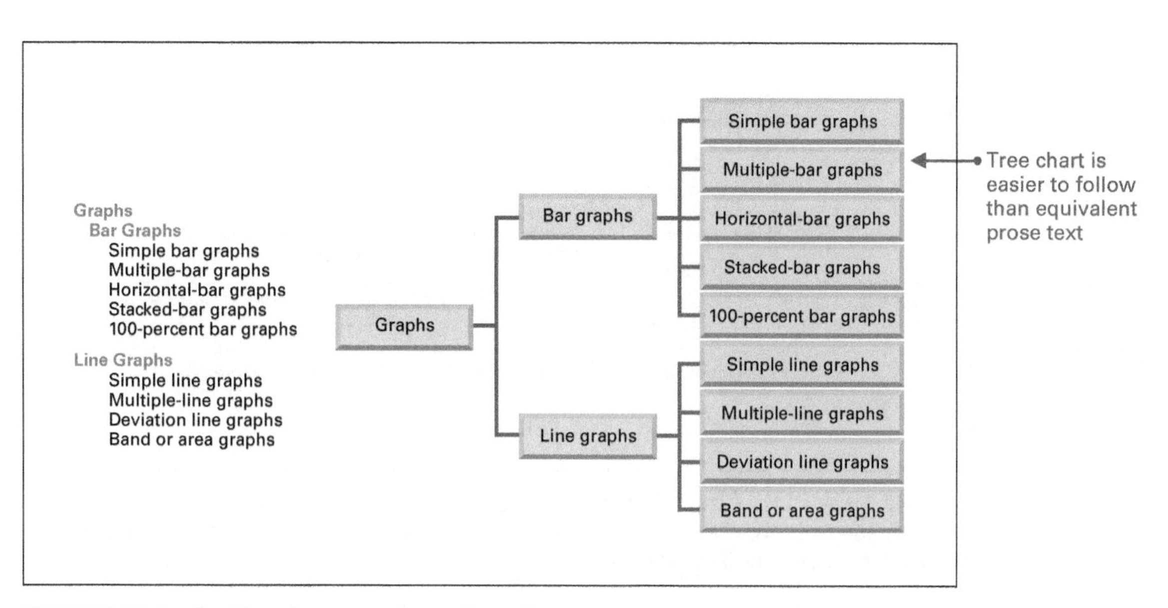

FIGURE 17 **An Outline Converted to a Tree Chart** Shows which items belong together and how they are connected.

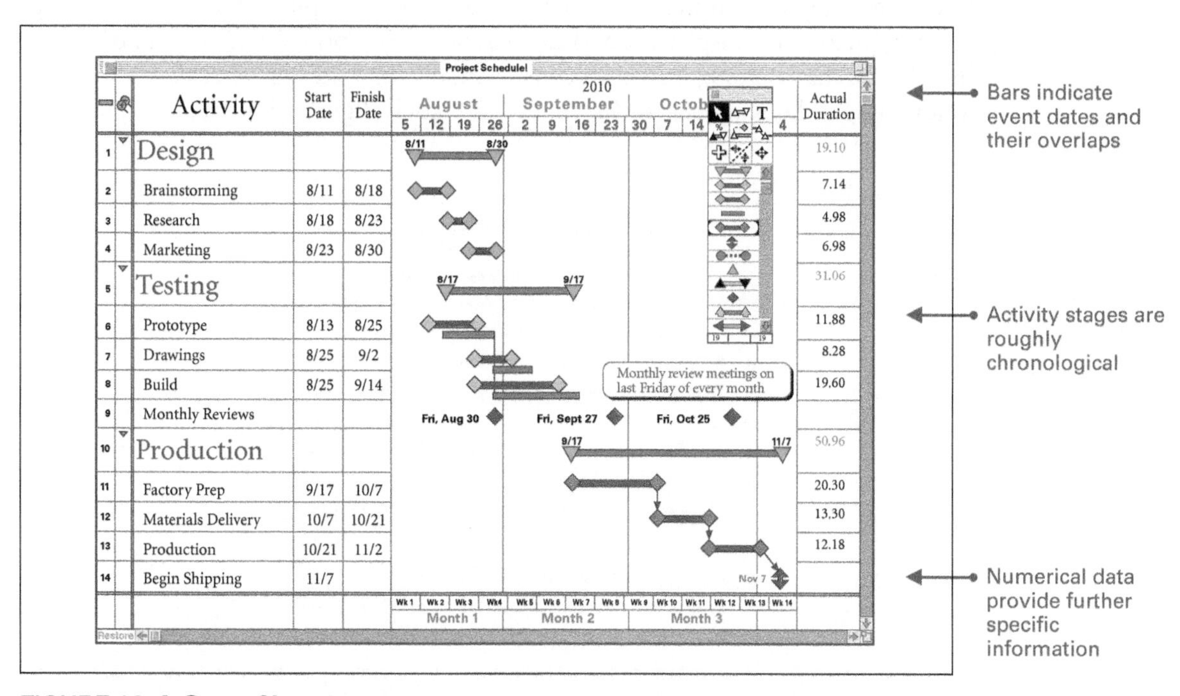

FIGURE 18 **A Gantt Chart** Depicts how the phases of a project interrelate.
Source: Chart created in *FastTrack Schedule™*. Reprinted by permission from AEC Software. Learn more about *FastTrack Schedule* at <www.aecsoftware.com>.

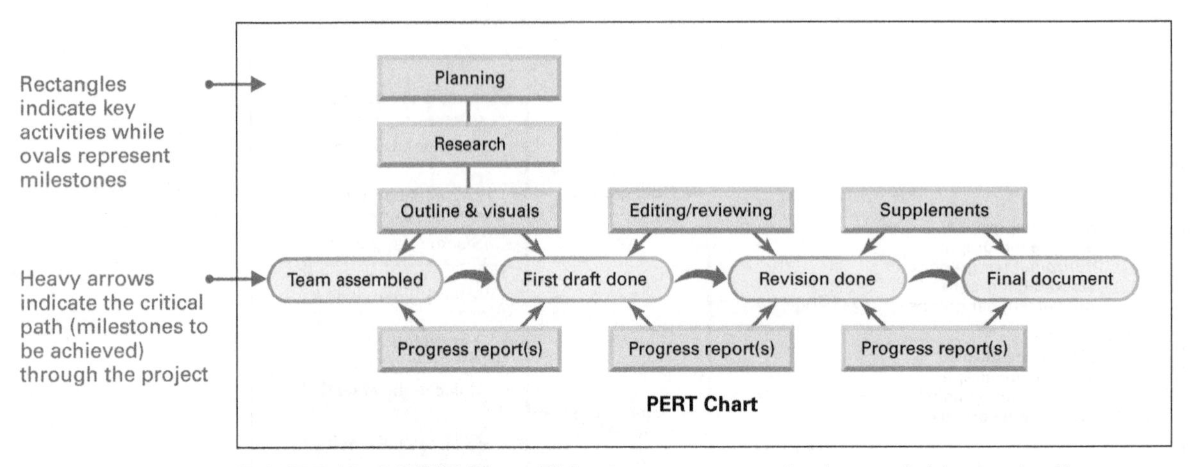

FIGURE 19 **A PERT Chart** This chart maps out the key activities and milestones ("Team assembled," "First draft done" and so on) for a major technical report to be produced by a collaborative team.

Pictograms

Pictograms use symbols to enhance a graph or chart

Pictograms are something of a cross between a line graph and a chart. Like line graphs, pictograms display numerical data, often by plotting it across *x* and *y* axes. But like a chart, pictograms use icons, symbols, or other graphic devices rather than simple lines or bars. In Figure 20 stick figures illustrate population

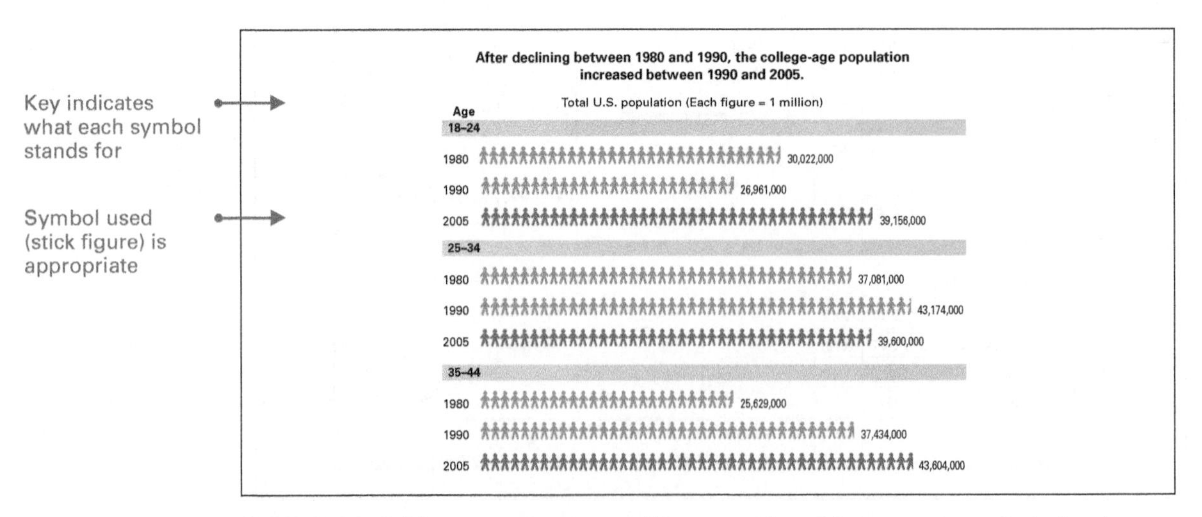

FIGURE 20 **A Pictogram** In place of lines and bars, icons and symbols lend appeal and clarity.
Source: U.S. Bureau of the Census.

changes during a given period. Pictograms are visually appealing and can be especially useful for nontechnical or multicultural audiences.

GUIDELINES for Creating Charts

Pie Charts

- **Make sure the parts of the pie add up to 100 percent.**
- **Differentiate and label each slice clearly.** Use different colors or shades for each slice, and label the category and percentage of each slice.
- **Keep all labels horizontal.** Make the chart easy to read.
- **Combine very small pie slices.** Group categories with very small percentages under "other."

Organization Charts

- **Move from top to bottom or left to right.** Place the highest level of hierarchy at the top (top-to-bottom chart) or at the left (left-to-right chart).
- **Use downward- or rightward-pointing arrows.** Arrows show the flow of hierarchy from highest to lowest.
- **Keep boxes uniform and text brief.** Shape may vary slightly according to how much text is in each box. Maintain a uniform look. Avoid too much text in any box.

Flowcharts, Tree Charts, and Gantt Charts

- **Move from top to bottom or left to right.** The process must start at the top (top-to-bottom chart) or left (left-to-right chart).
- **Use connector lines.** Show relationships between the parts.
- **Keep boxes uniform and text brief.** See the tips for organization charts above.

Pictograms

- **Follow the guidelines for bar graphs.**
- **Use symbols that are universally recognized.**
- **Keep the pictogram clean and simple (avoid too much visual clutter).**

GRAPHIC ILLUSTRATIONS

Illustrations can be diagrams, maps, drawings, icons, photographs, or any other visual that relies mainly on pictures rather than on data or words. For example, the diagram of a safety-belt locking mechanism in Figure 21 accomplishes what the verbal text alone cannot: it portrays the mechanism in operation.

Verbal text that requires a visual supplement

> The safety-belt apparatus includes a tiny pendulum attached to a lever, or locking mechanism. Upon sudden deceleration, the pendulum swings forward, activating the locking device to keep passengers from pitching into the dashboard.

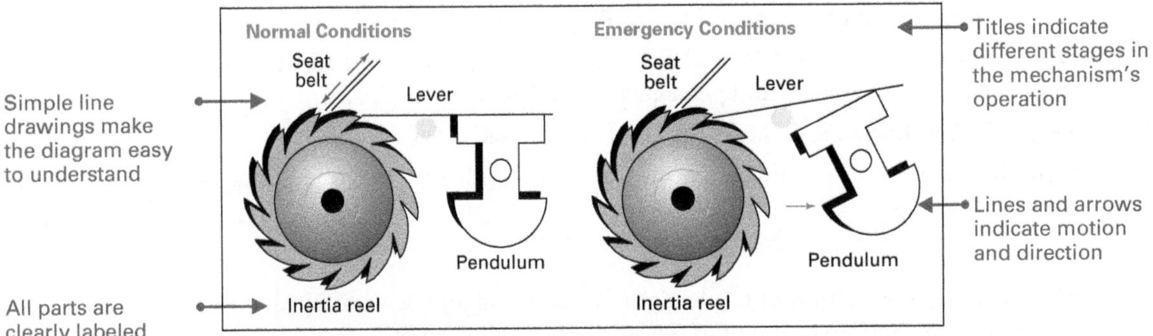

FIGURE 21 **A Diagram of a Safety-Belt Locking Mechanism** Shows how the basic parts work together.
Source: U.S. Department of Transportation.

Illustrations are invaluable when you need to convey spatial relationships or help your audience see what something actually looks like. Drawings can often illustrate more effectively than photographs because a drawing can simplify the view, omit unnecessary features, and focus on what is important.

Diagrams

Diagrams show how items function or are assembled

Diagrams are especially effective for presenting views that could not be captured by photographing or actually observing the item.

Exploded diagrams show how the parts of an item are assembled, as in Figure 22. These often appear in repair or maintenance manuals. Notice how parts are numbered for easy reference to the written instructions.

Cutaway diagrams show the item with its exterior layers removed to reveal interior sections, as in Figure 23. Unless the specific viewing perspective is immediately recognizable (as in Figure 23), name the angle of vision: "top view," "side view," and so on.

Block diagram model
(Go to *Student Resources>Chapter 12> Models and Templates*)

Block diagrams are simplified sketches that represent the relationship between the parts of an item, principle, system, or process. Because block diagrams are designed to illustrate *concepts* (such as current flow in a circuit), the parts are

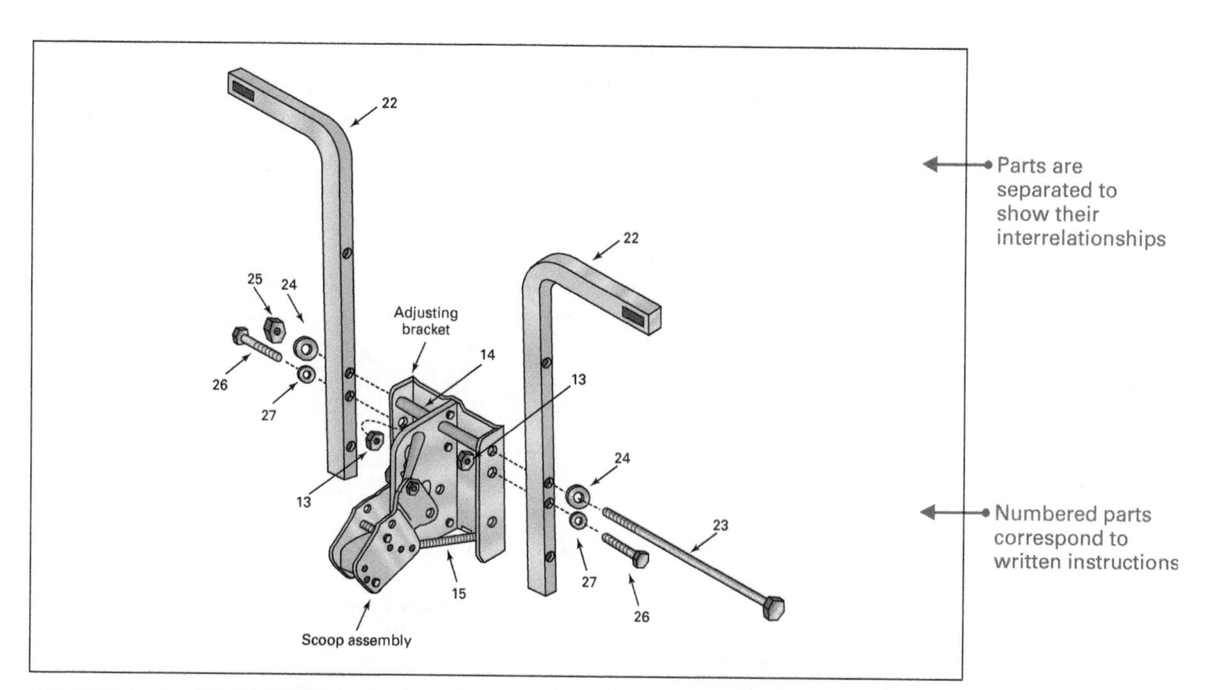

FIGURE 22 **An Exploded Diagram of a Brace for an Adjustable Basketball Hoop** Shows how the parts are assembled.
Source: Courtesy of Spalding.

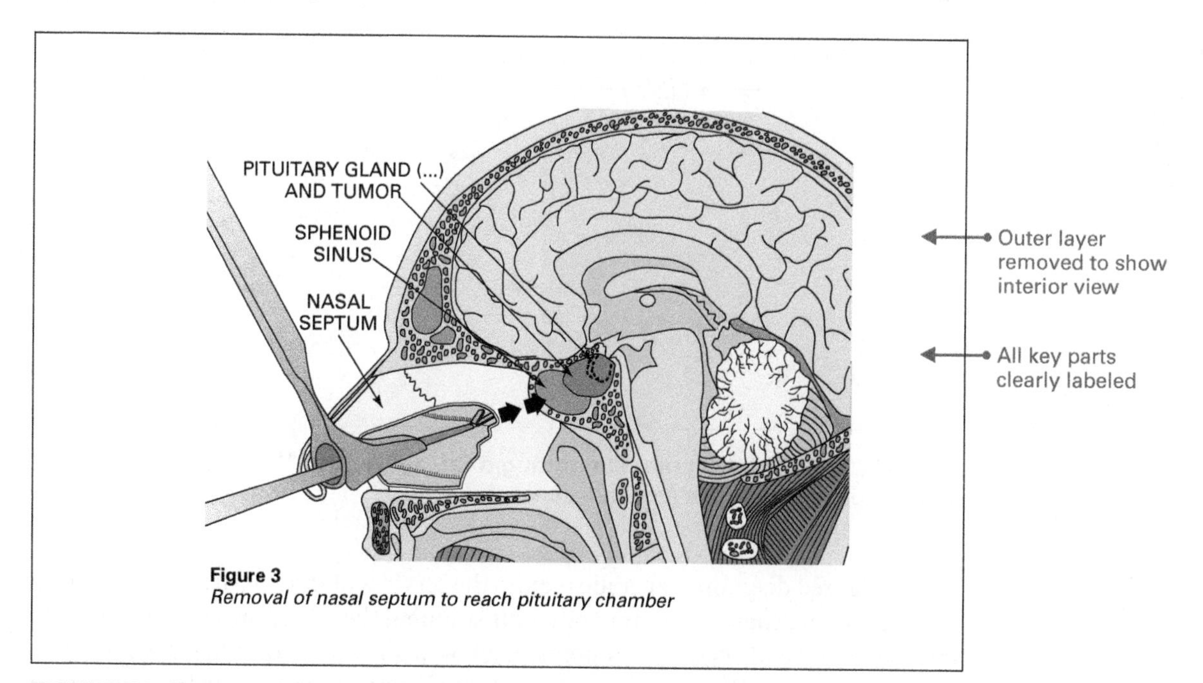

Figure 3
Removal of nasal septum to reach pituitary chamber

FIGURE 23 **Cutaway Diagram of a Surgical Procedure** Shows what is inside.
Source: Transsphenoidal Approach for Pituitary Tumor, © 1986 by The Ludann Co., Grand Rapids, MI.

represented as symbols or shapes. The block diagram in Figure 24 illustrates how any process can be controlled automatically through a feedback mechanism. Figure 25 shows the feedback concept applied as the cruise-control mechanism on a motor vehicle.

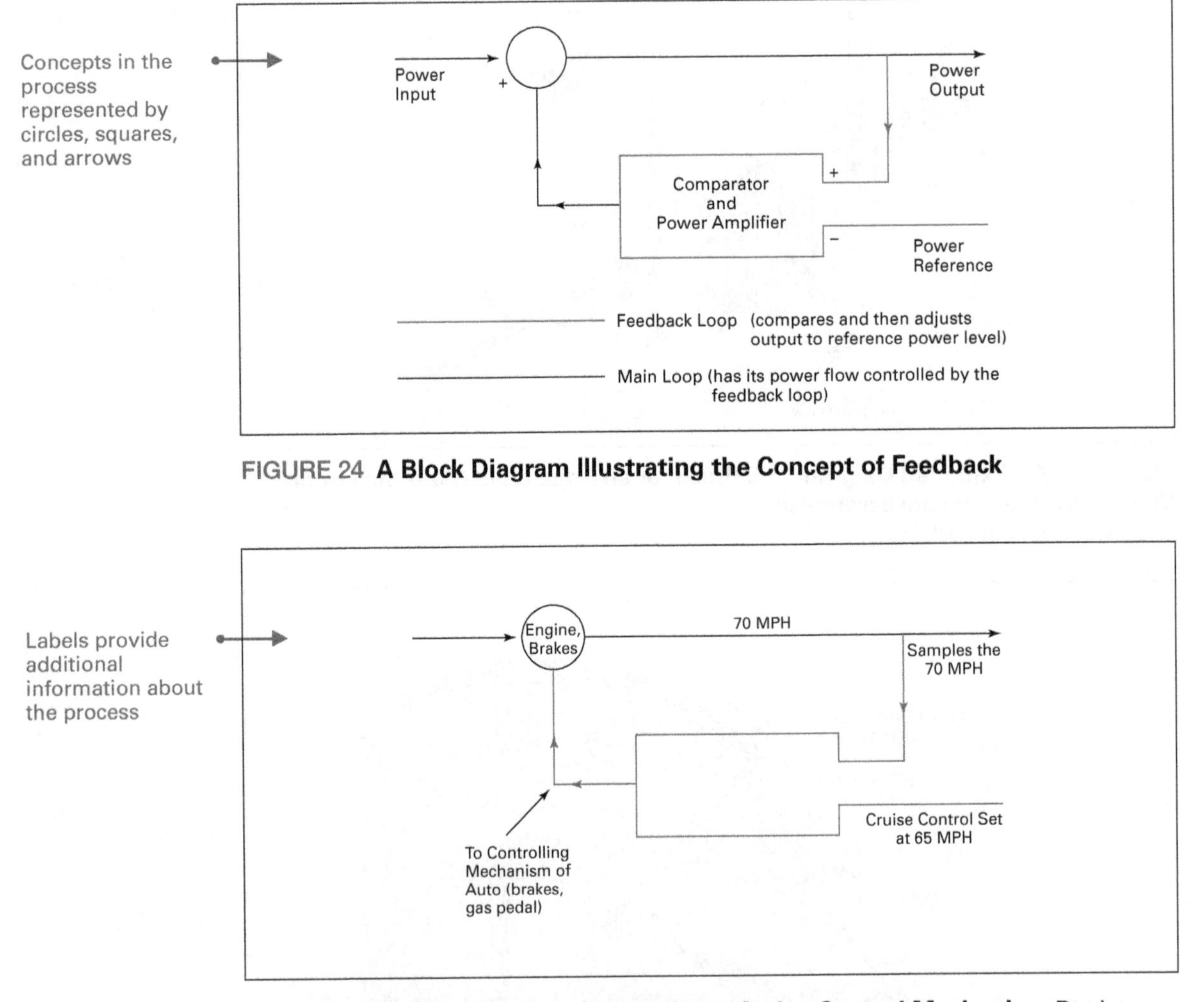

FIGURE 24 **A Block Diagram Illustrating the Concept of Feedback**

FIGURE 25 **A Block Diagram Illustrating a Cruise-Control Mechanism** Depicts a specific application of the feedback concept.

Specialized diagrams generally require the services of graphic artists or technical illustrators. The client requesting or commissioning the visual provides the art professional with an *art brief* (often prepared by writers and editors) that spells out the visual's purpose and specifications. The art brief is usually reinforced by a *thumbnail sketch,* a small, simple sketch of the visual being requested. For example, part of the brief addressed to the medical illustrator for Figure 23 might read as follows:

An art brief for Figure 23

- **Purpose:** to illustrate transsphenoidal adenomectomy for laypersons
- **View:** full cutaway, sagittal
- **Range:** descending from cranial apex to a horizontal plane immediately below the upper jaw and second cervical vertebra
- **Depth:** medial cross-section
- **Structures omitted:** cranial nerves, vascular and lymphatic systems
- **Structures included:** gross anatomy of bone, cartilage, and soft tissue—delineated by color, shading, and texture
- **Structures highlighted:** nasal septum, sphenoid sinus, and sella turcica, showing the pituitary embedded in a 1.5 cm tumor invading the sphenoid sinus via an area of herniation at the base of the pituitary fossa

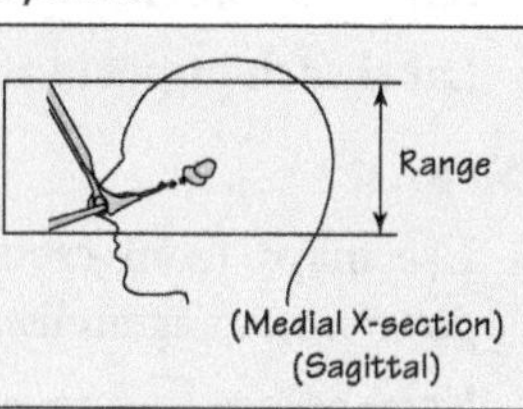

A thumbnail sketch of Figure 23

Maps

Besides being visually engaging, maps are especially useful for showing comparisons and for helping users *visualize* position, location, and relationships among various data. Figure 26 synthesizes statistical information in a format that is accessible and understandable. Color enhances the comparisons.

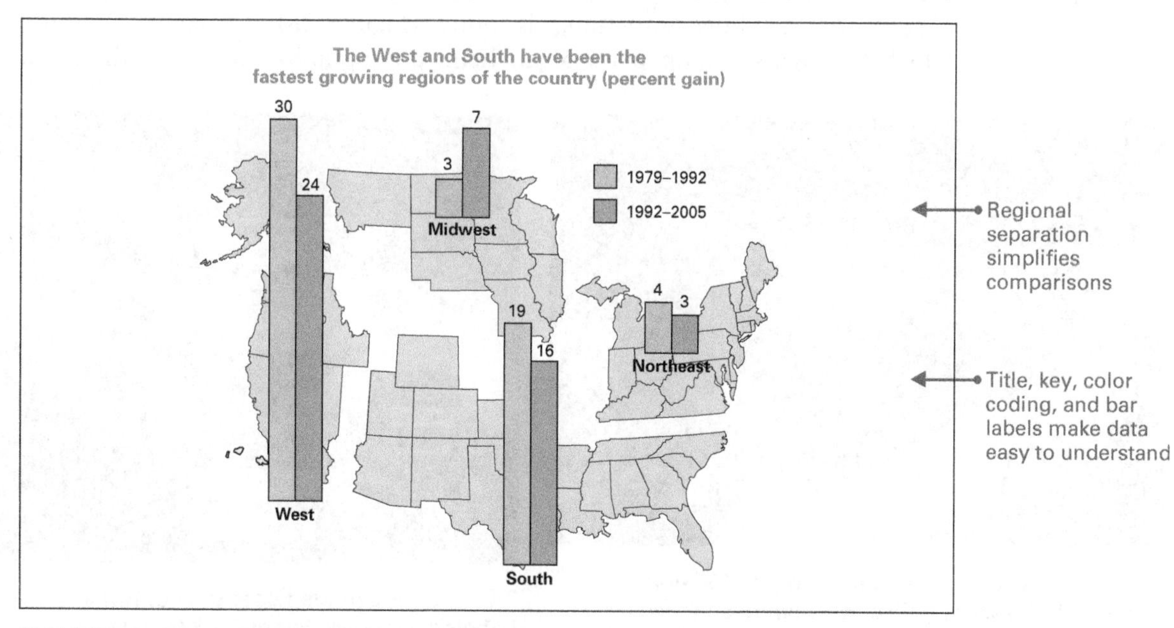

Regional separation simplifies comparisons

Title, key, color coding, and bar labels make data easy to understand

FIGURE 26 **A Map Rich in Statistical Significance** Shows the geographic distribution of data.

Source: U.S. Bureau of the Census.

GUIDELINES for Creating Graphic Illustrations

Drawings and Diagrams

- **Provide clear explanations.** Explain how diagram parts fit together or operate.
- **Use lines and arrows to indicate direction and motion.** For diagrams that show action, directional markers help viewers understand the action.
- **Keep diagram illustrations simple.** Only show viewers what they need to see.
- **Label each important part.**

Maps

- **Use maps from credible sources, such as the U.S. Census Bureau or other government agencies.**
- **Keep colors to a minimum, so that the maps are easy to read on a computer or in print.**

PHOTOGRAPHS

Photographs are especially useful for showing exactly how something looks (Figure 27) or how something is done (Figure 28). Unlike a diagram, which highlights certain parts of an item, photographs show everything. So

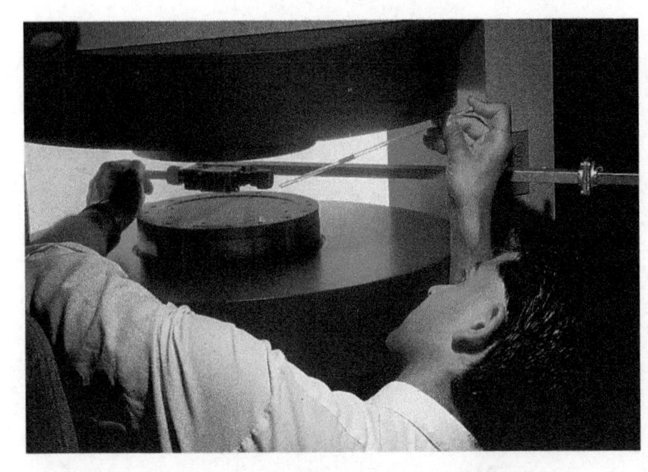

FIGURE 27 **Shows a Realistic Angle of Vision** Titration in Measuring Electron-Spin Resonance. (Shows object as well as person for sense of scale. Also shows angle that simulates operator's angle of vision. Photo has been cropped to remove needless detail.)
Source: SuperStock.

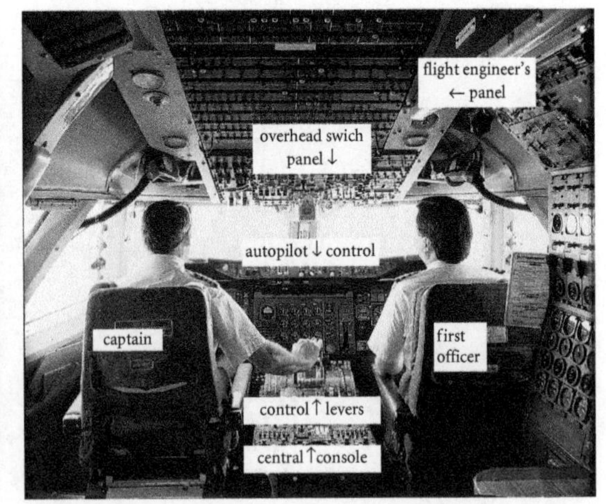

FIGURE 28 **Shows Essential Features Labeled** Standard Flight Deck for a Long-Range Jet.
Source: SuperStock.

while a photograph can be extremely useful, it also can provide too much detail or fail to emphasize the parts on which you want people to focus. For the most effective photographs, use a professional photographer who knows all about angles, lighting, lenses, and special film or digital editing options.

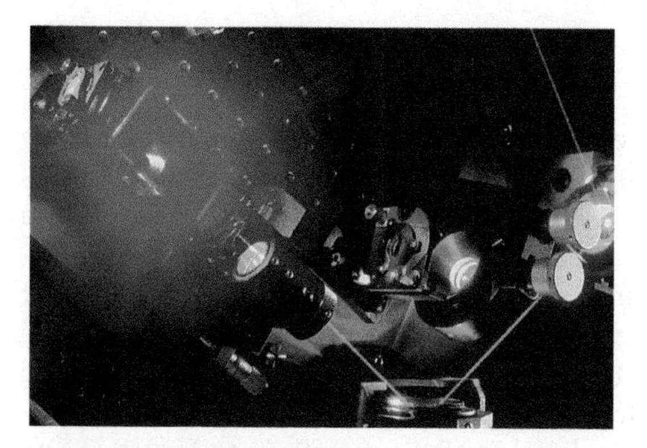

FIGURE 29 **Shows a Complex Mechanism** SapphireTunable Laser.
Source: SuperStock.

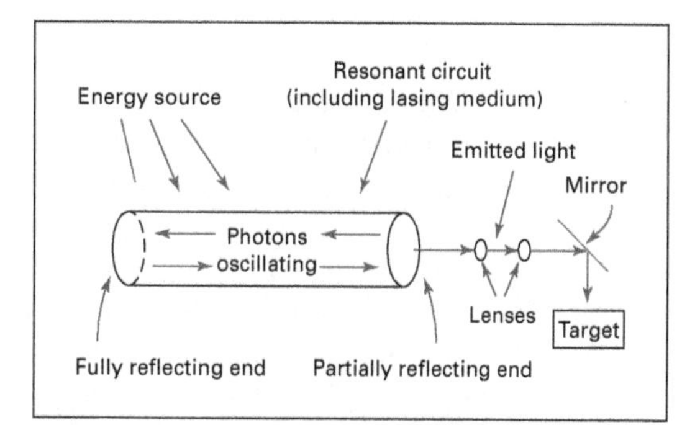

FIGURE 30 **A Simplified Diagram of Figure 29** Major Parts of the Laser.

GUIDELINES for Using Photographs

- **Simulate the readers' angle of vision.** Consider how they would view the item or perform the procedure (Figure 27).
- **Trim (crop) the photograph to eliminate needless detail** (Figure 27).
- **Provide a sense of scale for an object unfamiliar to readers.** Include a person, a ruler, or a familiar object (such as a hand) in the photo (Figure 27).
- **Label all the parts readers need to identify** (Figure 28).
- **Supplement the photograph with diagrams.** This way, you can emphasize selected features. (Figures 29 and 30).
- **If your document will be published, attend to the legal aspects.** Obtain a signed release from any person in the photograph and written permission from the copyright holder. Cite the photographer and/or the copyright holder.
- **Explain what readers should look for in the photo.** Do this in your discussion or use a caption.

Commercial vendors such as PhotoDisc, Inc. <www.photodisc.com> offer royalty-free stock photographs. For a fee, you can download photographs, edit or alter them as needed by using a program such as *Adobe Photoshop*, and then insert these images in your own documents.

> **NOTE** *Make sure you understand what is legally and ethically permissible before including altered images.*

VIDEOS

Videos show a full-motion view

Until recently, workplace videos were typically used only for training and safety purposes and were filmed by professional videographers. Today, with the advent of YouTube and similar sites, as well as the ease of filming with a small video camera or even a cell phone, organizations are using videos to supplement traditional documents such as user manuals. For instance, the video frame captured in Figure 31 is from a set of video instructions for a product called Dust-Aid (used to clean dust from the camera sensor of a digital SLR camera). The principles for using videos are similar to those for photographs, except that videos are altered via editing rather than cropping. For more advice, see the annotations to Figure 31 and the guidelines on the next page.

FIGURE 31 A Video Frame

Source: From "Dust-Aid: DSLR Camera Sensor Cleaning Video" by Ross Wordhouse from <www.youtube.com>. Reproduced by permission.

GUIDELINES for Using Video

- **Provide a sense of scale.** Try to show both the object and a person using it (or a ruler or a hand).
- **In showing a procedure, simulate the angle of vision of the person actually performing each step.** In other words allow the viewer to "look over the person's shoulder."
- **Show only what the viewer needs to see.** For example, in a video of a long procedure, focus only on the part of the procedure that is most relevant.
- **Edit out needless detail.** If you have editing software, shorten the video to include only the essentials.
- **Avoid excess office or background noise when recording sound.**

SOFTWARE AND DOWNLOADABLE IMAGES

Many of the tasks formerly performed by graphic designers and technical illustrators now fall to people with little or no training. Whatever your career, you could be expected to produce high-quality graphics for conferences, presentations, and in-house publications. This text offers only a brief introduction to these matters. Your best bet is to take a graphic design class.

Using the Software

The more you know about different graphics software packages, the more choices you will have when it comes to creating effective visuals.

A sampling of resources for electronic visual design

- **Graphics software,** such as *Adobe Illustrator* or *CorelDraw,* allows you to sketch, edit, and refine your diagrams and drawings.
- **Presentation software,** such as *Microsoft PowerPoint* or *Apple Keynote,* lets you create slides, computer presentations, and overhead transparency sheets. Using a program such as *Adobe Macromedia Director,* you can create multimedia presentations that include sound and video.
- **Spreadsheet software,** such as *Microsoft Excel* or *Apple Numbers,* makes it easy to create charts and graphs.
- **Word-processing programs,** such as *Microsoft Word* or *Google Docs,* include simple image editors ("draw" feature) and other tools for working with visuals. More sophisticated page layout programs, such as *Adobe InDesign,* also provide ways to work with visual design.

Using Symbols and Icons

Symbols and icons can convey information visually to a wide range of audiences. Because such visuals do not rely on text, they are often more easily understood by international audiences, children, or people who may have difficulty reading. Symbols and icons are used in airports and other public places as well as in documentation, manuals, or training material. Some of these images are developed and approved by the International Standards Organization (ISO). The ISO makes sure the images have universal appeal and conform to a single standard, whether used in a printed document or on an elevator wall.

How symbols and icons differ

The words *symbol* and *icon* are often used interchangeably. Technically, icons tend to resemble the item they represent: An icon of a file folder on your computer, for example, looks like a real file folder. Symbols can be more abstract. Symbols still get the meaning across but may not resemble, precisely, what they represent. Figure 32 shows some familiar icons and symbols.

Simple drawings reduce chances for confusion

The first three images are icons (representative); the last two are symbols (abstract)

FIGURE 32 **Internationally Recognized Icons and Symbols**

Limitations of clip art

Ready-to-use icons and symbols can be found in clip-art collections, from which you can import and customize images by using a drawing program. Because of its generally unpolished appearance, consider using clip art only for in-house documents or for situations in which your schedule or budget preclude obtaining original artwork.

NOTE *Be sure the image you choose is "intuitively recognizable" to multicultural users ("Using Icons" 3).*

Using Web Sites for Graphics Support

Following is a sampling of useful Web sites and gateways for finding visuals.

- **Clip art:** <www.clipart.com>
- **Photographs and video:** <www.gettyimages.com>
- **Maps:** <www.nationalgeographic.com/maps>
- **International symbols:** <www.iso.org>

NOTE *Be cautious about downloading and using visuals from the Web. Originators of any work, including Web-based visuals, own the work and the copyright. Even "free" clip art may be protected by copyright. Pay attention to the copyright and licensing information on the site* *where you obtain the visual. Check out the Creative Commons site for visuals and audio that are licensed for re-use at <www.creativecommons.org>.*

USING COLOR

Color often makes a presentation more interesting, focusing viewers' attention and helping them identify various elements. In Figure 18, for example, color helps viewers sort out the key schedule elements of a Gantt chart for a major project: activities, time lines, durations, and meetings.

Color can help clarify a concept or dramatize how something works. In Figure 33, bright colors against a darker, duller background enable users to *visualize* the "heat mirror" concept.

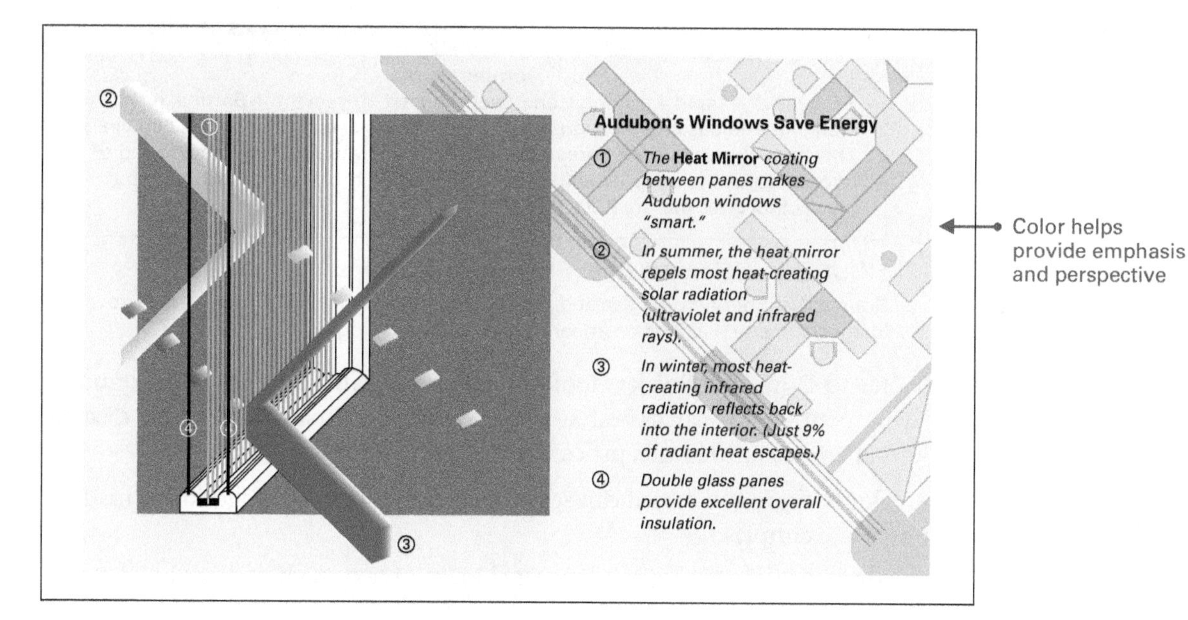

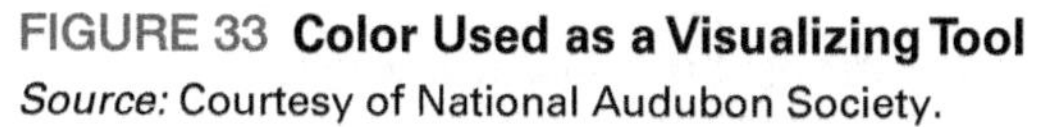

FIGURE 33 Color Used as a Visualizing Tool
Source: Courtesy of National Audubon Society.

Color can help clarify complex relationships. In Figure 34, a world map using distinctive colors allows comparisons at a glance.

Color also can help guide readers through the material. Used effectively on a printed page, color helps organize the reader's understanding, provides orientation, and emphasizes important material. On a Web page, color can mirror the site's main theme or "personality," orient the reader, and provide cues for navigating the site.

Following are just a few possible uses of color in page design (White, *Color* 39–44; Keyes 647–49).

Color and shading help readers make instant comparisons

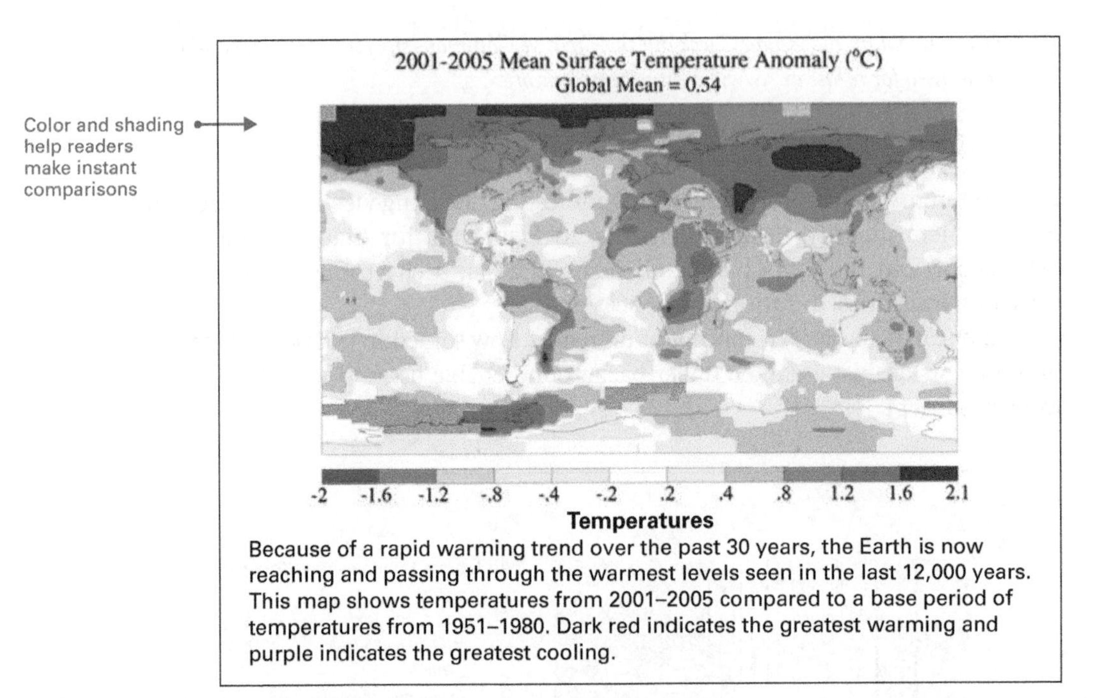

FIGURE 34 **Colors Used to Show Relationships**

Source: National Aeronautics and Space Administration (NASA) <www.nasa.gov/images/content/158226main_mean_surface_temp_lg.jpg>.

Use Color to Organize Readers look for ways of organizing their understanding of a document. Color can reveal structure and break material up into discrete blocks that are easier to locate, process, and digest.

How color reveals organization

- A color background screen can set off like elements such as checklists, instructions, or examples.
- Horizontal colored rules can separate blocks of text, such as sections of a document or areas of a page.
- Vertical rules can set off examples, quotations, captions, and so on.

Color used to organize

Color screens | Horizontal color rules | Vertical color rules

Use Color to Orient Readers look for signposts that help them find their place or locate what they need.

How color provides orientation

- Color can help headings stand out from the text and differentiate major headings from minor ones.
- Color tabs and boxes can serve as location markers.
- Color sidebars (for marginal comments), callouts (for labels), and leader lines (dotted lines for connecting a label to its referent) can guide the eyes.

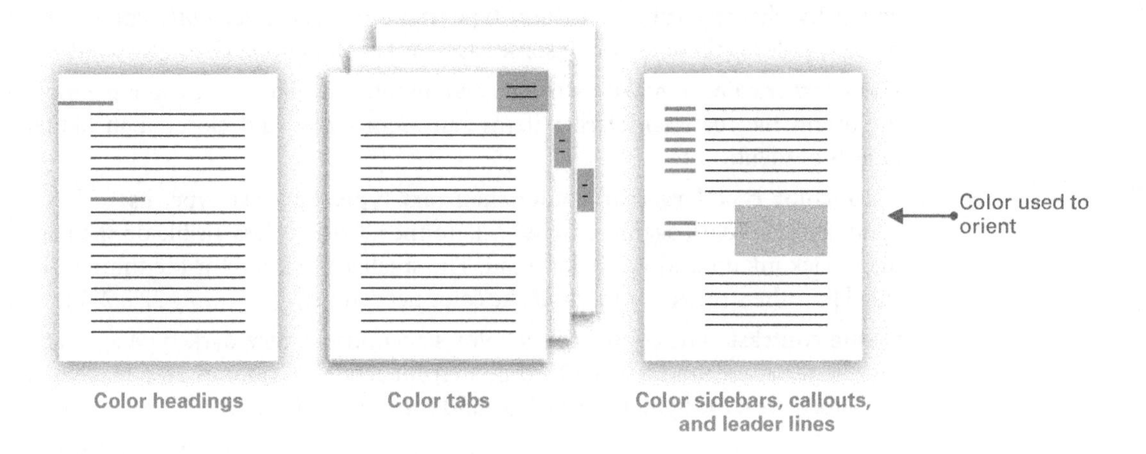

Use Color to Emphasize Readers look for places to focus their attention in the document.

How color emphasizes

- Color type can highlight key words or ideas.
- Color can call attention to cross-references or to links on a Web page.
- A color, ruled box can frame a warning, caution, note, hint, or any other item that needs to stick in people's minds.

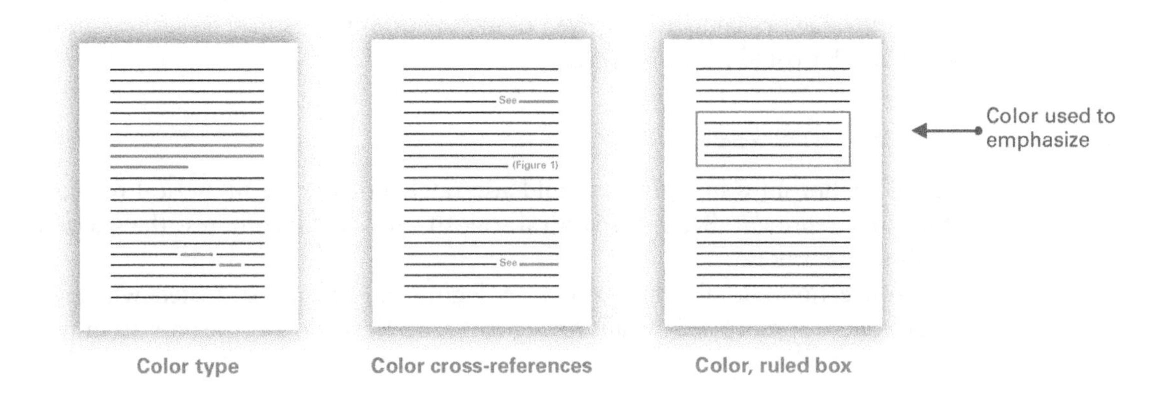

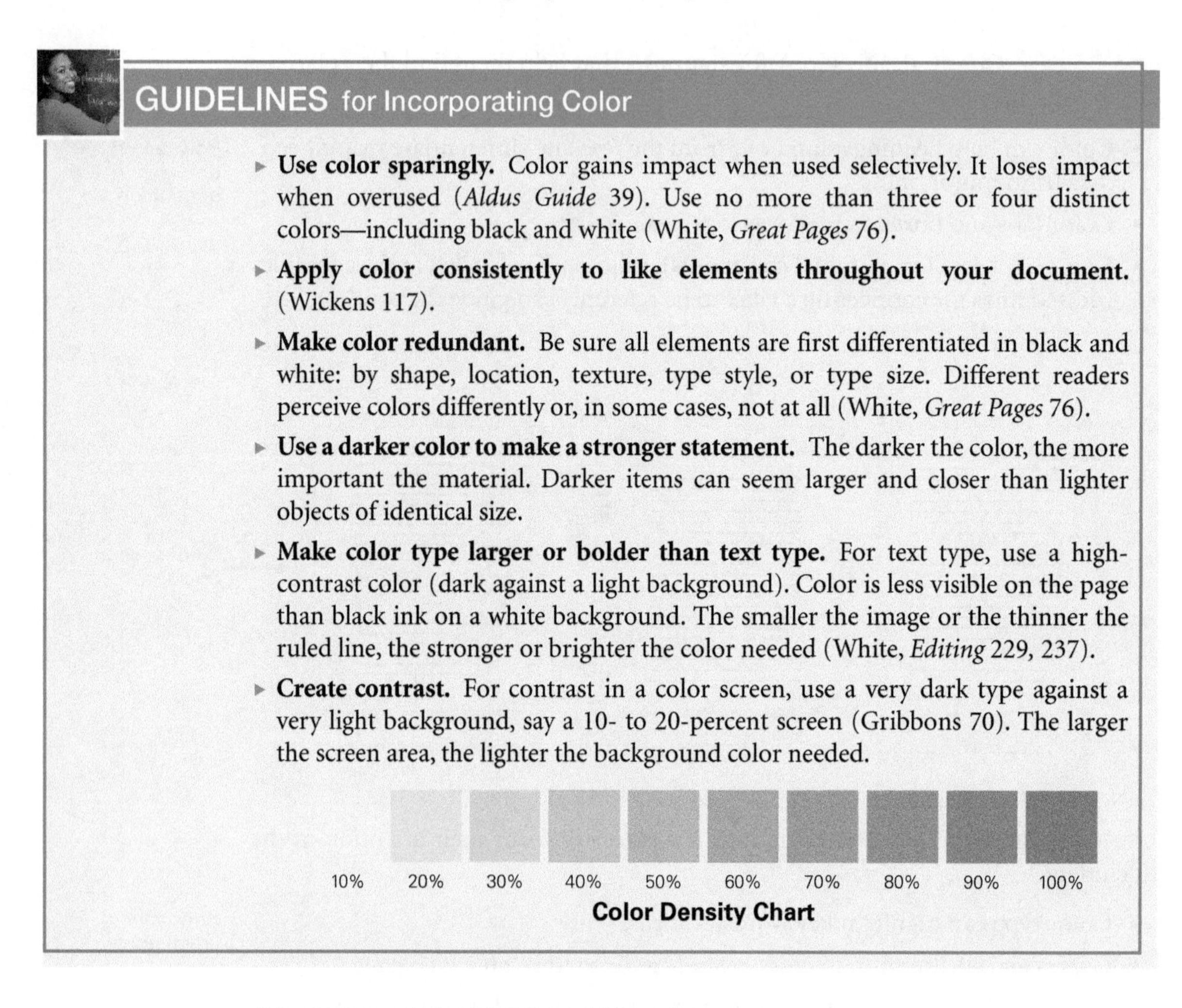

GUIDELINES for Incorporating Color

- **Use color sparingly.** Color gains impact when used selectively. It loses impact when overused (*Aldus Guide* 39). Use no more than three or four distinct colors—including black and white (White, *Great Pages* 76).
- **Apply color consistently to like elements throughout your document.** (Wickens 117).
- **Make color redundant.** Be sure all elements are first differentiated in black and white: by shape, location, texture, type style, or type size. Different readers perceive colors differently or, in some cases, not at all (White, *Great Pages* 76).
- **Use a darker color to make a stronger statement.** The darker the color, the more important the material. Darker items can seem larger and closer than lighter objects of identical size.
- **Make color type larger or bolder than text type.** For text type, use a high-contrast color (dark against a light background). Color is less visible on the page than black ink on a white background. The smaller the image or the thinner the ruled line, the stronger or brighter the color needed (White, *Editing* 229, 237).
- **Create contrast.** For contrast in a color screen, use a very dark type against a very light background, say a 10- to 20-percent screen (Gribbons 70). The larger the screen area, the lighter the background color needed.

Color Density Chart

ETHICAL CONSIDERATIONS

Although you may be perfectly justified in presenting data in its best light, you are ethically responsible for avoiding misrepresentation. Any one set of data can support contradictory conclusions. Even though your numbers may be accurate, your visual display could be misleading.

Present the Real Picture

Visual relationships in a graph should accurately portray the numerical relationships they represent. Begin the vertical scale at zero. Never compress the scales to reinforce your point.

Notice how visual relationships in Figure 35 become distorted when the value scale is compressed or fails to begin at zero. In version A, the bars accurately

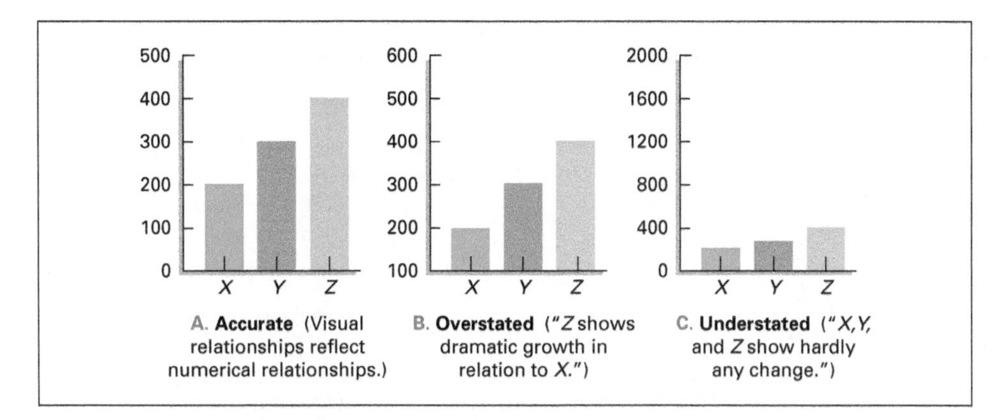

FIGURE 35 **An Accurate Bar Graph and Two Distorted Versions** Absence of a zero baseline in B shrinks the vertical axis and exaggerates differences among the data. In C, the excessive value range of the vertical axis dwarfs differences among the data.

depict the numerical relationships measured from the value scale. In version B, item *Z* (400) is depicted as three times *X* (200). In version C, the scale is overly compressed, causing the shortened bars to understate the quantitative differences.

Deliberate distortions are unethical because they imply conclusions that are contradicted by the actual data.

Present the Complete Picture

An accurate visual should include all essential data, without getting bogged down in needless detail. Figure 36 shows how distortion occurs when data that would provide a complete picture are selectively omitted. Version A accurately depicts the numerical relationships measured from the value scale. In version B, too few points are plotted. Always decide carefully what to include and what to leave out.

Don't Mistake Distortion for Emphasis

When you want to emphasize a point (a sales increase, a safety record, etc.), be sure your data support the conclusion implied by your visual. For instance, don't use inordinately large visuals to emphasize good news or small ones to downplay bad news. When using clip art, pictograms, or drawn images to dramatize a comparison, be sure the relative size of the images or icons reflects the quantities being compared.

A visual accurately depicting a 100-percent increase in phone sales at your company might look like version A in Figure 37. Version B overstates the good news by depicting the larger image four times the size, instead of twice the size, of the smaller image. Although the larger image is twice the height, it is also twice the *width,* so the total area conveys the visual impression that sales have *quadrupled.*

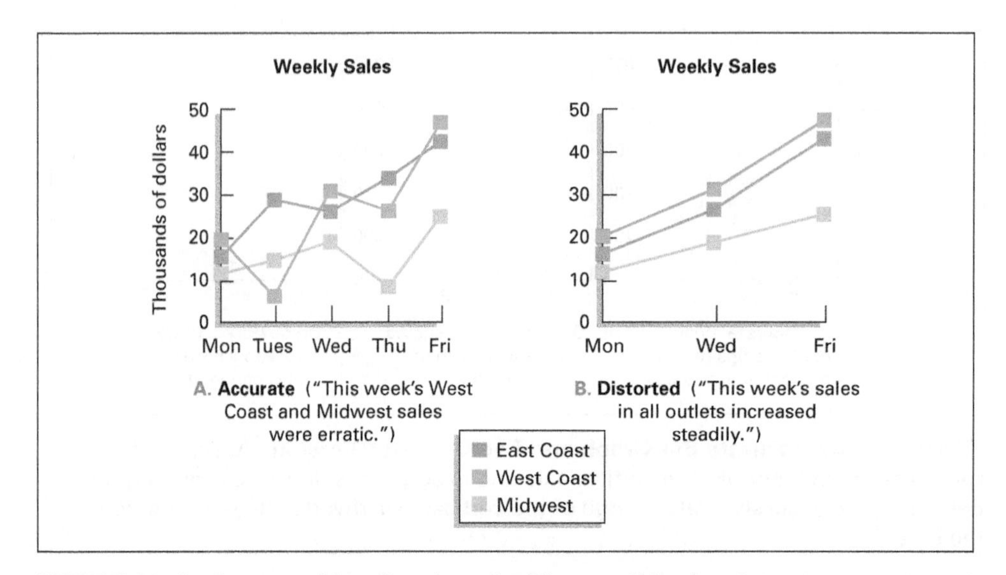

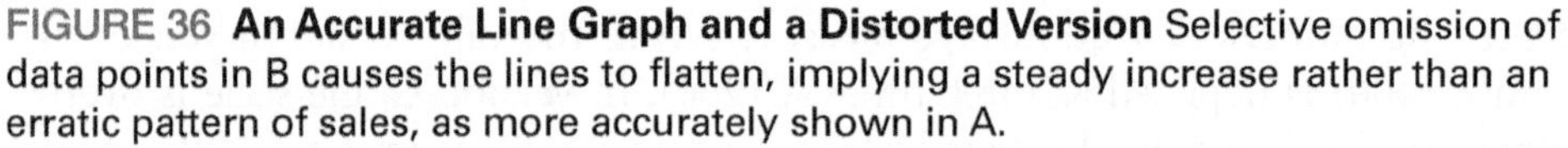
FIGURE 36 **An Accurate Line Graph and a Distorted Version** Selective omission of data points in B causes the lines to flatten, implying a steady increase rather than an erratic pattern of sales, as more accurately shown in A.

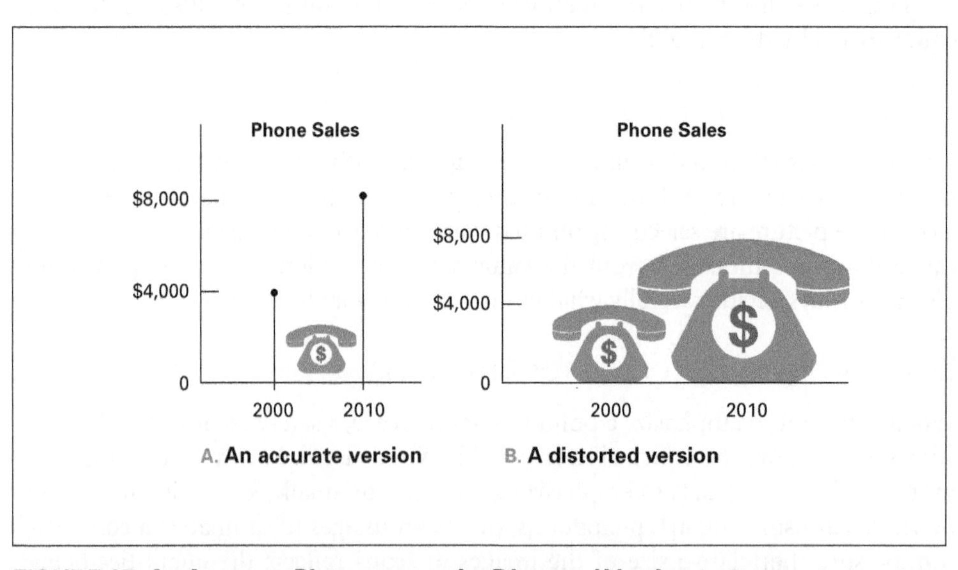

FIGURE 37 **An Accurate Pictogram and a Distorted Version** In B, the relative sizes of the images are not equivalent to the quantities they represent.

Visuals have their own rhetorical and persuasive force, which you can use to advantage—for positive or negative purposes, for the reader's benefit or detriment (Van Pelt 2). Avoiding visual distortion is ultimately a matter of ethics.

For additional guidance, use the planning sheet in Figure 38, and the checklist on visuals.

Focusing on Your Purpose

- What is this visual's purpose (to instruct, persuade, create interest)? ____________________
- What forms of information (numbers, shapes, words, pictures, symbols) will this visual depict? ____________________
- What kind of relationship(s) will the visual depict (comparison, cause-effect, connected parts, sequence of steps)? ____________________
- What judgment, conclusion, or interpretation is being emphasized (that profits have increased, that toxic levels are rising, that *X* is better than *Y*)? ____________________
- Is a visual needed at all? ____________________

Focusing on Your Audience

- Is this audience accustomed to interpreting visuals? ____________________
- Is the audience interested in specific numbers or an overall view? ____________________
- Should the audience focus on one exact value, compare two or more values, or synthesize a range of approximate values? ____________________
- Which type of visual will be most accurate, representative, accessible, and compatible with the type of judgment, action, or understanding expected from the audience? ____________________
- In place of one complicated visual, would two or more straightforward ones be preferable? ____________________
- Are there any specific cultural considerations? ____________________

Focusing on Your Presentation

- What enhancements, if any, will increase audience interest (colors, patterns, legends, labels, varied typefaces, shadowing, enlargement or reduction of some features)? ____________________
- Which medium—or combination of media—will be most effective for presenting this visual (slides, transparencies, handouts, large-screen monitor, flip chart, report text)? ____________________
- For greatest utility and effect, where in the presentation does this visual belong? ____________________

FIGURE 38 **A Planning Sheet for Preparing Visuals**

GUIDELINES for Obtaining and Citing Visual Material

Copyright

The Internet is a rich source for all kinds of visuals. It's tempting to simply cut and paste a visual from a Web page directly into your document. Most material on the Internet is subject to copyright laws, however. To avoid copyright problems when working with visuals, follow these guidelines:

- **Look for visuals that are copyright-free.** Many Web sites, such as <www.shutterstock.com>, offer images that don't require copyright permission.
- **Use public domain sources.** Some government sites, such as the U.S. Census Bureau, are a good source of charts, graphs, and tables that don't require copyright permission.
- **Follow fair use guidelines,** which allow for limited use of copyrighted material without permission (for example, for a class project that will not have widespread distribution).

Citing visuals created by someone else

- **Cite the source of the visual.** Even if you are following copyright guidelines, you should still properly cite the source of the visuals you use. *Failing to cite the source of a visual could constitute plagiarism.*
- **If the visual is available on the Internet, provide the Web address or other information so your reader can locate it.**

Attributing the source of your original visual

- **Cite the source of the data you used to create your visual.** Even if you create a visual yourself, the data for that visual may come from another source. For example, in Figure 9, the graph was created by a writer using Excel, but she used data downloaded from the U.S. Bureau of Labor Statistics.
- **If the data is available on the Internet, provide the Web address or other information so your reader can check the original source.**

CULTURAL CONSIDERATIONS

Meaning is in the eye of the beholder

Visual communication can serve as a universal language—as long as the graphic or image is not misinterpreted. For example, not all cultures read left to right, so a chart designed to be read left to right that is read in the opposite direction could be misunderstood. Color is also a cultural consideration: For instance, U.S. audiences associate red with danger and green with safety. But in Ireland, green or orange carry strong political connotations. In Muslim cultures, green is a holy color (Cotton 169). Icons and symbols as well can have offensive connotations. Hand gestures are especially problematic: some Arab cultures consider the left hand unclean; a pointing index finger—on either hand—signifies rudeness in Venezuela or Sri Lanka (Bosley 5–6).

GUIDELINES for Fitting Visuals with Text

- **Place the visual where it will best serve your readers.** If it is central to your discussion, place the visual as close as possible to the material it clarifies. (Achieving proximity often requires that you ignore the traditional "top or bottom" design rule for placing visuals on a page.) If the visual is peripheral to your discussion or of interest to only a few readers, place it in an appendix. Tell readers when to consult the visual and where to find it.
- **Never refer to a visual that readers cannot easily locate.** In a long document, don't be afraid to repeat a visual if you discuss it a second time.
- **Never crowd a visual into a cramped space.** Frame the visual with plenty of white space, and position it on the page for balance. To achieve proportion with the surrounding text, consider the size of each visual and the amount of space it will occupy.
- **Number the visual and give it a clear title and labels.** Your title should tell readers what they are seeing. Label all the important material and cite the source of data or of graphics.
- **Match the visual to your audience.** Don't make it too elementary for specialists or too complex for nonspecialists.
- **Introduce and interpret the visual.** In your introduction, tell readers what to expect:

  As Table 2 shows, operating costs have increased 7 percent annually since 1990. — Informative

  See Table 2. — Uninformative

  Visuals alone make ambiguous statements (Girill, "Technical Communication and Art" 35); pictures need to be interpreted. Instead of leaving readers to struggle with a page of raw data, explain the relationships displayed. Follow the visual with a discussion of its important features:

  This cost increase means that . . .

  Always tell readers what to look for and what it means.
- **Use prose captions to explain important points made by the visual.** Use a smaller type size so that captions don't compete with text type (*Aldus Guide* 35).
- **Eliminate "visual noise."** Excessive lines, bars, numbers, colors, or patterns will overwhelm readers. In place of one complicated visual, use two or more straightforward ones.
- **Be sure the visual can stand alone.** Even though it repeats or augments information already in the text, the visual should contain everything readers will need to interpret it correctly.

CHECKLIST: Visuals

Content

- ☐ Does the visual serve a valid purpose (clarification, not mere ornamentation)?
- ☐ Is the level of complexity appropriate for the audience?
- ☐ Is the visual titled and numbered?
- ☐ Are all patterns identified by label or legend?
- ☐ Are all values or units of measurement specified (grams per ounce, millions of dollars)?
- ☐ Do the visual relationships represent the numeric relationships accurately?
- ☐ Are captions and explanatory notes provided as needed?
- ☐ Are all data sources cited?
- ☐ Has written permission been obtained for reproducing or adapting a visual from a copyrighted source?
- ☐ Is the visual introduced, discussed, interpreted, integrated with the text, and referred to by number?
- ☐ Can the visual itself (along with any captions and labels) stand alone in terms of meaning?

Style

- ☐ Is this the best type of visual for my purpose and audience?
- ☐ Are all decimal points in each column of a table aligned vertically?
- ☐ Is the visual uncrowded, uncluttered, and free of "visual noise"?
- ☐ Is color used tastefully and appropriately?
- ☐ Is the visual ethically acceptable?
- ☐ Does the visual respect readers' cultural values?

Placement

- ☐ Is the visual easy to locate?
- ☐ Do all design elements (title, line thickness, legends, notes, borders, white space) achieve balance?
- ☐ Is the visual positioned on the page to achieve balance?
- ☐ Is the visual set off by adequate white space or borders?
- ☐ Does the left side of a broadside table face the bottom of the page?
- ☐ Is the visual placed near the text it is helping to describe?

Chapter quiz, Exercises, Web links, and Flashcards
(Go to *Student Resources>Chapter 12*)

Document design/visuals Activities, Case studies, and Quizzes
(Go to *Document Design and Graphics*)

Projects

GENERAL

1. The following statistics are based on data from three colleges in a large western city. They compare the number of applicants to each college over six years.

   - In 2006, *X* college received 2,341 applications for admission, *Y* college received 3,116, and *Z* college 1,807.
   - In 2007, *X* college received 2,410 applications for admission, *Y* college received 3,224, and *Z* college 1,784.
   - In 2008, *X* college received 2,689 applications for admission, *Y* college received 2,976, and *Z* college 1,929.
   - In 2009, *X* college received 2,714 applications for admission, *Y* college received 2,840, and *Z* college 1,992.
   - In 2010, *X* college received 2,872 applications for admission, *Y* college received 2,615, and *Z* college 2,112.
   - In 2011, *X* college received 2,868 applications for admission, *Y* college received 2,421, and *Z* college 2,267.

   Display these data in a line graph, a bar graph, and a table. Which version seems most effective for someone who (a) wants exact figures, (b) wonders how overall enrollments are changing, or (c) wants to compare enrollments at each college in a certain year? Include a caption interpreting each version.

2. Devise a flowchart for a process in your field or area of interest. Include a title and a brief discussion.
3. Devise an organization chart showing the lines of responsibility and authority in an organization where you work.
4. Devise a pie chart to depict your yearly expenses. Title and discuss the chart.
5. Obtain enrollment figures at your college for the past five years by gender, age, race, or any other pertinent category. Construct a stacked-bar graph to illustrate one of these relationships over the five years.
6. In textbooks or professional journal articles, locate each of these visuals: a table, a multiple-bar graph, a multiline graph, a diagram, and a photograph. Evaluate each according to the revision checklist, and discuss the most effective visual in class.
7. Choose the most appropriate visual for illustrating each of these relationships.

   a. A comparison of three top brands of skis, according to cost, weight, durability, and edge control.
   b. A breakdown of your monthly budget.
   c. The changing cost of an average cup of coffee, as opposed to that of an average cup of tea, over the past three years.
   d. The percentage of college graduates finding desirable jobs within three months after graduation, over the last ten years.
   e. The percentage of college graduates finding desirable jobs within three months after graduation, over the last ten years—by gender.
   f. An illustration of automobile damage for an insurance claim.
   g. A breakdown of the process of corn-based ethanol production.
   h. A comparison of five cereals on the basis of cost and nutritional value.
   i. A comparison of the average age of students enrolled at your college in summer, day, and evening programs, over the last five years.
   j. Comparative sales figures for three items made by your company.

8. Display each of these sets of information in the visual format most appropriate for the stipulated

audience. Complete the planning sheet in Figure 38 for each visual. Explain why you selected the type of visual as most effective for that audience. Include with each visual a caption that interprets and explains the data.

a. (For general readers.) Assume that the Department of Energy breaks down energy consumption in the United States (by source) into these percentages: In 1980, coal, 18.5; natural gas, 32.8; hydro and geothermal, 3.1; nuclear, 1.2; oil, 44.4. In 1990, coal, 20.3; natural gas, 26.9; hydro and geothermal, 3.8; nuclear, 4.0; oil, 45.0. In 2000, coal, 23.5; natural gas, 23.8; hydro and geothermal, 7.3; nuclear, 4.1; oil, 41.3. In 2010, coal, 20.3; natural gas, 25.2; hydro and geothermal, 9.6; nuclear, 6.3; oil, 38.6.

b. (For experienced investors in rental property.) As an aid in estimating annual heating and air-conditioning costs, here are annual maximum and minimum temperature averages from 1975 to 2010 for five Sunbelt cities (in Fahrenheit degrees): In Jacksonville, the average maximum was 78.4; the minimum was 57.6. In Miami, the maximum was 84.2; the minimum was 69.1. In Atlanta, the maximum was 72.0; the minimum was 52.3. In Dallas, the maximum was 75.8; the minimum was 55.1. In Houston, the maximum was 79.4; the minimum was 58.2. (From U.S. National Oceanic and Atmospheric Administration.)

c. (For the student senate.) Among the students who entered our school four years ago, here are the percentages of those who graduated, withdrew, or are still enrolled: In Nursing, 71 percent graduated; 27.9 percent withdrew; 1.1 percent are still enrolled. In Engineering, 62 percent graduated; 29.2 percent withdrew; 8.8 percent are still enrolled. In Business, 53.6 percent graduated; 43 percent withdrew; 3.4 percent are still enrolled. In Arts and Sciences, 27.5 percent graduated; 68 percent withdrew; 4.5 percent are still enrolled.

d. (For the student senate.) Here are the enrollment trends from 1999 to 2011 for two colleges in our university. In Engineering: 1999, 455 students enrolled; 2000, 610; 2001, 654; 2002, 758; 2003, 803; 2004, 827; 2005, 1046; 2006, 1200; 2007, 1115; 2008, 1075; 2009, 1116; 2010, 1145; 2011, 1177. In Business: 1999, 922; 2000, 1006; 2001, 1041; 2002, 1198; 2003, 1188; 2004, 1227; 2005, 1115; 2006, 1220; 2007, 1241; 2008, 1366; 2009, 1381; 2010, 1402; 2011, 1426.

9. Anywhere on campus or at work, locate a visual that needs revision for accuracy, clarity, appearance, or appropriateness. Look in computer manuals, lab manuals, newsletters, financial aid or admissions or placement brochures, student or faculty handbooks, newspapers, or textbooks. Using the planning sheet in Figure 38 and the checklist as guides, revise the visual. Submit a copy of the original, along with a memo explaining your improvements. Be prepared to discuss your revision in class.

10. Locate a document (news, magazine, or journal article, brief instructions) that lacks adequate or appropriate visuals. Analyze the document and identify where visuals would be helpful. In a memo to the document's editor or author, provide an art brief and a thumbnail sketch for each visual you recommend, specifying its exact placement in the document.

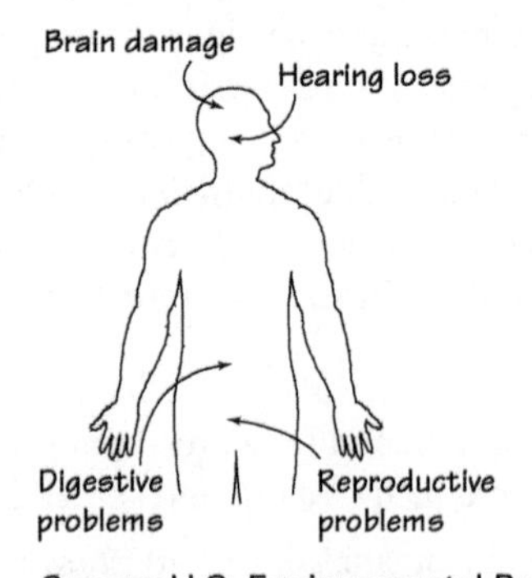

Source: U.S. Environmental Protection Agency. *Protect Your Family from Lead in Your Home,* 1995. 3.

Note: Be sure to provide enough detail for your audience to understand your suggestion clearly. For example, instead of merely recommending a "diagram of the toxic effects of lead on humans," stipulate a "diagram showing a frontal outline of the human body with the head turned sideways in profile view. Labels and arrows point to affected body areas to indicate brain damage, hearing problems, digestive problems, and reproductive problems."

11. Locate a Web page that uses color effectively to mirror the site's main theme or personality, to orient the reader, and to provide cues for easy navigation. Download the page and print it. Prepare a brief memo justifying your choice.
Note: In a computer classroom, consider doing your presentation electronically.

TEAM

Assume that your instructor is planning to purchase five copies of a graphics software package for students to use in designing their documents. The instructor has not yet decided which general-purpose package would be most useful. Your group's task is to test one package and to make a recommendation.

In small groups, visit your school's computer lab and ask for a listing of available graphics packages. Select one package and learn how to use it. Design at least four representative visuals. In a memo or presentation to your instructor and classmates, describe the package briefly and tell what it can do. Would you recommend purchasing this package for general-purpose use by writing students? Explain. Submit your report, along with the sample graphics you have composed.

DIGITAL

Compile a list of six Web sites that offer graphics support by way of advice, image banks, design ideas, artwork catalogs, and the like. Provide the address for each site, along with a description of the resources offered and their approximate cost. Report your findings in the format stipulated by your instructor.

GLOBAL

The International Organization for Standardization (ISO) is a group devoted to standardizing a range of material, including technical specifications and visual information. If you've ever been in an airport and seen the many international signs directing travelers to the restroom or informing them not to smoke, you have seen ISO signs. Go to the ISO Web site at <www.iso.org> to learn about ISO icons and symbols. Show some of the icons and symbols, and explain why these work for international audiences.

For more support in mastering the objectives of this chapter, go to **www.mytechcommlab.com**

Proposals

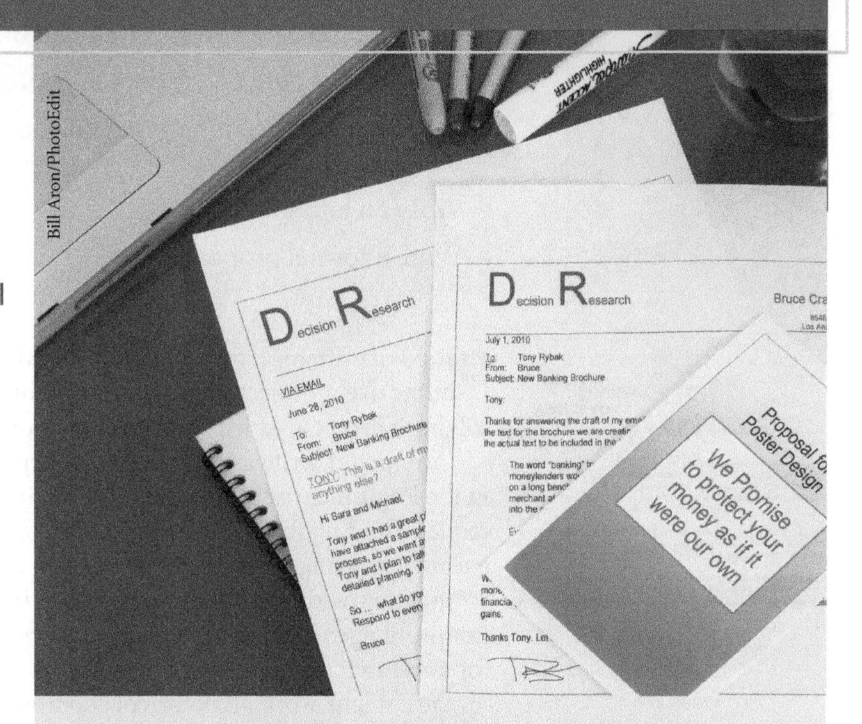

Bill Aron/PhotoEdit

"My work is all about proposal writing—it's my full-time job. While some of our museum's financial support comes from private donors, most of it is generated from grants. I mainly write for panels or committees reviewing grant proposals to decide whether to fund them: for example, corporate officers making a decision on a corporate gift, trustees of private foundations deciding on a foundation gift, and so on. Any such proposal (prepared for, say, The National Endowment for the Arts) usually has to be submitted on a yearly basis in order for funding to continue. And each proposal must compete yearly with proposals from similar institutions. It's a continuous challenge!"

—Ellen Catabia,
Grant Writer for a major museum

LEARNING OBJECTIVES FORTHIS CHAPTER

- Understand the persuasive purpose of proposals
- Understand the expectations of people who read proposals
- Differentiate between solicited and unsolicited proposals
- Differentiate between formal and informal proposals
- Understand the different functions of planning, research, and sales proposals
- Write an informal proposal
- Write a formal proposal

Chapter overview
(Go to *Student Resources>Chapter 24*)

Proposals attempt to *persuade* an audience to take some form of action: to authorize a project, accept a service or product, or support a specific plan for solving a problem or improving a situation.

You might write as a proposal a letter to your school board to suggest changes in the English curriculum; you might write a memo to your firm's vice president to request funding for a training program for new employees; or you might work on a team preparing an extensive document to bid on a Defense Department contract (competing with proposals from other firms). As a student or as an intern at a nonprofit agency, you might submit a *grant proposal*, requesting financial support for a research or community project.

You might work alone or collaboratively. Developing and writing the proposal might take hours or months. If your job depends on funding from outside sources, proposals might be the most important documents you produce.

CONSIDERING AUDIENCE AND PURPOSE

Audience considerations

In science, business, government, or education, proposals are written for decision makers: managers, executives, directors, clients, board members, or community leaders. Inside or outside your organization, these people review various proposals and then decide whether a specific plan is worthwhile, whether the project will materialize, or whether the service or product is useful.

Before accepting a particular proposal, reviewers look for persuasive answers to these basic questions:

What proposal reviewers want to know

- What exactly is the problem or need, and why is this such a big deal?
- Why should we spend time, money, and effort on this?
- What exactly is your plan, and how do we know it is feasible?

- Why should we accept the items that seem costly about your plan?
- What action are we supposed to take?

Connect with your audience by addressing the previous questions early and systematically. Here are the persuasive tasks involved:

A proposal involves these basic persuasive tasks

1. **Spell out the problem (and its causes) clearly and convincingly.** Supply enough detail for your audience to appreciate the problem's importance.
2. **Point out the benefits of solving the problem.** Explain specifically what your readers stand to gain.
3. **Offer a realistic, cost-effective solution.** Stick to claims or assertions you can support.
4. **Address anticipated objections to your solution.** Consider carefully your audience's level of skepticism about this issue.
5. **Convince your audience to act.** Decide exactly what you want your readers to do and give reasons why they should be the ones to take action.

Later in this chapter are examples and strategies for completing each of these tasks.

Purpose considerations

The singular purpose of your proposal is to convince your audience to accept your plan: "Yes. Let's move ahead on this."

How proposals and reports differ in purpose

While they may contain many of the same basic elements as a report, proposals have a primarily *persuasive* purpose. Of course, reports can also contain persuasive elements, as in recommending a specific course of action or justifying an equipment purchase. But reports typically serve a variety of *informative* purposes as well—such as keeping track of progress, explaining why something happened, or predicting an outcome.

A report often precedes a proposal. For example, a report on high levels of chemical pollution in a major waterway typically leads to various proposals for cleaning up that waterway. In short, once the report has *explored* a particular need, a proposal will be developed to *sell* the idea for meeting that need.

THE PROPOSAL PROCESS

Proposals in the commercial sector

The basic proposal process can be summarized like this: Someone offers a plan for something that needs to be done. This process has three stages:

Stages in the proposal process

1. Client *X* needs a service or product.
2. Firms *A*, *B*, and *C* propose a plan for meeting the need.
3. Client *X* awards the job to the firm offering the best proposal.

Following is a typical scenario.

CASE Submitting a Competitive Proposal

You manage a mining engineering firm in Tulsa, Oklahoma. You regularly read the *Commerce Business Daily*, an essential online reference tool for anyone whose firm seeks government contracts. This publication lists the government's latest needs for services (salvage, engineering, maintenance) and for supplies, equipment, and materials (guided missiles, engine parts, and so on). On Wednesday, February 19, you spot this announcement:

> **Development of Alternative Solutions to Acid Mine Water Contamination from Abandoned Lead and Zinc Mines** near Tar Creek, Neosho River, Ground Lake, and the Boone and Roubidoux aquifers in northeastern Oklahoma. This will include assessment of environmental effects of mine drainage followed by development and evaluation of alternate solutions to alleviate acid mine drainage in receiving streams. An optional portion of the contract to be bid on as an add-on and awarded at the discretion of the OWRB will be to prepare an Environmental Impact Assessment for each of three alternative solutions as selected by the OWRB. The project is expected to take six months to accomplish, with an anticipated completion date of September 30, 20XX. The projected effort for the required task is thirty person-months. The request for proposal is available at www.owrb.gov. Proposals are due March 1.
>
> Oklahoma Water Resources Board
> P.O. Box 53585
> 1000 Northeast 10th Street
> Oklahoma City, OK 73151
> (405) 555–2541

Your firm has the personnel, experience, and time to do the job, so you decide to compete for the contract. Because the March 1 deadline is fast approaching, you immediately download the request for proposal (RFP). The RFP will give you the guidelines for developing and submitting the proposal—guidelines for spelling out your plan to solve the problem (methods, timetables, costs).

You then get right to work with the two staff engineers you have appointed to your proposal team. Because the credentials of your staff could affect the client's acceptance of the proposal, you ask team members to update their résumés for inclusion in an appendix to the proposal.

In situations like the one above, the client will award the contract to the firm submitting the best proposal, based on the following criteria (and perhaps others):

Criteria by which reviewers evaluate proposals

- understanding of the client's needs, as described in the RFP
- clarity and feasibility of the plan being offered
- quality of the project's organization and management
- ability to complete the job by deadline
- ability to control costs

- firm's experience on similar projects
- qualifications of staff to be assigned to the project
- firm's performance record on similar projects

A client's specific evaluation criteria are often listed (in order of importance or on a point scale) in the RFP. Although these criteria may vary, every client expects a proposal that is *clear*, *informative*, and *realistic*.

Proposals in the nonprofit sector

In contrast to proposals prepared for commercial purposes, museums, community service groups, and other nonprofit organizations prepare *grant proposals* that request financial support for worthwhile causes. Government and charitable granting agencies such as the Department of Health and Human Services, the Pugh Charitable Trust, or the Department of Agriculture solicit proposals for funding in areas such as medical research, educational TV programming, and rural development. Submission and review of grant proposals follow the same basic process used for commercial proposals.

Submitting paperless proposals

In both the commercial and nonprofit sectors, the proposal process increasingly occurs online. The National Science Foundation's *Fastlane* Web site <www.fastlane.nsf.gov>, for example, allows grant applicants to submit proposals in electronic format. This enables applicants to include sophisticated graphics, to revise budget estimates, to update other aspects of the plan as needed, and to maintain real-time contact with the granting agency while the proposal is being reviewed.

TYPES OF PROPOSALS

Solicited and unsolicited proposals

Proposals may be either *solicited* or *unsolicited*. Solicited proposals are those that have been requested by a manager, client, or customer. Unsolicited proposals are those that have not been requested. If you are a new advertising agency in town, you may send out unsolicited proposals to local radio stations to suggest they use your agency for their advertising.

Proposals project
(Go to *Student Resources> Chapter 24> Projects and Case Studies>Start a Simulated Consulting Firm*)

Because the audience for a solicited proposal has made a specific request, you will not need to spend time introducing yourself or providing background on the product or service. For an unsolicited proposal (sometimes termed a "cold call" in sales), you will need to catch readers' attention quickly and provide incentives for them to continue reading—perhaps by printing a price comparison of your fees on the first page, for example.

Informal and formal proposals

Proposals may also be *informal* or *formal*. Informal proposals can take the form of an email or memo (if distributed within an organization), or a letter (when sent outside of an organization). Formal proposals, meanwhile, take on the same format as formal reports, including front matter, the proposal text, and end matter, if applicable.

Proposals models and template
(Go to *Student Resources> Chapter 24> Models and Templates*)

Both solicited and unsolicited proposals, whether informal or formal, fall into three categories: planning proposals, research proposals, and sales proposals.

Planning Proposals

The role of planning proposals

Planning proposals offer solutions to a problem or suggestions for improvement. A planning proposal might be a request for funding to expand the campus newspaper (as in the formal proposal in this chapter), an architectural plan for new facilities at a ski area, or a plan to develop energy alternatives to fossil fuels.

Figure 1 is a solicited, informal planning proposal that will be used in the following situation: The XYZ Corporation is about to contract with a team of communication consultants to design in-house writing workshops, and the consultants must persuade the client (the company's education and training manager) that their methods will succeed. After briefly introducing the problem, the authors develop their proposal under two headings and several subheadings, making the document easy-to-read and to the point. Because this proposal is addressed to an external reader, it is cast as a letter. (To save space, only the salutation and letter text are shown here.)

Notice that the word choice ("thanks," "what we're doing," "Jack and Terry") creates an informal, familiar tone—appropriate in this external document only because the consultants and client have spent many hours in conferences, luncheons, and phone conversations. Notice also that the "Limitations" section indicates that these authors are careful to promise no more than they can deliver.

Research Proposals

The role of research proposals

Research (or grant) proposals request approval (and often funding) for some type of study. For example, a university chemist might address a research proposal to the Environmental Protection Agency to request funds to identify toxic contaminants in local groundwater. Research proposals are solicited by many agencies, including the National Science Foundation and the National Institutes of Health. Each agency has its own requirements and guidelines for proposal format and content. Successful research proposals follow those guidelines and carefully articulate the goals of the project. In these cases, proposal readers will generally be other scientists; therefore, writers can use language that is appropriate for other experts.

Other research proposals might be submitted by students requesting funds or approval for, say, independent study, or a thesis project. A technical writing student usually submits an informal research proposal that will lead to the term project. For example, in the following research proposal (Figure 2), Tom Dewoody requests his instructor's authorization to do a feasibility study that will produce an analytical report for potential investors. Dewoody's proposal clearly answers the questions about *what, why, how, when,* and *where.* Because this proposal is addressed to an internal reader, it is cast as a memo.

Dear Mary:

Thanks for sending the writing samples from your technical support staff. Here is what we're doing to design a targeted approach. ← States purpose

Needs Assessment

After conferring with technicians in both Jack's and Terry's groups and then analyzing their writing samples, we identified this hierarchy of needs: ← Identifies problem

- improving readability
- achieving precise diction
- summarizing information
- organizing a set of procedures
- formulating various memo reports
- analyzing audiences for upward communication
- writing persuasive bids for transfer or promotion
- writing persuasive suggestions

Proposed Plan

Based on the needs listed above, we have limited our instruction package to seven carefully selected and readily achievable goals. ← Proposes solution

Course Outline. Each three-hour session is structured as follows: ← Details what will be done

1. achieving sentence clarity and conciseness
2. achieving fluency and precise diction
3. writing summaries and abstracts
4. outlining manuals and procedures
5. editing manuals and procedures
6. designing various reports for various purposes
7. analyzing the audience and writing persuasively

Classroom Format. The first three meetings will be lecture-intensive with weekly exercises to be done at home and edited in class. The remaining four weeks will combine lectures and exercises with group editing of work-related documents. We also plan to remain flexible so we can respond to needs that arise. ← Details how it will be done

Limitations

Given our limited contact time, we cannot realistically expect to turn out a batch of polished communicators. By the end of the course, however, our students will have begun to appreciate writing as a deliberate process. ← Sets realistic expectations

If you have any suggestions for refining this plan, please let us know. ← Encourages reader response

FIGURE 1 **A Planning Proposal**

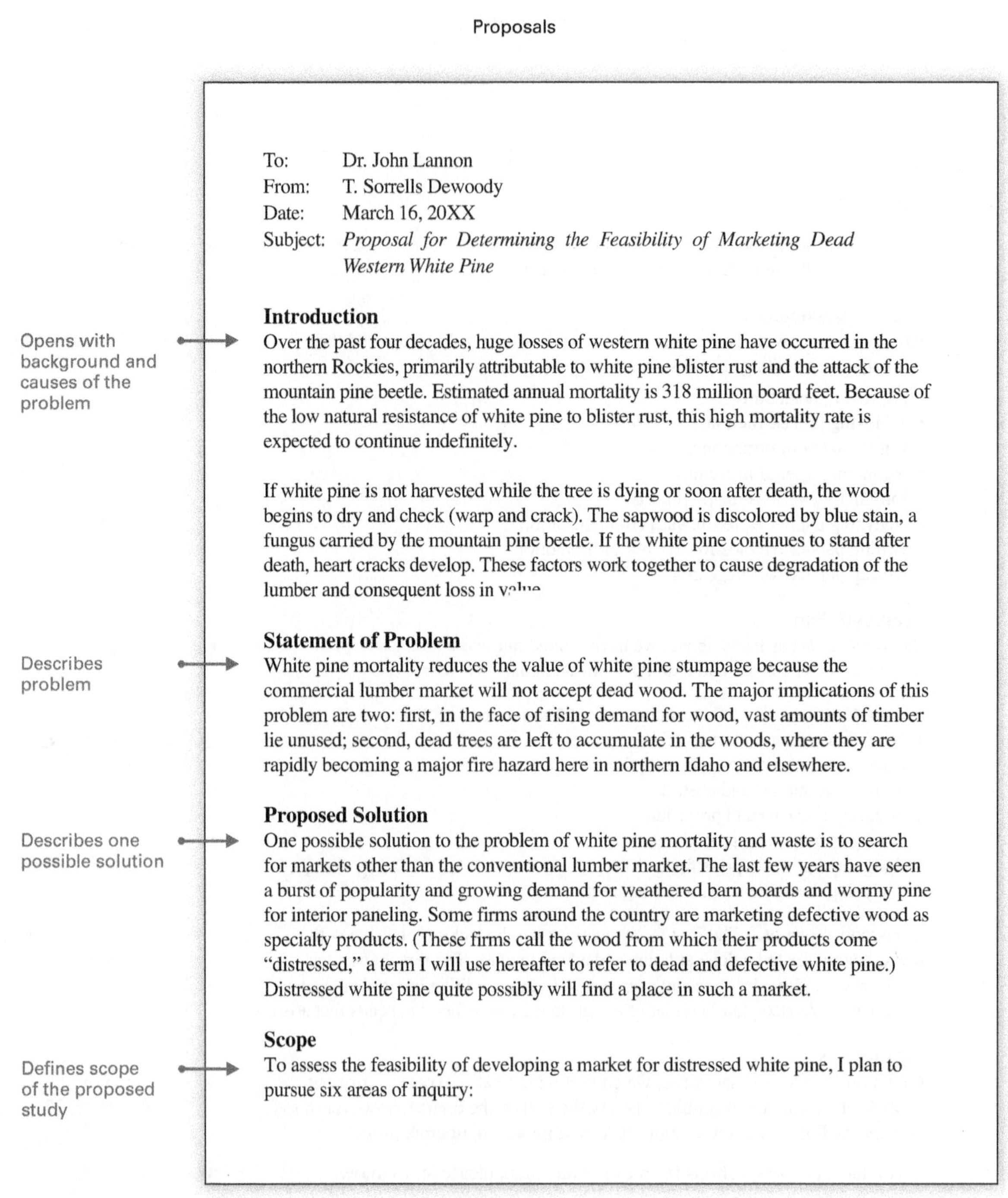

To: Dr. John Lannon
From: T. Sorrells Dewoody
Date: March 16, 20XX
Subject: *Proposal for Determining the Feasibility of Marketing Dead Western White Pine*

Introduction

Over the past four decades, huge losses of western white pine have occurred in the northern Rockies, primarily attributable to white pine blister rust and the attack of the mountain pine beetle. Estimated annual mortality is 318 million board feet. Because of the low natural resistance of white pine to blister rust, this high mortality rate is expected to continue indefinitely.

If white pine is not harvested while the tree is dying or soon after death, the wood begins to dry and check (warp and crack). The sapwood is discolored by blue stain, a fungus carried by the mountain pine beetle. If the white pine continues to stand after death, heart cracks develop. These factors work together to cause degradation of the lumber and consequent loss in value.

Statement of Problem

White pine mortality reduces the value of white pine stumpage because the commercial lumber market will not accept dead wood. The major implications of this problem are two: first, in the face of rising demand for wood, vast amounts of timber lie unused; second, dead trees are left to accumulate in the woods, where they are rapidly becoming a major fire hazard here in northern Idaho and elsewhere.

Proposed Solution

One possible solution to the problem of white pine mortality and waste is to search for markets other than the conventional lumber market. The last few years have seen a burst of popularity and growing demand for weathered barn boards and wormy pine for interior paneling. Some firms around the country are marketing defective wood as specialty products. (These firms call the wood from which their products come "distressed," a term I will use hereafter to refer to dead and defective white pine.) Distressed white pine quite possibly will find a place in such a market.

Scope

To assess the feasibility of developing a market for distressed white pine, I plan to pursue six areas of inquiry:

FIGURE 2 **A Research Proposal**

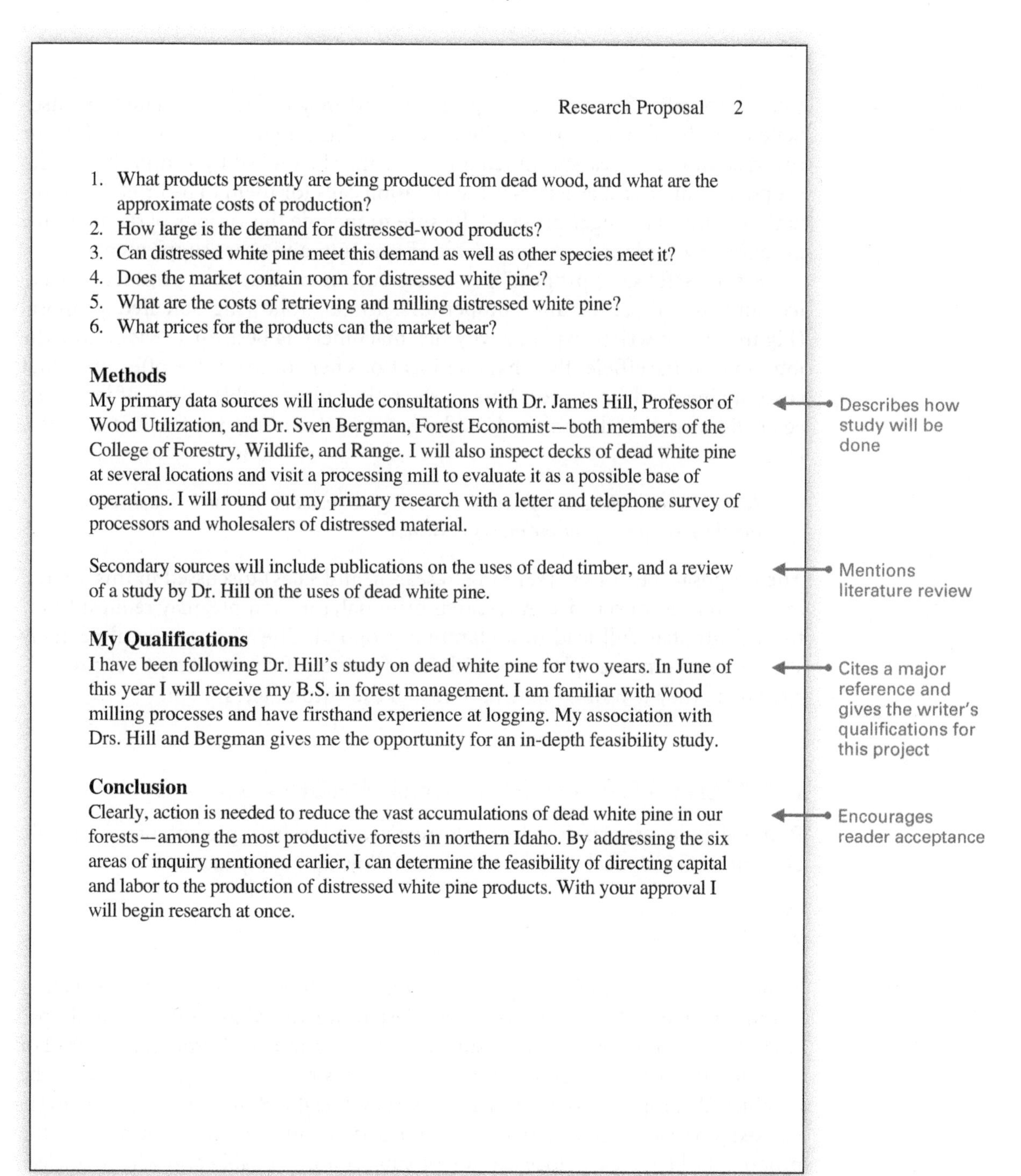

Research Proposal 2

1. What products presently are being produced from dead wood, and what are the approximate costs of production?
2. How large is the demand for distressed-wood products?
3. Can distressed white pine meet this demand as well as other species meet it?
4. Does the market contain room for distressed white pine?
5. What are the costs of retrieving and milling distressed white pine?
6. What prices for the products can the market bear?

Methods

My primary data sources will include consultations with Dr. James Hill, Professor of Wood Utilization, and Dr. Sven Bergman, Forest Economist—both members of the College of Forestry, Wildlife, and Range. I will also inspect decks of dead white pine at several locations and visit a processing mill to evaluate it as a possible base of operations. I will round out my primary research with a letter and telephone survey of processors and wholesalers of distressed material.

Secondary sources will include publications on the uses of dead timber, and a review of a study by Dr. Hill on the uses of dead white pine.

My Qualifications

I have been following Dr. Hill's study on dead white pine for two years. In June of this year I will receive my B.S. in forest management. I am familiar with wood milling processes and have firsthand experience at logging. My association with Drs. Hill and Bergman gives me the opportunity for an in-depth feasibility study.

Conclusion

Clearly, action is needed to reduce the vast accumulations of dead white pine in our forests—among the most productive forests in northern Idaho. By addressing the six areas of inquiry mentioned earlier, I can determine the feasibility of directing capital and labor to the production of distressed white pine products. With your approval I will begin research at once.

FIGURE 2 *(Continued)*

Sales Proposals

The role of sales proposals

Sales proposals offer services or products and may be either solicited or unsolicited. If the proposal is solicited, several firms may be competing for the contract; in such cases, submitted proposals may be ranked by a committee. Sales proposals can be cast as letters if the situation calls for them to be brief. If the situation requires a longer proposal, be sure to include the various parts of formal proposals (cover letter, title page, table of contents, and other supplements).

A successful sales proposal persuades customers that your product or service surpasses those of any competitors. In the following solicited proposal (Figure 3), the writer explains why her machinery is best for the job, how the job can be done efficiently, what qualifications her company can offer, and what costs are involved. To protect herself, she points out possible causes of increased costs. Because this document is addressed to an external reader, it is cast as a letter.

NOTE *Never underestimate costs by failing to account for and acknowledge all variables—a sure way to lose money or clients.*

The proposal categories (planning, research, and sales) discussed in this section are not mutually exclusive. A research proposal, for example, may request funds for a study that will lead to a planning proposal. The Vista proposal partially shown here combines planning and sales features; if clients accept the preliminary plan, they will hire the firm to install the automated system.

ELEMENTS OF A PERSUASIVE PROPOSAL

Proposal reviewers expect a clear, informative, and realistic presentation. They will evaluate your proposal on the basis of the following quality indicators.

A Forecasting Title or Subject Line

Provide a clear forecast

Announce the proposal's purpose and content with an informative title such as "Recommended Wastewater Treatment System for the Mudpie Resorts and Spa" (for a formal proposal) or with a subject line (in an informal proposal). Instead of a vague title such as "Proposed Office Procedures for Vista Freight Company," be specific: "A Proposal for Automating Vista's Freight Billing System." An overworked reviewer facing a stack of proposals might very well decide that the proposal lacking a clear, focused title or subject line probably also will be unclear and unfocused in its content—and set it aside.

Modern Landscaping
23–44 18th Street
Sunnyside, NY 11104

October 4, 20xx

Martin Haver
35–66 114th Avenue
Jamaica, NY 11107

Subject: *Proposal to Dig a Trench and Move Boulders at Bliss Site*

Dear Mr. Haver:

I've inspected your property and would be happy to undertake the landscaping project necessary for the development of your farm.

Describes the subject and purpose

The backhoe I use cuts a span 3 feet wide and can dig as deep as 18 feet—more than an adequate depth for the mainline pipe you wish to lay. Because this backhoe is on tracks rather than tires and is hydraulically operated, it is particularly efficient in moving rocks. I have more than twelve years of experience with backhoe work and have completed many jobs similar to this one.

Gives the writer's qualifications

After examining the huge boulders that block access to your property, I am convinced they can be moved only if I dig out underneath and exert upward pressure with the hydraulic ram while you push forward on the boulders with your D-9 Caterpillar. With this method, we can move enough rock to enable you to farm that now inaccessible tract. Because of its power, my larger backhoe will save you both time and money in the long run.

Explains how the job will be done

Maintains a confident tone throughout

This job should take 12 to 15 hours, unless we encounter subsurface ledge formations. My fee is $200 per hour. The fact that I provide my own dynamiting crew at no extra charge should be an advantage to you because you have so much rock to be moved.

Gives a qualified cost estimate

Please phone or email me at your convenience for more information. I'm sure we can do the job economically and efficiently.

Encourages reader acceptance by emphasizing economy and efficiency

Sincerely yours,
Sharon Ingram
Sharon Ingram

Phone: (814) 555-1212 **Fax:** (814) 551-1222 **Email:** SCAPES@gmail.com

FIGURE 3 **A Sales Proposal**

Background Information

A background section can be brief or long. If the reader is familiar with the project, a quick reminder of the context is sufficient:

Brief background, for readers familiar with the context

> **Background**
>
> Vista provides two services: (1) It locates freight carriers for its clients. The carriers, in turn, pay Vista a 6 percent commission for each referral. (2) Vista handles all shipping paperwork for its clients. For this auditing service, clients pay Vista a monthly retainer.

In an unsolicited proposal, you may need to provide a longer introduction. If the topic warrants, the background section may take up several pages.

Statement of the Problem

The problem and its resolution form the backbone of any proposal. Show that you clearly understand your clients' problems and their expectations, and then offer an appropriate solution.

Describes problem and its effects

> **Statement of the Problem**
>
> Although Vista's business has increased steadily for the past three years, record keeping, accounting, and other paperwork are still done manually. These inefficient procedures have caused a number of problems, including late billings, lost commissions, and poor account maintenance. Updated office procedures seem crucial to competitiveness and continued growth.

Description of Solution

The proposal audience wants specific suggestions for meeting their specific needs. Their biggest question is: "What will this plan do for me?" In the following proposal for automating office procedures at Vista, Inc., Gerald Beaulieu begins with a clear assessment of needs and then moves quickly into a proposed plan of action.

Describes plan to solve the problem

> **Objective**
>
> This proposal offers a realistic and effective plan for streamlining Vista's office procedures. We first identify the burden imposed on your staff by the current system, and then we show how to reduce inefficiency, eliminate client complaints, and improve your cash flow by automating most office procedures.

A Clear Focus on Benefits

Do a detailed audience and use analysis to identify readers' major concerns and to anticipate likely questions and objections. Show that you understand what readers (or their organization) will gain by adopting your plan. The following list spells the exact tasks Vista employees will be able to accomplish once the proposed plan is implemented.

> Once your automated system is operational, you will be able to
>
> - identify cost-effective carriers
> - coordinate shipments (which will ensure substantial client discounts)
> - print commission bills
> - track shipments by weight, miles, fuel costs, and destination
> - send clients weekly audit reports on their shipments
> - bill clients on a 25-day cycle
> - produce weekly or monthly reports
>
> Additional benefits include eliminating repetitive tasks, improving cash flow, and increasing productivity.

Relates benefits directly to client's needs

(Each of these benefits will be described at length later in the "Plan" section.)

Honest and Supportable Claims

Because they typically involve expenditures of large sums of money as well as contractual obligations, proposals require a solid ethical and legal foundation. Clients in these situations often have doubts or objections about time and financial costs and a host of other risks involved whenever any important project is undertaken. Your proposal needs to address these issues openly and honestly. For example, if you are proposing to install customized virus-protection software, be clear about what this software cannot accomplish under certain circumstances. False or exaggerated promises not only damage reputations, but also invite lawsuits.

Promise only what you can deliver

Here is how the Vista proposal qualifies its promises:

> As countless firms have learned, imposing automated procedures on employees can create severe morale problems—particularly among senior staff who feel coerced and often marginalized. To diminish employee resistance, we suggest that your entire staff be invited to comment on this proposal. To help avoid hardware and software problems once the system is operational, we have included recommendations and a budget for staff training. (Adequate training is essential to the automation process.)

Anticipates a major objection and offers a realistic approach

If the best available solutions have limitations, say so. Notice how the above solutions are qualified ("diminish" and "help avoid" instead of "eliminate") so as not to promise more than the plan can achieve.

A proposal can be judged fraudulent if it misleads potential clients by

Major ethical and legal violations in a proposal

- making unsupported claims,
- ignoring anticipated technical problems, or
- knowingly underestimating costs or time requirements.

For a project involving complex tasks or phases, provide a realistic timetable (perhaps using a Gantt chart) to show when each major phase will begin and end. Also provide a realistic, accurate budget, with a detailed cost breakdown (for supplies and equipment, travel, research costs, outside contractors, or the like) to show clients exactly how the money is being spent. For a sample breakdown of costs, see the construction repair proposal.

NOTE *Be certain that you spend every dollar according to the allocations that have been stipulated. For example, if a grant award allocates a certain amount for "a research assistant," be sure to spend that exact amount for that exact purpose—unless you receive written permission from the granting agency to divert funds for other purposes. Keep strict accounting of all the money you spend. Proposal experts Friedland and Folt remind us that "Financial misconduct is never tolerated, regardless of intent" (161). Even an innocent mistake or accounting lapse on your part can lead to charges of fraud.*

Appropriate Detail

Vagueness in a proposal is fatal. Spell everything out. Instead of writing, "We will install state-of-the-art equipment," enumerate the products or services to be provided.

Spells out what will be provided

> To meet your requirements, we will install 12 iMac desktop computers, each with 500 GB hard drives. The system will be networked for secure file transfer between office locations. The plan also includes network printers with four HP LaserJet CP2020 color printers and one HP Deskjet 6940 color printer.

To avoid misunderstandings that could produce legal complications, a proposal must elicit *one* interpretation only.

Place support material (maps, blueprints, specifications, calculations) in an appendix so as not to interrupt the discussion.

NOTE *While concrete and specific detail is vital, never overburden reviewers with needless material. A precise audience and use analysis can pinpoint specific information needs.*

Readability

A readable proposal is straightforward, easy to follow, and understandable. Avoid language that is overblown or too technical for your audience.

A Tone That Connects with Readers

Your proposal should move people to action. Keep your tone confident and encouraging, not bossy and critical.

Visuals

Emphasize key points in your proposal with relevant tables, flowcharts, and other visuals, properly introduced and discussed.

As the flowchart (Figure 1) illustrates, Vista's routing and billing system creates redundant work for your staff. The routing sheet alone is handled at least six times. Such extensive handling leads to errors, misplaced paperwork, and late billing.

Visual repeats, restates, or reinforces the prose

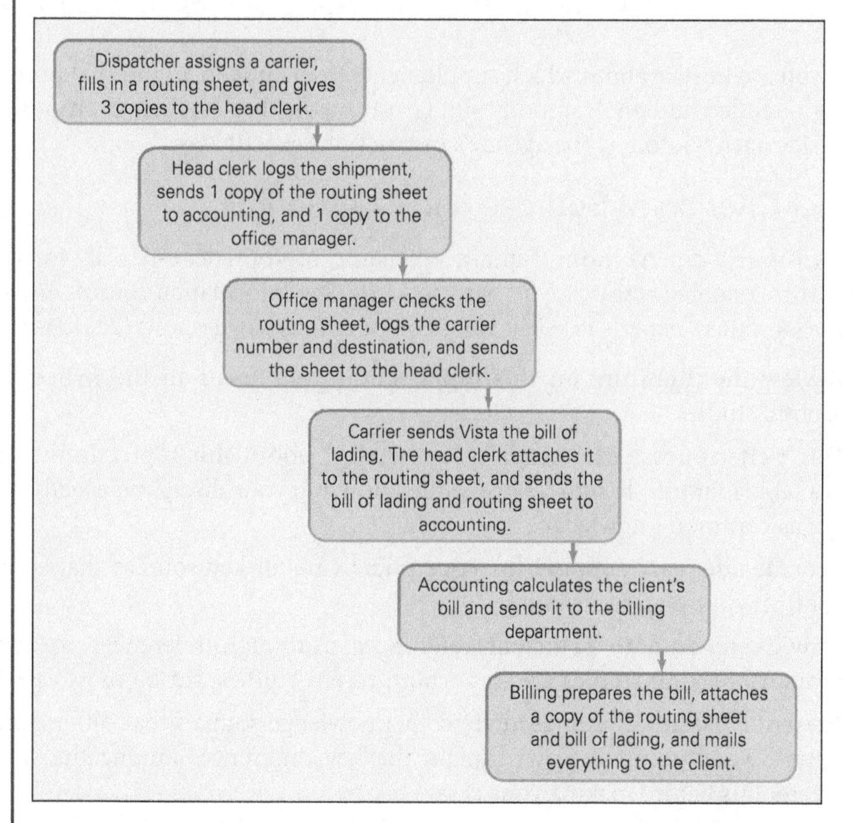

FIGURE 1 Flowchart of Vista's Manual Routing and Billing System

Accessible Page Design

Yours might be one of several proposals being reviewed. Help the audience to find what they need quickly.

Supplements Tailored for a Diverse Audience

Analyze the specific needs and interests of each major reviewer

A single proposal often addresses a diverse audience: executives, managers, technical experts, attorneys, politicians, and so on. Various reviewers are interested in different parts of your proposal. Experts look for the technical details. Others might be interested in the recommendations, costs, timetable, or expected results, but they will need an explanation of technical details as well.

Give each major reviewer what he or she expects

If the primary audience is expert or informed, keep the proposal text itself technical. For uninformed secondary reviewers (if any), provide an informative abstract, a glossary, and appendices explaining specialized information. If the primary audience has no expertise and the secondary audience does, write the proposal itself for laypersons, and provide appendices with the technical details (formulas, specifications, calculations) that experts will use to evaluate your plan.

If you are unsure about which supplements to include in an internal proposal, ask the intended audience or study similar proposals. For a solicited proposal (to an outside agency), follow the agency's instructions exactly.

Proper Citation of Sources and Contributors

Proposals rarely emerge from thin air. Whenever appropriate, especially for topics that involve ongoing research, you need to credit key information sources and contributors. Proposal experts Friedland and Folt offer these suggestions (22, 134–36):

How to cite sources and contributors

- **Review the literature on this topic.** Limit your focus to the major background studies.
- **Don't cite sources of "common knowledge" about this topic.** Information available in multiple sources or readily known in your discipline usually qualifies as common knowledge.
- **Provide adequate support for your plan.** Cite all key sources that serve to confirm your plan's feasibility.
- **Provide up-to-date principal references.** Although references to earlier, ground-breaking studies are important, recent studies can be most essential.
- **Present a balanced, unbiased view.** Acknowledge sources that differ from or oppose your point of view; explain the key differences among the various viewpoints before making your case.
- **Give credit to all contributors.** Recognize everyone who has worked on or helped with this proposal: for example, coauthors, editors, data gatherers, and people who contributed ideas.

Proper citation is not only an ethical requirement, but also an indicator of your proposal's feasibility.

AN OUTLINE AND MODEL FOR PROPOSALS

Depending on a proposal's complexity, each section contains some or all of the components listed in the following general outline:

I. Introduction
- A. Statement of Problem and Objective/Project Overview
- B. Background and Review of the Literature (as needed)
- C. Need
- D. Benefits
- E. Qualifications of Personnel
- F. Data Sources
- G. Limitations and Contingencies
- H. Scope

II. Plan
- A. Objectives and Methods
- B. Timetable
- C. Materials and Equipment
- D. Personnel
- E. Available Facilities
- F. Needed Facilities
- G. Cost and Budget
- H. Expected Results
- I. Feasibility

III. Conclusion
- A. Summary of Key Points
- B. Request for Action

IV. Works Cited

These components can be rearranged, combined, divided, or deleted as needed. Not every proposal will contain all components; however, each major section must persuasively address specific information needs as illustrated in the sample proposal that begins on the next page.

Introduction

From the beginning, your goal is *to sell your idea*—to demonstrate the need for the project, your qualifications for tackling the project, and your clear understanding of what needs to be done and how to proceed. Readers quickly lose interest in a wordy, evasive, or vague introduction.

Following is the introduction for a planning proposal titled "Proposal for Solving the Noise Problem in the University Library." Jill Sanders, a library work-study student, addresses her proposal to the chief librarian and the administrative staff. Because this proposal is unsolicited, it must first make the problem vivid through details that arouse concern and interest. This introduction is longer than it would be in a solicited proposal, whose audience would already agree on the severity of the problem.

NOTE *Title page, informative abstract, table of contents, and other front-matter and end-matter supplements that ordinarily accompany long proposals of this type are omitted here to save space.*

INTRODUCTION

Statement of Problem

Concise descriptions of problem and objective immediately alert the readers

During the October 20XX Convocation at Margate University, students and faculty members complained about noise in the library. Soon afterward, areas were designated for "quiet study," but complaints about noise continue. To create a scholarly atmosphere, the library should take immediate action to decrease noise.

Objective

This proposal examines the noise problem from the viewpoint of students, faculty, and library staff. It then offers a plan to make areas of the library quiet enough for serious study and research.

Sources

This section comes early because it is referred to in the next section

My data come from a university-wide questionnaire; interviews with students, faculty, and library staff; inquiry letters to other college libraries; and my own observations for three years on the library staff.

Details of the Problem

Details help readers understand the problem

This subsection examines the severity and causes of the noise.

Severity. Since the 20XX Convocation, the library's fourth and fifth floors have been reserved for quiet study, but students hold group study sessions at the large tables and disturb others working alone. The constant use of computer terminals on both floors adds to the noise, especially when students converse. Moreover, people often chat as they enter or leave study areas.

On the second and third floors, designed for reference, staff help patrons locate materials, causing constant shuffling of people and books, as well as loud conversation. At the computer service desk on the third floor, conferences between students and instructors create more noise.

Shows how campus feels about problem

The most frequently voiced complaint from the faculty members interviewed was about the second floor, where people using the Reference and Government Documents services converse loudly. Students complain about the lack of a quiet spot to study, especially in the evening, when even the "quiet" floors are as noisy as the dorms.

More than 80 percent of respondents (530 undergraduates, 30 faculty, 22 graduate students) to a university-wide questionnaire insisted that excessive noise discourages them from using the library as often as they would prefer. Of the student respondents, 430 cited quiet study as their primary reason for wishing to use the library.

Shows concern is widespread and pervasive

The library staff recognizes the problem but has insufficient personnel. Because all staff members have assigned tasks, they have no time to monitor noise in their sections.

Causes. Respondents complained specifically about these causes of noise (in descending order of frequency):

1. Loud study groups that often lapse into social discussions.
2. General disrespect for the library, with some students' attitudes characterized as "rude," "inconsiderate," or "immature."
3. The constant clicking of typing at computer terminals on all five floors, and of laptops on the first three.
4. Vacuuming by the evening custodians.

Identifies specific causes

All complaints converged on lack of enforcement by library staff. Because the day staff works on the first three floors, quiet-study rules are not enforced on the fourth and fifth floors. Work-study students on these floors have no authority to enforce rules not enforced by the regular staff. Small, black-and-white "Quiet Please" signs posted on all floors go unnoticed, and the evening security guard provides no deterrent.

Needs

Excessive noise in the library is keeping patrons away. By addressing this problem immediately, we can help restore the library's credibility and utility as a campus resource. We must reduce noise on the lower floors and eliminate it from the quiet-study floors.

This statement of need evolves logically and persuasively from earlier evidence

Scope

The proposed plan includes a detailed assessment of methods, costs and materials, personnel requirements, feasibility, and expected results.

Previews the plan

Body

The body (or plan section) of your proposal will receive the most audience attention. The main goal of this section is to prove your plan will work. Here you spell out your plan in enough detail for the audience to evaluate its soundness. If this section is vague, your proposal stands no chance of being accepted. Be sure that your plan is realistic and promises no more than you can deliver.

PROPOSED PLAN

This plan takes into account the needs and wishes of our campus community, as well as the available facilities in our library.

Phases of the Plan

Tells how plan will be implemented

Noise in the library can be reduced in three complementary phases: (1) improving publicity, (2) shutting down and modifying our facilities, and (3) enforcing the quiet rules.

Describes first phase

Improving Publicity. First, the library must publicize the noise problem. This assertive move will demonstrate the staff's interest. Publicity could include articles by staff members in the campus newspaper, leaflets distributed on campus, and a freshman library orientation acknowledging the noise problem and asking for cooperation from new students. All forms of publicity should detail the steps being taken by the library to solve the problem.

Describes second phase

Shutting Down and Modifying Facilities. After notifying campus and local newspapers, you should close the library for one week. To minimize disruption, the shutdown should occur between the end of summer school and the beginning of the fall term.

During this period, you can convert the fixed tables on the fourth and fifth floors to cubicles with temporary partitions (six cubicles per table). You could later convert the cubicles to shelves as the need increases.

Then you can take all unfixed tables from the upper floors to the first floor, and set up a space for group study. Plans are already under way for removing the computer terminals from the fourth and fifth floors.

Describes third phase

Enforcing the Quiet Rules. Enforcement is the essential long-term element in this plan. No one of any age is likely to follow all the rules all the time—unless the rules are enforced.

First, you can make new "Quiet" posters to replace the present, innocuous notices. A visual-design student can be hired to draw up large, colorful posters that attract attention. Either the design student or the university print shop can take charge of poster production.

Next, through publicity, library patrons can be encouraged to demand quiet from noisy people. To support such patron demands, the library staff can begin monitoring the fourth and fifth floors, asking study groups to move to the first floor, and revoking library privileges of those who refuse. Patrons on the second and third floors can be asked to speak in whispers. Staff members should set an example by regulating their own voices.

Costs and Materials

Estimates costs and materials needed

- The major cost would be for salaries of new staff members who would help monitor. Next year's library budget, however, will include an allocation for four new staff members.

- A design student has offered to make up four different posters for $200. The university printing office can reproduce as many posters as needed at no additional cost.
- Prefabricated cubicles for 26 tables sell for $150 apiece, for a total cost of $3,900.
- Rearrangement on various floors can be handled by the library's custodians.

The Student Fee Allocations Committee and the Student Senate routinely reserve funds for improving student facilities. A request to these organizations would presumably yield at least partial funding for the plan.

Personnel

The success of this plan ultimately depends on the willingness of the library administration to implement it. You can run the program itself by committees made up of students, staff, and faculty. This is yet another area where publicity is essential to persuade people that the problem is severe and that you need their help. To recruit committee members from among students, you can offer Contract Learning credits.

Describes personnel needed

The proposed committees include an Antinoise Committee overseeing the program, a Public Relations Committee, a Poster Committee, and an Enforcement Committee.

Feasibility

On March 15, 20XX, I mailed survey letters to twenty-five New England colleges, inquiring about their methods for coping with noise in the library. Among the respondents, sixteen stated that publicity and the administration's attitude toward enforcement were main elements in their success.

Assesses probability of success

Improved publicity and enforcement could work for us as well. And slight modifications in our facilities, to concentrate group study on the busiest floors, would automatically lighten the burden of enforcement.

Benefits

Publicity will improve communication between the library and the campus. An assertive approach will show that the library is aware of its patrons' needs and is willing to meet those needs. Offering the program for public inspection will draw the entire community into improvement efforts. Publicity, begun now, will pave the way for the formation of committees.

Offers a realistic and persuasive forecast of benefits

The library shutdown will have a dual effect: It will dramatize the problem to the community, and it will provide time for the physical changes. (An antinoise program begun with carpentry noise in the quiet areas would hardly be effective.) The shutdown will be both a symbolic and a concrete measure, leading to reopening of the library with a new philosophy and a new image.

Continued strict enforcement will be the backbone of the program. It will prove that staff members care enough about the atmosphere to jeopardize their friendly image in the eyes of some users, and that the library is not afraid to enforce its rules.

Conclusion

The conclusion reaffirms the need for the project and induces the audience to act. End on a strong note, with a conclusion that is assertive, confident, and encouraging—and keep it short.

CONCLUSION AND RECOMMENDATION

Reemphasizes need and feasibility and encourages action

The noise in Margate University Library has become embarrassing and annoying to the whole campus. Forceful steps are needed to restore the academic atmosphere.

Aside from the intangible question of image, close inspection of the proposed plan will show that it will work if the recommended steps are taken and—most important—if daily enforcement of quiet rules becomes a part of library policy.

In long, formal proposals, especially those beginning with a comprehensive abstract, the conclusion can be omitted.

GUIDELINES for Proposals

- **Understand the audience's needs.** Demonstrate a clear understanding of the audience's problem, and then offer an appropriate solution.
- **Perform research as needed.** For example, you might research the very latest technology for solving a problem; compare the costs, benefits, and drawbacks of various approaches; contact others in your field for their suggestions; or find out what competitors are up to.
- **Credit all information sources and contributors.** If anything in your proposal represents the work or input of others, document the sources.
- **Use an appropriate format.** For an informal proposal distributed internally, use email or memo format. For an informal proposal distributed externally, use letter format. For a formal proposal, include all the required front matter and end matter.
- **Provide a clear title or subject line and background information.** Tell readers what to expect, and orient them with the appropriate background information.
- **Spell out the problem (and its causes).** Answer the implied question, "Why is this such a big deal?"
- **Point out the benefits of solving the problem.** Answer the implied question, "Why should we spend time, money, and effort to do this?"
- **Offer a realistic solution.** Stick to claims or assertions you can support. Answer the implied question, "How do we know this will work?" If the solution involves accounting for costs, budgeting time, or proving your qualifications, include this information.

- **Address anticipated objections to your plan.** Decision makers typically approach a proposal with skepticism, especially if the project will cost them money and time. Answer the implied question, "Why should we accept the items that seem costly with your plan?"
- **Include all necessary details, but don't overload.** Include as much supporting detail as you need to induce readers to say yes. Leave nothing to guesswork. At the same time, don't overload readers with irrelevant information.
- **Write clearly and concisely.** Use action verbs and plain English. Avoid terms that are too technical for your audience. If necessary for a mixed audience with differing technical levels, include a glossary.
- **Express confidence.** You are trying to sell yourself, your ideas, or your services to a skeptical audience. Offer the supporting facts ("For the third year in a row, our firm has been ranked as the number 1 architecture firm in the Midwest") and state your case directly ("We know you will be satisfied with the results").
- **Make honest and supportable claims.** If the solutions you offer have limitations, make sure you say so.
- **Induce readers to act.** Decide exactly what you want readers to do, and give reasons why they should be the ones to act. In your conclusion, answer the implied question, "What action am I supposed to take?"

A SITUATION REQUIRING A FORMAL PROPOSAL

The proposal that follows is essentially a grant proposal, since it requests funding for a nonprofit enterprise. Notice how it adapts elements from the sample outline. As in any funding proposal, a precise, realistic plan and an itemized budget provide the justification for the requested financial support.

A Formal Proposal

The Situation. Southeastern Massachusetts University's newspaper, the SMU *Torch*, is struggling to meet rising production costs. The paper's yearly budget is funded by the Student Fee Allocation Committee, which disburses money to various campus organizations. Drastic budget cuts have resulted in reduced funding for all state schools. As a result, the newspaper has received no funding increase for the last three years. Meanwhile, production costs keep rising.

Bill Trippe, the *Torch's* business manager, has to justify a requested increase of 17.3 percent for the coming year's budget. Before drafting his proposal (Figure 4), Bill constructs an audience and use profile.

Audience and Use Profile. The primary audience includes all members of the Student Fee Allocation Committee. The secondary audience is the newspaper staff, who will implement the proposed plan—if it is approved by the committee.

The primary audience will use this document as perhaps the sole basis for deciding whether to grant the additional funds. Most of these readers have overseen the newspaper budget for years, and so they already know quite a bit about the newspaper's overall operation. But they still need an item-by-item explanation of the conditions created by problems with funding and ever-increasing costs. Probable questions Bill can anticipate:

- Why should the paper receive priority over other campus organizations?
- Just how crucial is the problem?
- Are present funds being used efficiently?
- Can any expenses be reduced?
- How would additional funds be spent?
- How much will this increase cost?
- Will the benefits justify the cost?

The primary audience often has expressed interest in this topic. But they are likely to object to any request for more money by arguing that everyone has to economize in these difficult times. Thus their attitude could be characterized as both receptive and hesitant. (Almost every campus organization is trying to make a case for additional funds.)

Bill knows most of the committee members pretty well, and he senses that they respect his management skills. But he still needs to spell out the problem and propose a realistic plan, showing that the newspaper staff is sincere in its intention to eliminate nonessential operating costs. At a time when everyone is expected to make do with less, this proposal needs to make an especially strong case for salary increases (to attract talented personnel).

The primary audience has solicited this proposal, and so it is likely to be carefully read—but also scrutinized and evaluated for its soundness. Especially in a budget request, this audience expects no shortcuts: Every expense will have to be itemized, and the Costs section should be the longest part of the proposal.

To further justify the budget request, the proposal needs to demonstrate just how well the newspaper manages its present funds. In the Feasibility section, Bill provides a detailed comparison of funding, expenditures, and the size of the *Torch* in relation to the size of the newspapers of the four other local colleges. These are the facts most likely to persuade readers that the plan is cost-effective.

To organize his document, Bill (1) identifies the problem, (2) establishes the need, (3) proposes a solution, (4) shows that the plan is cost-effective, and (5) concludes with a request for action.

This audience expects a confident and businesslike—but not stuffy—tone.

SMU *Torch*

Old Westport Road
North Dartmouth, Massachusetts 02747

May 1, 20XX

Charles Marcus, Chair
Student Fee Allocation Committee
Southeastern Massachusetts University
North Dartmouth, MA 02747

Dear Dean Marcus:

No one needs to be reminded about the effects of increased costs on our campus community. We are all faced with having to make do with less.

Letter of transmittal provides additional context and persuasion

Accordingly, we at the *Torch* have spent long hours devising a plan to cope with increased production costs—without compromising the newspaper's tradition of quality service. I think you and your colleagues will agree that our plan is realistic and feasible. Even the "bare-bones" operation that will result from our proposed spending cuts, however, will call for a $6,478.57 increase in next year's budget.

We have received no funding increase in three years. Our present need is absolute. Without additional funds, the *Torch* simply cannot continue to function as a professional newspaper. I therefore submit the following budget proposal for your consideration.

Respectfully,

William Trippe

William Trippe
Business Manager, SMU *Torch*

FIGURE 4 **A Formal Proposal**

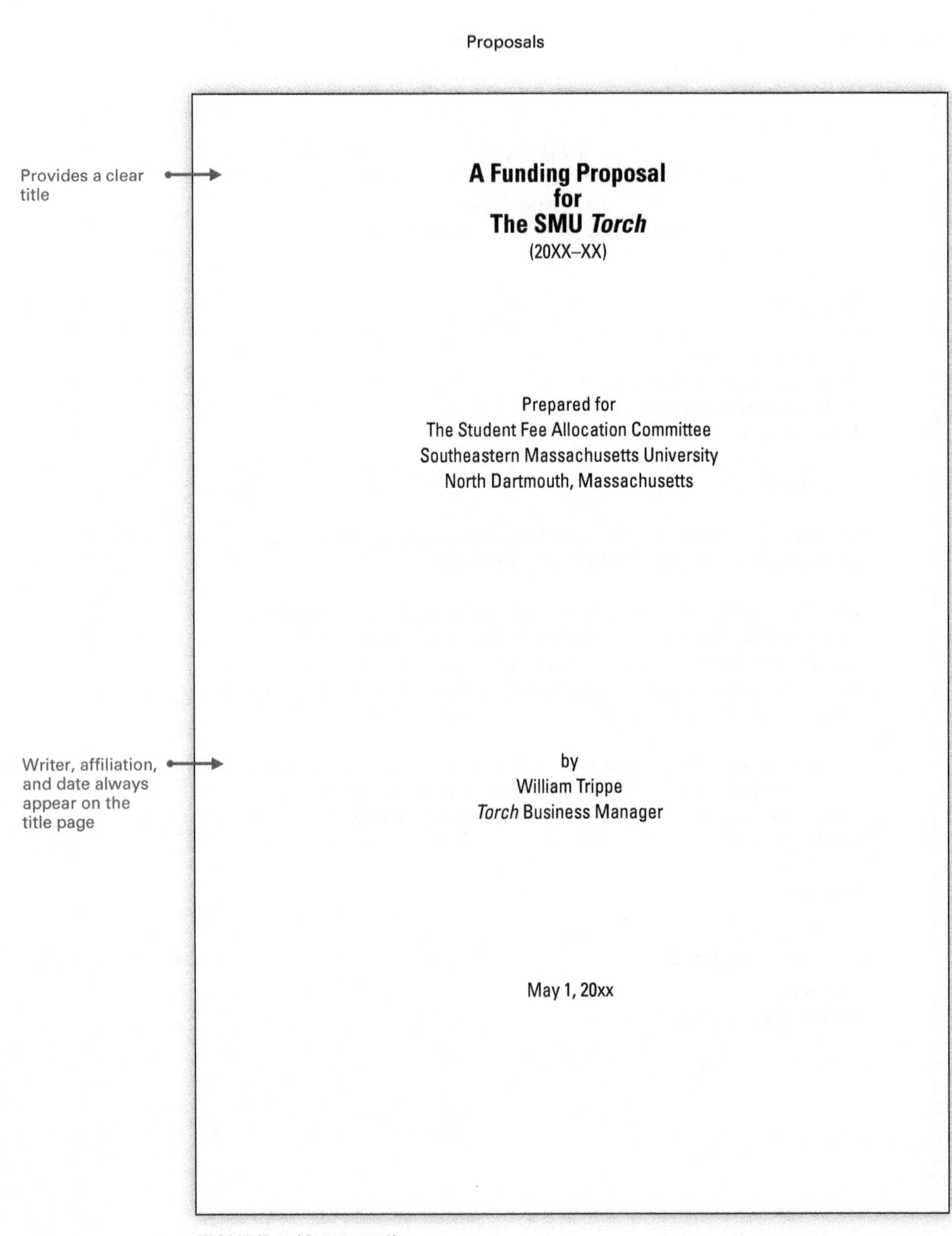

FIGURE 4 *(Continued)*

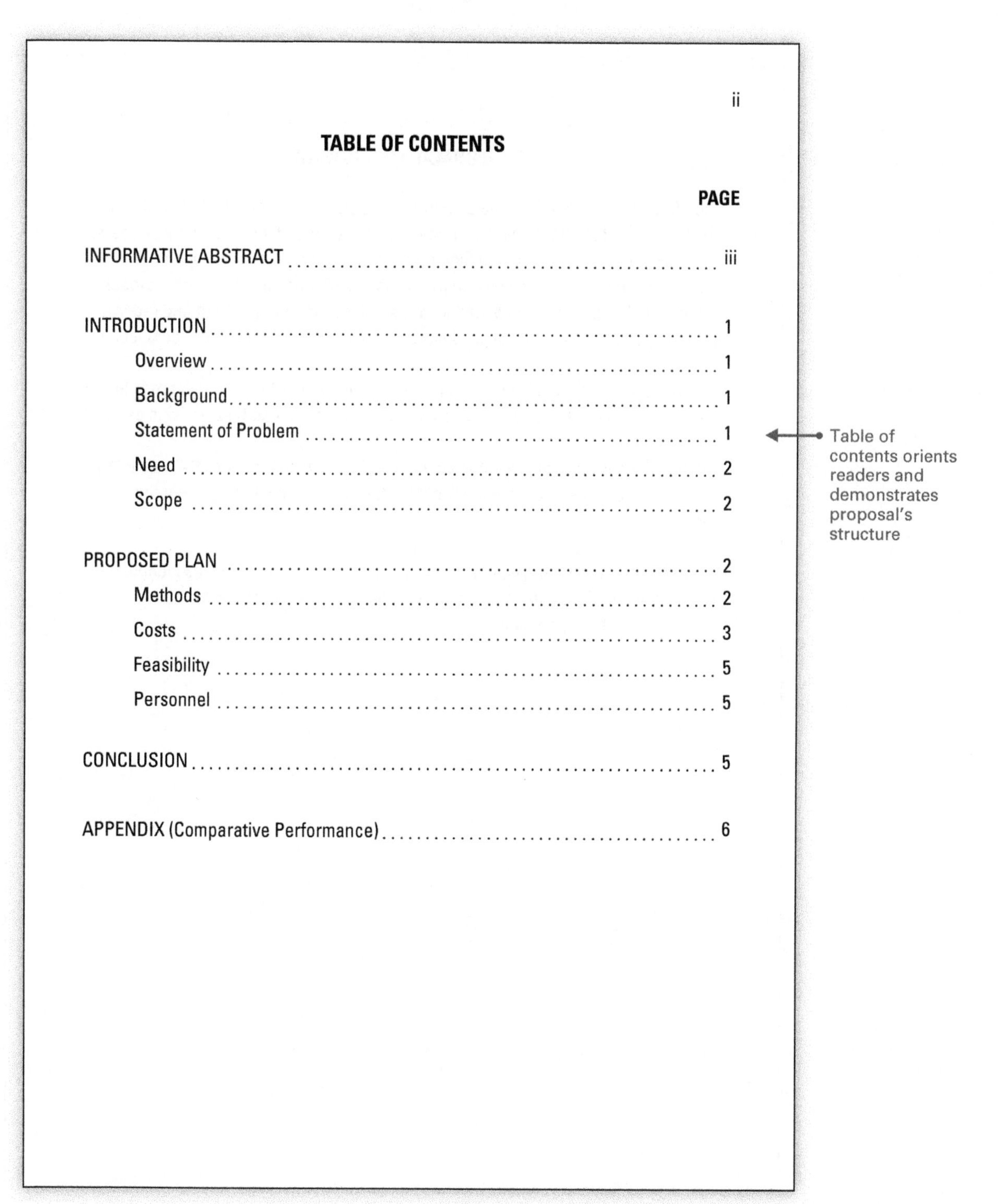
ii

TABLE OF CONTENTS

FIGURE 4 *(Continued)*

Abstract accurately encapsulates entire document

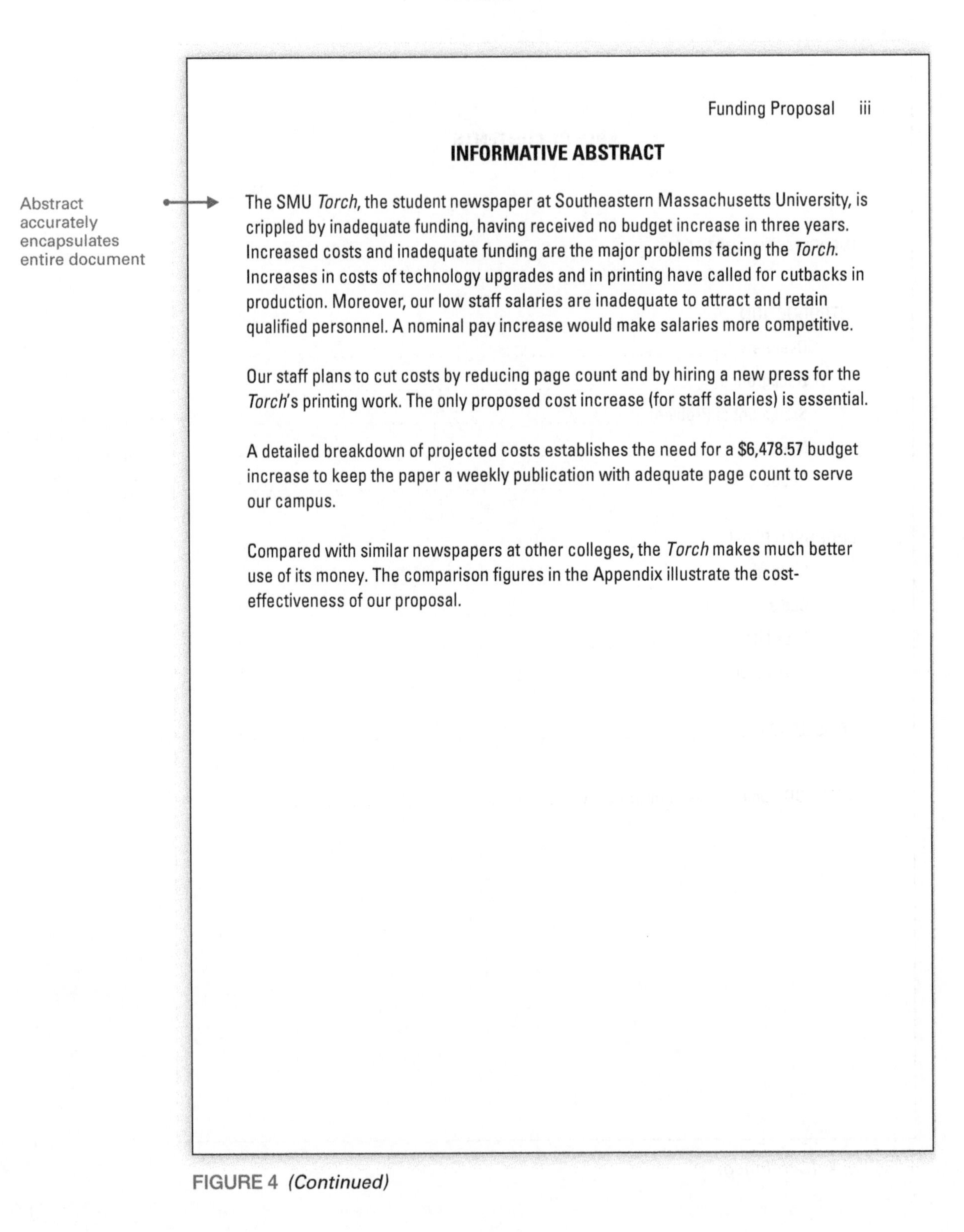

INFORMATIVE ABSTRACT

The SMU *Torch*, the student newspaper at Southeastern Massachusetts University, is crippled by inadequate funding, having received no budget increase in three years. Increased costs and inadequate funding are the major problems facing the *Torch*. Increases in costs of technology upgrades and in printing have called for cutbacks in production. Moreover, our low staff salaries are inadequate to attract and retain qualified personnel. A nominal pay increase would make salaries more competitive.

Our staff plans to cut costs by reducing page count and by hiring a new press for the *Torch*'s printing work. The only proposed cost increase (for staff salaries) is essential.

A detailed breakdown of projected costs establishes the need for a $6,478.57 budget increase to keep the paper a weekly publication with adequate page count to serve our campus.

Compared with similar newspapers at other colleges, the *Torch* makes much better use of its money. The comparison figures in the Appendix illustrate the cost-effectiveness of our proposal.

FIGURE 4 *(Continued)*

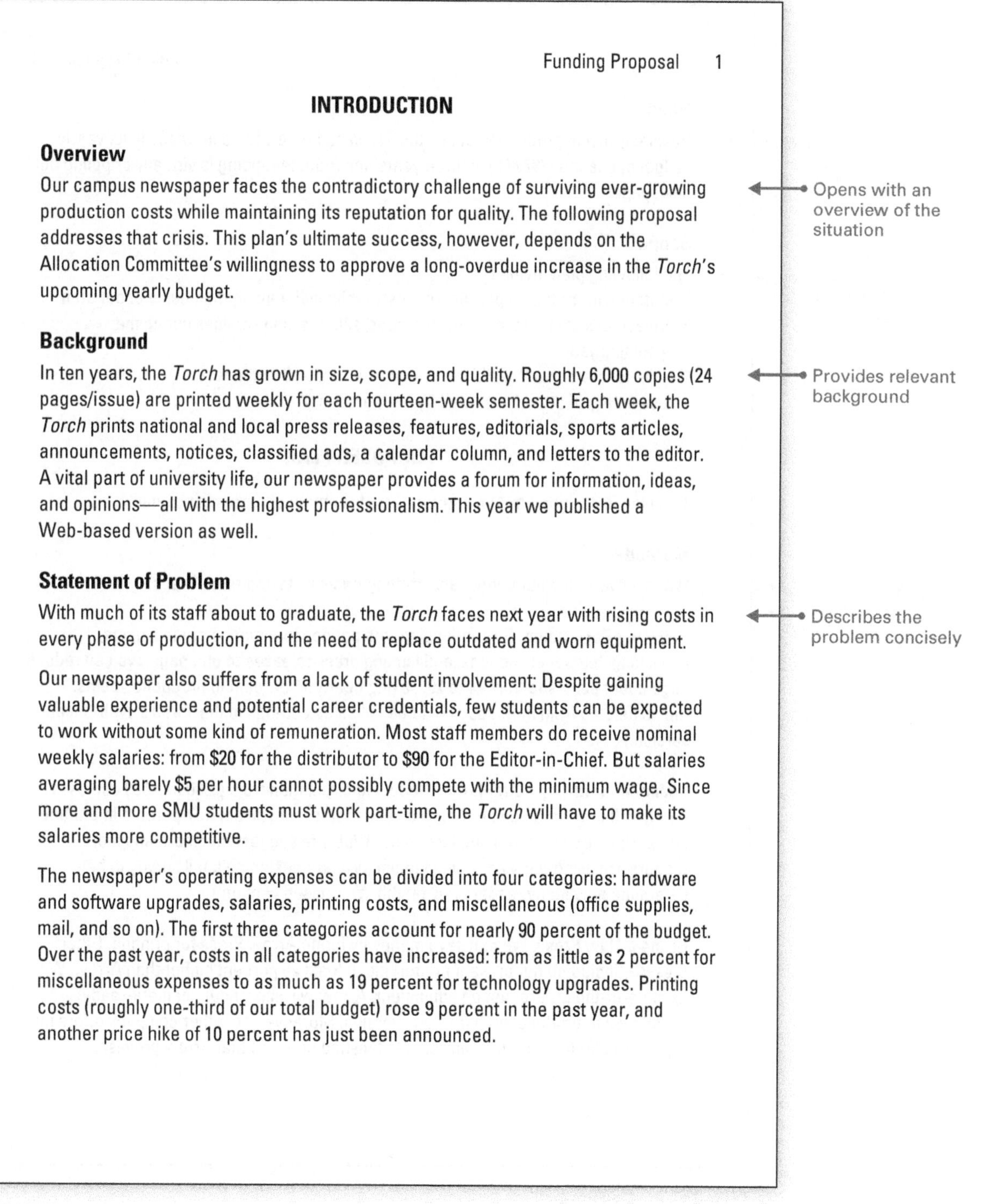

Funding Proposal 1

INTRODUCTION

Overview

Our campus newspaper faces the contradictory challenge of surviving ever-growing production costs while maintaining its reputation for quality. The following proposal addresses that crisis. This plan's ultimate success, however, depends on the Allocation Committee's willingness to approve a long-overdue increase in the *Torch*'s upcoming yearly budget.

Background

In ten years, the *Torch* has grown in size, scope, and quality. Roughly 6,000 copies (24 pages/issue) are printed weekly for each fourteen-week semester. Each week, the *Torch* prints national and local press releases, features, editorials, sports articles, announcements, notices, classified ads, a calendar column, and letters to the editor. A vital part of university life, our newspaper provides a forum for information, ideas, and opinions—all with the highest professionalism. This year we published a Web-based version as well.

Statement of Problem

With much of its staff about to graduate, the *Torch* faces next year with rising costs in every phase of production, and the need to replace outdated and worn equipment.

Our newspaper also suffers from a lack of student involvement: Despite gaining valuable experience and potential career credentials, few students can be expected to work without some kind of remuneration. Most staff members do receive nominal weekly salaries: from $20 for the distributor to $90 for the Editor-in-Chief. But salaries averaging barely $5 per hour cannot possibly compete with the minimum wage. Since more and more SMU students must work part-time, the *Torch* will have to make its salaries more competitive.

The newspaper's operating expenses can be divided into four categories: hardware and software upgrades, salaries, printing costs, and miscellaneous (office supplies, mail, and so on). The first three categories account for nearly 90 percent of the budget. Over the past year, costs in all categories have increased: from as little as 2 percent for miscellaneous expenses to as much as 19 percent for technology upgrades. Printing costs (roughly one-third of our total budget) rose 9 percent in the past year, and another price hike of 10 percent has just been announced.

FIGURE 4 *(Continued)*

Proposes a logical solution to the problem, based on evidence

Need

Despite growing production costs, the *Torch* has received no increase in its yearly budget allocation ($37,400) in three years. Inadequate funding is virtually crippling our newspaper.

Previews the plan before getting into details

Scope

The following plan includes

1. Methods for reducing production costs while maintaining the quality of our staff
2. Projected costs for technology upgrades, salaries, and services during the upcoming year
3. A demonstration of feasibility, showing our cost-effectiveness
4. A summary of attitudes shared by our personnel

PROPOSED PLAN

This plan is designed to trim operating costs without compromising quality.

Itemizes realistic ways to save money and retain staff

Methods

We can overcome our budget and staffing crisis by taking these steps:

Reducing Page Count. By condensing free notices for campus organizations, abolishing "personal" notices, and limiting press releases to one page, we can reduce page count per issue from 24 to 20, saving nearly 17 percent in production costs. (Items deleted from hard copy could be linked as add-ons in the *Torch's* Web-based version.)

Reducing Hard-Copy Circulation. Reducing circulation from 6,000 to 5,000 copies barely will cover the number of full-time students, but will save 17 percent in printing costs. The steadily increasing hits on our Web site suggest that more and more readers are using the electronic medium. (We are designing a fall survey to help determine how many readers rely on the Web-based version.)

Hiring a New Press. We can save money by hiring Arrow Press for printing. Other presses (including our present printer) bid at least 25 percent higher than Arrow. With its state-of-the art production equipment, Arrow will import our "camera-ready" digital files to produce the hard-copy version. Moreover, no other company offers the rapid turnover time (from submission to finished product) that Arrow promises.

FIGURE 4 *(Continued)*

Upgrading Our Desktop Publishing Technology. To meet Arrow's specifications for submitting digital files, we must upgrade our equipment. Upgrade costs will be largely offset the first year by reduced printing costs. Also, this technology will increase efficiency and reduce labor costs, resulting in substantial payback on investment.

Increasing Staff Salaries. Although we seek talented students who expect little money and much experience, salaries for all positions must increase by an average of 25 percent. Otherwise, any of our staff could earn as much money elsewhere by working only a little more than half the time. In fact, many students could exceed the minimum wage by working for local newspapers. To illustrate: The *Standard Beacon* pays $60 to $90 per news article and $30 per photo; the *Torch* pays nothing for articles and $6 per photo.

A striking example of low salaries is the $4.75 per hour we pay our desktop publishing staff. Our present desktop publishing cost of $3,038 could be as much as $7,000 or even higher if we had this service done by an outside firm, as many colleges do. Without this nominal salary increase, we cannot possibly attract qualified personnel.

Costs

Our proposed budget is itemized in Table 1, but the main point is clear: If the *Torch* is to remain viable, increased funding is essential for meeting our projected costs.

Table 1 Projected Costs and Requested Funding for Next Year's *Torch* Budget

PROJECTED COSTS	
Hardware/Software Upgrades	
Apple iMac w/ 4 GB RAM, 500 GB HD (3.06GHz processor)	$1,162.00
HP Pavilion 2709m 27" (second monitor)	355.00
Seagate 500 GB external hard drive (for backups)	128.99
Olympus Stylus 9000 digital camera	299.98
HP Scanjet 5000 sheet-feed scanner	799.00
Microsoft Office 2010 Professional Upgrade	499.00
Adobe Creative Suite 5 Master Collection	2,450.00
Subtotal	**$5,693.97**

Provides detailed breakdown of costs—the central issue in the situation

FIGURE 4 *(Continued)*

Wages and Salaries	
Desktop-publishing staff (35 hr/wk at $6.00/hr x 28 wk)	$5,880.00
Editor-in-Chief	3,150.00
News Editor	1,890.00
Features Editor	1,890.00
Advertising Manager	2,350.00
Advertising Designer	1,575.00
Webmaster	2,520.00
Layout Editor	1,890.00
Art Director	1,260.00
Photo Editor	1,890.00
Business Manager	1,890.00
Distributor	560.00
Subtotal	**$26,745.00**

Miscellaneous Costs	
Graphics by SMU art students (3/wk @ $10 each)	$ 840.00
Mailing	1,100.00
Telephone	1,000.00
Campus print shop services	400.00
Copier fees	100.00
Subtotal	**$3,440.00**

Fixed Printing Costs (5,000 copies/wk x 28/wk)	**$24,799.60**
TOTAL YEARLY COSTS	**$60,678.57**
Expected Advertising Revenue ($600/wk x 28 wks)	**($16,800.00)**
Total Costs Minus Advertising Revenue	**$45,109.39**
TOTAL FUNDING REQUEST	**$43,878.57**

FIGURE 4 *(Continued)*

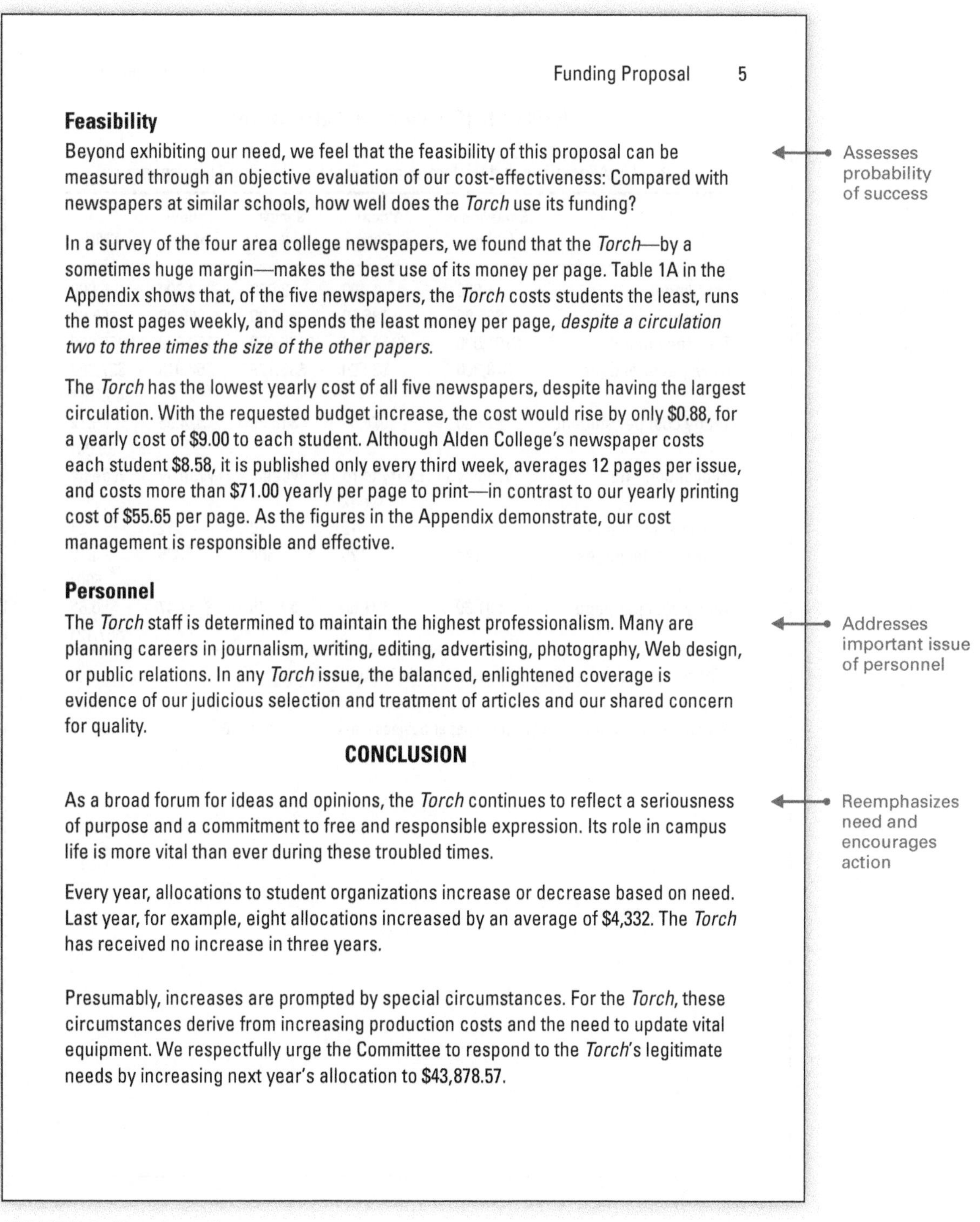

Funding Proposal 5

Feasibility

Beyond exhibiting our need, we feel that the feasibility of this proposal can be measured through an objective evaluation of our cost-effectiveness: Compared with newspapers at similar schools, how well does the *Torch* use its funding?

In a survey of the four area college newspapers, we found that the *Torch*—by a sometimes huge margin—makes the best use of its money per page. Table 1A in the Appendix shows that, of the five newspapers, the *Torch* costs students the least, runs the most pages weekly, and spends the least money per page, *despite a circulation two to three times the size of the other papers.*

The *Torch* has the lowest yearly cost of all five newspapers, despite having the largest circulation. With the requested budget increase, the cost would rise by only $0.88, for a yearly cost of $9.00 to each student. Although Alden College's newspaper costs each student $8.58, it is published only every third week, averages 12 pages per issue, and costs more than $71.00 yearly per page to print—in contrast to our yearly printing cost of $55.65 per page. As the figures in the Appendix demonstrate, our cost management is responsible and effective.

Personnel

The *Torch* staff is determined to maintain the highest professionalism. Many are planning careers in journalism, writing, editing, advertising, photography, Web design, or public relations. In any *Torch* issue, the balanced, enlightened coverage is evidence of our judicious selection and treatment of articles and our shared concern for quality.

CONCLUSION

As a broad forum for ideas and opinions, the *Torch* continues to reflect a seriousness of purpose and a commitment to free and responsible expression. Its role in campus life is more vital than ever during these troubled times.

Every year, allocations to student organizations increase or decrease based on need. Last year, for example, eight allocations increased by an average of $4,332. The *Torch* has received no increase in three years.

Presumably, increases are prompted by special circumstances. For the *Torch*, these circumstances derive from increasing production costs and the need to update vital equipment. We respectfully urge the Committee to respond to the *Torch*'s legitimate needs by increasing next year's allocation to $43,878.57.

FIGURE 4 *(Continued)*

APPENDIX (Comparative Performance)

Table 1A Allocations and Performance of Five Local College Newspapers

Appendix provides detailed breakdown of cost comparisons

	Stonehorse College	Alden College	Simms University	Fallow State	SMU
Enrollment	1,600	1,400	3,000	3,000	5,000
Fee paid (per year)	$65.00	$85.00	$35.00	$50.00	$65.00
Total fee budget	$104,000	$119,000	$105,000	$150,000	$325,000
Newspaper budget	$18,300	$8,580	$36,179	$52,910	$37,392 $45,109[a]
Yearly cost per student	$12.50	$8.58	$16.86	$24.66	$8.12 $9.00[a]
Publication rate	Weekly	Every third week	Weekly	Weekly	Weekly
Average no. of pages	8	12	18	12	24
Average total pages	224	120	504	336	672 560[a]
Yearly cost per page	$81.60	$71.50	$71.78	$157.47	$55.65 $67.12[a]

[a]These figures are next year's costs for the SMU *Torch*.

Source: Figures were quoted by newspaper business managers in April 20XX.

FIGURE 4 *(Continued)*

CHECKLIST: Proposals

Content

- ☐ Are all required proposal elements included?
- ☐ Does the title or subject line provide a clear forecast?
- ☐ Is the background section appropriate for this audience's needs?
- ☐ Is the problem clearly identified?
- ☐ Is the objective clearly identified?
- ☐ Does the proposal demonstrate a clear understanding of the client's problems and expectations?
- ☐ Is the proposed solution, service, or product stated clearly?
- ☐ Are the claims honest and supportable?
- ☐ Does the proposal maintain a clear focus on benefits?
- ☐ Does it address anticipated objections?
- ☐ Are the proposed solutions feasible and realistic?
- ☐ Are all foreseeable limitations and contingencies identified?
- ☐ Is every *relevant* detail spelled out?
- ☐ Is the cost and budget section accurate and easy to understand?
- ☐ Are visuals used effectively?
- ☐ Is each source and contribution properly cited?
- ☐ Is the proposal ethically acceptable?

Arrangement

- ☐ Does the introduction spell out the problem and preview the plan?
- ☐ Does the body section explain *how, where, when,* and *how much*?
- ☐ Does the conclusion encourage acceptance of the proposal?
- ☐ Is the informal proposal cast as a memo or letter, as appropriate?
- ☐ Does the formal proposal have adequate front matter and end matter supplements to serve the needs of different readers?

Style and Page Design

- ☐ Is the level of technicality appropriate for primary readers?
- ☐ Does the tone encourage acceptance of the proposal?
- ☐ Is the writing clear, concise, and fluent?
- ☐ Is the language precise?
- ☐ Is the proposal grammatical?
- ☐ Is the page design inviting and accessible?

TC WEB **Chapter quiz, Exercises, Web links, and Flashcards**
(Go to *Student Resources> Chapter 24*)

PEARSON mtcl **Proposals Activities, Case studies, Model documents, and Quiz**
(Go to *Technical Communication Documents*)

Projects

GENERAL

1. After identifying your primary and secondary audience, write a short planning proposal for improving an unsatisfactory situation in the classroom, on the job, or in your dorm or apartment (e.g., poor lighting, drab atmosphere, health hazards, poor seating arrangements). Choose a problem or situation whose solution or resolution is more a matter of common sense and lucid observation than of intensive research. Be sure to (a) identify the problem clearly, give a brief background, and stimulate interest; (b) clearly state the methods proposed to solve the problem; and (c) conclude with a statement designed to gain audience support.
2. Write a research proposal to your instructor (or an interested third party) requesting approval for your final term project (a formal analytical report or formal proposal). Verify that adequate primary and secondary sources are available. Convince your audience of the soundness and usefulness of the project.
3. As an alternate term project to the formal analytical report, develop a long proposal for solving a problem, improving a situation, or satisfying a need in your school, community, or job. Choose a subject sufficiently complex to justify a formal proposal, a topic requiring research (mostly primary). Identify an audience (other than your instructor) who will use your proposal for a specific purpose. Complete an audience and use profile.

TEAM

Working in groups of four, develop an unsolicited planning proposal for solving a problem, improving a situation, or satisfying a need in your school, community, or workplace. Begin by brainstorming as a group to come up with a list of possible issues or problems to address in your proposal. Narrow your list, and work as a group to focus on a specific issue or idea. Your proposal should address a clearly identified audience of decision makers and stakeholders in the given issue. Complete an audience and use profile.

DIGITAL

As noted earlier, solicited proposals are usually written in response to a formal "request for proposal" (RFP). Most RFPs are available on the Web. For instance, the National Science Foundation's site at <www.nsf.gov/funding/> provides links for all sorts of research funding opportunities. There is a link for undergraduate students, for graduate students, for K–12 educators, and for many program areas such as engineering, geosciences, and so on. Go to this site and click on a link that interests you and locate the RFP. Write a memo to your instructor explaining why you are interested in this research and what focus your proposal would take. For instance, you might have a good idea for a proposal in response to the Research Experiences for Undergraduates (REU) RFP. What topic would you choose and how would you make your best case?

GLOBAL

Compare the sorts of proposals regularly done in the United States with those created in other countries. For example, is the format the same? Are there more proposals for certain purposes in the United States than in another country? You can learn about this topic by interviewing an expert in international business (someone you meet on the job, during an internship, or through your adviser). You can also search the Web for information on international technical communication. Describe your findings in a short memo that you will share with your classmates.

For more support in mastering the objectives of this chapter, go to **www.mytechcommlab.com**

Thinking Critically about the Research Process

Thinking Critically about the Research Process

Robert Ginn/PhotoEdit

"As a freelance researcher, I search online databases and Web sites for any type of specialized information needed by my clients. For example, yesterday I did a search for a corporate attorney who needed the latest information on some specific product-liability issues, plus any laws or court decisions involving specific products. For the legal research I accessed LEXIS, the legal database that offers full-text copies of articles and cases. For the liability issue I began with Dow-Jones News/Retrieval and then double-checked by going into the Dialog database."

—Mark Casamonte,
Freelance Researcher

LEARNING OBJECTIVES FOR THIS CHAPTER

- Think critically about the research process
- Differentiate between procedural stages and inquiry stages of research
- Differentiate between primary and secondary research
- Explore online secondary sources using various search technologies
- Explore traditional secondary sources (books, periodicals, reference works)
- Explore primary sources (inquiries, interviews, surveys)
- Understand copyright in relation to research practices

Major decisions in the workplace are based on careful research, with the findings recorded in a written report. Some parts of the research process follow a recognizable sequence (Figure 1A). But research is not merely a numbered set of procedures. The procedural stages depend on the many decisions that accompany any legitimate inquiry (Figure 1B).[1] These decisions require you to *think critically* about each step of the process and about the information you gather for your research.

Chapter overview
(Go to *Student Resources>Chapter 7*)

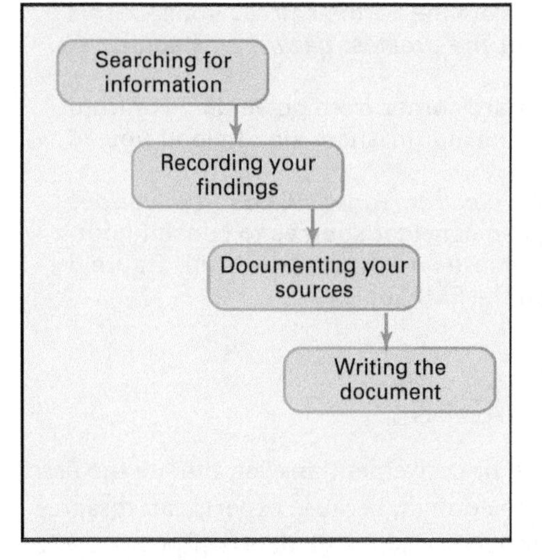

FIGURE 1A **The Procedural Stages of the Research Process**

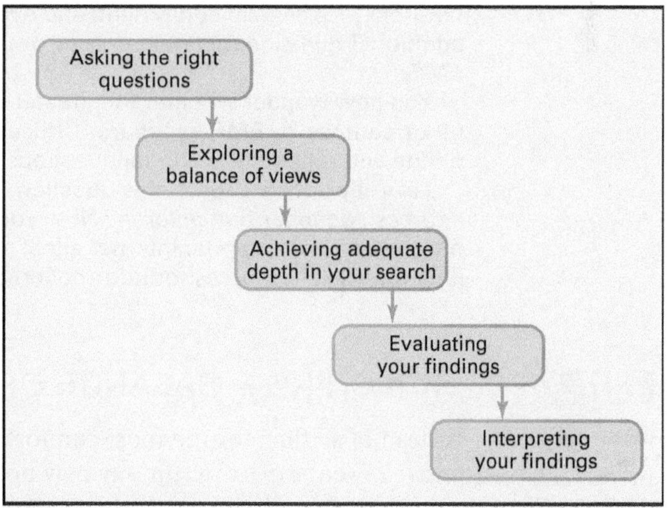

FIGURE 1B **Stages of Critical Thinking in the Research Process**

[1] Our thanks to University of Massachusetts Dartmouth librarian Shaleen Barnes for inspiring this chapter.

ASKING THE RIGHT QUESTIONS

The answers you uncover will only be as good as the questions you ask. Suppose, for instance, you face the following scenario:

CASE Defining and Refining a Research Question

You are the public health manager for a small, New England town in which high-tension power lines run within one hundred feet of the elementary school. Parents are concerned about danger from electromagnetic radiation (EMR) emitted by these power lines in energy waves known as electromagnetic fields (EMFs). Town officials ask you to research the issue and prepare a report to be distributed at the next town meeting in six weeks.

First, you need to identify your exact question or questions. Initially, the major question might be: *Do the power lines pose any real danger to our children?* After phone calls around town and discussions at the coffee shop, you discover that townspeople actually have three main questions about electromagnetic fields: *What are they? Do they endanger our children? If so, then what can be done?*

To answer these questions, you need to consider a range of subordinate questions, like those in the Figure 2 tree chart. Any *one* of those questions could serve as subject of a worthwhile research report on such a complex topic. As research progresses, this chart will grow. For instance, after some preliminary reading, you learn that electromagnetic fields radiate not only from power lines but from *all* electrical equipment, and even from the Earth itself. So you face this additional question: *Do power lines present the greatest hazard as a source of EMFs?*

You now wonder whether the greater hazard comes from power lines or from other sources of EMF exposure. Critical thinking, in short, has helped you to define and refine the essential questions.

Let's say you've chosen this question: *Do electromagnetic fields from various sources endanger our children?* Now you can consider sources to consult (journals, interviews, reports, Internet sites, database searches, and so on). Figure 3 illustrates likely sources for information on the EMF topic.

Research assignment tutorial
(Go to *The Research Process>Tutorials*)

EXPLORING A BALANCE OF VIEWS

Instead of settling for the most comforting or convenient answer, pursue the *best* answer. Even "expert" testimony may not be enough, because experts can disagree or be mistaken. To answer fairly and accurately, consider a balance of perspectives from up-to-date and reputable sources:

Try to consider all the angles

- What do informed sources have to say about this topic?
- On which points do sources agree?
- On which points do sources disagree?

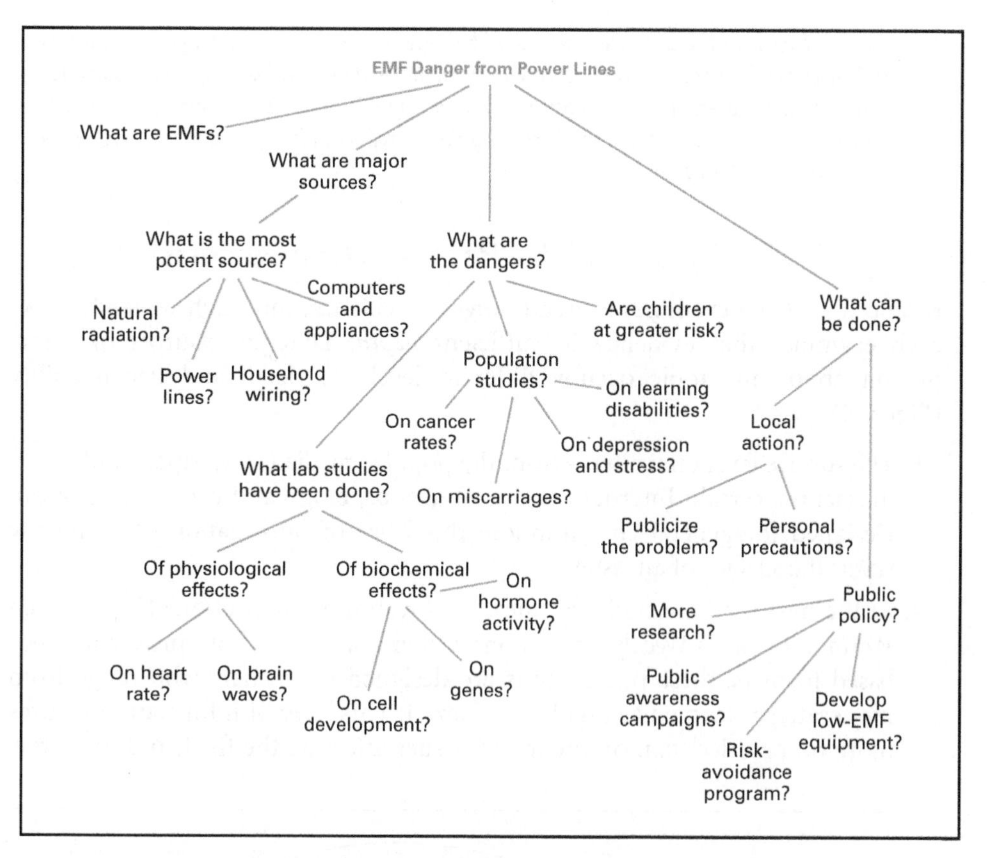

FIGURE 2 **How the Right Questions Help Define a Research Problem** You cannot begin to solve a problem until you have defined it clearly.

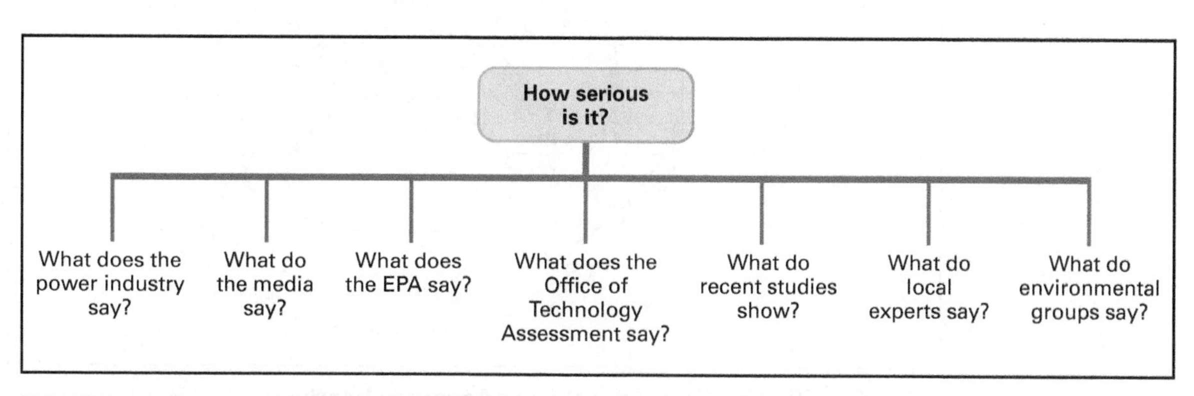

FIGURE 3 **A Range of Essential Viewpoints** No single source is likely to offer "the final word." Ethical researchers rely on evidence that represents a fair balance of views.

NOTE *Recognize the difference between "balance" (sampling a full range of opinions) and "accuracy" (getting at the facts). Government or power industry spokespersons, for example, might present a more positive view (or "spin") of the EMF issue than the facts warrant. Not every source is equal, nor should we report points of view as though they were equal (Trafford 137).*

ACHIEVING ADEQUATE DEPTH IN YOUR SEARCH[2]

Balanced research examines a broad *range* of evidence; thorough research, however, examines that evidence in sufficient *depth*. Different sources of information about any topic occupy different levels of detail and dependability (Figure 4).

The depth of a source often determines its quality

1. The surface level offers items from the popular media (newspapers, radio, TV, magazines, certain Internet discussion groups, blogs, and certain Web sites). Designed for general consumption, this layer of information often merely skims the surface of an issue.
2. At the next level are trade, business, and technical publications (*Frozen Food World*, *Publisher's Weekly*, and so on). Often available in both print and Web-based formats, these publications are designed for readers who range from moderately informed to highly specialized. This layer of information focuses more on practice than on theory, on issues affecting the field, and on public

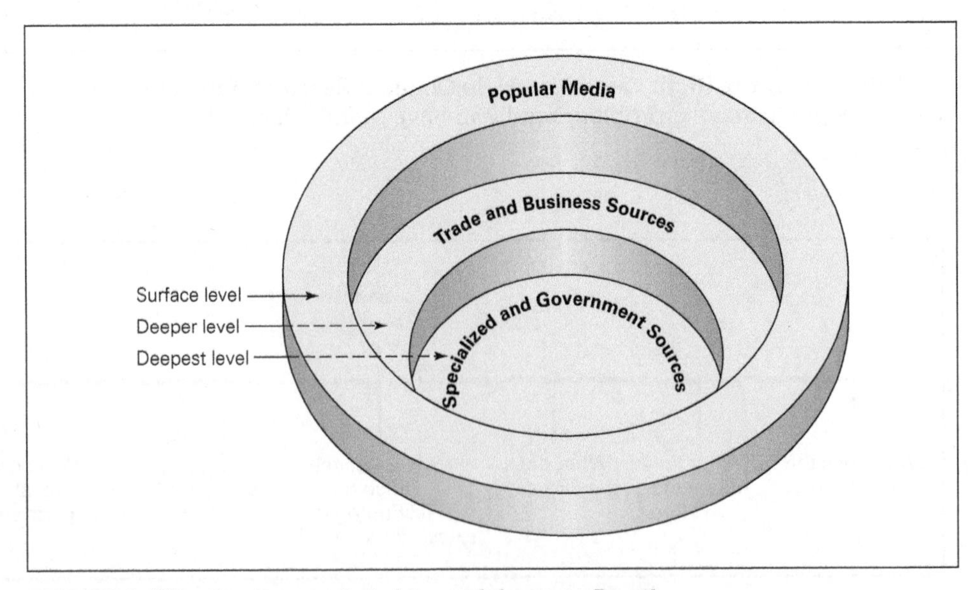

FIGURE 4 **Effective Research Achieves Adequate Depth**

[2] Our thanks to UMass Dartmouth librarian Ross LaBaugh for inspiring this section.

relations. While the information is usually accurate, the general viewpoints tend to reflect a field's particular biases.

3. At a deeper level is the specialized literature (journals from professional associations—academic, medical, legal, engineering). Designed for practicing professionals, this layer of information focuses on theory as well as on practice, on descriptions of the latest studies (written by the researchers themselves and scrutinized by peers for accuracy and objectivity), on debates among scholars and researchers, and on reviews, critiques, and refutations of prior studies and publications.

Also at this deepest level are government sources and corporate documents available through the Freedom of Information Act. Designed for anyone willing to investigate its complex resources, this information layer offers hard facts and detailed discussion, and (in many instances) *relatively* impartial views.

> **NOTE** *Web pages, of course, offer links to increasingly specific levels of detail. But the actual "depth" and quality of a Web site's information depend on the sponsorship and reliability of that site.*

How deep is deep enough? This depends on your purpose, your audience, and your topic. But the real story most likely resides at deeper levels. Research on the EMF issue, for example, would need to look beneath media headlines and biased special interests (say, electrical industry or environmental groups), focusing instead on studies by a wide range of experts.

EVALUATING YOUR FINDINGS

Not all findings have equal value. Some information might be distorted, incomplete, or misleading. Information might be tainted by *source bias*, in which a source understates or overstates certain facts, depending on whose interests that source represents (say, power company, government agency, parent group, or a reporter seeking headlines). To evaluate a particular finding, ask these questions:

TC WEB **Research project** (Go to *Student Resources>Chapter 7>Projects and Case Studies>Privacy at Work? Be Serious*)

Questions for evaluating a particular finding

- Is this information accurate, reliable, and relatively unbiased?
- Do the facts verify the claim?
- How much of the information is useful?
- Is this the whole or the real story?
- Do I need more information?

Instead of merely emphasizing findings that support their own biases or assumptions, ethical researchers seek out and report the most *accurate* answer.

INTERPRETING YOUR FINDINGS

Once you have decided which of your findings seem legitimate, you need to decide what they all mean by asking these questions:

Questions for interpreting your findings

- What are my conclusions and do they address my original research question?
- Do any findings conflict?
- Are other interpretations possible?
- Should I reconsider the evidence?
- What, if anything, should be done?

Research project
(Go to *Student Resources>Chapter 7> Projects and Case Studies>What Is Fair Maternity Leave?*)

NOTE *Never force a simplistic conclusion on a complex issue. Sometimes the best you can offer is an indefinite conclusion: "Although controversy continues over the extent of EMF hazards, we all can take simple precautions to reduce our exposure." A wrong conclusion is far worse than no definite conclusion at all.*

PRIMARY VERSUS SECONDARY SOURCES

How primary and secondary research differ

Primary research means getting information directly from the source by conducting interviews and surveys and by observing people, events, or processes in action. *Secondary research* is information obtained second hand by reading what other researchers have compiled in books and articles in print or online. Most information found on the Internet would be considered a secondary source. Some Web-based information is more accurate than others; for instance, a Web page created by a high school student might be interesting but not overly reliable, whereas a Web site that is the equivalent of a traditional secondary source (encyclopedia, research index, newspaper, journal) would be more reliable for your research.

Why you should combine primary and secondary research

Whenever possible, combine primary and secondary research. Typically, you would start by using secondary sources, because they are readily available and can help you get a full background understanding of your topic. However, don't neglect to add your own findings to existing ones by doing primary research.

Working with primary sources can help you expand upon what other people have already learned and add considerable credibility to your work. For instance, assume that your boss asks you to write a report about how well your company's new product is being received in the marketplace: You might consult sales reports and published print and online reviews of the product (secondary research), but you might also survey people who use the product and interview some of them individually (primary research).

EXPLORING SECONDARY SOURCES

(Go to *The Research Process> MySearchLab*)

Secondary sources include some Web sites; online news outlets and magazines; blogs and wikis; books in the library; journal, magazine, and newspaper articles; government publications; and other public records. Research assignments begin more effectively when you first uncover and sort through what is already known about your topic before adding to that knowledge yourself.

Web-based Secondary Sources

To find various sites on the Web, use two basic tools: *subject directories* and *search engines*.

Subject directories are maintained by editors

Internet searching help

- **Subject Directories.** Subject directories are indexes compiled by editors who sift through Web sites and sort the most useful links. Popular general subject directories include *Yahoo! Directory* <dir.yahoo.com>, *Google Directory* <www.google.com/dirhp>, and *About.com* <www.about.com>. Specialized directories focus on a single topic such as software, health, or employment. See *Beaucoup!*, a "directory of directories," at <www.beaucoup.com> for listings of specialized directories organized by category.
- **Search Engines.** Search engines, such as Yahoo <www.yahoo.com> and Google <www.google.com>, scan for Web sites containing key words. Even though search engines yield a lot more information than subject directories, much of it can be irrelevant. Some search engines, however, are more selective than others, and some focus on specialized topics.

Most search engines are maintained by computers, not people

Locating Secondary Sources Using Google

Most people today, from students to professionals, begin their research of secondary sources by doing a Google search. Google, the most popular of the search engines, searches Web pages, government documents, online news sites, and other sources. Google also has a large collection of books and journal articles that it makes available through agreements with publishers or by digitizing works that either are in the public domain or are out of copyright.

Refine your Google searches

It's fine to start with a Google search just to brainstorm ideas and develop approaches to get started. But you quickly will need to narrow down your findings and do some deeper digging. For instance, your search on "electromagnetic radiation" will yield thousands or even millions of results. Figure 5 outlines the process and results of a Google search. You should stick with sites from reliable sources such as universities or government research labs.

Locating Secondary Sources Using Wikipedia

Use Wikipedia as a starting point

The first two Web links in many Google searches are to Wikipedia, the popular online encyclopedia. Wikipedia's content is provided and edited by countless

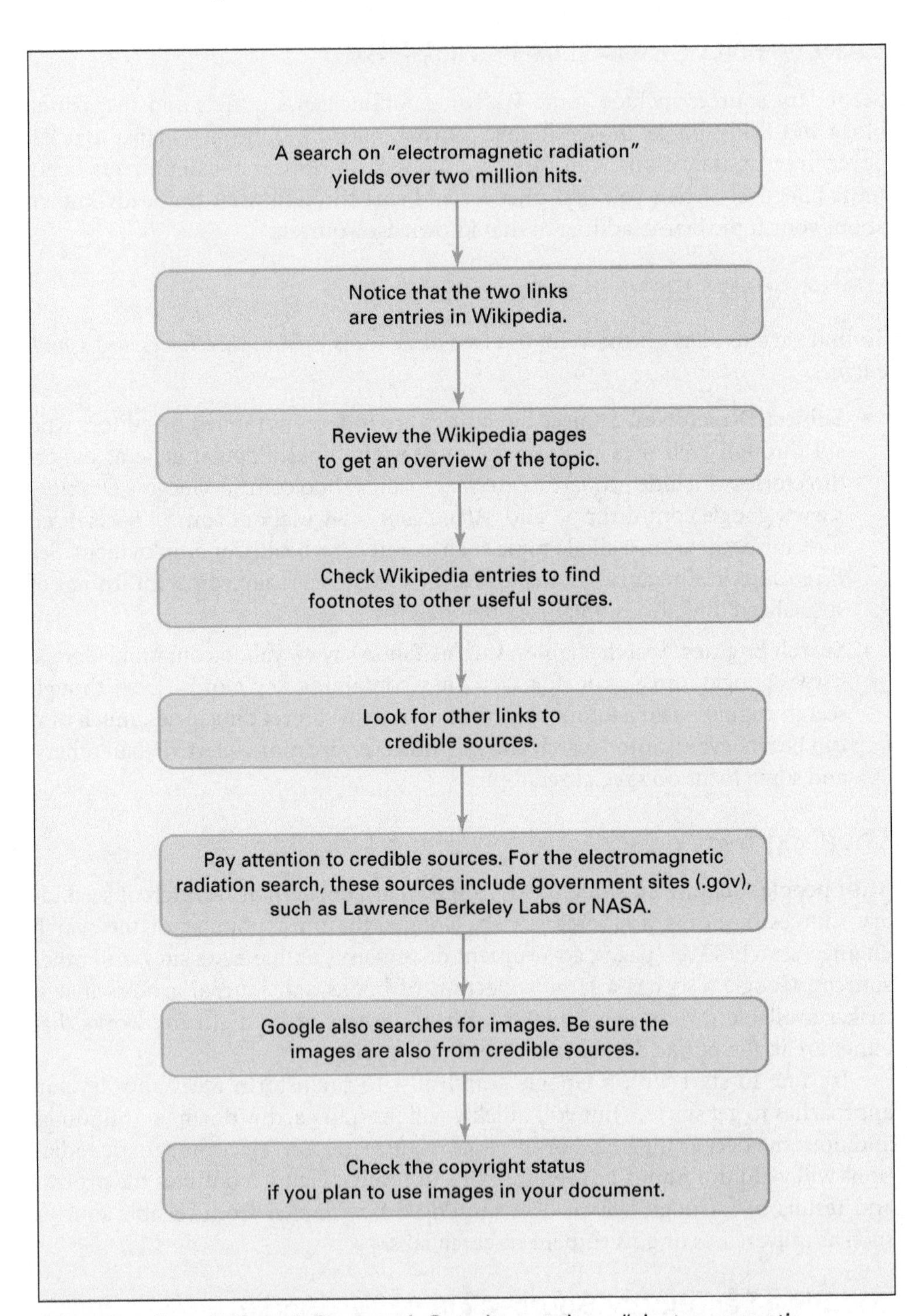

FIGURE 5 **Google Search Process** A Google search on "electromagnetic radiation" (or any other topic) will yield thousands if not more results. Links to government and science Web sites typically provide more trustworthy information than links to commercial sites.

people worldwide. Although these pages can provide a good starting point, the content may not be completely accurate. Use a Wikipedia entry to get an overview of the topic, and to help you locate other sources.

The Wikipedia page on electromagnetic radiation contains footnotes to other sources. You can track down these sources at the library or over the Internet. Think of Wikipedia as a place to get your research started, but not as your final destination.

Other Web-based Secondary Sources

Google and Wikipedia can help you get started with your research. But the more intensively you investigate the sources you find on the Internet, the more you will need to pay attention to what you are finding. Following are the principal categories of information sources on the Internet.

General Commercial, Organizational, and Academic Web Sites. Search engines pull up a wide variety of hits, most of which will be commercial (.com), organizational (.org), and academic (.edu) Web sites. If a commercial site looks relevant to your search, by all means use it, as long as you think critically about the information presented. Does the company's effort to sell you something affect the content? Be careful also of organizational Web sites, which are likely to be well-researched, but may have a particular social or political agenda. Academic Web sites tend to be credible. However, some academics may also have biases, so never stop thinking critically about what you find on the Web.

Government Web Sites. Search engines will also pull up government Web sites, but your best access route is through the United States government's Web portal at <www.usa.gov>. Most government organizations (local, state, and federal) offer online access to research and reports (Figure 6). Examples include the Food and Drug Administration's site at <www.fda.gov>, for information on food recalls, clinical drug trials, and countless related items; and the Federal Bureau of Investigation's site at <www.fbi.gov>, for information about fugitives, crime statistics, and much more. State and local sites provide information on auto licenses, state tax laws, and local property issues. From some of these sites you can link to specific government-sponsored research projects.

> **NOTE** *Be sure to check the dates of reports or data you locate on a government Web site, and find out how often the site is updated.*

Online News Outlets and Magazines. Most major news organizations offer online versions of their broadcasts and print publications. Examples include the *New York Times,* the *Wall Street Journal,* CNN, and National Public Radio. Magazines such as *Time, Newsweek,* and *Forbes* also offer Web versions. Some news is available online only, as in the online magazines *Slate* and *Salon.*

NOTE *Make sure you understand how the publication obtains and reviews information. Is it a major news site, such as CNN, or is it a smaller site run by a special-interest group? Each can be useful, but you must evaluate the source. Also keep in mind that many online magazines have a political bias.*

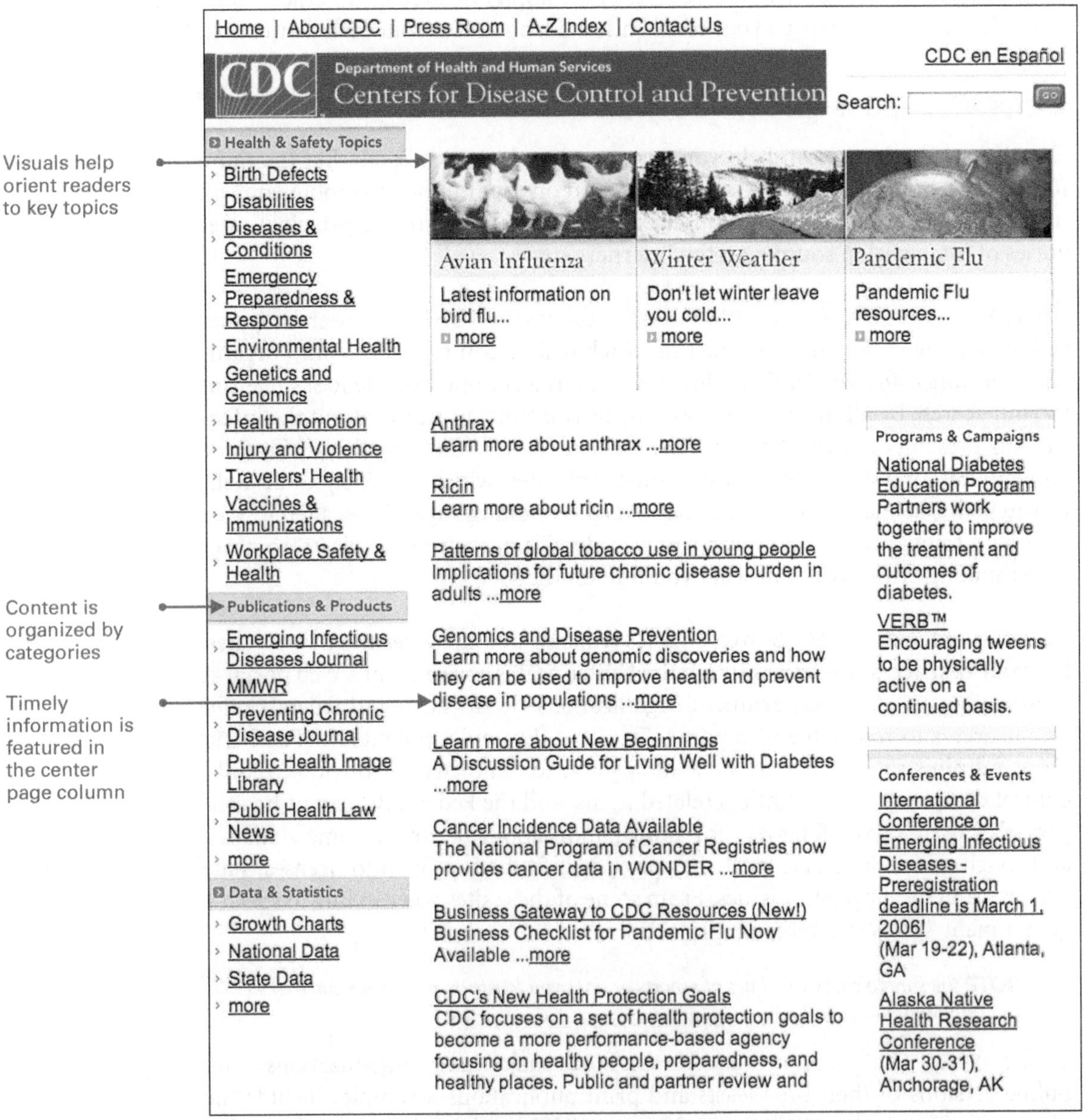

Home | About CDC | Press Room | A-Z Index | Contact Us

CDC en Español

CDC Department of Health and Human Services
Centers for Disease Control and Prevention

Search: GO

Health & Safety Topics
- Birth Defects
- Disabilities
- Diseases & Conditions
- Emergency Preparedness & Response
- Environmental Health
- Genetics and Genomics
- Health Promotion
- Injury and Violence
- Travelers' Health
- Vaccines & Immunizations
- Workplace Safety & Health

Publications & Products
- Emerging Infectious Diseases Journal
- MMWR
- Preventing Chronic Disease Journal
- Public Health Image Library
- Public Health Law News
- more

Data & Statistics
- Growth Charts
- National Data
- State Data
- more

Avian Influenza
Latest information on bird flu...
more

Winter Weather
Don't let winter leave you cold...
more

Pandemic Flu
Pandemic Flu resources...
more

Anthrax
Learn more about anthrax ...more

Ricin
Learn more about ricin ...more

Patterns of global tobacco use in young people
Implications for future chronic disease burden in adults ...more

Genomics and Disease Prevention
Learn more about genomic discoveries and how they can be used to improve health and prevent disease in populations ...more

Learn more about New Beginnings
A Discussion Guide for Living Well with Diabetes ...more

Cancer Incidence Data Available
The National Program of Cancer Registries now provides cancer data in WONDER ...more

Business Gateway to CDC Resources (New!)
Business Checklist for Pandemic Flu Now Available ...more

CDC's New Health Protection Goals
CDC focuses on a set of health protection goals to become a more performance-based agency focusing on healthy people, preparedness, and healthy places. Public and partner review and

Programs & Campaigns

National Diabetes Education Program
Partners work together to improve the treatment and outcomes of diabetes.

VERB™
Encouraging tweens to be physically active on a continued basis.

Conferences & Events

International Conference on Emerging Infectious Diseases - Preregistration deadline is March 1, 2006!
(Mar 19-22), Atlanta, GA

Alaska Native Health Research Conference
(Mar 30-31), Anchorage, AK

Visuals help orient readers to key topics

Content is organized by categories

Timely information is featured in the center page column

FIGURE 6 **Centers for Disease Control Home Page** The CDC home page provides Health & Safety Topics, disease information, and much more.
Source: Centers for Disease Control and Prevention home page, www.cdc.gov.

Blogs. *Blogs* (short for *Web logs*) are Web sites on which the blog's author posts ideas, and other readers reply. The postings and attached discussions are displayed in reverse chronological order. Links that the owner has selected also supply ways to connect to other blogs on similar topics. Blogs are great for finding current information about a specific topic from individuals, companies, and nonprofit organizations. Evaluate the information on individual blogs carefully and decide which ones are most relevant and reliable.

Colleges and universities also host blogs as a way to support classroom teaching, provide space for student discussion, allow faculty to collaborate on research projects, and more. One excellent example is the University of Minnesota's UThink Project at <blog.lib.umn.edu>.

Blogs nearly always represent the particular views of the blog author (whether an individual, company, organization, or academic institution) and of those who reply to the postings. Check any information you find on a blog against a professionally edited or peer-reviewed source.

Wikis. *Wikis* are community encyclopedias that allow anyone to add to or edit the content of a listing. The most popular wiki is *Wikipedia* <www.wikipedia.org>. The theory of a wiki is that if the information from one posting is wrong, someone else will correct it, and over time the site will reach a high level of accuracy and reliability.

Many wikis have no oversight. Aside from a few people who determine whether to delete articles based on requests from readers, the content on a wiki is not checked by editors for accuracy. Always check the information against other peer-reviewed or traditional sources. Remember that most of what is posted on a wiki has not been evaluated objectively.

Internet Forums and Electronic Mailing Lists. For almost any topic imaginable, you will find a Web forum, or discussion group. (See, for example, <discussions.apple.com/index.jspa>, for people who use Apple products.) Locate relevant forums by searching one of the major Internet forum providers. For instance, in researching a health-related issue such as stress among college students, you might visit *Google Groups* <groups.google.com> or *Yahoo! Groups* <groups.yahoo.com> and join a related group.

Most Internet forums offer two options: You may either subscribe to and visit the forum via the Web or subscribe to and receive messages directly into your email in-box. (Electronic mailing lists, or e-lists, are essentially the same as Internet forums.) Messages may be sent to the entire group or to individual participants.

Material from these sources may be insightful but biased. Visit a variety of forums and/or subscribe to multiple e-lists to get a broad perspective on the issue. Some information posted on forums or sent to e-list subscribers is not moderated (approved by a reviewer prior to being posted). Unmoderated material is usually less reliable.

E-Libraries. Entirely searchable via the Internet, e-libraries are excellent research tools. Aside from the online sites sponsored by public libraries, the most notable and reliable e-library is the Internet Public Library at <www.ipl.org>. E-libraries include links to online books, magazines, newspapers, periodical databases, and other resources including "live" librarians.

Although e-libraries can be efficient stand-ins for traditional, physical libraries, they can never replace such libraries. Resources available in electronic form will not include current books under copyright or a wide range of magazine and news articles and other publications. Supplement what you discover at an e-library with hard-copy materials from a traditional library.

Periodical Databases. Virtually all libraries have their own Web site where a library cardholder or student can access periodical databases. These are electronic collections of articles from newspapers, magazines, journals, and other publications. You can search by title, author, keyword, and so on.

Some of the most popular general periodical databases include *InfoTrac*, *NewsBank*, *ProQuest*, and *EBSCOHost*. Your library may also subscribe to specialized databases in a variety of subject areas.

Before initiating a periodical database search, meet with your reference librarian for a tour of the various databases and instructions for searching effectively. Also be aware that some databases may not be accessible from school or home—you may need to visit your library in person.

GUIDELINES for Researching on the Internet

- **Expect limited results from any one search engine or subject directory.** No single search engine can index more than a fraction of the material available on the Web. No subject directory will list the same Web sites as another.
- **When using a search engine, select keywords or search phrases that are varied and technical rather than general.** Some search terms generate more useful hits than others. In addition to "electromagnetic radiation," for example, try "electromagnetic fields," "power lines and health," or "electrical fields." Specialized terms (say, "vertigo" versus "dizziness") offer the best access to reliable sites. However, if you are not able to locate much by using a specialized term, widen your search somewhat.
- **When using Wikipedia or other online encyclopedias, check out the footnotes and other citations.** These references can direct you to other sources, such as government documents, books in the library, or published journal articles.

- **Consider the domain type (where the site originates).** Standard domain types in the United States include .com (commercial organization), .edu (educational institution), .gov or .mil (government or military organization), .net (general usage), and .org (nonprofit organization).
- **Identify the site's purpose and sponsor.** Is the intent merely to relay information, to sell something, or to promote an ideology or agenda? The domain type might alert you to bias or a hidden agenda. A .com site might provide accurate information but also some type of sales pitch. An .org site might reflect a political or ideological bias. Looking for a site's sponsor can also help you evaluate its postings. For example, a Web site about the dangers of bioengineered foods that is sponsored by an advocacy organization may be biased.
- **Look beyond the style of a site.** Sometimes the most reliable material resides in less attractive, text-only sites. The fact that a Web site may look professional doesn't always mean that its content is reliable.
- **Assess the currency of the site's materials.** When was the material created, posted, and updated? Many sites have not been updated in months or years.
- **Assess the author's credentials and assertions.** Check the author's reputation, expertise, and institutional affiliation (university, company, environmental group). Do not confuse the *author* (the person who wrote the material) with the *Webmaster* (the person who created and maintains the site). Follow links to other sites that mention the author. Where, on the spectrum of expert opinion and accepted theory, does this author fall? Is each assertion supported by solid evidence? Verify any extreme claim through other sources, such as a professor or expert in the field. Consider whether your own biases might predispose you to accept certain ideas.
- **Use bookmarks and hotlists for quick access to favorite Web sites.** It is always frustrating when you can't find a helpful Web site that you accessed earlier but didn't bookmark.
- **Save or print what you need before it changes or disappears.** Web sites often change their content or "go dead." Always record the URL and your access date.
- **Download only what you need; use it ethically; obtain permission; and credit your sources.** Unless they are crucial to your research, omit graphics, sound, and video files. Do not use material created by others in a way that harms the material's creator. For any type of commercial use of material from the Web, obtain written permission from the material's owner and credit the source exactly as directed by its owner.

Traditional Secondary Sources

As noted earlier, traditional secondary research tools are still of great value. Most hard-copy secondary sources are carefully reviewed and edited before they are published. Although the digitizing of hard-copy materials continues, many of these printed sources are not yet available on the Web, particularly the full texts of books.

Locate hard-copy secondary sources using your library's OPAC

Locate hard-copy sources by using your library's online public access catalog (OPAC). This catalog can be accessed through the Internet or at terminals in the library. You can search a library's holdings by subject, author, title, or keyword. Visit the library's Web site, or ask a librarian for help. To search catalogs from libraries worldwide, go to the *Library of Congress Gateway* at <www.loc.gov/z3950> or *LibrarySpot* at <www.libraryspot.com>.

Following are the principal categories of hard-copy sources found at libraries, as well as one type of source material (gray literature) that you will need to track down on your own.

Books and Periodicals. The larger or more specialized the library you visit, the more likely you are to find books by specialist publishers and periodicals that delve into more specific subject areas. When consulting books and periodicals, always check the copyright date and supplement the source with additional information from more recent sources, if necessary.

Reference Works. Reference works are general information sources that provide background and can lead to more specific information.

- **Bibliographies.** Bibliographies are lists of books and/or articles categorized by subject. To locate bibliographies in your field, begin by consulting the *Bibliographic Index Plus*, a list (by subject) of major bibliographies, which indexes over 500,000 bibliographies worldwide. You can also consult such general bibliographies as *Books in Print* or the *Readers' Guide to Periodical Literature*. Or, examine subject area bibliographies, such as *Bibliography of World War II History*, or highly focused bibliographies, such as *Health Hazards of Video Display Terminals: An Annotated Bibliography*.
- **Indexes.** Book and article bibliographies may also be referred to as "indexes." Yet there are other types of indexes that collect information not likely found in standard bibliographies. Examples include the *Index to Scientific and Technical Proceedings*, which indexes conference proceedings in the sciences and engineering. While limited versions of some of these indexes may be available for free on the Internet, most are only available via a library subscription. Other indexes that may be useful for your research include the following:

- *Newspaper indexes.* Most major newspapers, such as the *New York Times*, have an index covering almost the entire span of the paper's publication.
- *Periodical indexes.* These indexes list articles from magazines and journals. The most commonly known periodical index is the *Readers' Guide to Periodical Literature.*
- *Citation indexes.* Using a citation index, you can track down the publications in which original material has been cited, quoted, or verified.
- *Technical report indexes.* These indexes allow you to look for government and private sector reports. One example would be the *Scientific and Technical Aerospace Reports* index.
- *Patent indexes.* Patents are issued to protect rights to new inventions, products, or processes. You can search for patents by using the *Index of Patents Issued from the United States Patent and Trademark Office* or other similar indexes that cover both U.S. and international patents.

- **Encyclopedias.** Encyclopedias are alphabetically arranged collections of articles. You may want to start by consulting a general encyclopedia, such as *Encyclopedia Britannica* or the *Columbia Encyclopedia*, but then examine more subject-focused encyclopedias, such as *Encyclopedia of Nutritional Supplements, Encyclopedia of Business and Finance,* or *Illustrated Encyclopedia of Aircraft.*
- **Dictionaries.** Dictionaries are alphabetically arranged lists of words, including definitions, pronunciations, and word origins. If you can't locate a particular word in a general dictionary (e.g., a highly specialized term or jargon specific to a certain field), consult a specialized dictionary, such as *Dictionary of Engineering and Technology, Dictionary of Psychology*, or *Dictionary of Media and Communication Studies.*
- **Handbooks.** Handbooks offer condensed facts (formulas, tables, advice, examples) about particular fields. Examples include the *Civil Engineering Handbook* and *The McGraw-Hill Computer Handbook.*
- **Almanacs.** Almanacs are collections of factual and statistical data, usually arranged by subject area and published annually. Examples include general almanacs, such as the *World Almanac and Book of Facts*, or subject-specific almanacs, such as the *Almanac for Computers* or *Baer's Agricultural Almanac.*
- **Directories.** Directories provide updated information about organizations, companies, people, products, services, or careers, often listing addresses and phone numbers. Examples include *The Career Guide: Dun's Employment Opportunities Directory* and the *Directory of American Firms Operating in*

Foreign Countries. For electronic versions, ask your librarian about *Hoover's Company Capsules* (for basic information on thousands of companies) and *Hoover's Company Profiles* (for detailed information).

- **Abstracts.** Abstracts are collected summaries of books and/or articles. Reading abstracts can help you decide whether to read or skip an article and can save you from having to track down a journal you may not need. Abstracts usually are titled by discipline: *Biological Abstracts*, *Computer Abstracts*, and so on. For some current research, you might consult abstracts of doctoral dissertations in *Dissertation Abstracts International*.

Although the reference works mentioned here are available mainly as print documents, some are available on the Internet. Go to the Internet Public Library at <www.ipl.org> for links to many online reference works. When using a reference work, check the copyright date to make sure you are accessing the most current information available.

Access Tools for Government Publications. The federal government publishes maps, periodicals, books, pamphlets, manuals, research reports, and other information. An example would be the *Journal of Research of the National Bureau of Standards*. These publications may be available in digital as well as hard-copy formats. To help you find what you are looking for, you will need to use an access tool such as the following. (A librarian can teach you to use these tools.)

- The *Monthly Catalog of the United States Government* is the major pathway to government publications and reports.
- The *Government Reports Announcements and Index* is a listing (with summaries) of more than one million federally sponsored published research reports and patents issued since 1964.
- The *Statistical Abstract of the United States*, updated yearly, offers statistics on population, health, employment, and many other areas. It can be accessed via the Web. CD-ROM versions are now available.

Gray Literature. Some useful printed information may be unavailable at any library. This is known as "gray literature," or materials that are unpublished or not typically catalogued. Examples include pamphlets published by organizations or companies (such as medical pamphlets or company marketing materials), unpublished government documents (available under the Freedom of Information Act), dissertations by graduate students, papers presented at professional conferences, or self-published works.

The only way to track down gray literature is to contact those who produce such literature and request anything available in your subject area. For instance, you could contact a professional organization and request any papers on your topic that were delivered at their recent annual conference, or contact a government agency for statistics relevant to your topic. Before doing so, be knowledgeable about your topic and know specifically whom to contact. Don't make vague, general requests.

Keep in mind that gray literature, like much material found on the Web, is often not carefully scrutinized for content by editors. Therefore, it may be unreliable and should be backed up by information from other sources.

EXPLORING PRIMARY SOURCES

Types of primary sources

Once you have explored your research topic in depth by finding out what others have uncovered, supplement that knowledge with information you discover yourself by doing primary research. Primary sources include unsolicited inquiries, informational interviews, surveys, and observations or experiments.

Unsolicited Inquiries

Unsolicited inquiries uncover basic but important information

The most basic form of primary research is a simple, unsolicited inquiry. Letters, phone calls, or email inquiries to experts listed in Web pages or to people you identify in other ways can clarify or supplement information you already have. Try to contact the right individual instead of a company or department. Also, ask specific questions that cannot be answered elsewhere. Be sure what you ask about is not confidential or otherwise sensitive information.

Unsolicited inquiries, especially by phone or email, can be intrusive or even offensive. Therefore, limit yourself to a few questions that don't require extensive research or thought on the part of the person you contact.

Informational Interviews

Informational interviews can lead to original, unpublished material

An excellent primary source of information is the informational interview. Much of what an expert knows may never be published. Therefore, you can uncover highly original information by spending time with your respondent and asking pertinent questions. In addition, an interviewee might refer you to other experts or sources of information.

Expert opinion is not always reliable

Of course, an expert's opinion can be just as mistaken or biased as anyone else's. Like patients who seek second opinions about medical conditions, researchers must seek a balanced range of expert opinions about complex problems or controversial issues. In researching the effects of electromagnetic fields (EMFs), for example, you would seek opinions not only from a company engineer and environmentalist, but also from presumably more objective third parties such as a professor or journalist who has studied the issue. Figure 7 provides a partial text of an interview about persuasive challenges faced by a corporation's manager.

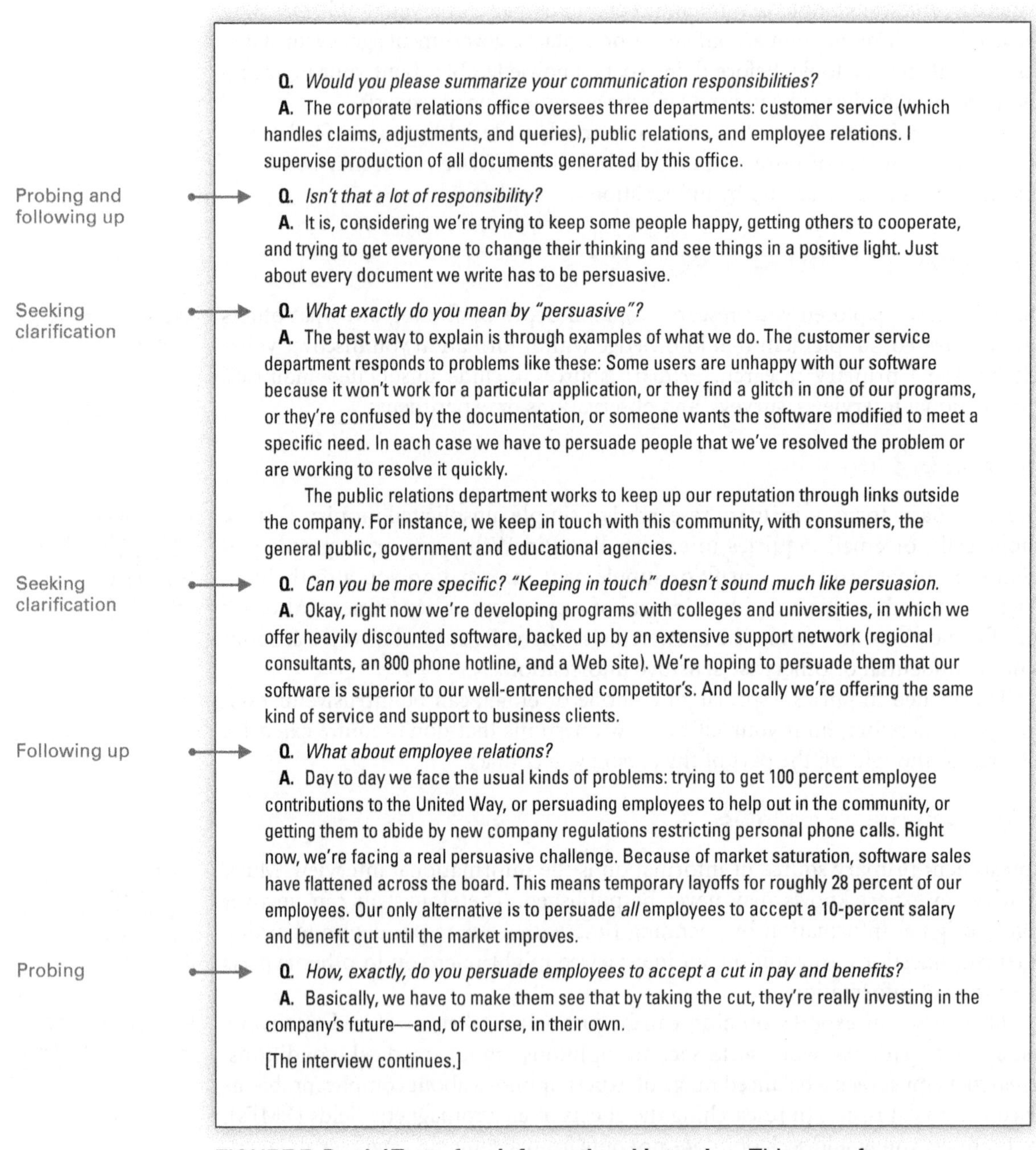

Q. *Would you please summarize your communication responsibilities?*

A. The corporate relations office oversees three departments: customer service (which handles claims, adjustments, and queries), public relations, and employee relations. I supervise production of all documents generated by this office.

Q. *Isn't that a lot of responsibility?*

A. It is, considering we're trying to keep some people happy, getting others to cooperate, and trying to get everyone to change their thinking and see things in a positive light. Just about every document we write has to be persuasive.

Q. *What exactly do you mean by "persuasive"?*

A. The best way to explain is through examples of what we do. The customer service department responds to problems like these: Some users are unhappy with our software because it won't work for a particular application, or they find a glitch in one of our programs, or they're confused by the documentation, or someone wants the software modified to meet a specific need. In each case we have to persuade people that we've resolved the problem or are working to resolve it quickly.

The public relations department works to keep up our reputation through links outside the company. For instance, we keep in touch with this community, with consumers, the general public, government and educational agencies.

Q. *Can you be more specific? "Keeping in touch" doesn't sound much like persuasion.*

A. Okay, right now we're developing programs with colleges and universities, in which we offer heavily discounted software, backed up by an extensive support network (regional consultants, an 800 phone hotline, and a Web site). We're hoping to persuade them that our software is superior to our well-entrenched competitor's. And locally we're offering the same kind of service and support to business clients.

Q. *What about employee relations?*

A. Day to day we face the usual kinds of problems: trying to get 100 percent employee contributions to the United Way, or persuading employees to help out in the community, or getting them to abide by new company regulations restricting personal phone calls. Right now, we're facing a real persuasive challenge. Because of market saturation, software sales have flattened across the board. This means temporary layoffs for roughly 28 percent of our employees. Our only alternative is to persuade *all* employees to accept a 10-percent salary and benefit cut until the market improves.

Q. *How, exactly, do you persuade employees to accept a cut in pay and benefits?*

A. Basically, we have to make them see that by taking the cut, they're really investing in the company's future—and, of course, in their own.

[The interview continues.]

FIGURE 7 **Partial Text of an Informational Interview** This page from an informational interview shows you how to use clear, specific questions and how to follow up and seek clarification to answers.

GUIDELINES for Informational Interviews

Planning the Interview

- **Know exactly what you're looking for from whom.** Write out your plan.

  > I will interview Anne Hector, Chief Engineer at Northport Electric, to ask about the company's approaches to EMF (electromagnetic field) risk avoidance—in the company as well as in the community.

  Audience and purpose statement

- **Do your homework.** Learn all you can. Be sure the information this person might provide is unavailable in print.
- **Make arrangements by phone, letter, or email.** Ask whether this person objects to being quoted or taped. If possible, submit your questions beforehand.

Preparing the Questions

- **Make each question clear and specific.** Avoid questions that can be answered "yes" or "no":

  > In your opinion, can technology find ways to decrease EMF hazards?

  An unproductive question

  Instead, phrase your question to elicit a detailed response:

  > Of the various technological solutions being proposed or considered, which do you consider most promising?

  A clear and specific question

- **Avoid loaded questions.** A loaded question invites or promotes a particular bias:

  > Wouldn't you agree that EMF hazards have been overstated?

  A loaded question

  Ask an impartial question instead:

  > In your opinion, have EMF hazards been accurately stated, overstated, or understated?

  An impartial question

- **Save the most difficult, complex, or sensitive questions for last.**
- **Write out each question on a separate notecard.** Use the notecard to summarize the responses during the interview.

Conducting the Interview

- **Make a courteous start.** Express your gratitude; explain why you believe the respondent can be helpful; explain exactly how you will use the information.
- **Respect cultural differences.** Consider the level of formality, politeness, directness, and other behaviors appropriate in the given culture.
- **Let the respondent do most of the talking.**
- **Be a good listener.**

▶▶

GUIDELINES *continued*

- **Stick to your interview plan.** If the conversation wanders, politely nudge it back on track (unless the peripheral information is useful).
- **Ask for clarification if needed.** Keep asking until you understand.

Clarifying questions

| —Could you go over that again?
| —What did you mean by [*word*]?

- **Repeat major points in your own words and ask if your interpretation is correct.** But do not put words into the respondent's mouth.
- **Be ready with follow-up questions.**

Follow-up questions

| —Why is it like that?
| —Could you say something more about that?
| —What more needs to be done?

- **Keep note taking to a minimum.** Record statistics, dates, names, and other precise data, but don't record every word. Jot key terms or phrases that can refresh your memory later.

Concluding the Interview

- **Ask for closing comments.** Perhaps these can point to additional information.

Concluding questions

| —Would you care to add anything?
| —Is there anyone else I should talk to?
| —Can you suggest other sources that might help me better understand this issue?

- **Request permission to contact your respondent again, if new questions arise.**
- **Invite the respondent to review your version for accuracy.** If the interview is to be published, ask for the respondent's approval of your final draft. Offer to provide copies of any document in which this information appears.
- **Thank your respondent and leave promptly.**
- **As soon as possible, write a complete summary (or record one verbally).**

Surveys

Surveys provide multiple, fresh viewpoints on a topic

Surveys help you form impressions of the concerns, preferences, attitudes, beliefs, or perceptions of a large, identifiable group (a *target population*) by studying representatives of that group (a *sample*). While interviews allow for greater clarity and depth, surveys offer an inexpensive way to get the viewpoints of a large group. Respondents can answer privately and anonymously—and often more candidly than in an interview.

The tool for conducting surveys is the questionnaire. See Figures 8 and 9 for a sample questionnaire cover letter and questionnaire.

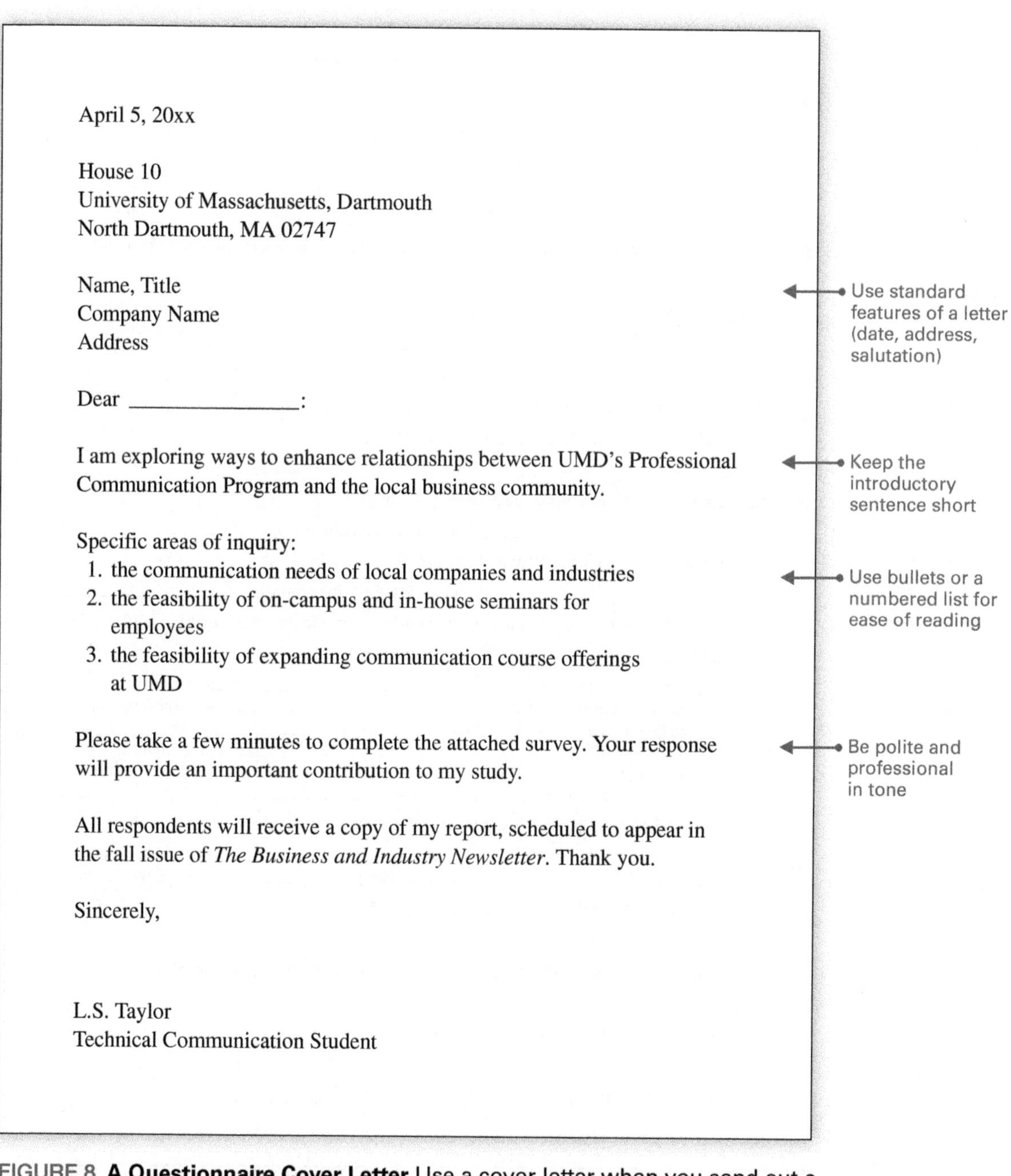

April 5, 20xx

House 10
University of Massachusetts, Dartmouth
North Dartmouth, MA 02747

Name, Title
Company Name
Address

Dear _______________:

I am exploring ways to enhance relationships between UMD's Professional Communication Program and the local business community.

Specific areas of inquiry:

1. the communication needs of local companies and industries
2. the feasibility of on-campus and in-house seminars for employees
3. the feasibility of expanding communication course offerings at UMD

Please take a few minutes to complete the attached survey. Your response will provide an important contribution to my study.

All respondents will receive a copy of my report, scheduled to appear in the fall issue of *The Business and Industry Newsletter*. Thank you.

Sincerely,

L.S. Taylor
Technical Communication Student

FIGURE 8 **A Questionnaire Cover Letter** Use a cover letter when you send out a questionnaire. If the questionnaire will be sent electronically, you can use email to write and send the cover letter.

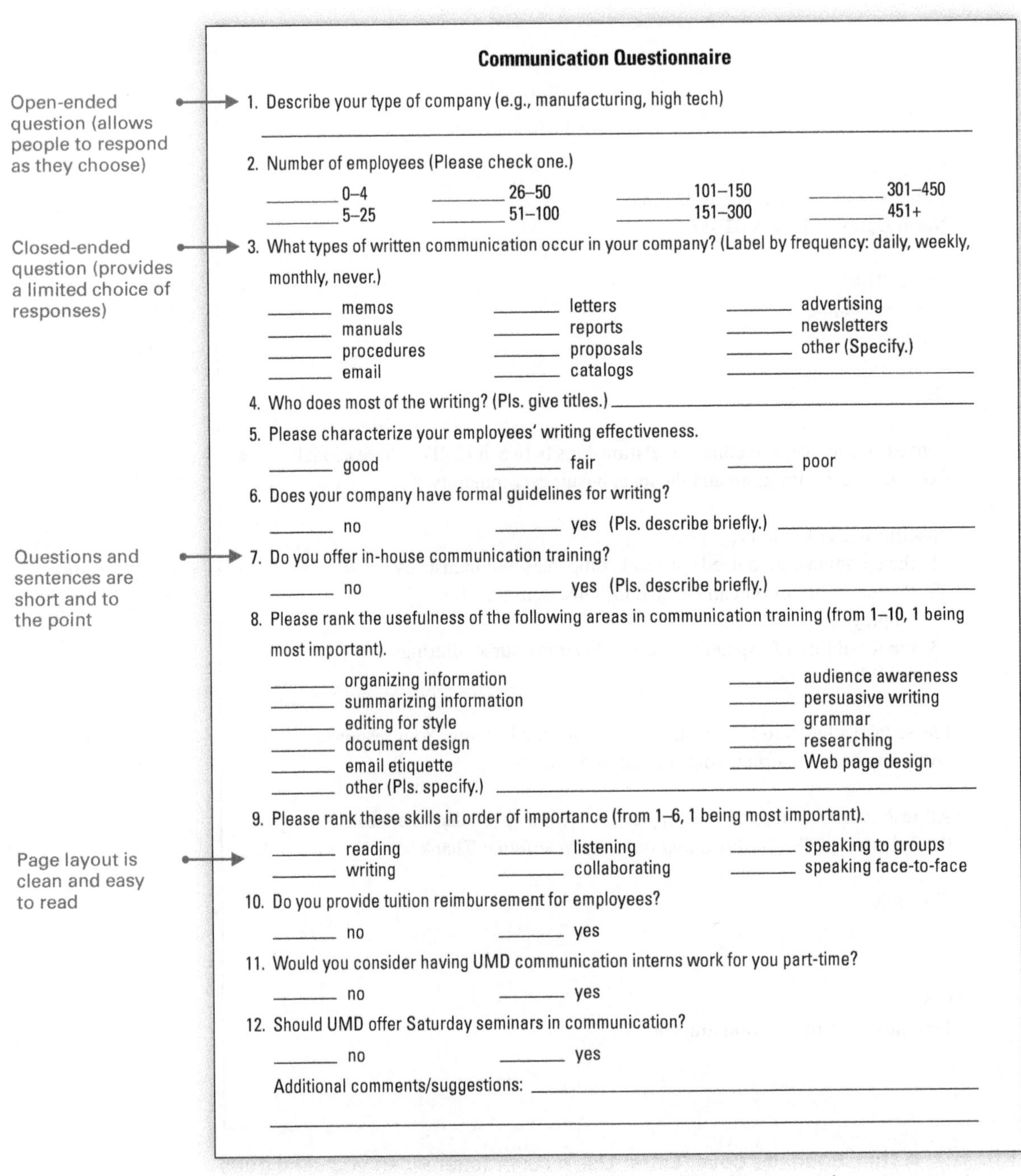

FIGURE 9 **A Questionnaire** A questionnaire will help you gather answers to specific questions and topics.

GUIDELINES for Surveys

- **Define the survey's purpose and target population.** Ask yourself, "Why is this survey being performed?" "What, exactly, is it measuring?" "How much background research do I need?" "How will the survey findings be used?" and "Who is the exact population being studied?"
- **Identify the sample group.** Determine how many respondents you need. Generally, the larger the sample surveyed the more dependable the results (assuming a well-chosen and representative sample). Also determine how the sample will be chosen. Will they be randomly chosen? In the statistical sense, *random* does not mean "haphazard": A random sample means that each member of the target population stands an equal chance of being in the sample group.
- **Define the survey method.** How will the survey be administered—by phone, by mail, or online? Each method has benefits and drawbacks: Phone surveys yield fast results and high response rates; however, they take longer than written surveys. Also, many people find them annoying and tend to be less candid when responding in person. Mail surveys promote candid responses, but many people won't bother returning the survey, and results can arrive slowly. Surveys via the Web or email yield quick results, but computer connections can fail, and (with Web surveys) you have less control over how often the same person responds.
- **Decide on types of questions.** Questions can be *open-* or *closed-ended.* Open-ended questions allow respondents to answer in any way they choose. Measuring the data gathered from such questions is more time-consuming, but they do provide a rich source of information. An open-ended question is worded like this:

  How much do you know about electromagnetic radiation at our school?

  Open-ended question

  Closed-ended questions give people a limited number of choices, and the data gathered are easier to measure. Here are some types of closed-ended questions:

  Are you interested in joining a group of concerned parents?

  YES____ NO____

  Rate your degree of concern about EMFs at our school.

  HIGH____ MODERATE____ LOW____ NO CONCERN ____

  Closed-ended questions

  Circle the number that indicates your view about the town's proposal to spend $20,000 to hire its own EMF consultant.

  1....2....3....4....5....6....7

  Strongly Disapprove | No Opinion | Strongly Approve

  How often do you . . . ?

  ALWAYS____ OFTEN ____ SOMETIMES ____ RARELY ____ NEVER____

  To measure exactly where people stand on an issue, choose closed-ended questions.

GUIDELINES *continued*

- **Develop an engaging introduction and provide appropriate information.** Persuade respondents that the questionnaire relates to their concerns, that their answers matter, and that their anonymity is ensured:

A survey introduction

> Your answers will help our school board to speak accurately for your views at our next town meeting. All answers will be kept confidential. Thank you.

Researchers often include a cover letter with the questionnaire, as in Figure 8.

Begin with the easiest questions, usually the closed-ended ones. Respondents who commit to these are likely to answer later, more difficult questions.

- **Make each question unambiguous.** All respondents should be able to interpret identical questions identically. An ambiguous question allows for misinterpretation:

An ambiguous question

> Do you favor weapons for campus police? YES______ NO______

"Weapons" might mean tear gas, clubs, handguns, tasers, or some combination of these. The limited "yes/no" format reduces an array of possible opinions to an either/or choice. Here is an unambiguous version:

A clear and incisive question

> ______ **Do you favor** (check all that apply):
> ______ Having campus police carry mace and a club?
> ______ Having campus police carry nonlethal "stun guns"?
> ______ Having campus police store handguns in their cruisers?
> ______ Having campus police carry handguns?
> ______ Having campus police carry large-caliber handguns?
> ______ Having campus police carry no weapons?
> ______ Don't know

To account for all possible responses, include options such as "Other," "Don't know," or an "Additional Comments" section.

- **Avoid biased questions:**

A loaded question

> Should our campus tolerate the needless endangerment of innocent students by lethal weapons? YES_____ NO_____

Avoid emotionally loaded and judgmental words ("endangerment," "innocent," "needless"), which can influence a person's response (Hayakawa 40).

- **Make it brief, simple, and inviting.** Long questionnaires usually get few replies. And people who do reply tend to give less thought to their answers. Limit the number and types of questions. Include a stamped, return-addressed envelope, and stipulate a return date.
- **Have an expert review your questionnaire before use, whenever possible.**

Observations and Experiments

Observations or experiments should be your final step, because you now know exactly what to look for.

When you make observations, have a plan in place. Know how, where, and when to look, and jot down or record your observations immediately. You might even take photos or draw sketches of what you observe.

Experiments are controlled forms of observations designed to verify assumptions (e.g., the role of fish oil in preventing heart disease) or to test something untried (e.g., the relationship between background music and productivity). Each field has its own guidelines for conducting experiments (e.g., you must use certain equipment, scrutinize your results in a certain way); follow those guidelines to the letter when conducting your own experiments.

Remember that observations and experiments are not foolproof. During observation or experimentation, you may be biased about what you see (focusing on the wrong events, ignoring something important). In addition, if you are observing people or experimenting with human subjects, they may be conscious of being observed and may alter their normal behaviors.

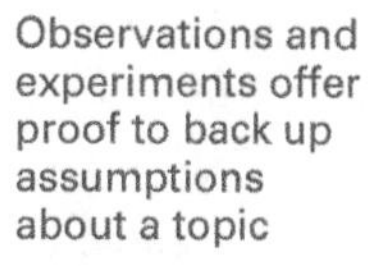

Observations and experiments offer proof to back up assumptions about a topic

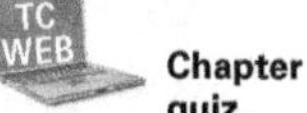

Chapter quiz, Exercises, Web links, and Flashcards
(Go to *Student Resources>Chapter 7*)

Research Activities, Case studies, Quizzes, and Model documents
(Go to *The Research Process*)

CONSIDER THIS: Frequently Asked Questions about Copyright

Research often involves working with copyrighted materials. Copyright laws have an ethical purpose: to balance the reward for intellectual labors with the public's right to use information freely.

1. *What is a copyright?*

   A copyright is the exclusive legal right to reproduce, publish, and sell a literary, dramatic, musical, or artistic work that is fixed in a tangible medium (digital or print). Written permission must be obtained to use all copyrighted material except where fair use applies or in cases where the copyright holder has stated other terms of use. For example, a musician might use a Creative Commons "attribution" license as part of a song released on the Internet. This license allows others to copy, display, and perform the work without permission, but only if credit is given. For more about Creative Commons and types of licenses, see <creativecommons.org/about/licenses>.

2. *What are the limits of copyright protection?*

   Copyright protection covers the exact wording of the original, but not the ideas or information it conveys. For example, Einstein's theory of relativity has no protection but his exact wording does (Abelman 33; Elias 3). Also, paraphrasing Einstein's ideas but failing to cite him as the source would constitute plagiarism.

3. *How long does copyright protection last?*

   Works published before January 1, 1978 are protected for 95 years. Works published on or after January 1, 1978 are copyrighted for the author's life plus 70 years.

(*Continued*)

CONSIDER THIS: *(continued)*

4. *Must a copyright be officially registered in order to protect a work?*

   No. Protection begins as soon as a work is created.

5. *Must a work be published in order to receive copyright protection?*

   No.

6. *What is "fair use"?*

   "Fair use" is the legal and limited use of copyrighted material without permission. The source should, of course, be acknowleged. Fair use does not ordinarily apply to case studies, charts and graphs, author's notes, or private letters ("Copyright Protection" 30).

7. *How is fair use determined?*

   In determining fair use, the courts ask these questions:

   - *Is the material being used for commercial or for nonprofit purposes?* For example, nonprofit educational use is viewed more favorably than for-profit use.
   - *Is the copyrighted work published or unpublished?* Use of published work is viewed more favorably than use of unpublished essays, correspondence, and so on.
   - *How much, and which part, of the original work is being used?* The smaller the part, the more favorably its use will be viewed. Never considered fair, however, is the use of a part that "forms the core, distinguishable, creative effort of the work being cited" (*Author's Guide* 30).
   - *How will the economic value of the original work be affected?* Any use that reduces the potential market value of the original will be viewed unfavorably.

8. *What is the exact difference between copyright infringement and fair use?*

   Although using ideas from an original work is considered fair, a paraphrase that incorporates too much of the original expression can be infringement—even when the source is cited (Abelman 41). Reproduction of a government document that includes material previously protected by copyright (graphs, images, company logos, slogans) is considered infringement. The United States Copyright Office offers this caution:

   > There is no specific number of words, lines, or notes that may safely be taken without permission.
   >
   > Acknowledging the source of the copyrighted material does not substitute for obtaining permission. ("Fair Use" 1–2)

   When in doubt, obtain written permission.

9. *What is material in the "public domain"?*

   "Public domain" refers to material not protected by copyright or material on which copyright has expired. Works published in the United States 95 years before the current year are in the public domain. Most government publications and commonplace information, such as height and weight charts or a metric conversion table, are in the public domain. These works might contain copyrighted material (used with permission and properly acknowledged). If you are not sure whether an item is in the public domain, request permission ("Copyright Protection" 31).

10. *What about international copyright?*

    Copyright protection varies among individual countries, and some countries offer little or no protection for foreign works:

> There is no such thing as an "international copyright" that will automatically protect an author's writings throughout the world. ("International Copyright" 1–2)
>
> In the United States all foreign works that meet certain requirements are protected by copyright (Abelman 36).

11. *Who owns the copyright to a work prepared as part of one's employment?*

A work prepared in the service of one's employer or under written contract for a client is a "work made for hire." The employer or client is legally considered the author and therefore holds the copyright (Abelman 33–34). For example, a manual researched, designed, and written as part of one's employment would be a work made for hire.

For latest developments, visit the United States Copyright Office <www.loc.gov/copyright>.

Projects

GENERAL

Begin researching for the analytical report due at semester's end.

Phase One: Preliminary Steps

- **a.** Choose a topic that affects you, your workplace, or your community directly.
- **b.** Develop a tree chart to help you ask the right questions.
- **c.** Complete an audience and use profile.
- **d.** Narrow your topic, checking with your instructor for approval and advice.
- **e.** Make a working bibliography to ensure sufficient primary and secondary sources.
- **f.** List what you already know about your topic.
- **g.** Write an audience and purpose statement and submit it in a research proposal.
- **h.** Make a working outline.

Phase Two: Collecting, Evaluating, and Interpreting Data

- **a.** In your research, begin with general works for an overview, and then consult more specific sources.
- **b.** Skim the sources, looking for high points.
- **c.** Take notes selectively, summarize, and record each source.
- **d.** Plan and administer questionnaires, interviews, and inquiries.
- **e.** Try to conclude your research with direct observation.
- **f.** Evaluate each finding for accuracy, reliability, fairness, and completeness.
- **g.** Decide what your findings mean.
- **h.** Reassess your methods, interpretation, and reasoning.

Phase Three: Organizing Your Data and Writing the Report

- **a.** Revise your working outline as needed.
- **b.** Document each source of information.
- **c.** Write your final draft.
- **d.** Proofread carefully. Add front and end matter supplements.

Due Dates: To Be Assigned by Your Instructor

List of possible topics due:

Final topic due:

Proposal memo due:

Working bibliography and working outline due:

Notecards (or note files) due:

Copies of questionnaires, interview questions, and inquiry letters due:

Revised outline due:

First draft of report due:

Final version with supplements and full documentation due:

TEAM

Divide into groups according to majors. Assume that several employers in your field are holding a job fair on campus next month and will be interviewing entry-level candidates. Each member of your group is assigned to develop a profile of *one* of these companies or organizations by researching its history, record of mergers and stock value, management style, financial condition, price/earnings ratio of its stock, growth prospects, products and services, multinational affiliations, ethical record, environmental record, employee relations, pension plan, employee stock options or profit-sharing plans, commitment to affirmative action, number of women and minorities in upper management, or any other features important to a prospective employee. The entire group will then edit each profile and assemble them in one single document to be used as a reference for students in your major.

DIGITAL

Using Wikipedia as a starting point, research a topic for this class or another class. Select a topic that is "big" (for example, global warming). Use the footnotes in the Wikipedia article to help you narrow your focus. (For instance, you might discover a footnote to an article about global warming and biodiversity.) Use your college library or the Internet, or both, to locate the articles, reports, and other publications cited in these footnotes. Write a short report (3–4 pages) describing your research process.

GLOBAL

Using the Guidelines for Informational Interviews, write an email to an interviewee who speaks fluent English but comes from another country. How might you approach the request for an interview differently? In addition to research about your topic and your respondent's background prior to the interview, what other research might you do? How might you compose your interview questions with your interviewee's nationality and/or culture in mind? Compare approaches in class.

For more support in mastering the objectives of this chapter, go to **www.mytechcommlab.com**

Evaluating and Interpreting Information

Kutay Tanir/Getty Images

"Our clients make investment decisions based on feasibility and strategy for marketing new products. Our job is to research consumer interest in these potential products (say, a new brand of low-calorie chocolate). In designing surveys, I have to translate the client's information needs into precise questions. I have to be certain that the respondents are answering *exactly* the question I had in mind, and not inventing their own version of the question. Then I have to take these data and translate them into accurate interpretations and recommendations for our clients."

—Jessica North, Senior Project Manager, market research firm

LEARNING OBJECTIVES FOR THIS CHAPTER

- Appreciate the role of critical thinking in evaluating research findings
- Assess the dependability of information sources
- Assess the quality of your evidence
- Interpret your findings accurately and without bias
- Understand that "certainty" in research is an elusive goal
- Recognize common errors in reasoning and statistical analysis
- Understand that research carries the potential for error

Determine if your research sources are valid and reliable

Chapter overview
(Go to *Student Resources>Chapter 8*)

Not all information is equal. Not all interpretations are equal either. For instance, if you really want to know how well the latest innovation in robotic surgery works, you need to check with other sources besides, say, the device's designer (from whom you could expect an overly optimistic or insufficiently critical assessment).

Whether you work with your own findings or the findings of other researchers, you need to decide if the information is valid and reliable. Then you need to decide what your information means. Figure 1 outlines your critical thinking decisions, and the potential for error at any stage in this process.

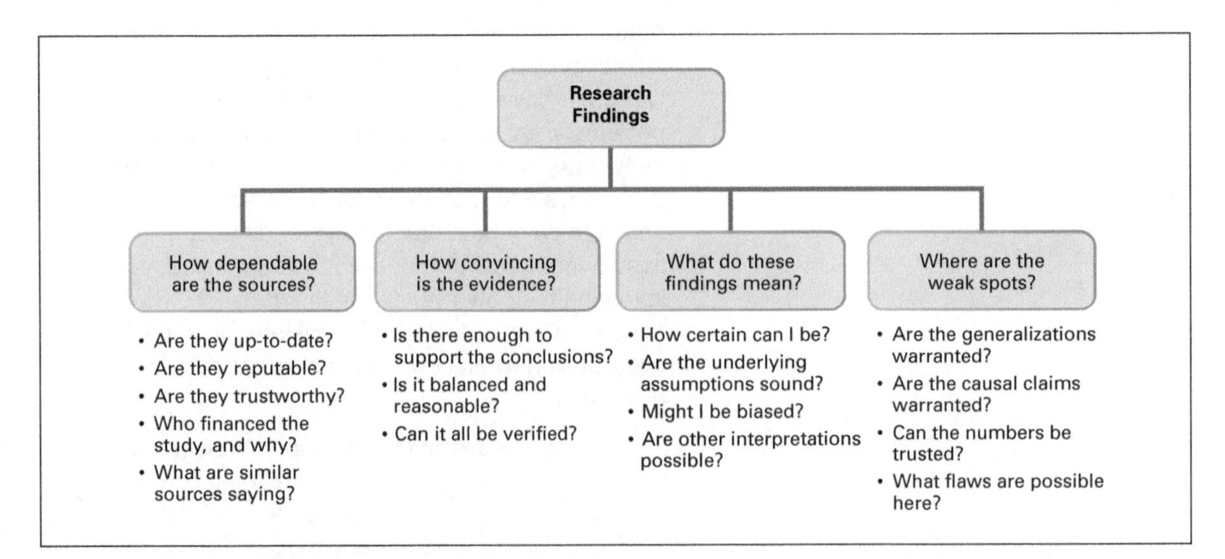

FIGURE 1 **Critical Thinking Decisions in Evaluating and Interpreting Information** Collecting information is often the easiest part of the research process. Your larger challenge is in getting the exact information you need, making sure it's accurate, figuring out what it means, and then double-checking for possible errors along the way.

EVALUATE THE SOURCES

Not all sources are equally dependable. A source might offer information that is out-of-date, inaccurate, incomplete, mistaken, or biased.

- **Determine the currency of the source.** Even newly published books contain information that can be more than a year old, and journal articles typically undergo a lengthy process of peer review before they are published.

"Is the source up-to-date?"

NOTE *The most recent information is not always the most reliable—especially in scientific research, a process of ongoing inquiry in which what seems true today may be proven false tomorrow. Consider, for example, the recent discoveries of fatal side effects from some of the latest "miracle" drugs.*

- **Assess the reputation of a printed source.** Check the publication's copyright page. Is the work published by a university, professional society, museum, or respected news organization? Is the publication *refereed* (all submissions reviewed by experts before acceptance)? Does the bibliography or list of references indicate how thoroughly the author has researched the issue (Barnes)? Also check citation indexes to see what other experts have said about this particular source. Many periodicals also provide brief biographies or descriptions of authors' earlier publications and achievements.

"Is the printed source reputable?"

- **Assess the perspective of an Internet or database source.** The Internet offers information that may never appear elsewhere, for example, from blogs and Web sites. But remember that the Internet does not have an editorial board—almost anyone can publish anything online. Depending on the sponsoring organization or author, the material you find may reflect only the perspective of the groups that provide it. For instance, the Web site in Figure 2 offers information and opinions about the uses of genetically modified foods from the perspective of a consumer advocacy group. If using this site as a source, you should also look for information from an organization that takes a different stance on the topic, so that you can assess a balance of viewpoints.

  Even in a commercial database such as *Dialog,* decisions about what to include and what to leave out depend on the biases, priorities, or interests of those who assemble that database.

"Is the electronic source trustworthy?"

NOTE *Because a special-interest Web site may advocate only one particular point of view, it can also provide you with useful clues about the ideas and opinions of its sponsors. Balance this information with information from a variety of sources, including peer reviewed publications, government Web sites, and special-interest sites that offer differing perspectives.*

- **Consider the possible motives of those who have funded the study.** Much of today's research is paid for by private companies or special-interest groups

"Who financed the study, and why?"

that have their own agendas (Crossen 14, 19). Medical research may be financed by drug or tobacco companies; nutritional research, by food manufacturers; environmental research, by oil or chemical companies. Instead of a neutral and balanced inquiry, this kind of "strategic research" is designed to support one special interest or another (132–34). Research financed by opposing groups can produce opposing results. Try to determine exactly what those who have funded a particular study stand to gain or lose from the results (234).

FIGURE 2 **A Web Site That Offers a Particular Perspective** This information seems convincing, but it still needs to be balanced with research from sources that take a different view or from sources that are neutral on the issue.

Source: Courtesy Institute for Responsible Technology.

NOTE *Keep in mind that any research ultimately stands on its own merits. Thus, funding by a special interest should not automatically discredit an otherwise valid and reliable study. Also, financing from a private company often sets the stage for beneficial research that might otherwise be unaffordable, as when research funded by Quaker Oats led to other studies proving that oats can lower cholesterol (Raloff 189).*

- **Cross-check the source against other, similar sources.** Most studies have some type of flaw or limitation. Instead of relying on a single source or study, you should seek a consensus among various respected sources.

"What are similar sources saying?"

EVALUATE THE EVIDENCE

Evidence is any finding used to support or refute a particular claim. Although evidence can serve the truth, it can also distort, misinform, and deceive. For example:

Questions that invite distorted evidence

- How much money, material, or energy does recycling really save?
- How well are public schools educating children?
- Which investments or automobiles are safest?
- How safe and effective are herbal medications?

Competing answers to such questions often rest on evidence that has been chosen to support a particular view or agenda.

- **Determine the sufficiency of the evidence.** Evidence is sufficient when nothing more is needed to reach an accurate judgment or conclusion. Say you are researching the stress-reducing benefits of low-impact aerobics among employees at a fireworks factory. You would need to interview or survey a broad sample: people who have practiced aerobics for a long time; people of both genders, different ages, different occupations, different lifestyles before they began aerobics; and so on. But responses even from hundreds of practitioners might be insufficient unless those responses were supported by laboratory measurements of metabolic and heart rates, blood pressure, and so on.

"Is there enough evidence?"

NOTE *Although anecdotal evidence ("This worked great for me!") may offer a starting point, personal experience rarely provides enough evidence from which to generalize.*

- **Differentiate hard from soft evidence.** "Hard evidence" consists of facts, expert opinions, or statistics that can be verified. "Soft evidence" consists of uninformed opinions or speculations, data that were obtained or analyzed unscientifically, and findings that have not been replicated or reviewed by experts.

"Can the evidence be verified?"

- **Decide whether the presentation of evidence is balanced and reasonable.** Evidence may be overstated, such as when overzealous researchers exaggerate their achievements without revealing the limitations of their study. Or vital facts may be omitted, as when acetaminophen pain relievers are

"Is this claim too good to be true?"

promoted as "safe," even though acetaminophen is the leading cause of U.S. drug fatalities (Easton and Herrara 42–44).

Is the glass "half full" or "half empty"?

- **Consider how the facts are being framed.** A *frame of reference* is a set of ideas, beliefs, or views that influences our interpretation or acceptance of other ideas. In medical terms, for example, is a "90-percent survival rate" more acceptable than a "10-percent mortality rate"? Framing sways our perception (Lang and Secic 239–40). For instance, what we now call a financial "recession" used to be a "depression"—a term that was coined as a euphemism for "panic" (Bernstein 183).

  Whether the language is provocative ("rape of the environment," "soft on terrorism"), euphemistic ("teachable moment" versus "mistake"), or demeaning to opponents ("bureaucrats," "tree huggers"), deceptive framing—all too common in political "spin" strategies—obscures the real issues.

INTERPRET YOUR FINDINGS

"What does this all mean?"

Interpreting means trying to reach the truth of the matter: an overall judgment about what the findings mean and what conclusion or action they suggest.

Unfortunately, research does not always yield answers that are clear or conclusive. Instead of settling for the most *convenient* answer, we must pursue the most *reasonable* answer by critically examining a full range of possible meanings.

Identify Your Level of Certainty

Research can yield three distinct and very different levels of certainty:

1. The ultimate truth—the *conclusive answer:*

A practical definition of "truth"

> Truth is *what is so* about something, as distinguished from what people wish, believe, or assert to be so. In the words of Harvard philosopher Israel Scheffler, truth is the view "which is fated to be ultimately agreed to by all who investigate."[1] The word *ultimately* is important. Investigation may produce a wrong answer for years, even for centuries. For example, in the second century A.D., Ptolemy's view of the universe placed the earth at its center—and though untrue, this judgment was based on the best information available at that time. And Ptolemy's view survived for 13 centuries, even after new information had discredited this belief. When Galileo proposed a more truthful view in the fifteenth century, he was labeled a heretic.
>
> One way to spare yourself further confusion about truth is to reserve the word *truth* for the final answer to an issue. Get in the habit of using the words *belief, theory,* and *present understanding* more often. (Ruggiero, 3rd ed. 21–22)

Conclusive answers are the research outcome we seek, but often we have to settle for answers that are less than certain.

[1] From *Reason and Teaching*. New York: Bobbs-Merrill, 1973.

2. The *probable answer:* the answer that stands the best chance of being true or accurate, given the most we can know at this particular time. Probable answers are subject to revision in light of new information. This is especially the case with *emergent science,* such as gene therapy or food irradiation.
3. The *inconclusive answer:* the realization that the truth of the matter is more elusive, ambiguous, or complex than we expected.

We need to decide what level of certainty our findings warrant. For example, we are *certain* about the perils of smoking and sunburn, *reasonably certain* about the health benefits of fruits and vegetables, but *less certain* about the perils of genetically modified food or the benefits of vitamin supplements.

"Exactly how certain are we?"

Examine the Underlying Assumptions

Assumptions are notions we take for granted, ideas we often accept without proof. The research process rests on assumptions such as these: that a sample group accurately represents a larger target group, that survey respondents remember facts accurately, that mice and humans share many biological similarities. For a study to be valid, the underlying assumptions have to be accurate.

Consider this example: You are an education consultant evaluating the accuracy of IQ testing as a predictor of academic performance. Reviewing the evidence, you perceive an association between low IQ scores and low achievers. You then verify your statistics by examining a cross-section of reliable sources. Can you justifiably conclude that IQ tests do predict performance accurately? This conclusion might be invalid unless you verify the following assumptions:

How underlying assumptions affect research validity

1. That no one—parents, teachers, or children—had seen individual test scores, which could produce biased expectations.
2. That, regardless of score, each child had completed an identical curriculum, instead of being "tracked" on the basis of his or her score.

NOTE *Assumptions can be easier to identify in someone else's thinking than our own. During team discussions, ask members to help you identify your own assumptions.*

Be Alert for Personal Bias

To support a particular version of the truth, our own bias might cause us to overestimate (or deny) the certainty of our findings.

Personal bias is a fact of life

> Unless you are perfectly neutral about the issue, an unlikely circumstance, at the very outset . . . you will believe one side of the issue to be right, and that belief will incline you to . . . present more and better arguments for the side of the issue you prefer. (Ruggiero 134)

Because personal bias is hard to transcend, *rationalizing* often becomes a substitute for *reasoning*:

Reasoning versus rationalizing

> You are reasoning if your belief follows the evidence—that is, if you examine the evidence first and then make up your mind. You are rationalizing if the evidence follows your belief—if you first decide what you'll believe and then select and interpret evidence to justify it. (Ruggiero 44)

Personal bias is often unconscious until we examine our attitudes long held but never analyzed, assumptions we've inherited from our backgrounds, and so on. Recognizing our own biases is a crucial first step in managing them.

Consider Other Possible Interpretations

"What else could this mean?"

Settling on a final meaning can be difficult—and sometimes impossible. For example, issues such as the need for defense spending or the causes of inflation are always controversial and will never be resolved. Although we can get verifiable data and can reason persuasively on many subjects, no close reasoning by any expert and no supporting statistical analysis will "prove" anything about a controversial subject. Some problems are simply more resistant to solution than others, no matter how dependable the sources.

NOTE *Not all interpretations are equally valid. Never assume that any interpretation that is possible is also allowable—especially in terms of its ethical consequences.*

CONSIDER THIS: Standards of Proof Vary for Different Audiences

How much evidence is enough to "prove" a particular claim? This often depends on who is making the inquiry:

- **The scientist** demands at least 95 percent certainty. A scientific finding must be evaluated and replicated by other experts. Good science looks at the entire picture. Findings are reviewed before they are reported. Even then, answers in science are never "final," but open-ended and ongoing.
- **The juror** demands evidence that indicates only 51 percent certainty (a "preponderance of the evidence"). Jurors are not scientists. Instead of the entire picture, jurors get only the information revealed by lawyers and witnesses. A jury bases its verdict on evidence that exceeds "reasonable doubt" (Monastersky, "Courting" 249; Powell 32+). Based on such evidence, courts must make final decisions.
- **The executive** demands immediate (even if insufficient) evidence. In a global business climate of overnight developments (in world markets, political strife, natural disasters), business decisions are often made on the spur of the moment. On the basis of incomplete or unverified information—or even hunches—executives must react to crises and try to seize opportunities (Seglin 54).
- **Specific cultures** have their own standards for evidence. "For example, African cultures rely on storytelling for authenticity. Arabic persuasion is dependent on universally accepted truths. And Chinese value ancient authorities over recent empiricism" (Byrd and Reid 109).

AVOID DISTORTED OR UNETHICAL REASONING

Finding the truth, especially in a complex issue or problem, often is a process of elimination, of ruling out or avoiding errors in reasoning. As we interpret, we make *inferences:* We derive conclusions about what we don't know by reasoning from what we do know (Hayakawa 37). For example, we might infer that a drug that boosts immunity in laboratory mice will boost immunity in humans, or that a rise in campus crime statistics is caused by the fact that young people have become more violent. Whether a particular inference is on target or dead wrong depends largely on our answers to one or more of these questions:

Questions for testing inferences

- To what extent can these findings be generalized?
- Is *Y* really caused by *X*?
- To what extent can the numbers be trusted, and what do they mean?

Three major reasoning errors that can distort our interpretations are faulty generalization, faulty causal reasoning, and faulty statistical analysis.

Faulty Generalization

The temptation to generalize on the basis of limited evidence can be hard to resist. Consider, for example, the highly controversial war in Iraq. Our political leaders initially justified this war by citing limited and often inaccurate evidence to support the conclusion that Iraq possessed weapons of mass destruction and had collaborated with al-Qaeda in planning the 9/11 attacks on New York City and Washington, D.C.

We engage in faulty generalization when we jump from a limited observation to a sweeping conclusion. Even "proven" facts can invite mistaken conclusions, as in the following examples:

Factual observations

1. "Some studies have shown that gingko [an herb] improves mental functioning in people with dementia [mental deterioration caused by maladies such as Alzheimer's Disease]" (Stix 30).
2. "For the period 1992–2005, two thirds of the fastest-growing occupations [called] for no more than a high-school degree" (Harrison 62).
3. "Adult female brains are significantly smaller than male brains—about 8% smaller, on average" (Seligman 74).

Invalid conclusions

1. Gingko is food for the brain!
2. Higher education . . . Who needs it?!
3. Women are the less intelligent gender.

"How much can we generalize from these findings?"

When we accept findings uncritically and jump to conclusions about their meaning (as in points 1 and 2, above) we commit the error of *hasty generalization.* When we overestimate the extent to which the findings reveal some larger truth (as in point 3, above) we commit the error of *overstated generalization.*

NOTE *We often need to generalize, and we should. For example, countless studies support the generalization that fruits and vegetables help lower cancer risk. But we ordinarily limit general claims by inserting qualifiers such as "usually," "often," "sometimes," "probably," "possibly," or "some."*

Faulty Causal Reasoning

Causal reasoning tries to explain why something happened or what will happen, often in very complex situations. Sometimes a *definite cause is apparent* ("The engine's overheating is caused by a faulty radiator cap"). We reason about definite causes when we explain why the combustion in a car engine causes the wheels to move, or why the moon's orbit makes the tides rise and fall. However, causal reasoning often explores *causes that are not so obvious, but only possible or probable.* In these cases, much analysis is needed to isolate a specific cause.

Suppose you ask: "Why are there no children's daycare facilities on our college campus?" Brainstorming yields these possible causes:

"Did *X* possibly, probably, or definitely cause *Y*?"

lack of need among students
lack of interest among students, faculty, and staff
high cost of liability insurance
lack of space and facilities on campus
lack of trained personnel
prohibition by state law
lack of government funding for such a project

Assume that you proceed with interviews, surveys, and research into state laws, insurance rates, and availability of personnel. As you rule out some items, others appear as probable causes. Specifically, you find a need among students, high campus interest, an abundance of qualified people for staffing, and no state laws prohibiting such a project. Three probable causes remain: high insurance rates, lack of funding, and lack of space. Further inquiry shows that high insurance rates and lack of funding *are* issues. You think, however, that these obstacles could be eliminated through new sources of revenue such as charging a modest fee per child, soliciting donations, and diverting funds from other campus organizations. Finally, after examining available campus space and speaking with school officials, you conclude that one definite cause is lack of space and facilities. In reporting your findings, you would follow the sequence shown in Figure 3.

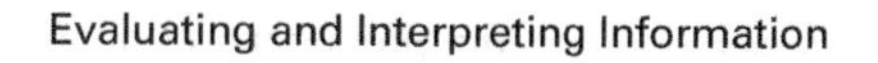

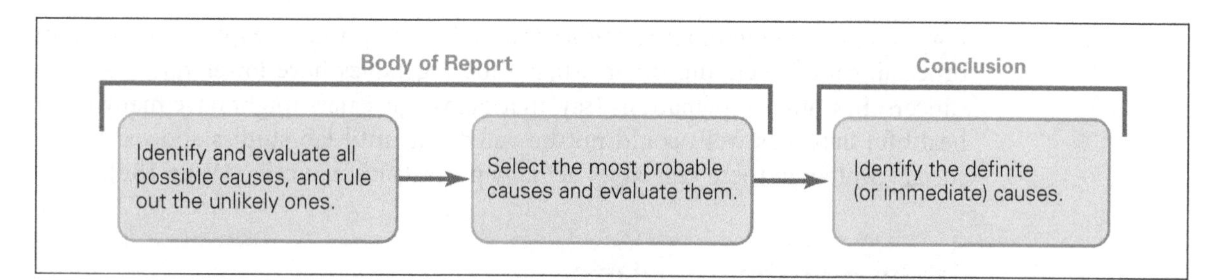

FIGURE 3 **The Reporting Sequence in a Causal Analysis** Be sure readers can draw conclusions identical to your own on the basis of the reasoning you present.

The persuasiveness of your causal argument will depend on the quality of evidence you bring to bear, as well as on your ability to explain the links in the chain of your reasoning. Also, you must convince audiences that you haven't overlooked important alternative causes.

> **NOTE** *Any complex effect is likely to have more than one cause. You have to make sure that the cause you have isolated is the right one. In the daycare scenario, for example, you might argue that lack of space and facilities somehow is related to funding. And the college's inability to find funds or space might be related to student need or interest, which is not high enough to exert real pressure. Lack of space and facilities, however, does seem to be the immediate cause.*

Here are common errors that distort or oversimplify cause-effect relationships:

Ignoring other causes

> Investment builds wealth. [*Ignores the roles of knowledge, wisdom, timing, and luck in successful investing.*]

Ignoring other effects

> Running improves health. [*Ignores the fact that many runners get injured and that some even drop dead while running.*]

Inventing a causal sequence

> Right after buying a rabbit's foot, Felix won the state lottery. [*Posits an unwarranted causal relationship merely because one event follows another.*]

Confusing correlation with causation

> Women in Scandinavian countries drink a lot of milk. Women in Scandinavian countries have a high incidence of breast cancer. Therefore, milk must be a cause of breast cancer. [*The association between these two variables might be mere coincidence and might obscure other possible causes, such as environment, fish diet, and genetic predisposition* (Lemonick 85).]

Rationalizing

> My grades were poor because my exams were unfair. [*Denies the real causes of one's failures.*]

Media researcher Robert Griffin identifies three criteria for demonstrating a causal relationship:

> Along with showing correlation [say, an association between smoking and cancer], evidence of causality requires that the alleged causal agent occurs prior to the condition it causes (e.g., that smoking precedes the development of cancers) and—the most difficult task—that other explanations are discounted or accounted for (240).

For example, epidemiological studies found this correlation: People who eat lots of broccoli, cauliflower, and other cruciferous vegetables have lower rates of some cancers. But other explanations (say, that big veggie eaters might have many other healthful habits as well) could not be ruled out until lab studies showed how a special protein in these vegetables actually protects human cells (Wang 182).

Faulty Statistical Analysis

How numbers can mislead

The purpose of statistical analysis is to determine the meaning of a collected set of numbers. In primary research, our surveys and questionnaires often lead to some kind of numerical interpretation ("What percentage of respondents prefer X?" "How often does Y happen?"). In secondary research, we rely on numbers collected by survey researchers.

Numbers seem more precise, more objective, more scientific, and less ambiguous than words. They are easier to summarize, measure, compare, and analyze. But numbers can be totally misleading. For example, radio or television phone-in surveys often produce distorted data: Although "90 percent of callers" might express support for a particular viewpoint, people who bother to respond tend to have the greatest anger or extreme feelings—representing only a fraction of overall attitudes (Fineman 24). Mail-in or Internet surveys can produce similar distortion. Before relying on any set of numbers, we need to know exactly where they come from, how they were collected, and how they were analyzed.

Common statistical fallacies

Faulty statistical reasoning produces conclusions that are unwarranted, inaccurate, or deceptive. Following are typical fallacies.

"Exactly how well are we doing?"

The Sanitized Statistic. Numbers can be manipulated (or "cleaned up") to obscure the facts. For instance, the College Board's 1996 "recentering" of SAT scores has raised the "average" math score from 478 to 500 and the average verbal score from 424 to 500 (boosts of almost 5 and 18 percent, respectively), although actual student performance remains unchanged (Samuelson, "Merchants" 44).

"How many rats was that?"

The Meaningless Statistic. Exact numbers can be used to quantify something so inexact or vaguely defined that it should only be approximated (Huff 247; Lavin 278): "Boston has 3,247,561 rats." "Zappo detergent makes laundry 10 percent brighter." An exact number looks impressive, but it can hide the fact that certain subjects (child abuse, cheating in college, drug and alcohol abuse, eating habits) cannot be quantified exactly because respondents don't always tell the truth (on account of denial or embarrassment or guessing). Or they respond in ways they think the researcher expects.

The Undefined Average. The mean, median, and mode can be confused in representing an "average" (Huff 244; Lavin 279): (1) The *mean* is the result of adding up the values of items in a set of numbers, and then dividing that total by the number of items in the set. (2) The *median* is the result of ranking all the values from high to low, then identifying the middle value (or the 50th percentile, as in calculating SAT scores). (3) The *mode* is the value that occurs most often in a set of numbers.

Three ways of reporting an "average"

Each of these three measurements represents some kind of average. But unless we know which "average" (mean, median, or mode) is being presented, we cannot possibly interpret the figures accurately.

Assume, for instance, that we want to determine the average salary among female managers at XYZ Corporation (ranked from high to low):

Manager	Salary
"A"	$90,000
"B"	$90,000
"C"	$80,000
"D"	$65,000
"E"	$60,000
"F"	$55,000
"G"	$50,000

In the above example, the *mean* salary (total salaries divided by number of salaries) is $70,000; the *median* salary (middle value) is $65,000; the *mode* (most frequent value) is $90,000. Each is, legitimately, an "average," and each could be used to support or refute a particular assertion (for example, "Women managers are paid too little" or "Women managers are paid too much").

"Why is everybody griping?"

Research expert Michael R. Lavin sums up the potential for bias in the reporting of averages:

> Depending on the circumstances, any one of these measurements may describe a group of numbers better than the other two. . . . [But] people typically choose the value which best presents their case, whether or not it is the most appropriate to use. (279)

Although the mean is the most commonly computed average, this measurement is misleading when one or more values on either end of the scale (*outliers*) are extremely high or low. Suppose, for instance, that manager "A" (above) was paid a $200,000 salary. Because this figure deviates so far from the normal range of salary figures for "B" through "G," it distorts the average for the whole group, increasing the mean salary by more than 20 percent (Plumb and Spyridakis 636).

"Is 51 percent really a majority?"

The Distorted Percentage Figure. Percentages are often reported without explanation of the original numbers used in the calculation (Adams and Schvaneveldt 359; Lavin 280): "Seventy-five percent of respondents prefer our brand over the competing brand"—without mention that, say, only four people were surveyed.

> **NOTE** *In small samples, percentages can mislead because the percentage size can dwarf the number it represents: "In this experiment, 33% of the rats lived, 33% died, and the third rat got away" (Lang and Secic 41). When your sample is small, report the actual numbers: "Five out of ten respondents agreed . . . ."*

"How large is the margin of error?"

Another fallacy in reporting percentages occurs when the *margin of error* is ignored. This is the margin within which the true figure lies, based on estimated sampling errors in a survey. For example, a claim that "most people surveyed prefer Brand X" might be based on the fact that 51 percent of respondents expressed this preference; but if the survey carried a 2 percent margin of error, the real figure could be as low as 49 percent or as high as 53 percent. In a survey with a high margin of error, the true figure may be so uncertain that no definite conclusion can be drawn.

"Which car should we buy?"

The Bogus Ranking. This distortion occurs when items are compared on the basis of ill-defined criteria (Adams and Schvaneveldt 212; Lavin 284). For example, the statement "Last year, the Batmobile was the number-one selling car in America" does not mention that some competing car makers actually sold *more* cars to private individuals and that the Batmobile figures were inflated by hefty sales—at huge discounts—to rental-car companies and corporate fleets. Unless we know how the ranked items were chosen and how they were compared (the *criteria*), a ranking can produce a seemingly scientific number based on a completely unscientific method.

"Does *X* actually cause *Y*?"

Confusion of Correlation with Causation. *Correlation* is a numerical measure of the strength of the relationship between two variables (say smoking and increased lung cancer risk, or education and income). *Causation* is the demonstrable production of a specific effect (smoking causes lung cancer). Correlations between smoking and lung cancer or between education and income signal a causal relationship that has been demonstrated by many studies. But not every correlation implies causation. For instance, a recently discovered correlation between moderate alcohol consumption and decreased heart disease risk offers no sufficient proof that moderate drinking *causes* less heart disease.

"Could something else have caused *Y*?"

In any type of causal analysis, be on the lookout for *confounding factors*, which are other possible reasons or explanations for a particular outcome. For instance, studies indicating that regular exercise improves health might be overlooking the confounding factor that healthy people tend to exercise more than those who are unhealthy ("Walking" 3–4).

Many highly publicized correlations are the product of *data mining:* In this process, computers randomly compare one set of variables (say, eating habits) with another set (say, range of diseases). From these countless comparisons, certain relationships or associations are revealed (say, between coffee drinking and pancreatic cancer risk). As dramatic as such isolated correlations may be, they constitute no proof of causation and often lead to hasty conclusions (Ross, "Lies" 135).

NOTE *Despite its limitations, data mining is invaluable for "uncovering correlations that require computers to perceive but that thinking humans can evaluate and research further" (Maeglin).*

The Biased Meta-Analysis. In a meta-analysis, researchers examine a whole range of studies that have been done on one topic (say, high-fat diets and cancer risk). The purpose of this "study of studies" is to decide the overall meaning of the collected findings. Because results ultimately depend on which studies have been included and which omitted, a meta-analysis can reflect the biases of the researchers who select the material. Also, because small studies have less chance of being published than large ones, they may get overlooked (Lang and Secic 174–76).

"Who selected which studies to include?"

The Fallible Computer Model. Computer models process complex *assumptions* to predict or estimate costs, benefits, risks, and probable outcomes. But answers produced by any computer model depend on the assumptions (and data) programmed in. Assumptions might be influenced by researcher bias or the sponsors' agenda. For example, a prediction of human fatalities from a nuclear reactor meltdown might rest on assumptions about the availability of safe shelter, evacuation routes, time of day, season, wind direction, and the structural integrity of the containment unit. But these assumptions could be manipulated to overstate or understate the risk (Barbour 228). For computer-modeled estimates of accident risk (oil spill, plane crash) or of the costs and benefits of a proposed project or policy (international space station, health care reform), consumers rarely know the assumptions behind the numbers.

"How have assumptions influenced this computer model?"

Misleading Terminology. The terms used to interpret statistics sometimes hide their real meaning. For instance, the widely publicized figure that people treated for cancer have a "50 percent survival rate" is misleading in two ways; (1) *Survival* to laypersons means "staying alive," but to medical experts, staying alive for only five years after diagnosis qualifies as survival; (2) the "50 percent" survival figure covers *all* cancers, including certain skin or thyroid cancers that have extremely high *cure rates,* as well as other cancers (such as lung or ovarian) that are rarely curable and have extremely low *survival rates* ("Are We" 6).

"Do we all agree on what these terms mean?"

Even the most valid and reliable statistics require that we interpret the reality behind the numbers. For instance, the overall cancer rate today is "higher" than it

"Is this news good, bad, or insignificant?"

was in 1910. What this may mean is that people are living longer and thus are more likely to die of cancer and that cancer today rarely is misdiagnosed—or mislabeled because of stigma ("Are We" 4). The finding that rates for certain cancers "double" after prolonged exposure to electromagnetic waves may really mean that cancer risk actually increases from 1 in 10,000 to 2 in 10,000.

The numbers may be "technically accurate" and may seem highly persuasive in the interpretations they suggest. But the actual "truth" behind these numbers is far more elusive. Any interpretation of statistical data carries the possibility that other, more accurate interpretations have been overlooked or deliberately excluded (Barnett 45).

ACKNOWLEDGE THE LIMITS OF RESEARCH

Legitimate researchers live with uncertainty. They expect to be wrong far more often than right. Following is a brief list of things that go wrong with research and interpretation.

Obstacles to Validity and Reliability

What makes a survey valid

Validity and *reliability* determine the dependability of any research (Adams and Schvaneveldt 79–97; Crossen 22–24). *Valid research* produces correct findings. A survey, for example, is valid when (1) it measures what you want it to measure, (2) it measures accurately and precisely, and (3) its findings can be generalized to the target population. Valid survey questions enable each respondent to interpret each question exactly as the researcher intended; valid questions also ask for information respondents are qualified to provide.

Why survey responses can't always be trusted

Survey validity depends largely on trustworthy responses. Even clear, precise, and neutral questions can produce mistaken, inaccurate, or dishonest answers. People often see themselves as more informed, responsible, or competent than they really are. Respondents are likely to suppress information that reflects poorly on their behavior, attitudes, or will power when answering such leading questions as "How often do you take needless sick days?" "Would you lie to get ahead?" "How much TV do you watch?" They might exaggerate or invent facts or opinions that reveal a more admirable picture when answering the following types of questions: "How much do you give to charity?" "How many books do you read?" "How often do you hug your children?" Even when respondents don't know, don't remember, or have no opinion, they often tend to guess in ways designed to win the researcher's approval.

What makes a survey reliable

Reliable research produces findings that can be replicated. A survey is reliable when its results are consistent; for instance, when a respondent gives identical answers to the same survey given twice or to different versions of the same questions. Reliable survey questions can be interpreted identically by all respondents.

Much of your communication will be based on the findings of other researchers, so you will need to assess the validity and reliability of their research as well as your own.

Flaws in Research Studies

Although some types of studies are more reliable than others, each type has limitations (Cohn 106; Harris, Richard 170–72; Lang and Secic 8–9; Murphy 143):

- **Epidemiological studies.** Epidemiologists study various populations (human, animal, or plant) to find correlations (say, between computer use and cataracts). Conducted via observations, interviews, surveys, or records review, these studies are subject to faulty sampling techniques and observer bias (seeing what one wants to see). Even with a correlation that is 99 percent certain, an epidemiological study alone doesn't "prove" anything. (The larger the study, however, the more credible.)

Common flaws in epidemiologic studies

- **Laboratory studies.** Although a laboratory offers controlled conditions, these studies also carry limitations. For example, the reactions of experimental mice to a specific treatment or drug often are not generalizable to humans. Also, the reaction of an isolated group of cells does not always predict the reaction of the entire organism.

Common flaws in laboratory studies

- **Human exposure studies** *(clinical trials).* These studies compare one group of people receiving medication or treatment with an untreated group, the *control group*. Limitations include the possibility that the study group may be non-representative or too different from the general population in overall health, age, or ethnic background. (For example, even though gingko may slow memory loss in sick people, that doesn't mean it will boost the memory of healthy people.) Also, anecdotal reports are unreliable. Respondents often invent answers to questions such as "How often do you eat ice cream?" or "Do you sometimes forget to take your medication?"

Common flaws in clinical trials

Deceptive Reporting

"Has bad or embarrassing news been suppressed?"

One problem in reviewing scientific findings is "getting the story straight." Intentionally or not, the public often is given a distorted picture. For instance, although twice as many people in the United States are killed by medications as by auto accidents—and countless others harmed—doctors rarely report adverse drug reactions. For example, one Rhode Island study identified roughly 26,000 adverse reactions noted in doctors' files, of which only 11 had been reported to the Food and Drug Administration (Freundlich 14).

Some promising but unconventional topics, such as herbal remedies, are rarely the topics of intensive research "partly because few 'respectable' scientists are willing

"Is the topic 'too weird' for researchers?"

to risk their reputations to do the testing required, and partly because few firms would be willing to pay for it if they were." Drug companies have little interest because "herbal medicines, not being new inventions, cannot be patented" ("Any Alternative?" 83).

Even bad science makes good news

Spectacular claims that are even remotely possible are more appealing than spectacular claims that have been disproven. Examples include "Giant Comet Headed for Earth!" and "Insects may carry the AIDS virus!"

NOTE *Does all this potential for error mean we shouldn't believe anything? Of course not. But we need to be discerning about what we do choose to believe. Critical thinking is essential.*

GUIDELINES for Evaluating and Interpreting Information

Evaluate the Sources

- **Check the posting or publication date.** The latest information is not always the best, but keeping up with recent developments is vital.
- **Assess the reputation of each printed source.** Check the copyright page for background on the publisher, the bibliography for the quality of research, and (if available) the author's brief biography.
- **Assess the quality of your source material.**
- **Identify the study's sponsor.** If a study proclaiming the crashworthiness of the Batmobile has been sponsored by the Batmobile Auto Company, be skeptical about the study's findings.
- **Look for corroborating sources.** A single study rarely produces definitive findings. Learn what other sources say, why they agree or disagree, and where most experts stand.

Evaluate the Evidence

- **Decide whether the evidence is sufficient.** Evidence should surpass personal experience, anecdote, or media reports. Reasonable and informed observers should be able to agree on its credibility.
- **Look for a fair and balanced presentation.** Suspect any claims about "breakthroughs" or "miracle cures" or the like.
- **Try to verify the evidence.** Examine the facts that support the claims. Look for replication of findings.

Interpret Your Findings

- **Don't expect "certainty."** Complex questions are mostly open-ended, and a mere accumulation of facts doesn't "prove" anything. Even so, the weight of evidence usually suggests some reasonable conclusion.
- **Examine the underlying assumptions.** As opinions taken for granted, assumptions are easily mistaken for facts.
- **Identify your personal biases.** Examine your own assumptions. Don't ignore evidence simply because it contradicts your original assumptions.
- **Consider alternative interpretations.** What else might this evidence mean?

Check for Weak Spots

- **Scrutinize all generalizations.** Decide whether the evidence supports the generalization. Suspect any general claim not limited by a qualifier such as "often," "sometimes," or "rarely."
- **Treat causal claims skeptically.** Differentiate correlation from causation, as well as possible from probable or definite causes. Consider confounding factors (other explanations for the reported outcome).
- **Look for statistical fallacies.** Determine where the numbers come from, and how they were collected and analyzed—information that legitimate researchers routinely provide. Note the margin of error.
- **Consider the limits of computer analysis.** Data mining often produces intriguing but random correlations; a meta-analysis might be biased; a computer model is only as accurate as the assumptions and data that were programmed in.
- **Look for misleading terminology.** Examine terms that beg for precise definition in their specific context: "survival rate," "success rate," "customer satisfaction," "risk factor," and so on.
- **Interpret the reality behind the numbers.** Consider the possibility of alternative, more accurate, interpretations of the data.
- **Consider the study's possible limitations.** Small, brief studies are less reliable than large, extended ones; epidemiological studies are less reliable than laboratory studies (which have their own flaws); and animal exposure studies are often not generalizable to human populations.
- **Look for the whole story.** Consider whether bad news may be underreported; good news, exaggerated; bad science, camouflaged and sensationalized; or research on promising but unconventional topics (say, alternative energy sources) ignored.

CHECKLIST: The Research Process

Methods

- ☐ Did I ask the right questions?
- ☐ Are the sources appropriately up-to-date?
- ☐ Is each source reputable, trustworthy, relatively unbiased, and borne out by other, similar sources?
- ☐ Does the evidence clearly support all of the conclusions?
- ☐ Is a fair balance of viewpoints represented?
- ☐ Can all the evidence be verified?
- ☐ Has my research achieved adequate depth?
- ☐ Has the entire research process been valid and reliable?

Interpretation and Reasoning

- ☐ Am I reasonably certain about the meaning of these findings?
- ☐ Can I discern assumption from fact?
- ☐ Am I reasoning instead of rationalizing?
- ☐ Can I discern correlation from causation?
- ☐ Is this the most reasonable conclusion (or merely the most convenient)?
- ☐ Can I rule out other possible interpretations or conclusions?
- ☐ Have I accounted for all sources of bias, including my own?
- ☐ Are my generalizations warranted by the evidence?
- ☐ Am I confident that my causal reasoning is accurate?
- ☐ Can I rule out confounding factors?
- ☐ Can all of the numbers, statistics, and interpretations be trusted?
- ☐ Have I resolved (or at least acknowledged) any conflicts among my findings?
- ☐ Can I rule out any possible error or distortion in a given study?
- ☐ Am I getting the whole story, and getting it straight?

Documentation

- ☐ Is my documentation consistent, complete, and correct?
- ☐ Is all quoted material clearly marked throughout the text?
- ☐ Are direct quotations used sparingly and appropriately?
- ☐ Are all quotations accurate and integrated grammatically?
- ☐ Are all paraphrases accurate and clear?
- ☐ Have I documented all sources not considered common knowledge?

Chapter quiz, Exercises, Web links, and Flashcards (Go to *Student Resources>Chapter 8*)

Projects

GENERAL

From media, personal experience, or the Internet, identify an example of each of the following sources of distortion or of interpretive error:

- a study with questionable sponsorship or motives
- reliance on insufficient evidence
- unbalanced presentation
- deceptive framing of facts
- overestimating the level of certainty
- biased interpretation
- rationalizing
- unexamined assumptions
- faulty causal reasoning
- hasty generalization
- overstated generalization
- sanitized statistic
- meaningless statistic
- undefined average
- distorted percentage figure
- bogus ranking
- fallible computer model
- misinterpreted statistic
- deceptive reporting

Hint: For examples of faulty (as well as correct) statistical reasoning in the news, check out Dartmouth College's *Chance Project* at <www.dartmouth.edu/~chance>.

Submit your examples to your instructor along with a memo explaining each error, and be prepared to discuss your material in class.

TEAM

Projects from the previous or following section may be done as team projects.

DIGITAL

Uninformed opinions are usually based on assumptions we've never really examined. Examples of popular assumptions that are largely unexamined:

- "Bottled water is safer and better for us than tap water."
- "Forest fires should always be prevented or suppressed immediately."
- "The fewer germs in their environment, the healthier the children."
- "The more soy we eat, the better."

Identify and examine one popular assumption for accuracy. For example, you might tackle the bottled water assumption by visiting the FDA Web site <www.fda.gov> and the Sierra Club site <www.sierra.org>, for starters. (Unless you get stuck, work with an assumption not listed above.) Trace the sites and links you followed to get your information, and write up your findings in a memo to be shared with the class.

GLOBAL

As indicated in the Consider This box, specific cultures have their own standards for credible evidence. In other words, different cultures reason differently. Using Google, research this phenomenon by conducting a search on "cultural differences in reasoning." Learn how at least two cultures may reason differently from North Americans of European descent, and report your findings.

For more support in mastering the objectives of this chapter, go to **www.mytechcommlab.com**

Organizing for Readers

Organizing for Readers

"I have to make sure that whatever I'm writing is clear *to me* first, and that the way I've organized it makes sense *to me*. Then I take that material and become more objective. I try to understand how my audience thinks: 'How can I make this logical to my audience? Will they understand what I want them to understand?'

Organizing is the key. Develop the type of outlining or listing or brainstorming tool that works best for you, but *find* one that works, and use it consistently. Then you'll be comfortable with that general strategy whenever you sit down to write, especially under a rigid deadline."

—Anne Brill,
Environmental Engineer

LEARNING OBJECTIVES FOR THIS CHAPTER

- Work from an introduction-body-conclusion structure
- Create informal and formal outlines
- Prepare a storyboard for a long document
- Shape effective paragraphs
- Determine the best sequence for your material
- Chunk information into discrete units
- Provide overviews of longer documents

Chapter overview
(Go to *Student Resources>Chapter 10*)

In order to comprehend your thinking, readers need information organized in a way that makes sense to *them*. But data rarely materializes or thinking rarely occurs in neat, predictable sequences. Instead of forcing readers to make sense of unstructured information, we shape this material for their understanding. As we organize a document, we face questions such as these:

Questions in organizing for readers

- What relationships do the collected data suggest?
- What should I emphasize?
- In which sequence will users approach this material?
- What belongs where?
- What do I say first? Why?
- What comes next?
- How do I end the presentation?

To answer these questions, we rely on a variety of organizing strategies.

THE TYPICAL SHAPE OF WORKPLACE DOCUMENTS

Standard introduction/body/conclusion pattern

Organize your material to make the document logical from the reader's point of view. Begin with the basics: Useful documents of any length (memo, letter, long report, and so on) typically follow the pattern shown in Figure 1: *introduction*, *body*, and *conclusion*. The introduction attracts the reader's attention, announces the writer's viewpoint, and previews what will follow. The body delivers on the promise implied in the introduction. The body explains and supports the writer's viewpoint, achieving *unity* by remaining focused on that viewpoint and *coherence* by carrying a line of thought from sentence to sentence in a logical order. Finally, the conclusion has various purposes: it might reemphasize key points, take a position, predict an outcome, offer a solution, or suggest further study. Good conclusions give readers a clear perspective on what they have just read.

Powell Rabkin

MEMORANDUM

To: Department Managers
From: Jill McCreary, General Manager J.M.
Date: December 8, 20XX
Subject: *Diversity training initiative*

Introduction announces the topic and provides an overview of what will follow

As part of our ongoing efforts to highlight the company's commitment to diversity, we recently conducted two surveys—one directed to company employees and one to our retail buyers. We have just received the survey results from our outside analysts. The employee survey indicates that the members of all departments appreciate our efforts to create a diverse and comfortable work environment. The customer survey indicates that our company is well regarded for marketing products in ways that appeal to diverse buyers. However, both surveys also illuminate areas in which we could do even better. As a result, we will be initiating a new series of diversity training workshops early next year. Let me explain the survey findings that have led to this initiative.

Body provides the evidence and data to support the claims made in the introduction

First, the employee survey indicates that our workforce is rated "highly diverse" in terms of gender, with nearly equal representation of male and female employees in both managerial and nonmanagerial positions; however, we could do better in terms of minority representation at the managerial level. Meanwhile, the customer survey demonstrates that our customers are "very satisfied" with the diversity of our marketing materials, but that we fail to provide enough materials for our native Spanish-speaking buyers.

Conclusion summarizes by taking a position and making recommendations

Those are the survey highlights—see the attached analysis for a more detailed picture. Again, we are doing well, but could do better. We feel that the best solution to address our weaker areas is to conduct a second series of diversity training workshops in the upcoming 12 months. We hope that these workshops—which are often illuminating to both new employees and those who have attended diversity trainings earlier—will help keep the word "diversity" at the forefront of everyone's thoughts when hiring and mentoring employees and creating marketing materials. More information will follow, but for now please emphasize to your department employees the importance and value of these workshops.

FIGURE 1 **Document with a Standard Introduction/Body/Conclusion Structure**

A nonstandard structure can also be effective in certain cases

There are many ways of adapting this standard structure. For example, Figure 2 provides visual features (columns, colors), headings, and an engaging layout. Although organized differently from the previous document, Figure 2 does provide an introduction, a body, and a conclusion. The heading "What is arsenic?"

JUST THE FACTS FOR CONSUMERS

ARSENIC IN YOUR DRINKING WATER

What is arsenic?

Arsenic is a toxic chemical element that is unevenly distributed in the Earth's crust in soil, rocks, and minerals.

How does arsenic get into my drinking water?

Arsenic occurs naturally in the environment and as a by-product of some agricultural and industrial activities. It can enter drinking water through the ground or as runoff into surface water sources.

How is arsenic in drinking water regulated?

In 1974, Congress passed the Safe Drinking Water Act. This law directs EPA to issue non-enforceable health goals and enforceable drinking water regulations for contaminants that may cause health problems. The goals, which reflect the level at which no adverse health effects are expected, are called maximum contaminant level goals (MCLGs). The MCLG for arsenic is 0 parts per billion (ppb).

The enforceable standard for arsenic is a maximum contaminant level (MCL). MCLs are set as close to the health goals as possible, considering cost, benefits, and the ability of public water systems to detect and remove contaminants using suitable treatment technologies.

Why should I be concerned about arsenic in my drinking water?

Although short-term exposures to high doses (about a thousand times higher than the drinking water standard) cause adverse effects in people, such exposures do not occur from public water supplies in the U.S. that comply with the arsenic MCL.

Some people who drink water containing arsenic in excess of EPA's standard over many years could experience skin damage or problems with their circulatory system, and may have an increased risk of getting cancer. Health effects might include:

- Thickening and discoloration of the skin, stomach pain, nausea, vomiting, diarrhea, and liver effects;
- Cardiovascular, pulmonary, immunological, neurological (e.g., numbness and partial paralysis), reproductive, and endocrine (e.g., diabetes) effects;
- Cancer of the bladder, lungs, skin, kidney, nasal passages, liver, and prostate.

What is EPA's standard for arsenic in drinking water?

To protect consumers served by public water systems from the health risks of long-term (chronic) arsenic exposure, EPA recently lowered the arsenic MCL from 50 ppb to 10 ppb.

Use of visuals, color, and columns makes the organization clear

"What is arsenic?" paragraph is placed above subsequent sections, indicating that it is the introduction

These lengthier sections are balanced in the middle of the page to indicate the body

"What is EPA's standard?" section is placed at the bottom of the page, indicating that it is a conclusion

FIGURE 2 **Document with a Nonstandard, But Well-Organized Structure**
Source: Environmental Protection Agency <www.epa.gov>

represents a form of introduction. The next several headings answer the question posed in the introduction, forming, in essence, the body of the document. The final heading, asking about EPA standards, represents a form of conclusion, moving beyond data and description to the topic of policy and use.

In organizing any document, we typically begin with the time-tested strategy known as *outlining*.

OUTLINING

Outlining is essential

Even basic documents require at least an introduction-body-conclusion outline done in your head and/or a few ideas jotted down in list form. Longer documents require a more detailed outline so that you can visualize your document overall and ensure that ideas flow logically from point to point.

An Outlining Strategy

Start by searching through the information you have gathered and creating a random list of key topics your document should include. For instance, in preparing the drinking water document in Figure 2, you might start by simply listing all the types of information you think readers need or expect:

Start by creating a list of essential information

- explain what the EPA is doing about arsenic in drinking water
- define what arsenic is
- explain how arsenic gets into drinking water
- list some of the effects of arsenic (stomach, heart, cancer)
- include specific data
- mention/explain the Safe Water Drinking Act
- refer to/define MCLGs

Now you can reorganize this list, as shown below.

A simple list like the one above usually suffices for organizing a short document like the memo in Figure 1. However, for a more complex document, transform your list into a deliberate map that will guide readers from point to point. Create an introduction, body, and conclusion and then decide how you will divide each of these parts into subtopics. An outline for Figure 2 might look like this:

Then organize the information into an outline

I. Introduction—Define arsenic.

II. Body

  A. Explain how arsenic gets into drinking water.

  B. Explain how it is regulated (1974 Safe Drinking Water Act/MCLGs, Maximum Contaminant Level Goals).

  C. List some of the health effects of arsenic (visible effects, diseases, cancers).

III. Conclusion—Describe the EPA's standards.

The Formal Outline

In planning a long document, an author or team rarely begins with a formal outline. But eventually in the writing process, a long or complex document calls for much more than a simple list. Figure 3 shows a formal outline for a report examining the health effects of electromagnetic fields.

Long documents call for formal outlines

NOTE *Long reports often begin directly with a statement of purpose. For the intended audience (i.e., generalists) of the report outlined in Figure 3, however, the technical topic must first be defined so that readers understand the context. Also, each level of division yields at least two items. If you cannot divide a major item into at least two subordinate items, retain only your major heading.*

A formal outline easily converts to a table of contents for the finished document.

NOTE *Because they serve mainly to guide the writer, minor outline headings (such as items [a] and [b] under II.A.2 in Figure 3) may be omitted from the table of contents or the report itself. Excessive headings make a document seem fragmented.*

In technical documents, alphanumeric notation often is replaced by decimal notation. Compare the following with part "A" of the DATA SECTION from Figure 3.

2.0 DATA SECTION
- 2.1 Sources of EMF Exposure
  - 2.1.1 power lines
  - 2.1.2 home and office
    - 2.1.2.1 kitchen
    - 2.1.2.2 workshop [and so on]
  - 2.1.3 natural radiation
  - 2.1.4 risk factors
    - 2.1.4.1 current intensity
    - 2.1.4.2 source proximity [and so on]

Part of a formal outline using decimal notation

The decimal outline makes it easier to refer users to specifically numbered sections ("See section 2.1.2"). Decimal notation is usually preferred in the workplace.

You may wish to expand your *topic outline* into a *sentence outline*, in which each sentence serves as a topic sentence for a paragraph in the document:

2.0 DATA SECTION

2.1 Although the 2 million miles of power lines crisscrossing the United States have been the focus of the EMF controversy, potentially harmful waves also are emitted by household wiring, appliances, electric blankets, and computer terminals.

A sentence outline

Sentence outlines are used mainly in collaborative projects in which various team members prepare different sections of a long document.

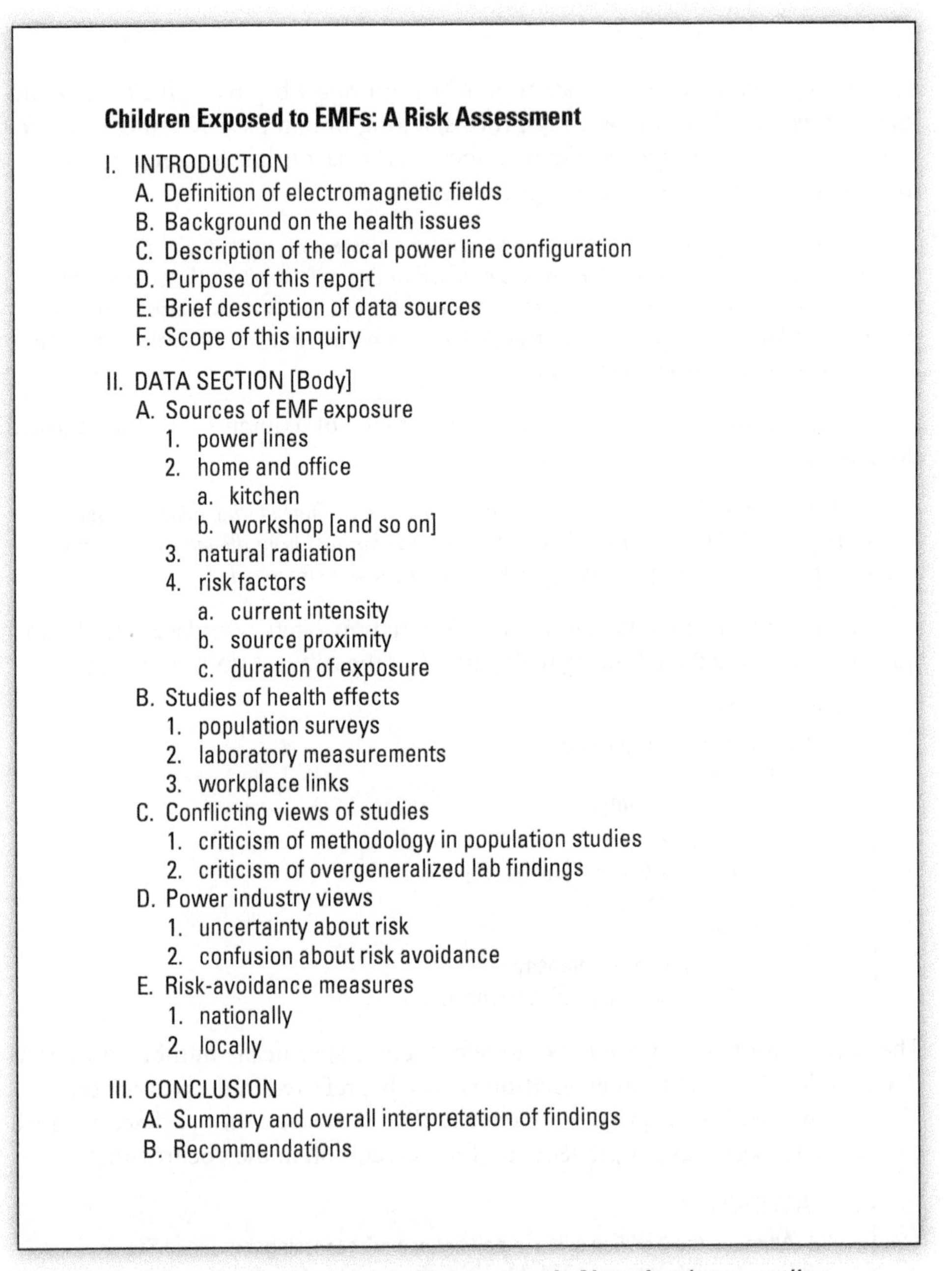

Children Exposed to EMFs: A Risk Assessment

I. INTRODUCTION
  A. Definition of electromagnetic fields
  B. Background on the health issues
  C. Description of the local power line configuration
  D. Purpose of this report
  E. Brief description of data sources
  F. Scope of this inquiry

II. DATA SECTION [Body]
  A. Sources of EMF exposure
    1. power lines
    2. home and office
      a. kitchen
      b. workshop [and so on]
    3. natural radiation
    4. risk factors
      a. current intensity
      b. source proximity
      c. duration of exposure
  B. Studies of health effects
    1. population surveys
    2. laboratory measurements
    3. workplace links
  C. Conflicting views of studies
    1. criticism of methodology in population studies
    2. criticism of overgeneralized lab findings
  D. Power industry views
    1. uncertainty about risk
    2. confusion about risk avoidance
  E. Risk-avoidance measures
    1. nationally
    2. locally

III. CONCLUSION
  A. Summary and overall interpretation of findings
  B. Recommendations

FIGURE 3 **A Formal Outline Using Alphanumeric Notation** In an outline, *alphanumeric notation* refers to the use of letters and numbers.

NOTE *The neat and ordered outlines in this text show the final* ***products*** *of writing and organizing, not the* ***process,*** *which is often initially messy and chaotic. Many writers don't start out with an outline at all! Instead, they scratch and scribble with pencil and paper or click away at the keyboard, making lots of false starts as they hammer out some kind of acceptable draft; only then do they outline to get their thinking straight.*

Not until you finish the final draft of a long document do you compose the finished outline. This outline serves as a model for your table of contents, as a check on your reasoning, and as a way of revealing to readers a clear line of thinking.

NOTE *No single form of outline should be followed slavishly. The organization of any document ultimately is determined by the reader's needs and expectations. In many cases, specific requirements about a document's organization and style are spelled out in a company's style guide.*

GUIDELINES for Outlining

- **List key topics and subtopics to be included in your document.** Determine what information is important to include.
- **Set up a standard outline.** Start with a typical introduction, body, and conclusion structure, even if you plan to vary the structure later.
- **Place key topics and subtopics where they fit within your standard outline.** Keep your introduction brief, setting the stage for the rest of your document. Include your specific data in the body section, to back up what you promised in your introduction. Do not introduce new data in the conclusion.
- **Use alphanumeric or decimal notation consistently throughout the outline.**
- **Avoid excessive subtopics.** If you find that your outline is getting into multiple levels of detail too often, think of ways to combine information. Do not go to another level unless there are at least two distinct subtopics at that level.
- **Refine your outline as you write your document.** Continue revising the outline until you complete the document.

STORYBOARDING

As you prepare a long document, one useful organizing tool is the *storyboard,* a sketch of the finished document.

Visualize each section of your outline

Figure 4 displays one storyboard module based on Section II.A of the outline. Much more specific and visual than an outline, a storyboard

section title	Sources of EMF Exposure
text	Discuss milligauss measurements as indicators of cancer risk
text	Brief lead-in to power line emissions
visual	EPS table comparing power line emissions at various distances
text	Discuss EMF sources in home and office
visual	Table comparing EMF emissions from common sources
text	Discuss major risk factors: Voltage versus current; proximity versus duration of exposure; sporadic, high-level exposure versus constant, low-level exposure
visual	Line graph showing strength of exposure in relation to distance from electrical appliances
text	Focus on the key role of proximity to the EMF source in risk assessment

Special considerations:

- Define all specialized terms (current, voltage, milligauss, and so on) for a general audience.
- Emphasize that no "safe" level of EMF exposure has been established.
- Emphasize that even the earth's magnetic field emits significant electromagnetic radiation.

FIGURE 4 **One Module from a Storyboard** Notice how the module begins with the section title, describes each text block and each visual, and includes suggestions about special considerations.

maps out each section (or module) of your outline, topic by topic, to help you see the shape and appearance of the entire document in its final form. Working from a storyboard, you can rearrange, delete, and insert material as needed—without having to wrestle with a draft of the entire document.

Storyboarding is especially helpful when people collaborate to prepare various parts of a document and then get together to edit and assemble their material. In such cases, storyboard modules may be displayed on whiteboards, posterboards, flip charts, or computer screens.

> **NOTE** *Try creating a storyboard after writing a full draft, for a bird's-eye view of the document's organization.*

PARAGRAPHING

¶

Readers look for orientation, for shapes they can recognize. But a document's larger design (introduction, body, conclusion) depends on the smaller design of each paragraph.

Shape information into paragraphs

Paragraphs have various shapes and purposes (introduction, conclusion, or transition), but the focus here is on standard *support paragraphs*. Although part of the document's larger design, each support paragraph can usually stand alone in meaning.

The Support Paragraph

All the sentences in a standard support paragraph relate to the main point, which is expressed as the *topic sentence:*

Topic sentences

> As sea levels rise, New York City faces increasing risk of hurricane storm surge.

> A video display terminal can endanger the operator's health.

> Chemical pesticides and herbicides are both ineffective and hazardous.

Each topic sentence introduces an idea, judgment, or opinion. But in order to grasp the writer's exact meaning, people need explanation. Consider the third statement:

> Chemical pesticides and herbicides are both ineffective and hazardous.

Imagine that you are a researcher for the Epson Electric Light Company, assigned this question: Should the company (1) begin spraying pesticides and herbicides under its power lines, or (2) continue with its manual (and nonpolluting) ways of minimizing foliage and insect damage to lines and poles? If you simply responded with the preceding assertion, your employer would have further questions:

- Why, exactly, are these methods ineffective and hazardous?
- What are the problems? Can you explain?

To answer the previous questions and to support your assertion, you need a fully developed paragraph:

Introduction (1-topic sentence)

Body (2–6)

Conclusion (7–8)

> [1]**Chemical pesticides and herbicides are both ineffective and hazardous.** [2]Because none of these chemicals has permanent effects, pest populations invariably recover and need to be resprayed. [3]Repeated applications cause pests to develop immunity to the chemicals. [4]Furthermore, most of these products attack species other than the intended pest, killing off its natural predators, thus actually increasing the pest population. [5]Above all, chemical residues survive in the environment (and living tissue) for years, often carried hundreds of miles by wind and water. [6]This toxic legacy includes such biological effects as birth deformities, reproductive failures, brain damage, and cancer. [7]Although intended to control pest populations, these chemicals ironically threaten to make the human population their ultimate victims. [8]I therefore recommend continuing our manual control methods.

Most standard support paragraphs in technical writing have an introduction-body-conclusion structure. They begin with a clear topic (or orienting) sentence stating a generalization. Details in the body support the generalization.

ts The Topic Sentence

Readers look to a paragraph's opening sentences for the main idea. The topic sentence should appear *first* (or early) in the paragraph, unless you have good reason to place it elsewhere. Think of your topic sentence as "the one sentence you would keep if you could keep only one" (U.S. Air Force Academy 11). In some instances, a main idea may require a "topic statement" consisting of two or more sentences, as in this example:

A topic statement can have two or more sentences

> The most common strip-mining methods are open-pit mining, contour mining, and auger mining. The specific method employed will depend on the type of terrain that covers the coal.

The topic sentence or topic statement should focus and forecast. Don't write *Some pesticides are less hazardous and often more effective than others* when you mean *Organic pesticides are less hazardous and often more effective than their chemical counterparts.* The first version is vague; the second helps us focus and tells us what to expect from the paragraph.

¶un Paragraph Unity

A paragraph is unified when all its content belongs—when every word, phrase, and sentence directly expands on the topic sentence.

Solar power offers an efficient, economical, and safe solution to the Northeast's energy problems. To begin with, solar power is highly efficient. Solar collectors installed on fewer than 30 percent of roofs in the Northeast would provide more than 70 percent of the area's heating and air-conditioning needs. Moreover, solar heat collectors are economical, operating for up to twenty years with little or no maintenance. These savings recoup the initial cost of installation within only ten years. Most important, solar power is safe. It can be transformed into electricity through photovoltaic cells (a type of storage battery) in a noiseless process that produces no air pollution—unlike coal, oil, and wood combustion. In contrast to its nuclear counterpart, solar power produces no toxic waste and poses no catastrophic danger of meltdown. Thus, massive conversion to solar power would ensure abundant energy and a safe, clean environment for future generations.

A unified paragraph

One way to damage unity in the paragraph above would be to veer from the focus on *efficient*, *economical*, and *safe* toward material about the differences between active and passive solar heating or the advantages of solar power over wind power.

Every topic sentence has a key word or phrase that carries the meaning. In the pesticide-herbicide paragraph, the key words are *ineffective* and *hazardous*. Anything that fails to advance their meaning throws the paragraph—and the readers—off track.

Paragraph Coherence

¶coh

In a coherent paragraph, everything not only belongs, but also sticks together: Topic sentence and support form a *connected line of thought*, like links in a chain.

Paragraph coherence can be damaged by (1) short, choppy sentences; (2) sentences in the wrong order; (3) insufficient transitions and connectors for linking related ideas; or (4) an inaccessible line of reasoning. Here is how the solar energy paragraph might become incoherent:

Solar power offers an efficient, economical, and safe solution to the Northeast's energy problems. Unlike nuclear power, solar power produces no toxic waste and poses no danger of meltdown. Solar power is efficient. Solar collectors could be installed on fewer than 30 percent of roofs in the Northeast. These collectors would provide more than 70 percent of the area's heating and air-conditioning needs. Solar power is safe. It can be transformed into electricity. This transformation is made possible by photovoltaic cells (a type of storage battery). Solar heat collectors are economical. The photovoltaic process produces no air pollution.

An incoherent paragraph

In the above paragraph, the second sentence, about safety, belongs near the end. Also, because of short, choppy sentences and insufficient links between ideas, the paragraph reads more like a list than a flowing discussion. Finally, a concluding sentence is needed to complete the chain of reasoning and to give readers a clear perspective on what they've just read.

Here, in contrast, is the original, coherent paragraph with sentences numbered for later discussion; transitions and connectors are shown in boldface. Notice how this version reveals a clear line of thought:

A coherent paragraph

> [1]Solar power offers an efficient, economical, and safe solution to the Northeast's energy problems. [2]**To begin with**, solar power is highly efficient. [3]Solar collectors installed on fewer than 30 percent of roofs in the Northeast would provide more than 70 percent of the area's heating and air-conditioning needs. [4]**Moreover**, solar heat collectors are economical, operating for up to twenty years with little or no maintenance. [5]**These savings** recoup the initial cost of installation within only ten years. [6]**Most important**, solar power is safe. [7]**It** can be transformed into electricity through photovoltaic cells (a type of storage battery) in a noiseless process that produces no air pollution—unlike coal, oil, and wood combustion. [8]**In contrast** to its nuclear counterpart, solar power produces no toxic waste and poses no danger of catastrophic meltdown. [9]**Thus**, massive conversion to solar power would ensure abundant energy and a safe, clean environment for future generations.

We can easily trace the sequence of thoughts in the previous paragraph:

1. The topic sentence establishes a clear direction.
2–3. The first reason is given and then explained.
4–5. The second reason is given and explained.
6–8. The third and major reason is given and explained.
9. The conclusion reemphasizes the main point.

To reinforce the logical sequence, related ideas are combined in individual sentences, and transitions and connectors signal clear relationships. The whole paragraph sticks together.

¶lgth

Paragraph Length

Paragraph length depends on the writer's purpose and the reader's capacity for understanding. Writing that contains highly technical information or complex instructions may use short paragraphs or perhaps a list. In writing that explains concepts, attitudes, or viewpoints, support paragraphs generally run from 100 to 300 words. But word count really means very little. What matters is *how thoroughly the paragraph makes your point.*

Try to avoid too much of anything. A clump of short paragraphs can make some writing seem choppy and poorly organized, but a stretch of long paragraphs can be tiring. A well-placed short paragraph—sometimes just one sentence—can highlight an important idea.

NOTE *In writing displayed on computer screens, short paragraphs and lists are especially useful because they allow for easy scanning and navigation.*

SEQUENCING

Arrange information in a logical progression

A logical sequence reveals a particular relationship: cause-and-effect, comparison-contrast, and so on. For instance, a progress report usually follows a *chronological* sequence (events in order of occurrence). An argument for a companywide exercise program would likely follow an *emphatic* sequence (benefits in order of importance—least to most, or vice versa).

A single paragraph usually follows one particular sequence. A longer document may use one sequence or a combination. Below are some common sequences illustrated in paragraph form.

Spatial Sequence

A spatial sequence begins at one location and ends at another. It is most useful in describing a physical item or a mechanism. You might describe the parts in the same sequence that readers would follow if they were actually looking at the item. Or you might follow the sequence in which each part functions (left to right, inside to outside, top to bottom). The following description of a hypodermic needle proceeds from the needle's base (hub) to its point.

"What are the parts, and how do they fit together?"

> A hypodermic needle is a slender, hollow steel instrument used to introduce medication into the body (usually through a vein or muscle). It is a single piece composed of three parts, all considered sterile: the hub, the cannula, and the point. The hub is the lower, larger part of the needle that attaches to the necklike opening on the syringe barrel. Next is the cannula (stem), the smooth and slender central portion. Last is the point, which consists of a beveled (slanted) opening, ending in a sharp tip. The diameter of a needle's cannula is indicated by a gauge number; commonly, a 24–25 gauge needle is used for subcutaneous injections. Needle lengths are varied to suit individual needs. Common lengths used for subcutaneous injections are 3/8, 1/2, 5/8, and 3/4 inch. Regardless of length and diameter, all needles have the same functional design.

Product and mechanism descriptions almost always have some type of visual to amplify the verbal description.

Chronological Sequence

A chronological sequence follows an actual sequence of events. Explanations of how to do something or how something happened generally follow a strict time sequence: first step, second step, and so on.

"In what order have things happened/should things happen?"

> Instead of breaking into a jog too quickly and risking injury, take a relaxed and deliberate approach. Before taking a step, spend at least ten minutes stretching and warming up, using any exercises you find comfortable. (After your first week, consult a jogging book for specialized exercises.) When you've completed your warmup, set a brisk pace walking. Exaggerate the distance between steps, taking long strides and swinging your arms briskly and loosely. After roughly one hundred yards at this brisk pace, you should feel ready to jog. Immediately break into a very slow trot: lean your torso forward and let one foot fall in front of the other (one foot barely leaving the ground while the other is on the pavement). Maintain the slowest pace possible, just above a walk. *Do not bolt out like a sprinter!* The biggest mistake is to start fast and injure yourself. While jogging, relax your body. Keep your shoulders straight and your head up, and enjoy the scenery—after all, it is one of the joys of jogging. Keep your arms low and slightly bent at your sides. Move your legs freely from the hips in an action that is easy, not forced. Make your feet perform a heel-to-toe action: land on the heel; rock forward; take off from the toe.

Effect-to-Cause Sequence

Problem-solving analyses typically use a sequence that first identifies a problem and then traces its causes.

"How did this happen?"

> Modern whaling techniques nearly brought the whale population to the threshold of extinction. In the nineteenth century, invention of the steamboat increased hunters' speed and mobility. Shortly afterward, the grenade harpoon was invented so that whales could be killed quickly and easily from the ship's deck. In 1904, a whaling station opened on Georgia Island in South America. This station became the gateway to Antarctic whaling for world nations. In 1924, factory ships were designed that enabled round-the-clock whale tracking and processing. These ships could reduce a ninety-foot whale to its by-products in roughly thirty minutes. After World War II, more powerful boats with remote sensing devices gave a final boost to the whaling industry. The number of kills had now increased far beyond the whales' capacity to reproduce.

Cause-to-Effect Sequence

A cause-to-effect sequence follows an action to its results. Below, the topic sentence identifies the causes, and the remainder of the paragraph discusses its effects.

"What will happen if I do this?"

> Some of the most serious accidents involving gas water heaters occur when a flammable liquid is used in the vicinity. The heavier-than-air vapors of a flammable liquid such as gasoline can flow along the floor—even the length of a basement—and be explosively ignited by the flame of the water heater's pilot light or burner. Because the victim's clothing frequently ignites, the resulting burn injuries are commonly serious and extremely painful. They may require long hospitalization, and can result in disfigurement or death. *Never, under any circumstances, use a flammable liquid near a gas heater or any other open flame.* (Consumer Product Safety Commission)

Emphatic Sequence

Emphasis makes important things stand out. Reasons offered in support of a specific viewpoint or recommendation often appear in workplace writing, as in the pesticide-herbicide paragraph or the solar energy paragraph. For emphasis, the reasons or examples are usually arranged in order of decreasing or increasing importance. In this paragraph, the most dramatic example appears last, for greatest emphasis.

> Although strip mining is safer and cheaper than conventional mining, it is highly damaging to the surrounding landscape. Among its effects are scarred mountains, ruined land, and polluted waterways. Strip operations are altering our country's land at the rate of 5,000 acres per week. An estimated 10,500 miles of streams have been poisoned by silt drainage in Appalachia alone. If strip mining continues at its present rate, 16,000 square miles of U.S. land will eventually be stripped barren.

"What should I remember most about this?"

Problem-Causes-Solution Sequence

The problem-solving sequence proceeds from description of the problem, through diagnosis, to a solution. After describing the cause of the problem, this next paragraph explains how the problem has been solved:

> On all waterfront buildings, the unpainted wood exteriors had been severely damaged by the high winds and sandstorms of the previous winter. After repairing the damage, we took protective steps against further storms. First, all joints, edges, and sashes were treated with water-repellent preservative to protect against water damage. Next, three coats of nonporous primer were applied to all exterior surfaces to prevent paint from blistering and peeling. Finally, two coats of wood-quality latex paint were applied over the nonporous primer. To keep coats of paint from future separation, the first coat was applied within two weeks of the priming coats, and the second within two weeks of the first. Two weeks after completion, no blistering, peeling, or separation has occurred.

"What was the problem, and how was it solved?"

Comparison-Contrast Sequence

Workplace writing often requires evaluation of two or more items on the basis of their similarities or differences.

> The ski industry's quest for a binding that ensures good performance as well as safety has led to development of two basic types. Although both bindings improve performance and increase the safety margin, they have different release and retention mechanisms. The first type consists of two units (one at the toe, another at the heel) that are spring-loaded. These units apply their retention forces directly to the boot sole. Thus the friction of boot against ski allows for the kind of ankle movement needed at high speeds over rough terrain, without causing the boot to

"How do these items compare?"

release. In contrast, the second type has one spring-loaded unit at either the toe or the heel. From this unit a boot plate travels the length of the boot to a fixed receptacle on its opposite end. With this plate binding, the boot has no part in release or retention. Instead, retention force is applied directly to the boot plate, providing more stability for the recreational skier, but allowing for less ankle and boot movement before releasing. Overall, the double-unit binding performs better in racing, but the plate binding is safer.

For comparing and contrasting more specific data on these bindings, two lists would be most effective.

The Salomon 555 offers the following features:

1. upward release at the heel and lateral release at the toe (thus eliminating 80 percent of leg injuries)
2. lateral antishock capacity of 15 millimeters, with the highest available return-to-center force
3. two methods of reentry to the binding: for hard and deep-powder conditions
4. five adjustments
5. (and so on)

The Americana offers these features:

1. upward release at the toe as well as upward and lateral release at the heel
2. lateral antishock capacity of 30 millimeters, with moderate return-to-center force
3. two methods of reentry to the binding
4. two adjustments, one for boot length and another for comprehensive adjustment for all angles of release and elasticity
5. (and so on)

Instead of this block structure (in which one binding is discussed and then the other), the writer might have chosen a point-by-point structure (in which points common to both items, such as "Reentry Methods" are listed together). The point-by-point comparison works best in feasibility and recommendation reports because it offers readers a meaningful comparison between common points.

CHUNKING

Break information down into smaller units

Each organizing technique discussed in this chapter is a way of *chunking* information: breaking it down into discrete, digestible units, based on the users' needs and the document's purpose. Well-chunked material generally is easier to follow and is more visually appealing.

Chunking enables us to show which pieces of information belong together and how the various pieces are connected. For example, a discussion about research in technical communication might be divided into two chunks:

- Procedural Stages
- Inquiry Stages

A major topic chunked into subtopics

Each of these units then divides into smaller chunks:

- Procedural Stages
  - Searching for Information
  - Recording Your Findings
  - Documenting Your Sources
  - Writing the Document
- Inquiry Stages
  - Asking the Right Questions
  - Exploring a Balance of Views
  - Achieving Adequate Depth in Your Search
  - Evaluating Your Findings
  - Interpreting Your Findings

Subtopics chunked into smaller topics

Any of these segments that become too long might be subdivided again.

NOTE *Chunking requires careful decisions about exactly how much is enough and what constitutes sensible proportions among the parts. Don't overdo it by creating such tiny segments that your document ends up looking fragmented and disconnected.*

In addition to chunking information verbally, we can chunk it visually.

Using visuals for chunking

Finally, we can chunk information by using white space, headings, or other forms of page design. A well-designed page provides immediate cues about where to look and how to proceed.

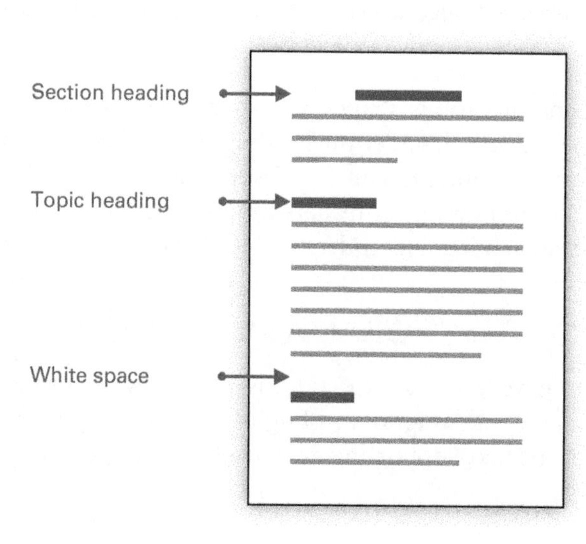

Using page design for chunking

Chunking on the Web versus chunking on a printed page

When you write for the Web, you chunk information differently than when you write for print. On Web pages, readers expect information in very short chunks because they don't like reading large blocks of text on a computer screen. Also, readers want the option of zeroing in on various parts of the page and of moving from link to link. In printed documents, however, readers tolerate longer passages of text because the printed page is easier on the eyes. Also, readers expect to *scan* a printed page sequentially rather than navigate a linked network.

PROVIDING AN OVERVIEW

Show the big picture

Once you've settled on a final organization for your document, give readers an immediate preview of its contents by answering their initial questions:

What readers want to know immediately

- What is the purpose of this document?
- Why should I read it?
- What information can I expect to find here?

Readers will have additional, more specific questions as well, but first they want to know what the document is all about and how it relates to them.

An overview should be placed near the beginning of a document, but you may also want to provide section overviews at the beginning of each section in a long document. The following is an overview of a long report on groundwater contamination.

A report overview

About This Report

This report contains five sections. Section One describes the scope and scale of groundwater contamination in Jackson county. Section Two offers background on previous legislation related to groundwater. Section Three shows the most recent data from the Jackson County Groundwater Project, and Section Four compares that data to national averages. Section Five offers recommendations and ideas for next steps.

Overviews come in various shapes and sizes. The overview for this text, for example, appears on page xxi, under the heading "How This Text is Organized." An informative abstract of a long document also provides an overview. Whatever its shape or size a good overview gives readers the "big picture" to help them navigate the document or presentation and understand its details.

ORGANIZING FOR GLOBAL AUDIENCES

Different cultures have varying expectations as to how information should be organized. For instance, a paragraph in English typically begins with a topic sentence, followed by related supporting sentences; any digression from this main idea is considered harmful to the paragraph's *unity.* But some cultures consider digression a sign of intelligence or politeness. To native readers of English, the long introductions and digressions in certain Spanish or Russian documents might seem tedious and confusing, but a Spanish or Russian reader might view the more direct organization of English as abrupt and simplistic (Leki 151).

Expectations differ even among same-language cultures. British correspondence, for instance, typically expresses the bad news directly up front, instead of taking the indirect approach preferred in the United States. A bad news letter or memo appropriate for a U.S. audience could be considered evasive by British readers (Scott and Green 19).

CHECKLIST for Organizing Information

- ☐ Does the document employ a standard or varied introduction/body/conclusion structure?
- ☐ Will the outline allow me to include all the necessary data for the document?
- ☐ Is this outline organized using alphanumeric or decimal notation?
- ☐ Have I created a storyboard to supplement my formal outline?
- ☐ Is the information chunked into discrete, digestible units for the proper medium (print or Web)?
- ☐ Does each paragraph include these features?
    - topic sentence (introduction)
    - unity (body that supports the topic sentence)
    - coherence (connected line of thought leading to a conclusion)
- ☐ Is the information in the correct sequence?
    - spatial: to describe a physical item or mechanism
    - chronological: to describe a sequence of events
    - cause-and-effect: to describe an incident and trace its causes or follow an action to its results
    - problem-causes-solution: to describe and diagnose a problem and offer a solution
    - emphatic: to arrange items in order of increasing or decreasing importance
    - comparison-contrast: to arrange items according to similarities or differences
- ☐ If appropriate, does the document include an overview, offering a larger picture of what will follow?
- ☐ Have I considered my audience's specific cultural expectations?

Chapter quiz, Exercises, Web links, and Flashcards
(Go to *Student Resources>Chapter 10*)

Projects

GENERAL

1. Locate, copy, and bring to class a paragraph that has the following features:
   - an orienting topic sentence
   - adequate development
   - unity
   - coherence
   - a recognizable sequence
   - appropriate length for purpose and audience

   Be prepared to identify and explain each of these features in a class discussion.

2. For each of the following documents, indicate the most logical sequence. (For example, a description of a proposed computer lab would follow a spatial sequence.)
   - instructions for operating a power tool
   - a campaign report describing your progress in political fund-raising
   - a report analyzing the weakest parts in a piece of industrial machinery
   - a report analyzing the desirability of a proposed nuclear power plant in your area
   - a detailed breakdown of your monthly budget to trim excess spending
   - a report investigating the reasons for student apathy on your campus
   - a report evaluating the effects of the ban on DDT in insect control
   - a report investigating the success of a no-grade policy at other colleges

TEAM

Assume your group is preparing a report titled "The Negative Effects of Strip Mining on the Cumberland Plateau Region of Kentucky." After brainstorming and researching, you all settle on four major topics:

- economic and social effects of strip mining
- description of the strip-mining process
- environmental effects of strip mining
- description of the Cumberland Plateau

Arrange these topics in the most sensible sequence.

Assume that subsequent research and further brainstorming produce this list of subtopics:

- method of strip mining used in the Cumberland Plateau region
- location of the region
- permanent land damage
- water pollution
- lack of educational progress
- geological formation of the region
- open-pit mining
- unemployment
- increased erosion
- auger mining
- natural resources of the region
- types of strip mining
- increased flood hazards
- depopulation
- contour mining

Arrange these subtopics under appropriate topic headings. Use decimal notation to create the body of a formal outline. Appoint one group member to present the outline in class.

Hint: Assume that your thesis is: "Decades of strip mining have devastated the Cumberland Plateau's environment, economy, and social structure."

DIGITAL

Locate a Web page and a print document (brochure, booklet, user guide) about the same product. Compare these, looking for the different ways in which material is organized on the Web versus in print.

Compare, for example, the use of headings, looking for differences. In class, give a short presentation on these differences.

GLOBAL

Find a document that presents the same information in several languages (assembly instructions, for example). Even without being able to understand all of the languages used, see if you can spot any changes made in the use of headings, the length of paragraphs, or the extent to which information is chunked. Interview a language professor on campus to find out why these choices may have been made.

For more support in mastering the objectives of this chapter, go to **www.mytechcommlab.com**

Designing and Testing Documents for Usability

Designing and Testing Documents for Usability

"When researching a topic for a manual, I focus on usability by trying to anticipate my audience's needs and asking the technical source person (usually a programmer or a systems analyst) specific questions keyed to my audience's needs: Who performs the task? What materials are required? What does the task accomplish? What can go wrong? Once a decent draft is written, our team asks potential readers to perform the tasks and to report any problems they encountered. Based on reader feedback, we revise and retest as often as needed until we get it right."

—Pam Herbert,
Technical Writer, software firm

LEARNING OBJECTIVES FOR THIS CHAPTER

- Know how usability testing helps your readers
- Understand why a usable design is essential
- Achieve a usable design
- Write, test, and revise your document
- Identify ethical and global issues that affect usability
- Differentiate usability of print versus online/multimedia documents

When you design and write any type of workplace or technical document, your end goal is for readers to be able to *use* the document effectively and easily. For instance, if you are creating a manual to accompany a lawnmower, you need to ensure that people who purchase the mower can assemble and operate it safely. But how can you be sure that the document works as you want it to?

Chapter overview
(Go to *Student Resources>Chapter 14> Overview*)

Definition of usability testing

To answer this question, companies routinely conduct what is called *usability testing* as a way to observe how people use a document. Information that is collected during this testing can be employed to revise and change the document before it becomes finalized.

A *usable* document is safe, dependable, and easy-to-read and navigate. Regardless of the type or format (print or digital) of the document, a usable document allows people to do three things (Coe, *Human Factors* 193; Spencer 74):

What a usable document enables readers to do

- easily locate the information they need
- understand the information immediately
- use the information safely and successfully

To assess the usability of a manual that accompanies a lawnmower, for example, you would ask: "How well do these instructions enable all readers of the document to assemble, operate, and maintain the mower safely, efficiently, and effectively?"

WHY USABLE DESIGN IS ESSENTIAL

From lawnmowers to consumer electronics, technology enables the creation of ever more elaborate products and gadgets. Unfortunately, with each new upgrade or innovation, many of these products seem to grow more complicated to use. The more complicated the product or task, the greater the need for usable documentation.

Flaws that reduce a document's usability

To keep their customers—and to avoid lawsuits—companies go to great lengths to eliminate flaws in their products and documents and to anticipate all the ways a product might fail or be misused. In any document, for example, usability can be compromised by inaccurate content, poor organization, unreadable style, inadequate visuals, or bad page design. Any such flaws—ranging from too much information to too few headings or hard-to-read type—can spell frustration or even disaster for people who use the document "in ways other than those intended" (van Der Meij 219).

ACHIEVING A USABLE DESIGN

A usable document needs to meet specific criteria. You can determine these criteria by asking and answering the following basic questions about the people who will use the document, the tasks they need to perform, and the setting where the document will be used.

Questions for achieving usability

- What tasks will people need to perform to achieve their goals?
- What do we know about the specific audience's abilities and limitations?
- In what setting will the document be read/used?

Figure 1 outlines specific ways of applying these questions.

The strategies that follow will help you answer the previous questions.

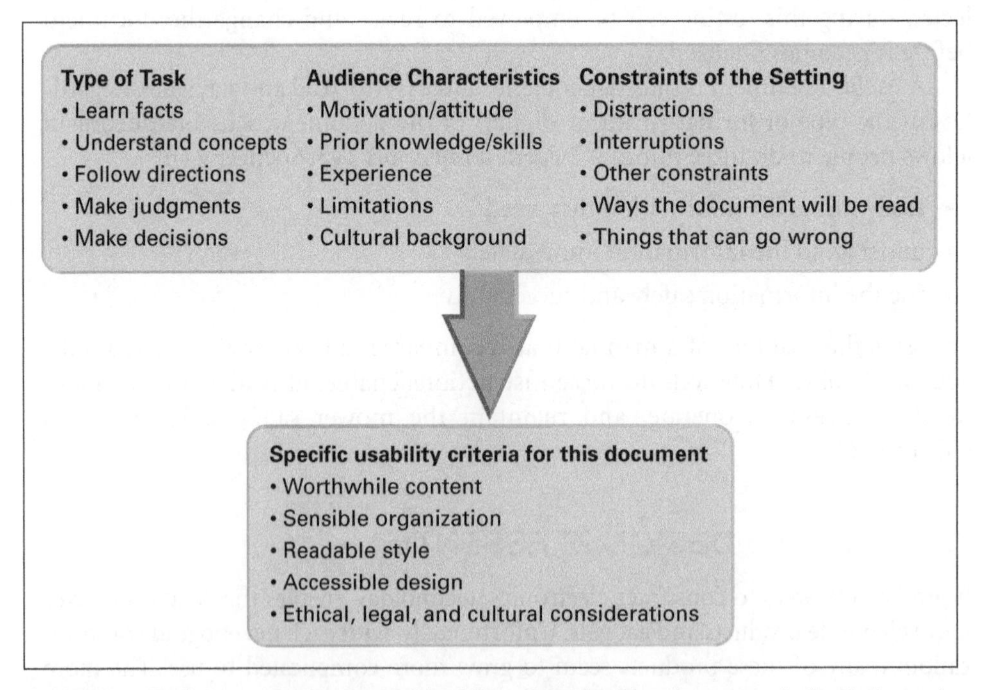

FIGURE 1 **Defining a Document's Usability Criteria** The document's final shape is based on careful analysis of the tasks involved, the people using the document, and the setting.

Analyze the Document's Audience, Purpose, and Setting

To identify the intended readers and their goals for your document, consult the Guidelines for Preparing and Testing a Document for Usability.

"Who are the readers?"

Once you have determined what readers will do with your information, write out a clear audience and purpose statement that will guide your planning and writing decision.

"What should this document accomplish?"

Also consider the conditions under which the document will be used: Will distractions or interruptions make it hard to pay attention? Will readers always have the document in front of them? Will they be scanning the document, studying it, or memorizing it? Will they read page-by-page or consult the document only randomly?

"How will the setting affect use of this document?"

Do the Research

Pinpoint the typical readers of the product being documented (age, education, and so on). For example, you might interview typical customers or survey previous purchasers of other models made by your company. Or observe first-time operators coping with a manual for an earlier model and then ask for their feedback. Find out how most injuries from lawnmowers occur. Check company records for customer complaints about safety problems. Consult retail dealers for their feedback. Ask your company's legal department about prior injury claims by customers. The more you know, the better.

"Have I learned all I can in advance?"

Identify the Performance Objectives for the Document

Spell out the *performance objectives*, the precise tasks that readers must accomplish successfully (or the precise knowledge they must acquire) (Carliner, "Physical" 564; Zibell 13). These tasks are most apparent when the document is a set of instructions, say, for installing software or for using a new piece of medical equipment. But other forms of communication, such as reports and memos, also involve tasks for the reader. For instance, a project manager might read daily progress reports to keep track of a team's work activities and to plan future activities; or the manager might study an accident report to learn all the facts before drafting a proposal for stricter safety procedures. A potential investor might need to understand the concept of gene therapy before deciding to invest in a biomedical company. In short, people read the document because they want to use this information to *do* something.

"What do I want my readers to do with this information?"

To define the tasks or topics your document will cover, develop an outline of steps and substeps (or of major points and supporting points). In preparing an instruction manual to accompany a lawnmower, for example, you might specify the performance objectives shown in the task outline in Figure 2.

Performance Objectives for Using the Model 76 Boban Lawnmower

1. Assemble the lawnmower
   a. Remove the unit from the carton.
   b. Assemble the handle.
   c. Assemble the cover plate.
   d. Connect the spark plug wire.
2. Operate the lawnmower
   a. Add oil and fuel.
   b. Adjust the cutting height.
   c. Adjust the engine control.
   d. Start the engine.
   e. Mow the grass.
   f. Stop the engine.
3. Maintain the lawnmower
   a. Clean the mower after each use.
   b. Keep oil level full and key parts lubricated.
   c. Replace the air filter as needed.
   d. Keep the blade sharpened.

FIGURE 2 **A Task Outline** You can determine these tasks by interviewing the lawnmower's designers and by watching "model" readers perform the actions.

Many of the substeps in Figure 2 can be divided further: For example, "Press primer bulb" and "Hold down control handle" are part of starting the engine.

Identify Possible Hazards or Sources of Error

"What are the trouble spots?"

How might the document be misinterpreted or misunderstood? Are there any potential "trouble spots" (material too complex for these readers, too hard to follow, or too loaded with information)?

CREATING A DESIGN PLAN

A document plan ensures you achieve usability

Once you have a clear picture of the audience, purpose, setting, background information, performance objectives, and possible trouble spots for your document, you can specify what the document should contain and how it should look.

Your *design plan* is your blueprint for achieving usability. A design plan is especially important in collaborative work, so that group members can coordinate their efforts throughout the document's production. In preparing the instruction manual to accompany the Boban Lawnmower, for example, you might submit the design plan shown in Figure 3.

NOTE *Depending on its complexity, some other type of document (say, a memo) would call for a far simpler design plan—perhaps merely a rough outline; a long proposal, on the other hand, would call for a far more intricate plan.*

WRITING, TESTING, AND REVISING YOUR DOCUMENT

Write, test, and revise after thorough planning

When your analysis and planning are complete, you can write, test, and revise the document. For a lawnmower manual, you would write the instructions, design the graphics, and select a medium (print, CD, Web—or some combination) for distributing the information.

Usability test and report (Go to *Student Resources>Chapter 14>Models and Templates*)

Once you have a workable draft, test the document on potential readers, if possible. Ask people what they find useful—or confusing. Or observe people using the material and then measure their performance. If someone trying to assemble a lawnmower, for instance, cannot locate a part because of unclear instructions, this information will be valuable as you revise your material.

The goal of usability testing is to keep what works in a project or a document and to fix what doesn't. Figure 4, for example, is designed to assess reader needs and preferences for the *Statistical Abstract of the United States*, a widely consulted publication that is updated yearly.

To obtain valuable reader feedback on your document, consult the guidelines later in this chapter. Based on reader feedback, revise your plan and your draft document. If readers find a technical term hard to understand, define it clearly, or use a simpler word or concept. If a graphic makes no sense, find one that does, and so on.

To guide your revision, consult the Usability Checklist. This checklist identifies broad usability standards that apply to virtually any document. In addition, specific elements (visuals, page layout) and specific document types (proposals, memos, instructions) have their own standards.

Boban Lawnmowers, Inc.

7/5/10

To: Manual Design Team
From: Jessica Brown and Fred Bowen, team leaders J.B., F.B.
Subject: **Audience/Use Profile and Design Plan for the Model 76 User Manual**

Based on the following analysis, we offer a design plan for the Model 76 user manual, which will provide safe and accurate instructions for assembling, operating, and maintaining the lawnmower.

PART ONE: AUDIENCE AND USE PROFILE

Audience
The audience is extremely diverse, ranging from early teens to retirees. Some may be using a walk-behind power mower for the first time; others are highly experienced. Some are mechanically minded; others are not. Some will mow with reasonable caution; others will not.

Setting and Hazards
The 76 mower will be used in the broadest variety of settings and conditions, ranging from manicured lawns to wet grass or rough terrain littered with branches, stones, and even small tree stumps. Also, the operator will need to handle gasoline on a regular basis.

Our research indicates that most user injuries fall into three categories, in descending order of frequency: foreign objects thrown into the eyes, contact with the rotating blade, and fire or explosion from gasoline.

Research also suggests that most users read a lawnmower instruction manual (with varying degrees of attention) before initially using the mower, and they consult it later only when the mower malfunctions. Therefore, our manual needs to highlight safety issues as early as the cover page.

Purpose
This manual has three purposes:

1. Instruct the user in assembling, operating, and maintaining the lawnmower.
2. Provide safety instructions that comply with legal requirements.
3. Provide a phone number, Web address, and other contact information for people who have questions or who need replacement parts.

Performance Objectives
This manual will address three main tasks:

1. **How to assemble the lawnmower.** This task involves four simple steps that have to be done correctly to avoid damage and ensure smooth operation.
2. **How to operate the lawnmower.** This task requires constant vigilance. Because this is the part of the procedure when most injuries occur, we need to stress safety at all times.

FIGURE 3 **A Design Plan for the Lawnmower Manual** Here you incorporate your analysis of the tasks, readers, and setting along with a specific proposal for the content, shape, style, and layout of your document.

Design team, 7/5/10, page 2

3. **How to maintain the lawnmower.** To keep the mower in good operating condition, users need to attend to these steps regularly and to be especially careful to wear eye protection if they sharpen their own blade.

PART TWO: DESIGN PLAN

For a readable and accessible manual, we recommend this plan:

Tentative Outline

- Size, page layout, and color: $8\frac{1}{2}$" × 11" trim size; two-column pages; black ink on white paper.
- *Cover page:* Includes a drawing of the 76 mower and a highlighted reference to safety instructions throughout the manual.
- *Safety considerations:* Cautions and warnings displayed prominently before a given step.
- *Visuals:* Drawings and/or diagrams to accompany each step as needed.
- *Inside front cover:* Table of contents and customer contact information.
- *Introduction:* A complete listing of all safety warnings that appear at various points in the manual.
- *Section One:* A numbered list of steps for assembling the mower.
- *Section Two:* A numbered list of steps for operating the mower.
- *Section Three:* A bulleted list of tasks for maintaining the mower.

Production Schedule
The first units of Model 76 are scheduled to ship May 4, 2011, with a manual included. To meet that deadline, we propose this schedule:

January 15: First draft is completed and tested on sample users.

February 15: Manual is revised based on results of usability test.

March 15: After copyediting, proofreading, and final changes, manual goes to compositor.

April 10: Page proofs and art proofs are reviewed and corrected.

April 17: Corrected proofs go to the printer.

April 30: Finished manual is packaged for May 4 shipment.

FIGURE 3 *(Continued)*

FORM S-555
(8-3-94)

STATISTICAL ABSTRACT SURVEY

U.S. DEPARTMENT OF COMMERCE
BUREAU OF THE CENSUS

Please take a few minutes to answer the questions below. Your voluntary cooperation will help us continue to serve your needs as data users. When completed, please refold, **apply tape to the open edges at the top,** and drop in the mail. Thank you.

1a. Which sections do you refer to frequently? *Mark (X) all that apply.*

☐ Population
☐ Vital statistics
☐ Health
☐ Education
☐ Law enforcement
☐ Geography
☐ Parks and recreation
☐ Elections
☐ Federal government
☐ State and local government
☐ National defense
☐ Social insurance
☐ Labor force
☐ Income
☐ Prices
☐ Banking
☐ Business
☐ Communications
☐ Energy
☐ Science
☐ Land transportation
☐ Air and water transportation
☐ Agriculture
☐ Forests and fisheries
☐ Mining
☐ Construction and housing
☐ Manufactures
☐ Domestic trade
☐ Foreign commerce
☐ Outlying areas
☐ International statistics

b. Indicate topics for which you would like to see more coverage.

2. To what degree do you find our current presentation of data in tables clear, meaningful, and easy to understand? *Mark (X) one.*

☐ Very much ☐ Somewhat ☐ Not at all

3. Which of the following do you feel currently interferes with the clarity of the tables presented? *Mark (X) all that apply.*

☐ Hard to understand column headings and row indentations
☐ Too many numbers in the tables—too much data to absorb
☐ Not clear what numbers mean when they are rounded ("In thousands" or "in millions," for example)
☐ Too many notes in the tables
☐ Some concepts too difficult to understand
☐ Other — Specify

4. Please indicate which of these features you might like to see expanded or reduced in future editions.

Mark (X) the appropriate column for each feature.

Feature	Expand	Reduce	OK as is
a. State rankings *(pp. xii–xxi)*			
b. Telephone contact list *(pp. xxii–xxiv)*			
c. Introductory text for sections			
d. Guide to Sources *(pp. 887–925)*			
e. Metropolitan Concepts and Components *(pp. 926–935)*			
f. Statistical Methodology (now called Limitations of the Data) *(pp. 936–950)*			
g. Index *(pp. 959–1011)*			
h. Charts and graphs			

5. Indicate your level of satisfaction with the Abstract. *Mark (X) one.*

☐ Very satisfied ☐ Satisfied ☐ Indifferent ☐ Unsatisfied ☐ Very unsatisfied

FIGURE 4 **A Usability Survey** This survey yields valuable data in the form of reader feedback that can be used for improving future editions of *The Statistical Abstract.*
Source: U.S. Department of Commerce, Bureau of the Census.

GUIDELINES for Preparing and Testing a Document for Usability

- **Identify the document's purpose.** Determine how much *learning* versus *performing* is required in carrying out the task—and assess the level of difficulty (Mirel et al. 79; Wickens 232, 243, 250):
  - *Merely provide facts.* "How rapidly is this virus spreading?"
  - *Explore concepts or theories.* "What biochemical mechanism enables this virus to mutate?"
  - *Provide directions.* "How do I inject the vaccine?"
  - *Guide a complex activity that requires decisions or judgments.* "Is this diagnosis accurate?" "Which treatment option should I select?"

- **Analyze the audience and setting.** Determine which characteristics of the reader and the work setting (*human factors*) enhance or limit performance (Wickens 3):
  - *Abilities/limitations.* What do these readers know already? How experienced are they in this area? How educated? What cultural differences could create misunderstanding?
  - *Attitudes.* How motivated or attentive are they? How anxious or defensive? Do readers need persuading to pay attention or be careful?
  - *Reading styles.* Will readers be scanning the document, studying it, or memorizing it? Will they read page by page or randomly?
  - *Workplace constraints.* Under what conditions will the document be read? What distractions or interruptions does the work setting pose? (for example, procedures for treating a choking victim, posted in a busy restaurant kitchen) Will readers always have the document in front of them during the task?
  - *Possible failures.* What could go wrong?

- **Design the usability test.** Focus on specific problems:
  - *Content.* Too much or too little information? Inaccuracies?
  - *Organization.* Anything out of sequence, or hard to find or follow?
  - *Style.* Anything hard to understand, inexact, too complex, or wordy?
  - *Design.* Any confusing headings, or too many or too few? Excessively long lists or paragraphs, or steps? Overly complex or misleading visuals? Anything that could be clarified by a visual? Anything cramped and hard to read?
  - *Ethical, legal, and cultural considerations.* Any distortion of the facts? Possible legal or cross-cultural problems?

▶▶

GUIDELINES

Figure 5 shows a sample usability survey (Carliner, "Demonstrating Effectiveness" 258). Notice how the phrasing encourages readers to respond with examples instead of just "yes" or "no."

- **Get reader feedback.** Have respondents perform the task. Ask them to identify difficulties they encountered in reading the instructions and in performing the task. Even in a classroom, one form of usability testing known as "think-aloud protocol" can be done like this: Working in small groups, write a simple set of instructions (say, for assembling a set of Legos® into some particular configuration such as a set of three specifically sized and colored cubes stacked in decreasing sizes []). Without showing them the actual structure your group has assembled, have members from another group "think out loud" and talk to you while they work with your instructions. Have them describe any problems they experience during the procedure.

ETHICAL AND GLOBAL ISSUES AFFECTING USABILITY

Be sure your message is ethically sound

In all aspects of technical communication, readers expect a document that will serve their best interests. For example, people often are given children's car seats by a relative whose children are too big for this size seat. The instruction manual usually is long gone. So, some companies now print the instructions on a label that is glued onto the back of the seat. Both the design and testing of these instructions could save a life.

Even a document that conveys bad news should be straightforward, honest, and easy to understand. The document should also provide readers with the same clear view and interpretation of the material that its writer enjoys.

Respect cultural differences

For those readers whose cultural backgrounds and/or native languages differ from the standard North American model, matters of ethics and usability become increasingly complex. Depending on the specific culture, a document may have to be redesigned and/or translated, for example. In such cases, the resulting document may—however inadvertently—create misunderstanding or result in some form of exploitation. And, of course, the long reach of the Internet only increases the potential for any posted document to be misinterpreted or misunderstood.

PDF of The Basic Usability Survey (Go to *Student Resources>Chapter 14> Forms and Checklists*)

Although various chapters address cross-cultural issues, the range of possible scenarios affecting a document's ethical soundness and usability are far too

Basic Usability Survey

1. Briefly describe why this document is used. ______
2. Evaluate the *content:*
   - Identify any irrelevant information. ______
   - Indicate any gaps in the information. ______
   - Identify any information that seems inaccurate. ______
   - List other problems with the content. ______
3. Evaluate the *organization:*
   - Identify anything that is out of order or hard to locate or follow. ______
   - List other problems with the organization. ______
4. Evaluate the *style:*
   - Identify anything you misunderstood on first reading. ______
   - Identify anything you couldn't understand at all. ______
   - Identify expressions that seem wordy, inexact, or too complex. ______
   - List other problems with the style. ______
5. Evaluate the *design:*
   - Indicate any headings that are missing, confusing, or excessive. ______
   - Indicate any material that should be designed as a list. ______
   - Give examples of material that might be clarified by a visual. ______
   - Give examples of misleading or overly complex visuals. ______
   - List other problems with design. ______
6. Identify anything that seems misleading or that could create legal problems or cross-cultural misunderstanding. ______
7. Please suggest other ways of making this document easier to use. ______

FIGURE 5 **A Basic Usability Survey** Versions of these questions can serve as a basis for testing (by the document's readers).

diverse for the scope of this chapter. And so our advice here must remain highly general: Research as needed for a clear understanding of both your particular writing situation and the needs and expectations of your specific audience. Design your document using internationally recognized symbols. When testing, be sure that your test group has a sufficiently diverse set of participants; if the document has an international readership, for example, be sure the group includes a good balance of native and non-native English speakers. Finally, do not release your document until it has been carefully tested and revised to reflect sound ethical judgment and cultural sensitivity.

USABILITY ISSUES IN ONLINE AND DIGITAL DOCUMENTS

In contrast to printed documents, online and digital documents pose unique usability considerations:

Usability in online or multimedia documents

- Online documents tend to focus more on "doing" than on detailed explanations. Workplace readers typically use online documents for reference or training rather than for study or memorizing.
- Online instructions rarely need to overtly persuade (asking people to pay attention or follow instructions, for example) because readers are guided interactively through each step of the procedure.
- Visuals play a huge role in online instruction.
- Online documents are typically organized to be read interactively and selectively rather than in linear sequence. Readers move from place to place, depending on their immediate needs. Organization, therefore, is flexible and modular, with small bits of easily accessible information that can be combined to suit a particular reader's needs and interests.
- Digital documents, such as books, newspapers, and magazines produced for e-book readers such as the iPad or Kindle, are organized differently from their print counterparts. Content is structured in sections and sub-sections and arranged for quick skimming and reading. For instance, the *New York Times* Kindle edition organizes information into major sections, listing how many articles are in each section. Readers select a section, then skim titles and brief article summaries. Most devices allow readers to "clip" an article, add bookmarks and notes, and access built-in-dictionaries to look up unfamiliar words and terms. These features, along with search options, need to be plentiful and complete, to keep readers from feeling lost.

Figure 6 shows the home page for a Web site that offers a wealth of information on usability. Although the emphasis here is on Web pages, much of this material also applies to other digital documents.

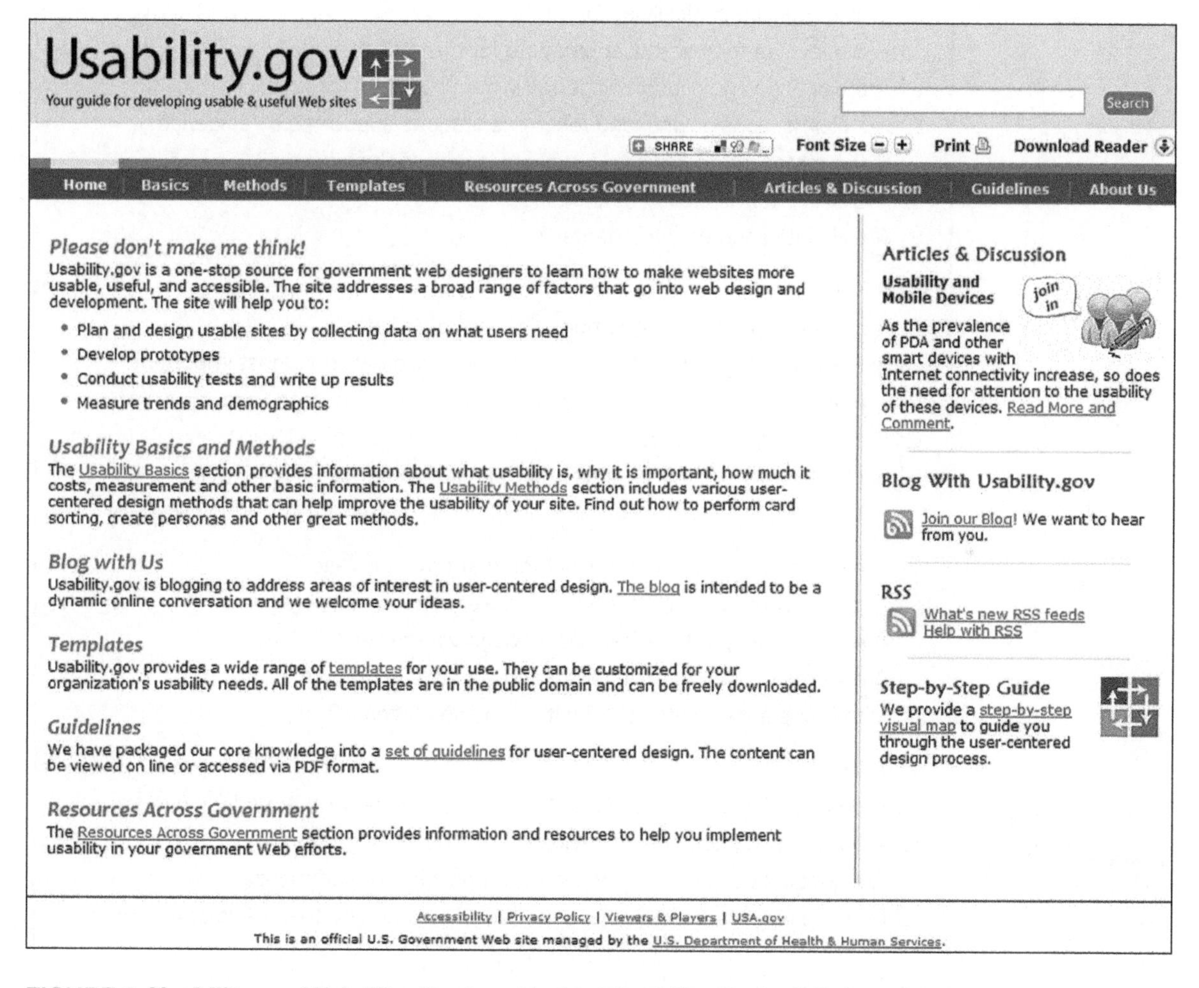

FIGURE 6 **Usability.gov Web Site** Begin with the "Usability Basics" link on this home page for up-to-date coverage of usability.

Source: www.usability.gov U.S. Department of Health.

CHECKLIST: Usability

Content

- ☐ Is all material relevant to this reader for this task?
- ☐ Is all material technically accurate?
- ☐ Is the level of technicality appropriate for this audience?
- ☐ Are warnings and cautions inserted where needed?
- ☐ Are claims, conclusions, and recommendations supported by evidence?
- ☐ Is the material free of gaps, foggy areas, or needless details?
- ☐ Are all key terms clearly defined?
- ☐ Are all data sources documented?

Organization

- ☐ Is the structure of the document visible at a glance?
- ☐ Is there a clear line of reasoning that emphasizes what is most important?
- ☐ Is material organized in the sequence readers are expected to follow?
- ☐ Is everything easy to locate?
- ☐ Is the material "chunked" into easily digestable parts?

Style

- ☐ Is each sentence understandable the first time it is read?
- ☐ Is rich information expressed in the fewest words possible?
- ☐ Are sentences put together with enough variety?
- ☐ Are words chosen for exactness, and not for camouflage?
- ☐ Is the tone appropriate for the situation and audience?

Page Design

- ☐ Is page design inviting, accessible, and appropriate for the readers' needs?
- ☐ Are there adequate aids to navigation (heads, lists, type styles)?
- ☐ Are adequate visuals used to clarify, emphasize, or summarize?
- ☐ Do supplements (front and end matter) accommodate the needs of a diverse audience?

Ethical, Legal, and Cultural Considerations

- ☐ Does the document reflect sound ethical judgment?
- ☐ Does the document comply with copyright law and other legal standards?
- ☐ Does the document respect readers' cultural diversity?

Chapter quiz, Exercises, Web links, and Flashcards (Go to *Student Resources> Chapter 14*)

Usability Case studies (Go to *Technical Communication Documents*)

Projects

GENERAL

1. As a class, identify an activity that could require instructions for a novice to complete (for example, surviving the first week of college as a commuter). Using the outline in Figure 2 as a model, prepare a task outline of the steps and substeps for this activity (for example, "1. Obtain essential items: campus map, ID card, parking sticker," and so on; "2. Get to know the library"; "3. Get to know your advisor"; "4. Establish a campus support network"). Exchange task outlines with another student in your class and critique each other's outlines. Revise your outline and be prepared to discuss it in class.
2. Find a set of instructions or some other technical document that is easy-to-use. Assume that you are Associate Director of Communications for the company that produced this document and you are doing a final review before the document is released. Using the Guidelines for Preparing and Testing a Document for Usability and the Checklist for Usability, identify those features that make the document usable and prepare a memo to your boss that justifies your decision to release the document.

   Following the identical scenario, find a document that is hard-to-use, and identify the features that need improving. Prepare a memo to your boss that spells out the needed improvements. Submit both memos and the examples to your instructor.

TEAM

Divide into teams. Test the usability of a document prepared for this course (submitted by one of your team members who has volunteered). As basis for your testing, refer to the guidelines, profile sheet, and checklist specified in General Project 2, and to whichever specific checklist applies to this particular document. As a team, revise the document based on your findings. Appoint a group member to explain the usability testing procedure and the results to the class.

DIGITAL

As Communications Director for your software company, you've decided to institute a "Usability Awareness" workshop for members of your writing team. As a first step, you've checked out the following Web sites on usability and decided to write a one-paragraph summary (or bulleted list) of the material to be found on each site. Your final memo will serve as a quick reference to usability resources for the writing team. Bring your completed memo to class for discussion.

Usability Resources on the Web

<www.useit.com>
<www.upassoc.org>
<www.plainlanguage.gov/howtoguidelines/bigdoc/testing.cfm>

GLOBAL

Assume that you are part of a team preparing a document for posting on your software company's Web site. This document describes the innovative features of your company's new line of architectural-design software for use by architects and structural engineers across the globe. Your assignment as a team member is to prepare a usable version of this basic document for an audience from a specific non-U.S. culture (choose one). Begin your project by googling "usability guidelines for global audiences" and searching out those sites that offer specific usability advice for your chosen audience. (Note: This search will require substantial effort on your part.) Make a one- or two-page list of the specific guidelines that pertain to your chosen audience, and convey this information in a memo to your team members. Be sure to cite the exact sources of your information.

For more support in mastering the objectives of this chapter, go to **www.mytechcommlab.com**

Technical Definitions

Mark Sykes/Alamy

"As a nurse practitioner, much of my working day is spent defining specialized terms for patients and their families: medical conditions, treatments and surgical procedures, medications and side effects, and so on. Most of today's patients—especially those facing complex health decisions—expect to be well-informed about the medical issues that affect their lives. Clear, understandable definitions are an important first step in providing the information people need."

—Dana Ballinger,
Nurse Practitioner in a primary-care clinic

LEARNING OBJECTIVES FOR THIS CHAPTER

- Appreciate the role of definition in technical communication
- Know how audience and purpose indicate the need for definition
- Consider the role of definitions within and beyond the workplace
- Differentiate among levels of detail in a definition
- Select the right level of detail as your situation requires
- Write an expanded definition
- Place definitions effectively in your document

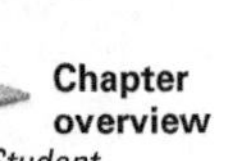

Chapter overview
(Go to *Student Resources>Chapter 19*)

Definitions explain terms or concepts that are specialized and may be unfamiliar to people who lack expertise in a particular field. In many cases, a term may have more than one meaning or different meanings in different fields. Consider a word such as *atmosphere*: To an astronomer, it would refer to the envelope of gases that surrounds a planet ("the Earth's atmosphere"); to a politician or office manager, it would typically mean the mood of the country or the workplace ("an atmosphere of high hopes"); to a physicist it would stand for a unit of pressure ("a standard atmosphere is 101,325 pascal"); and to a novelist it would be associated with the mood of a novel ("a gothic atmosphere").

Why definitions must be precise

Precision is particularly important in specialized fields, in which field-specific terminology is common and undefined terms may prevent the overall document from making sense. Engineers talk about *elasticity* or *ductility*; bankers discuss *amortization* or *fiduciary relationships*. These terms must be defined if people both inside and outside of those fields are to understand the document as a whole. Imagine if a doctor continually used the words *myocardial infarction* in a patient brochure without ever defining the term. The fact that a myocardial infarction is the medical name for one form of *heart attack* would be lost on patients who need to have a clear understanding of the brochure.

CONSIDERING AUDIENCE AND PURPOSE

Audience considerations

Definitions answer one of two questions: "What, exactly, is it?" or "What, exactly, does it entail?" The first question spells out what makes an item, concept, or process unique. For example, an engineering student needs to understand the distinction between *elasticity* and *ductility*. People in any audience have to grasp precisely what "makes a thing what it is and distinguishes that thing from all other things" (Corbett 38). The second question spells out for your audience how they are affected by the item defined. For example, a person buying a new computer needs to understand exactly what "manufacturer's guarantee" or "expandable memory" means in the context of that purchase.

Purpose considerations

Consider the purpose of defining particular terms in your document by answering the question "Why does my audience need to understand this term?" The level of technicality you use must match the audience's background and experience. For a group of mechanical engineering students, your definition of a *solenoid*, for example, can use highly technical language:

A highly technical version

> A solenoid is an inductance coil that serves as a tractive electromagnet.

For general audiences, your definition will require language they can understand:

A nontechnical version

> A solenoid is a metal coil that converts electrical energy to magnetic energy capable of performing mechanical functions.

Unless you are certain that your audience already knows the exact meaning, always define a term the first time you use it.

LEGAL, ETHICAL, SOCIETAL, AND GLOBAL IMPLICATIONS

Definitions have legal implications

Precise definition is essential, because you (or the organization, if you write a document on its behalf) are legally responsible for that document. For example, contracts are detailed (and legally binding) definitions of the specific terms of an agreement. If you lease an apartment or a car, the printed contract will define both the *lessee's* and *lessor's* specific responsibilities. Likewise, an employment contract or employee handbook will spell out responsibilities for both employer and employee. In preparing an employee handbook for your company, you would need to define such terms as *acceptable job performance*, *confidentiality*, *sexual harassment*, and *equal opportunity*.

Definitions have ethical implications

Definitions have ethical implications, too. For example, the term *acceptable risk* had an ethical impact on January 28, 1986, when the space shuttle *Challenger* exploded 73 seconds after launch, killing all seven crew members. (Two rubber O-ring seals in a booster rocket had failed, allowing hot exhaust gases to escape and igniting the adjacent fuel tank.) Hours earlier—despite vehement objections from the engineers—management had decided that going ahead with the launch was a risk worth taking. In this case, management's definition of *acceptable risk* was based not on the engineering facts but rather on bureaucratic pressure to launch on schedule. Agreeing on meaning in such cases rarely is easy, but you are ethically bound to convey an accurate interpretation of the facts as you understand them.

Definitions have societal implications

Clear and accurate definitions help the public understand and evaluate complex technical and social issues. For example, as a first step in understanding the debate over the term *genetic engineering*, we need at least the following basic definition:

A general but informative definition

> Genetic engineering refers to [an experimental] technique through which genes can be isolated in a laboratory, manipulated, and then inserted stably into another organism. Gene insertion can be accomplished mechanically, chemically, or by using biological vectors such as viruses. (Office of Technology Assessment 20)

Of course, to follow the debate, we would need increasingly detailed information (about specific procedures, risks, benefits, and so on). But the above definition gets us started on a healthy debate by enabling us to visualize the basic concept and to mutually agree on the basic meaning of the term.

Definitions have global implications

Ongoing threats to our planet's environment, the prospect of nuclear proliferation, and the perils of terrorism top a list of complex issues that make definitions vital to global communication. For example, on the environmental front, world audiences need a realistic understanding of concepts such as *greenhouse effect* or *ozone depletion*. On the nuclear proliferation front, the survival of our species could well depend on the clear definition of terms such as *nuclear non-proliferation treaty* or *non-aggression pact* by the nations who are parties to such agreements. On the terrorism front, the public wants to understand such terms as *biological terrorism* or *weapons of mass destruction*.

In short, definition is more than an exercise in busy work. Figure 1 illustrates the informative power of an effective definition.

TYPES OF DEFINITION

Three categories of definitions

Definitions fall into three distinct categories: *parenthetical*, *sentence*, and *expanded*. Decide how much detail your audience actually requires in order to grasp your exact meaning.

Parenthetical Definitions

When to use parenthetical definitions

Often, you can clarify the meaning of a word by using a more familiar synonym or a clarifying phrase in parentheses, as in these examples:

Parenthetical definitions

> The *leaching field* (sievelike drainage area) requires crushed stone.

> The trees on the site are mostly *deciduous* (shedding foliage at season's end).

On a Web page or online help system, these types of short definitions can be linked to the main word or phrase. Readers who click on *leaching field* would be taken to a window containing a brief definition.

DIRTY VERSUS NUCLEAR BOMBS

People sometimes confuse radiological with nuclear weapons.

A DIRTY BOMB is likely to be a primitive device in which TNT or fuel oil and fertilizer explosives are combined with highly radioactive materials. The detonated bomb vaporizes or aerosolizes the toxic isotopes, propelling them into the air.

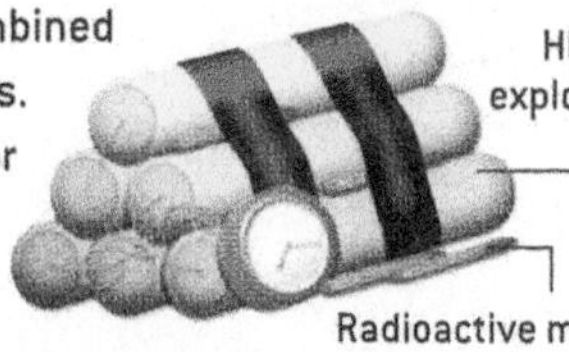

High explosives

Radioactive materials

A FISSION BOMB is a more sophisticated mechanism that relies on creating a runaway nuclear chain reaction in uranium 235 or plutonium 239. One type features tall, inward-pointing pyramids of plutonium surrounded by a shell of high explosives. When the bomb goes off, the explosives produce an imploding shock wave that drives the plutonium pieces together into a sphere containing a pellet of beryllium/polonium at the center, creating a critical mass. The resulting fission reaction causes the bomb to explode with tremendous force, sending high-energy electromagnetic waves and fallout into the air.

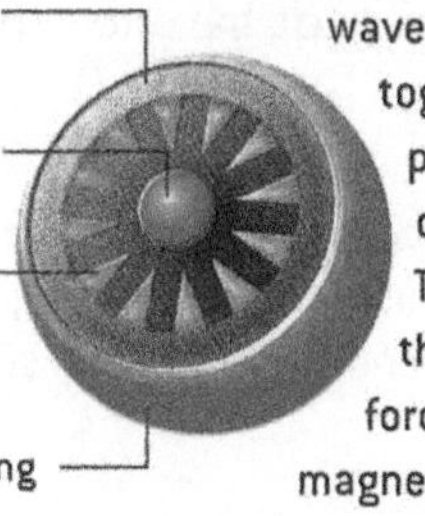

High explosives

Beryllium/polonium core

Plutonium pieces

Heavy casing

FIGURE 1 **Definition with Global Implications** In this example, two items are defined, to clarify an important distinction for the general public.

Source: 'Dirty Versus Nuclear Bomb' from "Weapons of Mass Disruption." Text by Henry C. Kelly and Michael A. Levi. Illustrations by Sara Chen. Published in Scientific American, November 2002.

Sentence Definitions

When to use sentence definitions

When a term requires more elaboration than a parenthetical definition can offer, use a sentence definition. Begin by stating the term. Then indicate the broader class to which this item belongs, followed by the features that distinguish it from other items in that general class. Here are examples:

Sentence definitions (term-class-features)

Term	**Class**	**Distinguishing Features**
A carburetor	a mixing device. . .	in gasoline engines that blends air and fuel into a vapor for combustion within the cylinders.

Diabetes	a metabolic disease...	caused by a disorder of the pituitary gland or pancreas and characterized by excessive urination, persistent thirst, and inability to metabolize sugar.
Stress	an applied force...	that strains or deforms a body.

The previous elements may be combined into one or more complete sentences:

A complete sentence definition

> Diabetes is a metabolic disease caused by a disorder of the pituitary gland or pancreas. This disease is characterized by excessive urination, persistent thirst, and inability to metabolize sugar.

Sentence definitions are especially useful if you plan to use a term often and need to establish a working definition that you will not have to repeat throughout the document:

A working definition

> Throughout this report, the term *disadvantaged student* will refer to all students who lack adequate funds to pay for on-campus housing, food services, and medical care, but who are able to pay for their coursework and books through scholarships and part-time work.

Expanded Definitions

When to use expanded definitions

Brief definitions are fine when your audience requires only a general understanding of a term. For example, the parenthetical definition of *leaching field* might be adequate in a progress report to a client whose house you're building. But a document that requires more detail, such as a public health report on groundwater contamination from leaching fields, would call for an expanded definition.

Likewise, the nontechnical definition of "solenoid" is adequate for a layperson who simply needs to know what a solenoid is. An instruction manual for mechanics, however, would define solenoid in much greater detail; mechanics need to know how a solenoid works and how to use and repair it.

Depending on audience and purpose, an expanded definition may be a short paragraph or may extend to several pages. For example, if a device, such as a digital dosimeter (used for measuring radiation exposure), is being introduced to an audience who needs to understand how this instrument works, your definition would require at least several paragraphs, if not pages.

METHODS FOR EXPANDING DEFINITIONS

An expanded definition can be created in any number of ways as described below. The method or methods you decide to use will depend on the questions you expect the audience will want answered, as illustrated in Figure 2.

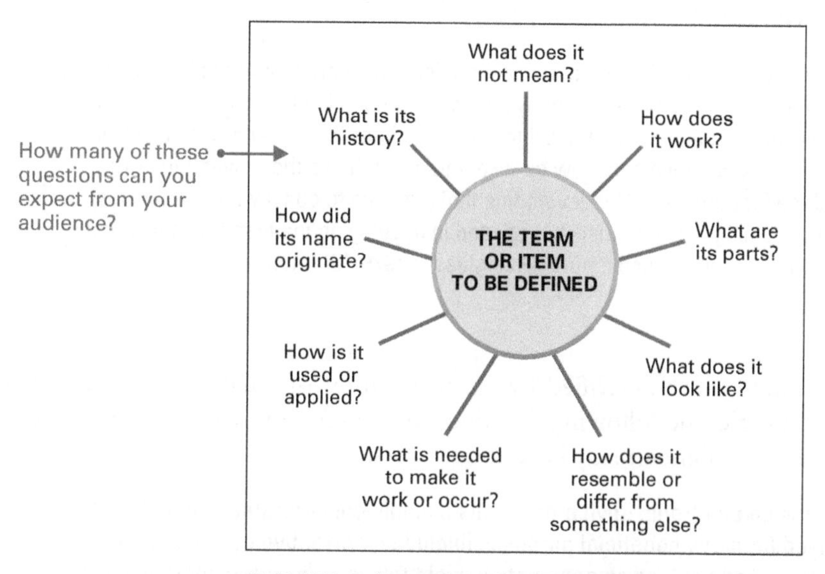

FIGURE 2 **Questions for Expanding a Definition**

As you read through the following sections, refer to the following sentence definition of the word *laser*, and consider how each expansion method provides detail in a different way:

> A laser is an electronic device that emits a highly concentrated beam of light.

Sentence definition

Etymology

Sometimes, a word's origin (its development and changing meanings), also known as the word's etymology, can help clarify its meaning. For example, *biometrics* (the statistical analysis of biological data) is a word derived from the Greek *bio*, meaning "life", and *metron*, meaning "measure." You can use a dictionary to learn the origins of most words. Not all words develop from Greek, Latin, or other roots, however. For example, some terms are acronyms, derived from the first letters or parts of several words. Such is the case with the word *laser* (derived from *light amplification by stimulated emission of radiation*); therefore, to expand the sentence definition of *laser*, you might phrase your definition as follows:

> The word *laser* is an acronym for *light amplification by stimulated emission of radiation*, and is the name for an electronic device that emits a highly concentrated beam of light.

"How did its name originate?"

History

In some cases, explaining the history of a term, concept, or procedure can be useful in expanding a definition. Specialized dictionaries and encyclopedias are good background sources. You might expand the definition of a laser by describing how the laser was invented:

"What is its history?"

> The early researchers in fiber optic communications were hampered by two principal difficulties—the lack of a sufficiently intense source of light and the absence of a medium which could transmit this light free from interference and with a minimum signal loss. Lasers emit a narrow beam of intense light, so their invention in 1960 solved the first problem. The development of a means to convey this signal was longer in coming, but scientists succeeded in developing the first communications-grade optical fiber of almost pure silica glass in 1970. (Stanton 28)

Negation

Some definitions can be clarified by an explanation of what the term *does not* mean. For example, the following definition of a laser eliminates any misconceptions an audience might already have about lasers:

"What does it not mean?"

> A laser is an electronic device that emits a highly concentrated beam of light. It is used for many beneficial purposes (including corrective eye and other surgeries), and not—as science fiction might tell you—as a transport medium to other dimensions.

Operating Principle

Anyone who wants to use a product correctly will need to know how it operates:

"How does it work?"

> Basically, a laser [uses electrical energy to produce] coherent light: light in which all the waves are in phase with each other, making the light hotter and more intense. (Gartaganis 23)

Analysis of Parts

To create a complete picture, be sure to list all the parts. If necessary, define individual parts as well, as in the following passage:

"What are its parts?"

> A laser is an electronic device that emits a highly concentrated beam of light. To get a better idea of how a laser works, consider its three main parts:
>
> 1. [Lasers require] a source of energy, [such as] electric currents or even other lasers.
> 2. A resonant circuit . . . contains the lasing medium and has one fully reflecting end and one partially reflecting end. The medium—which can be a solid, liquid, or gas—absorbs the energy and releases it as a stream of photons [electromagnetic particles that emit light]. The photons . . . vibrate between the fully and partially reflecting ends of the resonant circuit, constantly accumulating energy—that is,

they are amplified. After attaining a prescribed level of energy, the photons can pass through the partially reflecting surface as a beam of coherent light and encounter the optical elements.

3. Optical elements—lenses, prisms, and mirrors—modify size, shape, and other characteristics of the laser beam and direct it to its target. (Gartaganis 23)

Visuals

Make sure any visual you use is well labeled. Always introduce and explain your visual and place it near your discussion. If the visual is borrowed, credit the source. The following visual accompanies the previous analysis of parts:

"What does it look like?"

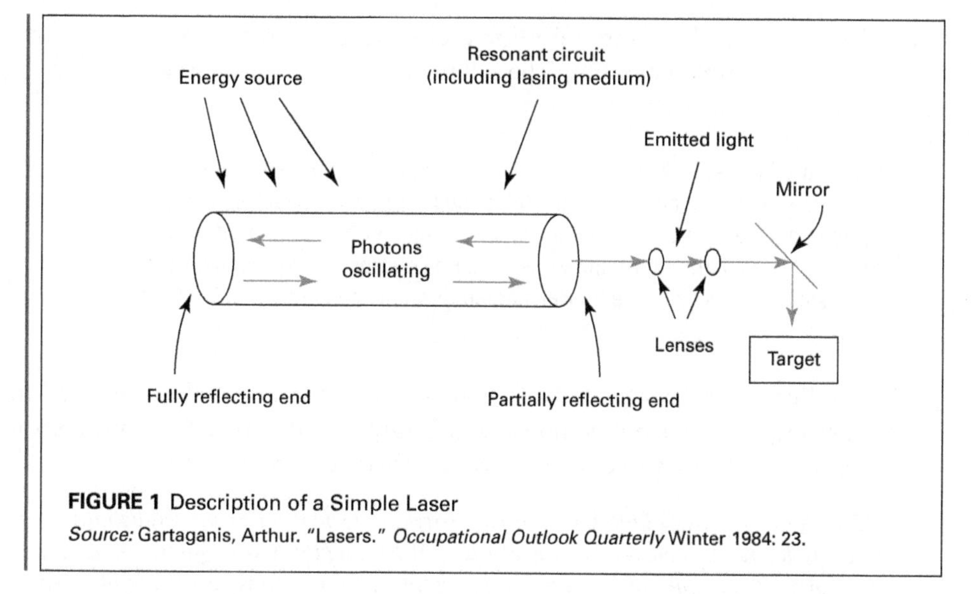

FIGURE 1 Description of a Simple Laser

Source: Gartaganis, Arthur. "Lasers." *Occupational Outlook Quarterly* Winter 1984: 23.

Comparison and Contrast

By comparing (showing similarities) or contrasting (showing differences) between new information and information your audience already understands, you help build a bridge between what people already know and what they don't. The following passage uses both comparison and contrast to expand upon a more basic definition of a laser:

"How does it resemble or differ from something else?"

Fiber optics technology results from the superior capacity of light waves to carry a communications signal. Sounds waves, radio waves, and light waves can all carry signals; their capacity increases with their frequency. Voice frequencies carried by telephone operate at 1000 cycles per second, or hertz. Television signals transmit at about 50 million hertz. Light waves, however, operate at frequencies in the hundreds of trillions of hertz. (Stanton 28)

Required Conditions

Some items or processes need special materials and handling, or they may have other requirements or restrictions. An expanded definition should include this important information:

"What is needed to make it work or occur?"

> In order to emit a highly concentrated beam of light, the laser must absorb energy through the reflecting end of a resonant circuit, amplify the photons produced between the reflecting and partially reflecting end of the resonant circuit, and release the photons as a beam of light via a set of lenses, prisms, and mirrors.

Examples

Examples are a powerful communication tool—as long as they are tailored to your audience's level of understanding. The following example shows how laser light is used in medical treatment:

"How is it used or applied?"

> Lasers are increasingly used to treat health problems. Thousands of eye operations involving cataracts and detached retinas are performed every year by ophthalmologists. . . . Dermatologists treat skin problems. . . . Gynecologists treat problems of the reproductive system, and neurosurgeons even perform brain surgery—all using lasers transmitted through optical fibers. (Gartaganis 24–25)

Use as many expansion methods as needed

Depending on the complexity of what you need to define, you may need to combine multiple expansion methods, as in Figures 3 and 4. Whichever expansion strategies you use, be sure to document your information sources.

NOTE *An increasingly familiar (and user-friendly) format for expanded definition, especially for readers on the Web, is a listing of Frequently Asked Questions (FAQ), which organizes chunks of information as responses to questions people are likely to ask. This question-and-answer format creates a conversational style and conveys to readers the sense that their particular concerns are being addressed. Consider using a FAQ list whenever you want to increase user interest and decrease resistance.*

SITUATIONS REQUIRING EXPANDED DEFINITIONS

The following two definitions (Figures 3 and 4) employ expansion methods suitable for their respective audiences' needs (and labeled in the margin). Like a good essay, both definitions are unified and coherent. Each paragraph is developed around one main idea and logically connected to other paragraphs. Transitions emphasize the connection between ideas. Visuals are incorporated. Each definition displays a level of technicality that is appropriate for the intended audience.

An Expanded Definition for Semitechnical Readers

The Situation. Ron Vasile, a lab assistant in his college's Electronics Engineering Technology program, has been asked to contribute to a reference manual for the program's incoming students. His first assignment is to prepare a section defining basic solenoid technology (Figure 3). As a way of getting started on this assignment, Ron creates the following audience and use profile.

Audience and Use Profile. The intended readers (future service technicians) are beginning student mechanics. Before they can repair a solenoid, they will need to know where the term *solenoid* comes from, what a solenoid looks like, how it works, how its parts operate, and how it is used. Diagrams will reinforce the explanations and enable readers to visualize this mechanism's parts and operating principle.

This definition is designed as an *introduction,* and so it offers only a general view of the mechanism. Because the readers are not engineering students, they do *not* need electromagnetic or mechanical theory (e.g., equations or graphs illustrating voltage magnitudes, joules, lines of force).

An Expanded Definition for Nontechnical Readers

The Situation. Amy Rogers has recently joined the public relations division of a government organization whose task is to explore the possible uses and applications of nanotechnology. She and other members of her division are helping to prepare a Web site that explains this complex topic to the general public. One of Amy's assignments is to prepare a definition of nanotechnology to be posted on the site. The definition shown in Figure 4 is written for hi-tech investors and other readers interested in new and promising technologies.

Audience and Use Profile. To understand *nanotechnology* and its implications, readers need an overview of what it is and how it developed, as well as its potential uses, present applications, health risks, and impact on the workforce. Question-type headings pose the questions in the same way readers are likely to ask them. Parenthetical definitions of *nanometer* and *micrometer* provide an essential sense of scale.

This audience would have little interest in the physics or physical chemistry involved, such as *carbon nanotubes* (engineered nanoparticles), *nanolasers* (advanced applications) or *computational nanotechnology* (theoretical aspects). They simply need the broadest possible picture, including a diagram that compares the size of nanoparticles with the size of more familiar items.

Each of these sample documents is developed from an audience and use profile.

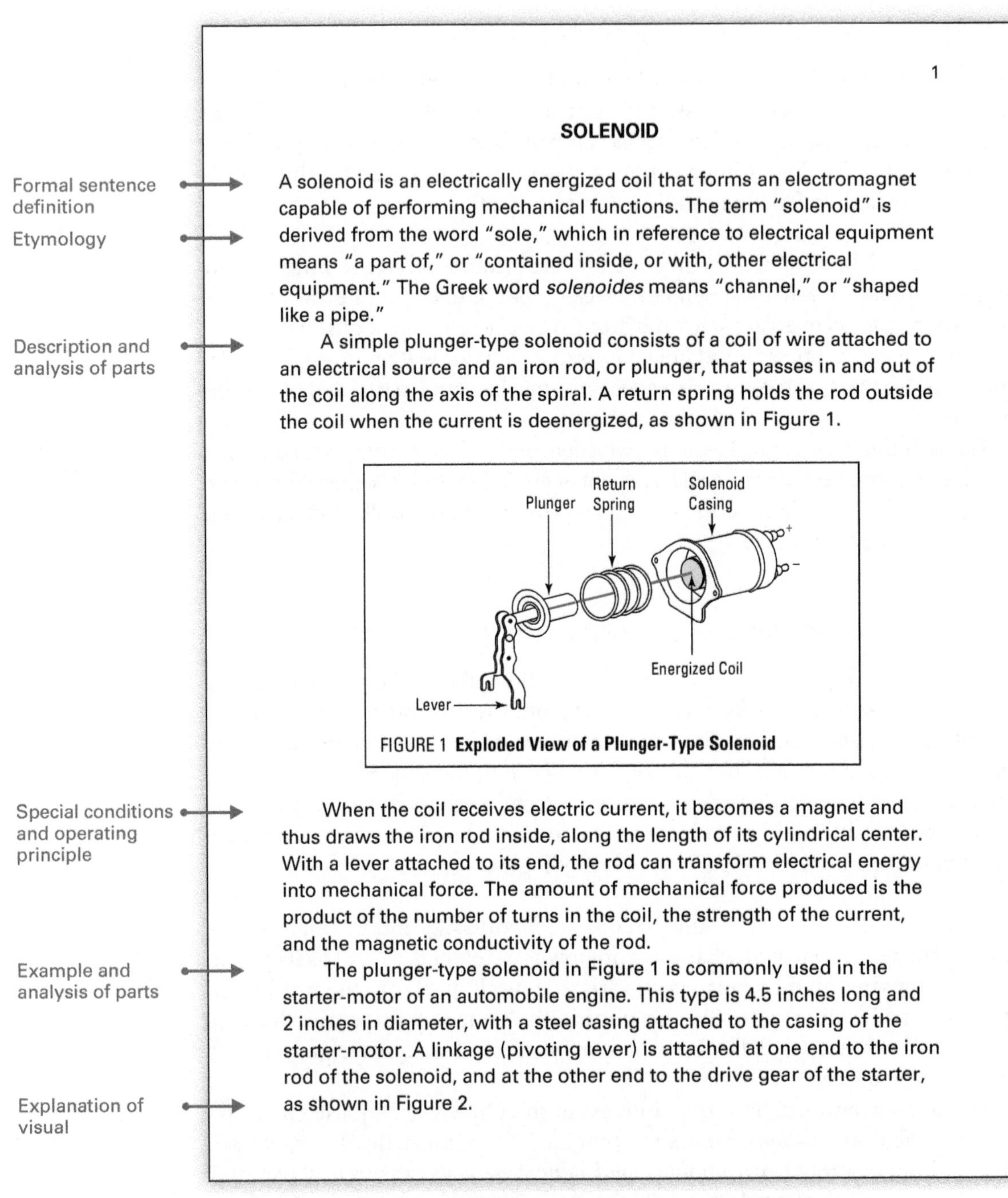

1

SOLENOID

A solenoid is an electrically energized coil that forms an electromagnet capable of performing mechanical functions. The term "solenoid" is derived from the word "sole," which in reference to electrical equipment means "a part of," or "contained inside, or with, other electrical equipment." The Greek word *solenoides* means "channel," or "shaped like a pipe."

A simple plunger-type solenoid consists of a coil of wire attached to an electrical source and an iron rod, or plunger, that passes in and out of the coil along the axis of the spiral. A return spring holds the rod outside the coil when the current is deenergized, as shown in Figure 1.

FIGURE 1 **Exploded View of a Plunger-Type Solenoid**

When the coil receives electric current, it becomes a magnet and thus draws the iron rod inside, along the length of its cylindrical center. With a lever attached to its end, the rod can transform electrical energy into mechanical force. The amount of mechanical force produced is the product of the number of turns in the coil, the strength of the current, and the magnetic conductivity of the rod.

The plunger-type solenoid in Figure 1 is commonly used in the starter-motor of an automobile engine. This type is 4.5 inches long and 2 inches in diameter, with a steel casing attached to the casing of the starter-motor. A linkage (pivoting lever) is attached at one end to the iron rod of the solenoid, and at the other end to the drive gear of the starter, as shown in Figure 2.

FIGURE 3 **An Expanded Definition for Semitechnical Readers**

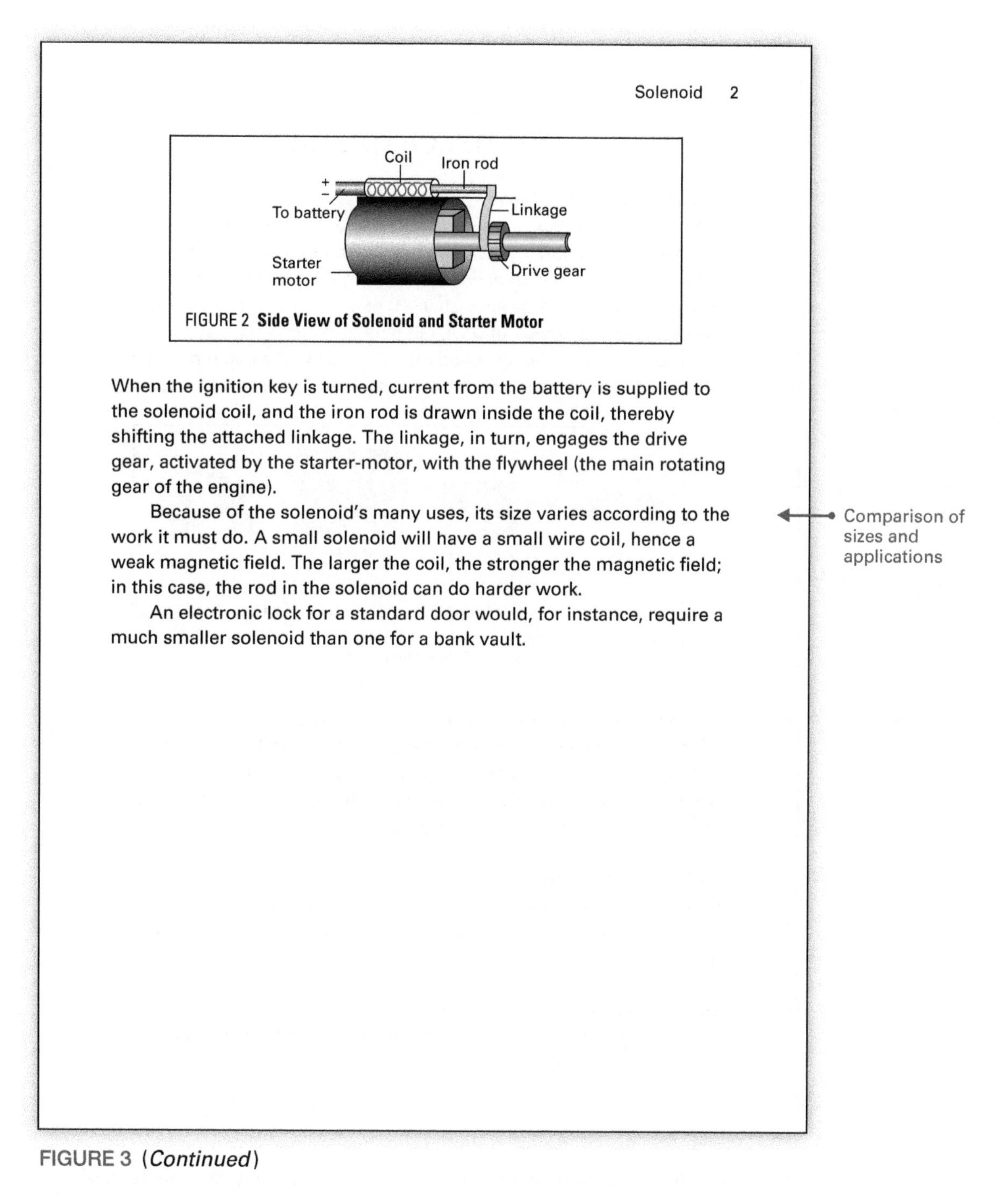

Solenoid 2

FIGURE 2 **Side View of Solenoid and Starter Motor**

When the ignition key is turned, current from the battery is supplied to the solenoid coil, and the iron rod is drawn inside the coil, thereby shifting the attached linkage. The linkage, in turn, engages the drive gear, activated by the starter-motor, with the flywheel (the main rotating gear of the engine).

Because of the solenoid's many uses, its size varies according to the work it must do. A small solenoid will have a small wire coil, hence a weak magnetic field. The larger the coil, the stronger the magnetic field; in this case, the rod in the solenoid can do harder work.

Comparison of sizes and applications

An electronic lock for a standard door would, for instance, require a much smaller solenoid than one for a bank vault.

FIGURE 3 (*Continued*)

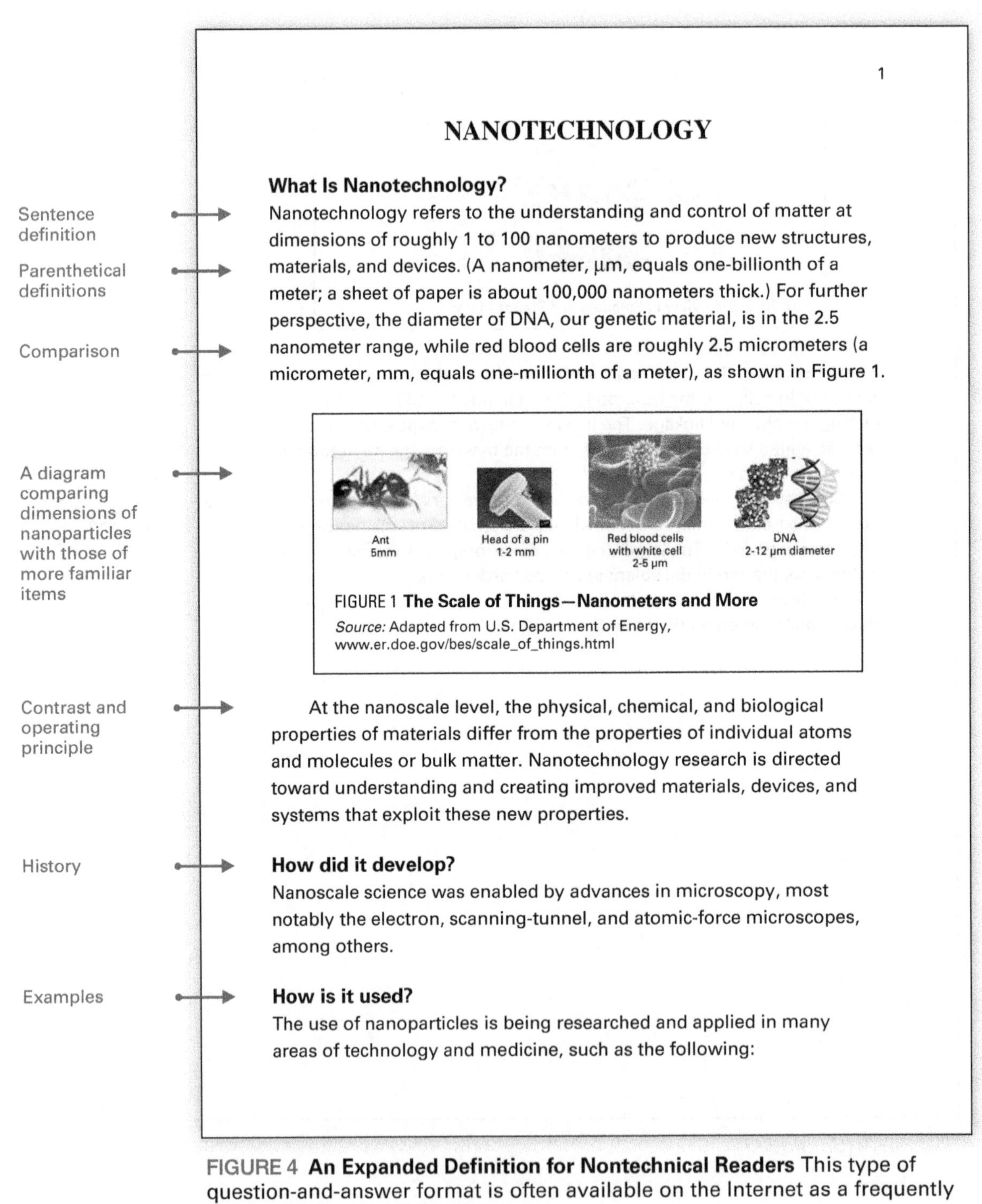

1

NANOTECHNOLOGY

What Is Nanotechnology?

Nanotechnology refers to the understanding and control of matter at dimensions of roughly 1 to 100 nanometers to produce new structures, materials, and devices. (A nanometer, μm, equals one-billionth of a meter; a sheet of paper is about 100,000 nanometers thick.) For further perspective, the diameter of DNA, our genetic material, is in the 2.5 nanometer range, while red blood cells are roughly 2.5 micrometers (a micrometer, mm, equals one-millionth of a meter), as shown in Figure 1.

FIGURE 1 **The Scale of Things—Nanometers and More**

Source: Adapted from U.S. Department of Energy, www.er.doe.gov/bes/scale_of_things.html

At the nanoscale level, the physical, chemical, and biological properties of materials differ from the properties of individual atoms and molecules or bulk matter. Nanotechnology research is directed toward understanding and creating improved materials, devices, and systems that exploit these new properties.

How did it develop?

Nanoscale science was enabled by advances in microscopy, most notably the electron, scanning-tunnel, and atomic-force microscopes, among others.

How is it used?

The use of nanoparticles is being researched and applied in many areas of technology and medicine, such as the following:

FIGURE 4 **An Expanded Definition for Nontechnical Readers** This type of question-and-answer format is often available on the Internet as a frequently asked questions, or FAQ, document.

Source: Adapted from Documents at the National Nanotechnology Initiative <www.nano.gov>.

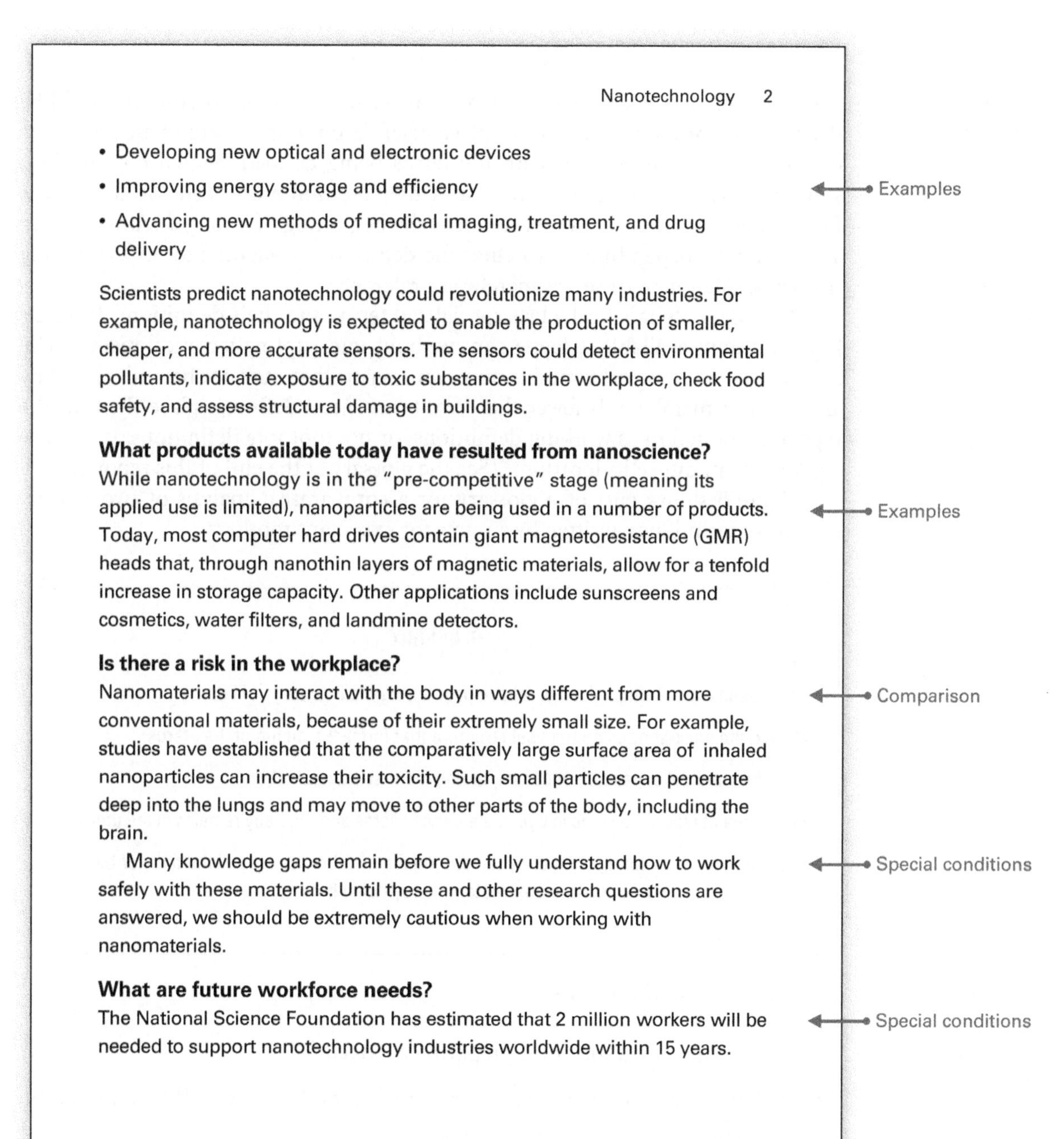

Nanotechnology 2

- Developing new optical and electronic devices
- Improving energy storage and efficiency
- Advancing new methods of medical imaging, treatment, and drug delivery

Scientists predict nanotechnology could revolutionize many industries. For example, nanotechnology is expected to enable the production of smaller, cheaper, and more accurate sensors. The sensors could detect environmental pollutants, indicate exposure to toxic substances in the workplace, check food safety, and assess structural damage in buildings.

What products available today have resulted from nanoscience?
While nanotechnology is in the "pre-competitive" stage (meaning its applied use is limited), nanoparticles are being used in a number of products. Today, most computer hard drives contain giant magnetoresistance (GMR) heads that, through nanothin layers of magnetic materials, allow for a tenfold increase in storage capacity. Other applications include sunscreens and cosmetics, water filters, and landmine detectors.

Is there a risk in the workplace?
Nanomaterials may interact with the body in ways different from more conventional materials, because of their extremely small size. For example, studies have established that the comparatively large surface area of inhaled nanoparticles can increase their toxicity. Such small particles can penetrate deep into the lungs and may move to other parts of the body, including the brain.

Many knowledge gaps remain before we fully understand how to work safely with these materials. Until these and other research questions are answered, we should be extremely cautious when working with nanomaterials.

What are future workforce needs?
The National Science Foundation has estimated that 2 million workers will be needed to support nanotechnology industries worldwide within 15 years.

FIGURE 4 (*Continued*)

PLACING DEFINITIONS IN A DOCUMENT

Placing printed definitions

Each time readers encounter an unfamiliar term or concept, that item should be defined. In a printed text, you can place brief definitions in parentheses or in the document's margin, aligned with the terms being defined. Sentence definitions should be part of the running text or, if they are numerous, listed in a glossary. Place an expanded definition either near the beginning of a long document or in an appendix—depending on whether the definition is essential to understanding the whole document or serves merely as a reference.

Using a glossary

A glossary alphabetically lists specialized terms and their definitions. It makes key definitions available to laypersons without interrupting technical readers. Use a glossary if your report contains numerous terms that may not be understood by all audience members. If fewer than five terms need defining, place them in the report introduction as working definitions, or use footnote definitions. If you use a glossary, announce its location: "(See the glossary at the end of this report)."

Figure 5 shows part of a glossary for a comparative analysis of two natural childbirth techniques, written by a nurse for expectant mothers.

GLOSSARY

Analgesic: a medication given to relieve pain during the first stage of labor.

Cervix: the neck-shaped anatomical structure that forms the mouth of the uterus.

Dilation: cervical expansion occurring during the first stage of labor.

First stage of labor: the stage in which the cervix dilates and the baby remains in the uterus.

Induction: the stimulating of labor by puncturing the membranes around the baby or by giving an oxytoxic drug (uterine contractant), or by doing both.

FIGURE 5 **A Partial Glossary**

How to prepare a glossary

Follow these suggestions for preparing a glossary:

- Define all terms unfamiliar to an intelligent layperson. When in doubt, overdefining is safer than underdefining.
- Define all terms by giving their class and distinguishing features, unless some terms need expanded definitions.
- List all terms in alphabetical order.
- On first use, place an asterisk in the text by each item defined in the glossary.
- List your glossary and its first page number in the table of contents.

On a Web site, you would use a link for each definition and/or provide a link to a separate glossary page. Hypertext and the Web (Figure 6) are perhaps the best answer to making definitions accessible, because readers can click on the item, read about it, and return to their original place on the page.

Using hyperlinked definitions

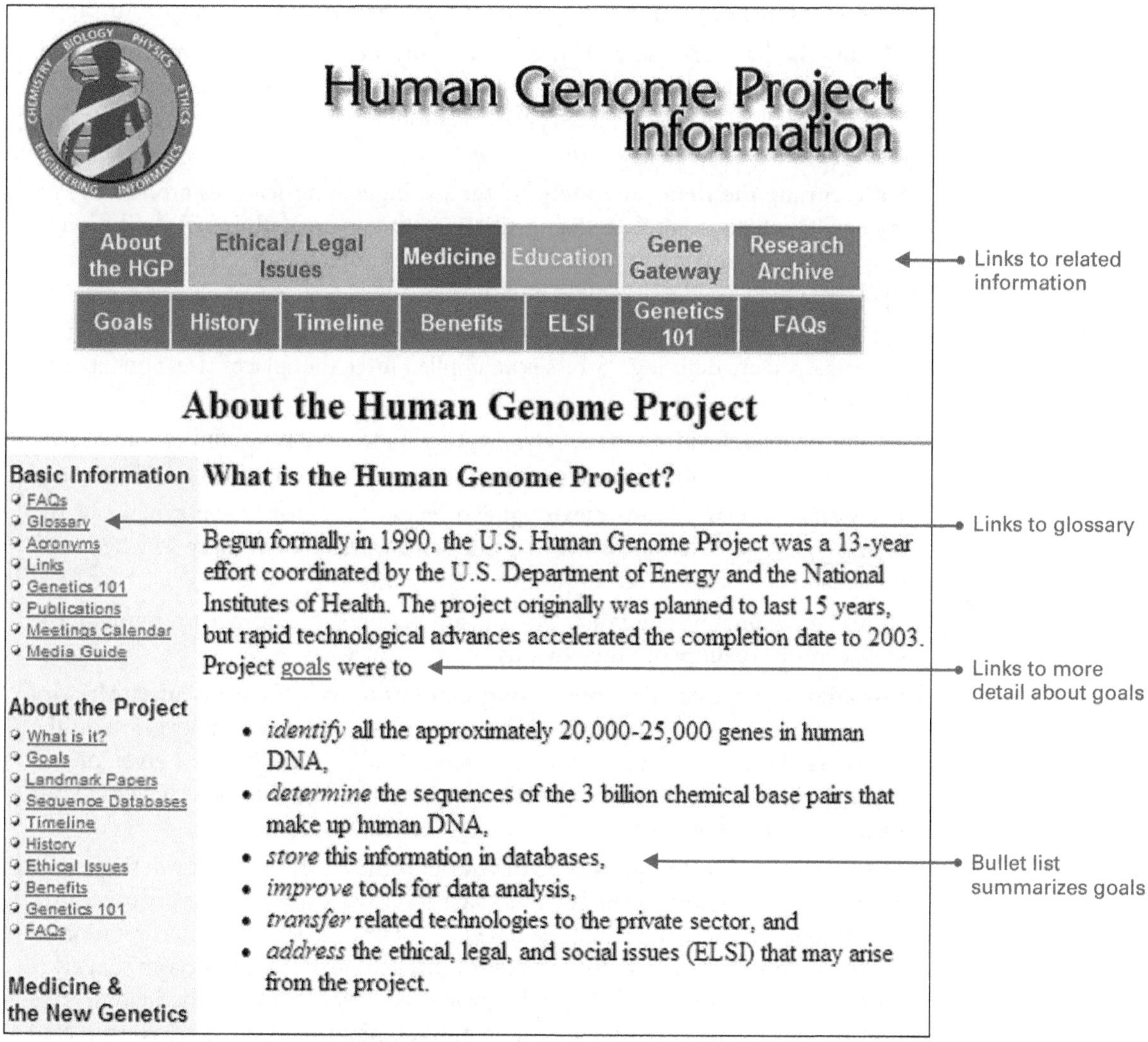

Human Genome Project Information

About the HGP | Ethical / Legal Issues | Medicine | Education | Gene Gateway | Research Archive

Goals | History | Timeline | Benefits | ELSI | Genetics 101 | FAQs

Links to related information

About the Human Genome Project

Basic Information
- FAQs
- Glossary
- Acronyms
- Links
- Genetics 101
- Publications
- Meetings Calendar
- Media Guide

About the Project
- What is it?
- Goals
- Landmark Papers
- Sequence Databases
- Timeline
- History
- Ethical Issues
- Benefits
- Genetics 101
- FAQs

Medicine & the New Genetics

What is the Human Genome Project?

Links to glossary

Begun formally in 1990, the U.S. Human Genome Project was a 13-year effort coordinated by the U.S. Department of Energy and the National Institutes of Health. The project originally was planned to last 15 years, but rapid technological advances accelerated the completion date to 2003. Project goals were to

Links to more detail about goals

- *identify* all the approximately 20,000-25,000 genes in human DNA,
- *determine* the sequences of the 3 billion chemical base pairs that make up human DNA,
- *store* this information in databases,
- *improve* tools for data analysis,
- *transfer* related technologies to the private sector, and
- *address* the ethical, legal, and social issues (ELSI) that may arise from the project.

Bullet list summarizes goals

FIGURE 6 **A Web-based Expanded Definition with Hyperlinks** This definition provides links to deeper levels (such as *Sequence Databases*).
Source: U.S. Department of Energy Office of Science, Office of Biological and Environmental Research, and Human Genome Program, http://www.ornl.gov/sci/techresources/Human_Genome/project/about.shtml.>

GUIDELINES for Definitions

- **Decide on the level of detail you need.** Definitions vary greatly in length and detail, from a few words in parentheses to a multipage document. How much does this audience need in order to follow your explanation or grasp your point?
- **Classify the item precisely.** The narrower your class, the clearer your meaning. *Stress* is classified as an applied force; to say that stress "is what . . ." or "takes place when . . ." fails to denote a specific classification. Diabetes is precisely classified as a *metabolic disease,* not as a *medical term.*
- **Differentiate the item accurately.** If the distinguishing features are too broad, they will apply to more than the particular item you are defining. A definition of *brief* as a "legal document used in court" fails to differentiate *brief* from all other legal documents (*wills, affidavits,* and the like).
- **Avoid circular definitions.** Do not repeat, as part of the distinguishing feature, the word you are defining. "Stress is an applied force that places stress on a body" is a circular definition.
- **Expand your definition selectively.** Begin with a sentence definition and select the best combination of development strategies for your audience and purpose.
- **Use visuals to clarify your meaning.** No matter how clearly you explain, as the saying goes, a picture can be worth a thousand words—even more so when used with readable, accurate writing.
- **Know "how much is enough."** Don't insult people's intelligence by giving needless details or spelling out the obvious.
- **Consider the legal implications of your definition.** What does an "unsatisfactory job performance" mean in an evaluation of a company employee: that the employee should be fired, required to attend a training program, or given one or more chances to improve ("Performance Appraisal 3–4)? Failure to spell out your meaning invites a lawsuit.
- **Consider the ethical implications of your definition.** Be sure your definition of a fuzzy or ambiguous term such as "safe levels of exposure," or "conservative investment," or "acceptable risk" is based on a fair and accurate interpretation of the facts. Consider, for example, a recent U.S. cigarette company's claim that cigarette smoking in the Czech Republic promoted "fiscal benefits," defined, in this case, by the fact that smokers die young, thus eliminating pension and health care costs for the elderly!
- **Place your definition in an appropriate location.** Allow users to access the definition and then return to the main text with as little disruption as possible.
- **Cite your sources as needed.**

CHECKLIST: Definitions

Content

- ☐ Is the type of definition (parenthetical, sentence, expanded) suited to its audience and purpose?
- ☐ Does the definition adequately classify the item?
- ☐ Does the definition adequately differentiate the item?
- ☐ Will the level of technicality connect with the audience?
- ☐ Have circular definitions been avoided?
- ☐ Is the expanded definition developed adequately for its audience?
- ☐ Is the expanded definition free of needless details for its audience?
- ☐ Are visuals used adequately and appropriately?
- ☐ Are all information sources properly documented?
- ☐ Is the definition ethically and legally acceptable?

Arrangement

- ☐ Is the expanded definition unified and coherent (like an essay)?
- ☐ Are transitions between ideas adequate?
- ☐ Is the definition appropriately located in the document?

Style and Page Design

- ☐ Is the definition in plain English?
- ☐ Are sentences clear, concise, and fluent?
- ☐ Is word choice precise?
- ☐ Is the definition grammatical?
- ☐ Is the page design inviting and accessible?

TC WEB **Chapter quiz, Exercises, Web links, and Flashcards** (Go to *Student Resources>Chapter 19*)

PEARSON mtcl **Definitions/descriptions Activities, Case studies, Model documents, and Quiz** (Go to *Technical Communication Documents*)

Projects

GENERAL

Choose a situation and an audience, and prepare an expanded definition designed for this audience's level of technical understanding. Use at least four expansion strategies, including at least one visual. In preparing your expanded definition, consult no fewer than four outside references. Cite and document each source.

TEAM

Divide into groups by majors or interests. Appoint one person as group manager. Decide on an item, concept, or process that would require an expanded definition for laypersons. Some examples follow:

From computer science: an algorithm, binary coding, or systems analysis
From nursing: a pacemaker, coronary bypass surgery, or natural childbirth

Complete an Audience and Use Profile. Once your group has decided on the appropriate expansion strategies, the group manager will assign each member to work on one or two specific strategies as part of the definition. As a group, edit and incorporate the collected material into an expanded definition, revising as often as needed. The group manager will assign one member to present the definition in class.

Your instructor may stipulate a brochure format for your definition, as in Figure 7.

DIGITAL

Convert your expanded definition from the General Project into a Web page. Include links to your information sources.

GLOBAL

Any definition you write may be read by someone for whom English is not a first language. Locate an expanded definition on Wikipedia that may be difficult for a non-American or non–native English speaker to understand for some reason (use of idioms, use of abbreviations, use of American metaphors such as sports metaphors not used in other countries). Explain how the definition could be reworded so that most readers would understand it.

For more support in mastering the objectives of this chapter, go to **www.mytechcommlab.com**

What is a generic drug?

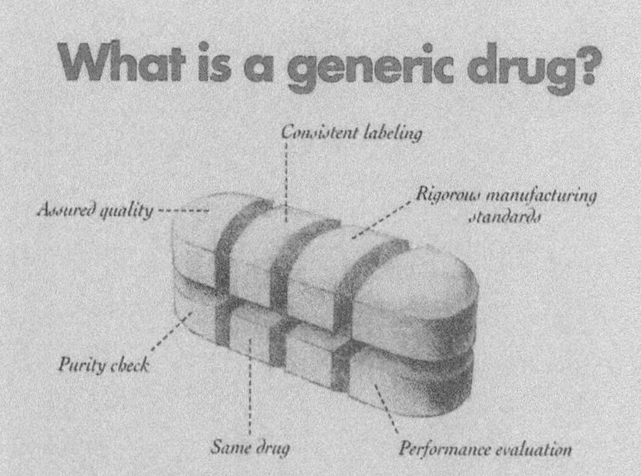

When a brand-name drug's patent protection expires, generic versions of the drug can be approved for sale. The generic version works like the brand-name drug in dosage, strength, performance and use, and must meet the same quality and safety standards. All generic drugs must be reviewed and approved by FDA.

How does FDA ensure that my generic drug is as safe and effective as the brand-name drug?

All generic drugs are put through a rigorous, multi-step review process that includes a review of scientific data on the generic drug's ingredients and performance. FDA also conducts periodic inspections of the manufacturing plant, and monitors drug quality—even after the generic drug has been approved.

If generic drugs and brand-name drugs have the same active ingredients, why do they look different?

Generic drugs look different because certain inactive ingredients, such as colors and flavorings, may be different. These ingredients do not affect the performance, safety or effectiveness of the generic drug. They look different because trademark laws in the U.S. do not allow a generic drug to look exactly like other drugs already on the market.

Is my generic drug made by the same company that makes the brand-name drug?

It is possible. Brand-name firms are responsible for manufacturing approximately 50 percent of generic drugs.

Are generic drugs always made in the same kind of facilities as brand-name drugs?

Yes. All generic drug manufacturing facilities must meet FDA's standards of good manufacturing practices. FDA will not permit drugs to be made in substandard facilities. FDA conducts about 3,500 inspections a year to ensure standards are met.

FDA makes it tough to become a generic drug in America so you can feel confident about taking your generic drugs. If you still want to learn more, talk with your doctor, pharmacist or other health care professional. Or call **1-888-INFO-FDA** or visit **www.fda.gov/cder** today.

Generic Drugs: Safe. Effective. FDA Approved.

FIGURE 7 **A Definition for Laypersons, Designed as a Two-Column Brochure**
Source: U.S. Department of Health and Human Services. Food and Drug Administration.

Instructions and Procedures

cultura/Corbis

"Clear, accurate instructions and procedures are essential to the work we do in aerospace engineering. We need to ensure that the mechanics, ground control personnel, and pilots have the information they need to perform tasks and conduct safety and operations checks. These instructional documents can't have too much detail or be too wordy, and they need a clear list of steps. Hazard and warning material needs to show up easily, usually through the use of a visual. At our company, teams of engineers and technical writers work together to design, write, and evaluate all of our instructions, which we then print on quick-reference cards and make available on CDs."

—Farid Akina, Aerospace Engineer, at an international aerospace design firm

LEARNING OBJECTIVES FOR THIS CHAPTER

- Know how instructions and procedures are used in the workplace
- Recognize the various formats for hard-copy instructions
- Understand how instructions have serious legal implications
- Compare the benefits of print, digital, online, and video instructions
- Write a set of instructions
- Understand how procedures differ from instructions
- Write a set of procedures

Chapter overview (Go to *Student Resources>Chapter 21*)

Instructions spell out the steps required for completing a task or a series of tasks (say, installing printer software on your computer or operating an electron microscope). The audience for a set of instructions might be someone who doesn't know how to perform the task or someone who wants to perform it more effectively. In either case, effective instructions enable people to complete a job safely and efficiently.

Procedures, a special type of instructions, serve also as official guidelines. Procedures ensure that all members of a group (such as employees at the same company) follow the same steps to perform a particular task. For example, many companies have procedures in place that must be followed for evacuating a building or responding to emergencies.

The role of instructions on the job

Almost anyone with a responsible job writes and reads instructions. For example, you might instruct new employees on how to activate their voice mail system or advise a customer about shipping radioactive waste. An employee going on vacation typically writes instructions for the person filling in. People who buy a computer or cell phone usually look at the print or online instruction manual to get started.

CONSIDERING AUDIENCE AND PURPOSE

Audience considerations

Before preparing instructions, find out how much your audience already knows about the task(s) involved. For example, technicians who have done this procedure often (say, fixing a jammed photocopier), will need only basic guidelines rather than detailed explanations. But a more general audience (say, consumers trying to set up and use a digital scanner), will need step-by-step guidance. A mixed audience (some experienced people and some novices) may require a layered approach: for instance, some initial basic information with a longer section later that has more details.

Purpose considerations

The general purpose of instructions is to help people perform a task. The task may be simple (inserting a new toner cartridge in a printer) or complex (using an electron microscope). Whatever the task, people will have some basic questions:

What people expect to learn from a set of instructions

- Why am I doing this?
- How do I do it?
- What materials and equipment will I need?
- Where do I begin?
- What do I do next?
- What could go wrong?

Because they focus squarely on the person who will "read" and then "do," instructions must meet the highest standards of excellence.

FORMATS FOR INSTRUCTIONAL DOCUMENTS

Manuals models and template (Go to *Student Resources>Chapter 21> Models and Templates*)

Instructional documents take various formats, in hard copy or electronic versions (usually as PDF documents on a company Web site). Here are some of the most commonly used:

Common formats for instructional documents

- **Manuals** (Figure 1) contain instructions for all sorts of tasks. A manual also may contain descriptions and specifications for the product, warnings, maintenance and troubleshooting advice, and any other information the reader is likely to need. For complex products (such as an ozone-mapping spectrometer) or procedures (such as cleaning a hazardous-waste site), the manual can be a sizable book. Most manuals (of any size) are available in both print and PDF format.
- **Brief reference cards** (Figure 2) typically fit on a single page or less. The instructions usually focus on the basic steps for people who want only enough information to start on a task and to keep moving through it.
- **Instructional brochures** (Figure 3) can be displayed, handed out, mailed, or otherwise distributed to a broad audience. They are especially useful for advocating procedures that increase health and safety.
- **Hyperlinked instructions** (Figure 4) enable people to explore various levels and layers of information and to choose the layers that match their needs.
- **Online instructions** (Figure 9) provide the contents of a hard copy manual as a link on a Web site. Whereas people with less experience tend to prefer paper documentation, online help is especially popular among people with more experience.

Regardless of its format, any set of instructions must meet the strict legal and usability requirements discussed on the following pages.

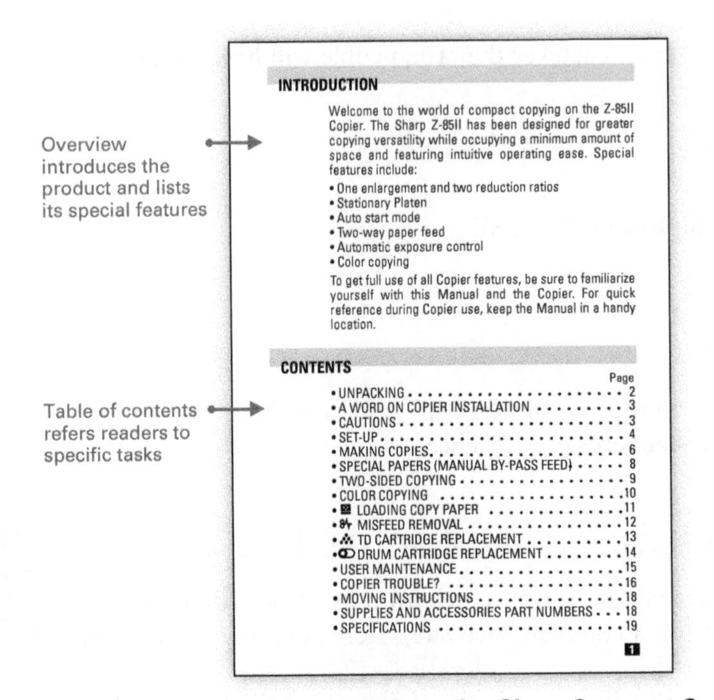

INTRODUCTION

Welcome to the world of compact copying on the Z-85II Copier. The Sharp Z-85II has been designed for greater copying versatility while occupying a minimum amount of space and featuring intuitive operating ease. Special features include:

- One enlargement and two reduction ratios
- Stationary Platen
- Auto start mode
- Two-way paper feed
- Automatic exposure control
- Color copying

To get full use of all Copier features, be sure to familiarize yourself with this Manual and the Copier. For quick reference during Copier use, keep the Manual in a handy location.

CONTENTS

1

FIGURE 1 **Table of Contents from the *Sharp Compact Copier Z-8511 Operation Manual***

Source: Used with permission of Sharp Electronics Corporation.

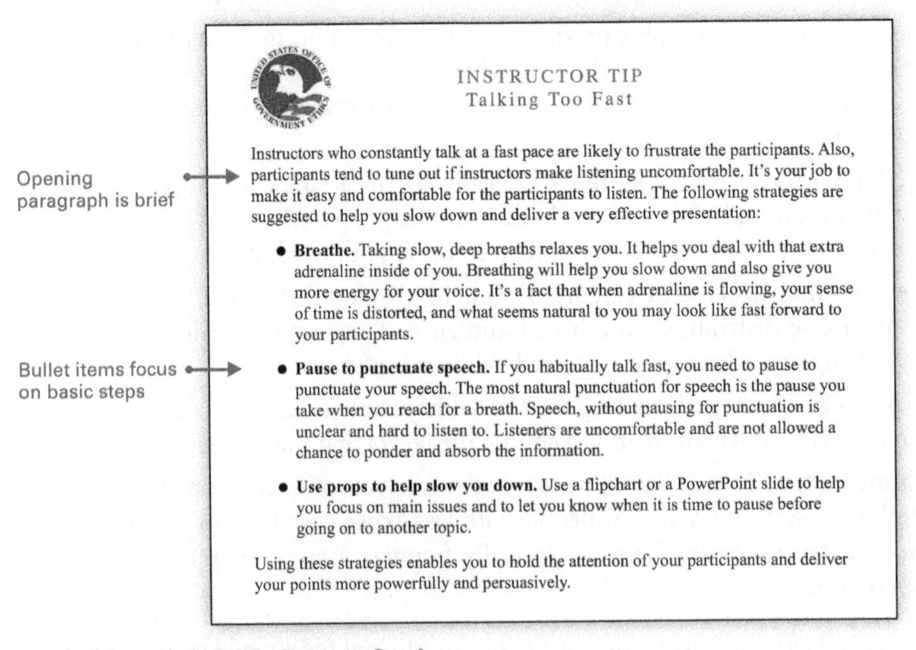

INSTRUCTOR TIP
Talking Too Fast

Instructors who constantly talk at a fast pace are likely to frustrate the participants. Also, participants tend to tune out if instructors make listening uncomfortable. It's your job to make it easy and comfortable for the participants to listen. The following strategies are suggested to help you slow down and deliver a very effective presentation:

- **Breathe.** Taking slow, deep breaths relaxes you. It helps you deal with that extra adrenaline inside of you. Breathing will help you slow down and also give you more energy for your voice. It's a fact that when adrenaline is flowing, your sense of time is distorted, and what seems natural to you may look like fast forward to your participants.
- **Pause to punctuate speech.** If you habitually talk fast, you need to pause to punctuate your speech. The most natural punctuation for speech is the pause you take when you reach for a breath. Speech, without pausing for punctuation is unclear and hard to listen to. Listeners are uncomfortable and are not allowed a chance to ponder and absorb the information.
- **Use props to help slow you down.** Use a flipchart or a PowerPoint slide to help you focus on main issues and to let you know when it is time to pause before going on to another topic.

Using these strategies enables you to hold the attention of your participants and deliver your points more powerfully and persuasively.

FIGURE 2 **A Brief Reference Card**

Source: Adapted from United States Office of Government Ethics <www.usoge.gov>.

BAC (foodborne bacteria) could make you and those you care about sick. In fact, even though you can't see BAC—or smell him, or feel him—he and millions more like him may have already invaded the food you eat. But you have the power to *Fight BAC!®*.

Foodborne illness can strike anyone. Some people are at a higher risk for developing foodborne illness, including pregnant women, young children, older adults and people with weakened immune systems. For these people the following four simple steps are critically important:

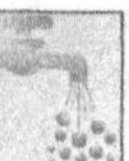

CLEAN: *Wash hands and surfaces often*

Bacteria can be spread throughout the kitchen and get onto hands, cutting boards, utensils, counter tops and food. To *Fight BAC!®*, always:

- Wash your hands with warm water and soap for at least 20 seconds before and after handling food and after using the bathroom, changing diapers and handling pets.
- Wash your cutting boards, dishes, utensils and counter tops with hot soapy water after preparing each food item and before you go on to the next food.
- Consider using paper towels to clean up kitchen surfaces. If you use cloth towels wash them often in the hot cycle of your washing machine.
- Rinse fresh fruits and vegetables under running tap water, including those with skins and rinds that are not eaten.
- Rub firm-skin fruits and vegetables under running tap water or scrub with a clean vegetable brush while rinsing with running tap water.

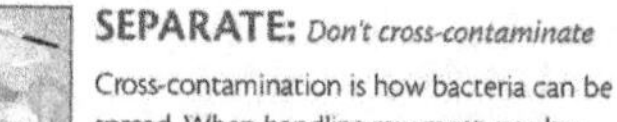

SEPARATE: *Don't cross-contaminate*

Cross-contamination is how bacteria can be spread. When handling raw meat, poultry, seafood and eggs, keep these foods and their juices away from ready-to-eat foods. Always start with a clean scene— wash hands with warm water and soap. Wash cutting boards, dishes, countertops and utensils with hot soapy water.

- Separate raw meat, poultry, seafood and eggs from other foods in your grocery shopping cart, grocery bags and in your refrigerator.
- Use one cutting board for fresh produce and a separate one for raw meat, poultry and seafood.
- Never place cooked food on a plate that previously held raw meat, poultry, seafood or eggs.

COOK: *Cook to proper temperatures*

Food is safely cooked when it reaches a high enough internal temperature to kill the harmful bacteria that cause illness. Refer to the chart on the back of this brochure for the proper internal temperatures.

- Use a food thermometer to measure the internal temperature of cooked foods. Make sure that meat, poultry, egg dishes, casseroles and other foods are cooked to the internal temperature shown in the chart on the back of this brochure.
- Cook ground meat or ground poultry until it reaches a safe internal temperature. Color is not a reliable indicator of doneness.
- Cook eggs until the yolk and white are firm. Only use recipes in which eggs are cooked or heated thoroughly.
- When cooking in a microwave oven, cover food, stir and rotate for even cooking. Food is done when it reaches the internal temperature shown on the back of this brochure.
- Bring sauces, soups and gravy to a boil when reheating.

CHILL: *Refrigerate promptly*

Refrigerate foods quickly because cold temperatures slow the growth of harmful bacteria. Do not over-stuff the refrigerator. Cold air must circulate to help keep food safe. Keeping a constant refrigerator temperature of 40°F or below is one of the most effective ways to reduce the risk of foodborne illness. Use an appliance thermometer to be sure the temperature is consistently 40°F or below. The freezer temperature should be 0°F or below.

- Refrigerate or freeze meat, poultry, eggs and other perishables as soon as you get them home from the store.
- Never let raw meat, poultry, eggs, cooked food or cut fresh fruits or vegetables sit at room temperature more than two hours before putting them in the refrigerator or freezer (one hour when the temperature is above 90°F).
- Never defrost food at room temperature. Food must be kept at a safe temperature during thawing. There are three safe ways to defrost food: in the refrigerator, in cold water, and in the microwave. Food thawed in cold water or in the microwave should be cooked immediately.
- Always marinate food in the refrigerator.
- Divide large amounts of leftovers into shallow containers for quicker cooling in the refrigerator.
- Use or discard refrigerated food on a regular basis. Check USDA cold storage information at ***www.fightbac.org*** for optimum storage times.

FIGURE 3 **A Foldout Instructional Brochure** The three inside panels of this *Fight BAC!* brochure offer "Four Simple Steps to Food Safety."

Source: Used by permission of Partnership for Food Safety Education <www.fightbac.org>.

FAULTY INSTRUCTIONS AND LEGAL LIABILITY

Ethical implications of instructions

Instructional documents carry serious ethical and legal obligations on the part of those who prepare such documents. As many as 10 percent of workers are injured each year on the job (Clement 149). Certain medications produce depression that can lead to suicide (Caher 5). Countless injuries also result from misuse of consumer products such as power tools, car jacks, or household cleaners—types of misuse that are often caused by defective instructions.

Legal implications of instructions

Any person injured because of unclear, inaccurate, or incomplete instructions can sue the writer as well as the manufacturer. Courts have ruled that a writing defect in product support literature carries the same type of liability as a design or manufacturing defect in the product itself (Girill, "Technical Communication and Law" 37).

Links provide quick access to other information

Numbered steps are easy to see

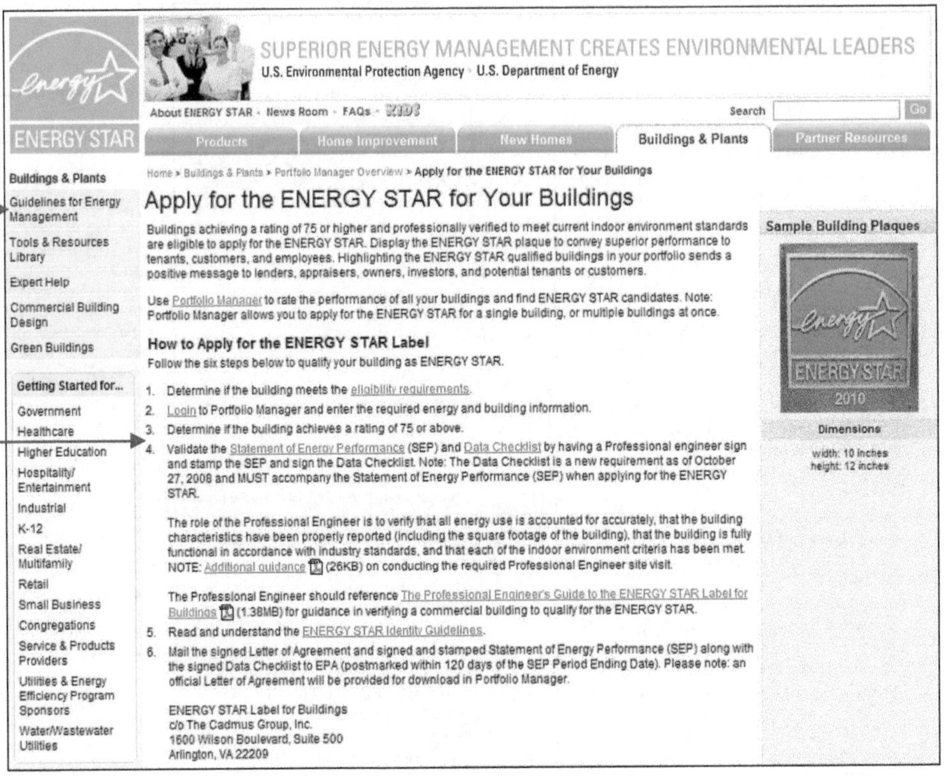

SUPERIOR ENERGY MANAGEMENT CREATES ENVIRONMENTAL LEADERS
U.S. Environmental Protection Agency · U.S. Department of Energy

ENERGY STAR

About ENERGY STAR · News Room · FAQs · Search Go

Products | Home Improvement | New Homes | Buildings & Plants | Partner Resources

Home » Buildings & Plants » Portfolio Manager Overview » Apply for the ENERGY STAR for Your Buildings

Buildings & Plants
Guidelines for Energy Management
Tools & Resources Library
Expert Help
Commercial Building Design
Green Buildings

Getting Started for...
Government
Healthcare
Higher Education
Hospitality/Entertainment
Industrial
K-12
Real Estate/Multifamily
Retail
Small Business
Congregations
Service & Products Providers
Utilities & Energy Efficiency Program Sponsors
Water/Wastewater Utilities

Apply for the ENERGY STAR for Your Buildings

Buildings achieving a rating of 75 or higher and professionally verified to meet current indoor environment standards are eligible to apply for the ENERGY STAR. Display the ENERGY STAR plaque to convey superior performance to tenants, customers, and employees. Highlighting the ENERGY STAR qualified buildings in your portfolio sends a positive message to lenders, appraisers, owners, investors, and potential tenants or customers.

Use Portfolio Manager to rate the performance of all your buildings and find ENERGY STAR candidates. Note: Portfolio Manager allows you to apply for the ENERGY STAR for a single building, or multiple buildings at once.

How to Apply for the ENERGY STAR Label

Follow the six steps below to qualify your building as ENERGY STAR.

1. Determine if the building meets the eligibility requirements.
2. Login to Portfolio Manager and enter the required energy and building information.
3. Determine if the building achieves a rating of 75 or above.
4. Validate the Statement of Energy Performance (SEP) and Data Checklist by having a Professional engineer sign and stamp the SEP and sign the Data Checklist. Note: The Data Checklist is a new requirement as of October 27, 2008 and MUST accompany the Statement of Energy Performance (SEP) when applying for the ENERGY STAR.

   The role of the Professional Engineer is to verify that all energy use is accounted for accurately, that the building characteristics have been properly reported (including the square footage of the building), that the building is fully functional in accordance with industry standards, and that each of the indoor environment criteria has been met. NOTE: Additional guidance (26KB) on conducting the required Professional Engineer site visit.

   The Professional Engineer should reference The Professional Engineer's Guide to the ENERGY STAR Label for Buildings (1.38MB) for guidance in verifying a commercial building to qualify for the ENERGY STAR.
5. Read and understand the ENERGY STAR Identity Guidelines.
6. Mail the signed Letter of Agreement and signed and stamped Statement of Energy Performance (SEP) along with the signed Data Checklist to EPA (postmarked within 120 days of the SEP Period Ending Date). Please note: an official Letter of Agreement will be provided for download in Portfolio Manager.

   ENERGY STAR Label for Buildings
   c/o The Cadmus Group, Inc.
   1600 Wilson Boulevard, Suite 500
   Arlington, VA 22209

Sample Building Plaques

ENERGY STAR 2010

Dimensions
width: 10 inches
height: 12 inches

FIGURE 4 **A Set of Web-Based (Hyperlinked) Instructions** Note the links to specific steps.

Source: Energy Star, a joint program of the U.S. Environmental Protection Agency and the U.S. Department of Energy, <http://www.energystar.gov>.

Those who prepare instructions are potentially liable for damage or injury resulting from information omissions such as the following (Caher 5–7; Manning 13; Nordenberg 7):

Examples of faulty instructions that create legal liability

- **Failure to instruct and caution users in the proper use of a product:** for example, a medication's proper dosage or possible interaction with other drugs or possible side effects.
- **Failure to warn against hazards from proper use of a product:** for example, the risk of repetitive stress injury resulting from extended use of a keyboard.
- **Failure to warn against the possible misuses of a product:** for example, the danger of child suffocation posed by plastic bags or the danger of toxic fumes from spray-on oven cleaners.
- **Failure to explain a product's benefits and risks in language that average consumers can understand.**

- **Failure to convey the extent of risk with forceful language.**
- **Failure to display warnings prominently.**

Some legal experts argue that defects in the instructions carry even greater liability than defects in the product because such deficits are more easily demonstrated to a nontechnical jury (Bedford and Stearns 128).

> **NOTE** *Among all technical documents, instructions have the strictest requirements for giving readers precisely what they need precisely when they need it. To design usable instructions, you must have a clear sense of (a) the specific tasks you want readers to accomplish, (b) the readers' abilities and limitations, and (c) the setting/circumstances in which people will be referring to this document.*

ELEMENTS OF EFFECTIVE INSTRUCTIONS

Clear and Limiting Title

Provide a clear and exact preview of the task. For example, the title "Instructions for Cleaning the Drive Head of a Laptop Computer" tells people what to expect: instructions for a specific procedure involving one selected part. But the title "The Laptop Computer" gives no such forecast; a document so titled might contain a history of the laptop, a description of each part, or a wide range of related information.

Give a forecast

Instructions project
(Go to *Student Resources>Chapter 21> Projects and Case Studies>Emergency Response and Survival*)

Informed Content

Make sure that you know exactly what you are talking about. Ignorance, inexperience, or misinformation on your part makes you no less liable for faulty or inaccurate instructions:

Know the procedure

> If the author of [a car repair] manual had no experience with cars, yet provided faulty instructions on the repair of the car's brakes, the home mechanic who was injured when the brakes failed may recover [damages] from the author. (Walter and Marsteller 165)

Ignorance provides no legal excuse

Unless you have performed the task often, do not try to write instructions for other people confronting this task.

Visuals

Instructions often include a persuasive dimension: to promote interest, commitment, or action. In addition to showing what to do, visuals attract the reader's attention and help keep words to a minimum.

Types of visuals especially suited to instructions include icons, representational and schematic diagrams, flowcharts, photographs, and prose tables.

Visuals to accompany instructions can be created using a variety of software packages. Other sources for instructional graphics include clip art, scanning, and downloading from the Internet.

To use visuals effectively, consider these suggestions:

How to use instructional visuals

- Illustrate any step that might be hard for readers to visualize. The less specialized your readers, the more visuals they are likely to need.
- Parallel the reader's angle of vision in performing the activity or operating the equipment. Name the angle (side view, top view) if you think people will have trouble figuring it out for themselves.
- Avoid illustrating any action simple enough for readers to visualize on their own, such as "PRESS RETURN" for anyone familiar with a keyboard.

Visuals can be used without words, too, especially for international audiences. Often called *wordless instructions*, these diagrams use clear, simple line drawings, arrows, and call-outs to let people see how to do something. Figure 5 shows a wordless instruction for setting up a printer.

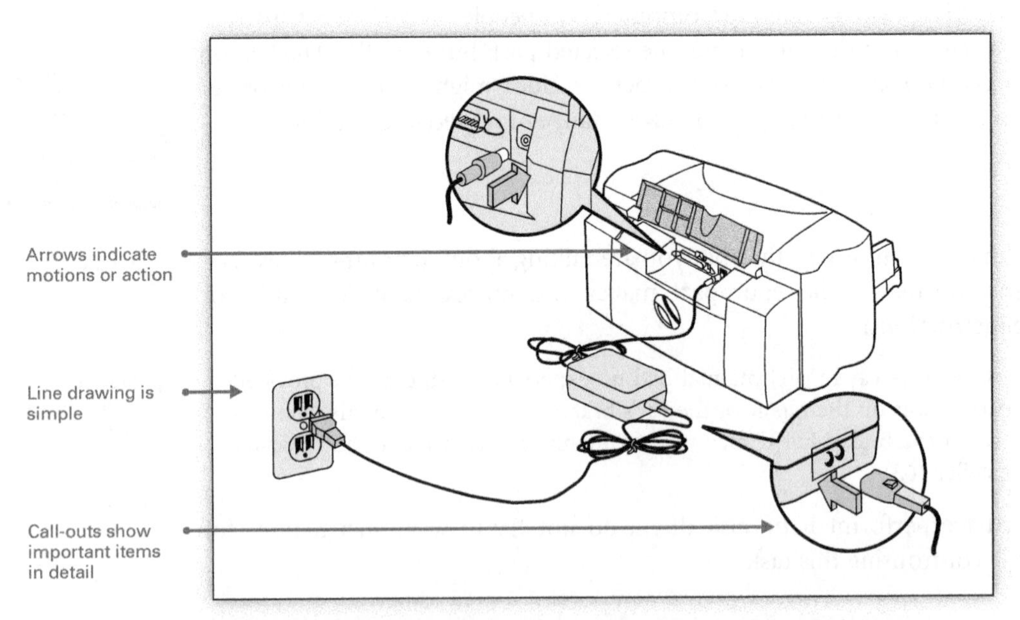

FIGURE 5 **Wordless Instructions** Instructions with only images, and no words, are suitable for most readers, including international audiences.

Source: Hewlett-Packard Co. Reprinted with permission.

Figure 6 presents an array of visuals and their specific instructional functions. Each of these visuals is easily constructed and some could be further enhanced, depending on your production budget and graphics capability.

HOW TO LOCATE SOMETHING

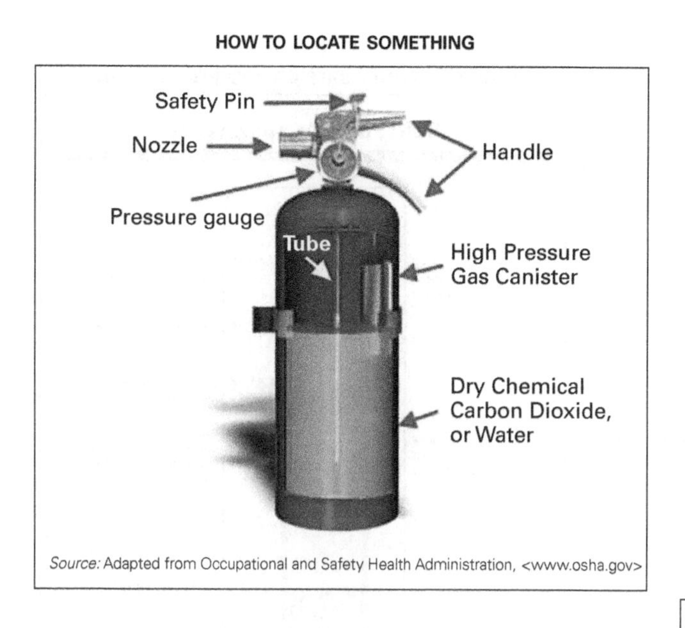

Source: Adapted from Occupational and Safety Health Administration, <www.osha.gov>

HOW TO OPERATE SOMETHING

Source: Superstock

HOW TO REPAIR SOMETHING

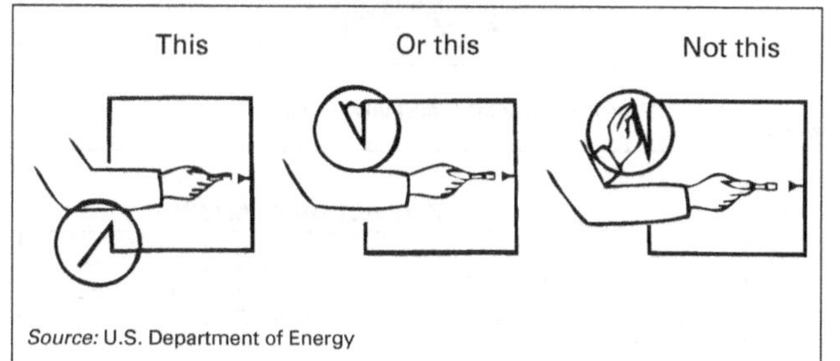

Source: U.S. Department of Energy

HOW TO ASSEMBLE SOMETHING

Extension Cord Retainer

1. Look into the end of the Switch Handle and you will see 2 slots. The WIDER end of the Retainer goes into the TOP slot (Figure 8).
2. Plug extension cord into Switch Handle and weave cord into Retainer, leaving a little slack (Figure 9).

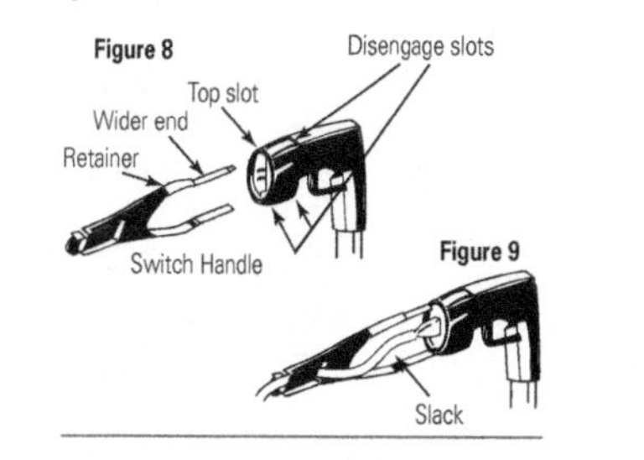

Source: Courtesy of Black & Decker® (U.S.), Inc.

HOW TO POSITION SOMETHING

Source: From U.S. Department of Energy, <www.nrel.gov/docs/fy01osti/28039.pdf>

HOW TO AVOID DAMAGE OR INJURY

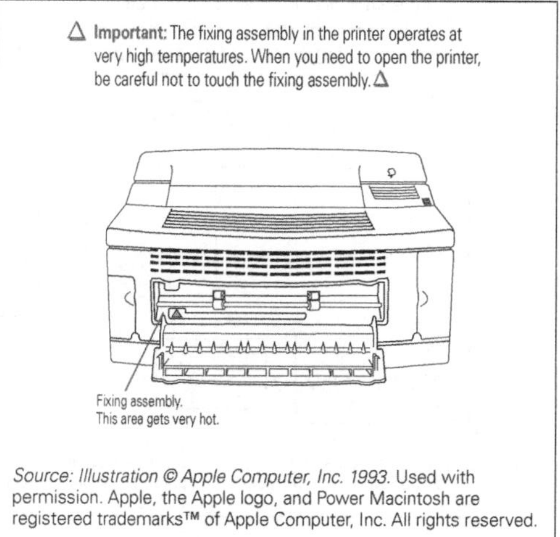

Source: Illustration © Apple Computer, Inc. 1993. Used with permission. Apple, the Apple logo, and Power Macintosh are registered trademarks™ of Apple Computer, Inc. All rights reserved.

FIGURE 6 **Common Types of Instructional Visuals and Their Functions**

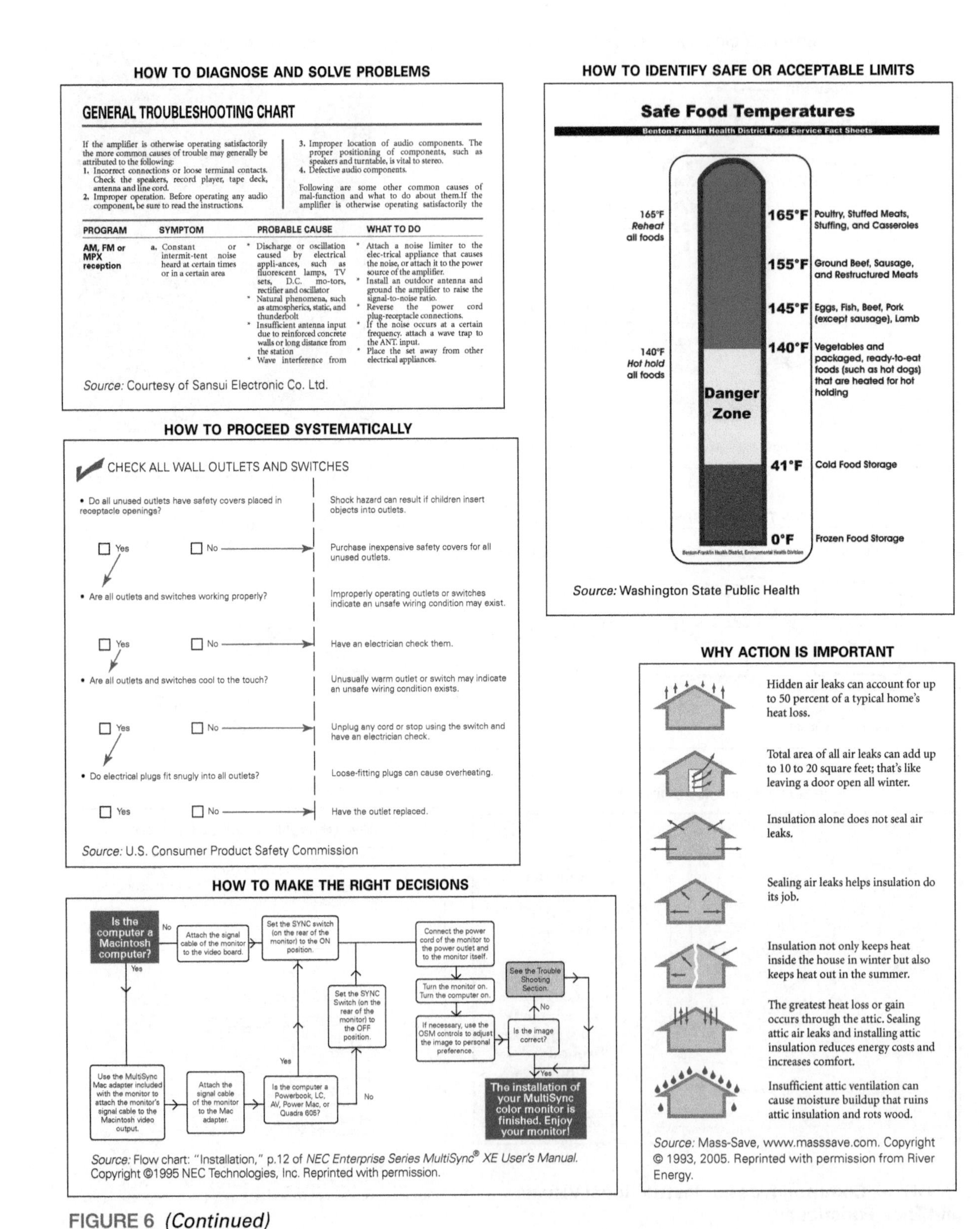

FIGURE 6 *(Continued)*

Appropriate Level of Detail and Technicality

Unless you know your readers have the relevant background and skills, write for a general audience, and do three things:

Provide exactly and only what readers need

1. Give readers enough background to understand why they need to follow these instructions.
2. Give enough detail to show *what* to do.
3. Give enough examples so each step can be visualized clearly.

These three procedures are explained and illustrated on the following pages.

1. **Provide Background.** Begin by explaining the purpose of the task.

Tell readers why they are doing this

> You might easily lose information stored on a flash drive if
>
> - the drive is damaged by repeated use, moisture, or extreme temperature;
> - the drive is erased by a power surge, a computer malfunction, or a user error; or
> - the stored information is scrambled by a nearby magnet (telephone, computer terminal, or the like).
>
> Always have backup storage for any important material.

Also, state your assumptions about your reader's level of technical understanding.

Spell out what readers should already know

> To follow these instructions, you should be able to identify these parts of your iMac: computer, monitor, keyboard (wireless or USB), mouse, and an external USB or FireWire hard drive (for backup).

Define any specialized terms that appear in your instructions.

Tell readers what each key term means

> *Initialize:* Before you can store or retrieve information on a new CD, you must initialize the disk. Initializing creates a format that computers and CD players can understand—a directory of specific memory spaces on the disk where you can store information and retrieve it as needed.

When the reader understands *what* and *why*, you are ready to explain *how* he or she can complete the task.

2. **Provide Adequate Detail.** Include enough detail for people to understand and perform the task successfully. Omit general information that readers probably know, but do not overestimate the audience's background, as in the following example.

Make instructions complete but not excessive

Inadequate detail for laypersons

First Aid for Electrical Shock

1. Check vital signs.
2. Establish an airway.
3. Administer CPR as needed.
4. Treat for shock.

Not only are the above details inadequate, but terms such as "vital signs" and "CPR" are too technical for laypersons. Such instructions posted for workers in a high-voltage area would be useless. Illustrations and explanations are needed, as in the partial instructions in Figure 7 for item 3 above, administering CPR.

Don't assume that people know more than they really do, especially when you can perform the task almost automatically. (Think about when a relative or friend taught you to drive a car—or perhaps you tried to teach someone else.) Always assume that your readers know less than you. A colleague will know at least a little less; a layperson will know a good deal less—maybe nothing—about this procedure.

Exactly how much information is enough? The following guidelines can help you find an answer:

GUIDELINES for Providing Appropriate Detail

- **Provide *all* the necessary information.** The instructions must be able to stand alone.
- **Don't provide unnecessary information.** Give only what readers need. Don't tell them how to build a computer when they only need to know how to copy a file.
- **Instead of focusing on the *product,* focus on the *task.*** "How does it work?" "How do I use it?" or "How do I do it?" (Grice, "Focus" 132).
- **Omit steps that are obvious.** "Seat yourself at the computer," for example.
- **Divide the task into simple steps and substeps.** Allow people to focus on one step at a time.
- **Adjust the *information rate.*** This is "the amount of information presented in a given page" (Meyer 17), adjusted to the reader's background and the difficulty of the task. For complex or sensitive steps, slow the information rate. Don't make people do too much too fast.
- **Reinforce the prose with visuals.** Don't be afraid to repeat information if it saves readers from going back to look something up.
- **Keep it simple.** When writing instructions for consumer products, assume "a barely literate reader" (Clement 151).
- **Recognize the persuasive dimension of the instructions.** Readers may need persuading that this procedure is necessary or beneficial, or that they can complete this procedure with relative ease and competence.

Methods of Cardiopulmonary Resuscitation (CPR)

Mouth-to-Mouth Breathing

Step 1: If there are no signs of breathing or there is no significant pulse, place one hand under the victim's neck and gently lift. At the same time, push with the other hand on the victim's forehead. This will move the tongue away from the back of the throat to open the airway. If available, a plastic "stoma," or oropharyngeal airway device, should be inserted now.

Adequate detail for laypersons

Step 2: While maintaining the backward head tilt position, place your cheek and ear close to the victim's mouth and nose. Look for the chest to rise and fall while you listen and feel for breathing. Check for about 5 seconds.

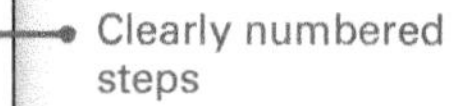

Clearly numbered steps

Step 3: Next, while maintaining the backward head tilt, pinch the victim's nose with the hand that is on the victim's forehead to prevent leakage of air, open your mouth wide, take a deep breath, seal your mouth around the victim's mouth, and blow into the victim's mouth with four quick but full breaths. For an infant, give gentle puffs and blow through the mouth and nose *and* do not tilt the head back as far as for an adult.

If you do not get an air exchange when you blow, it may help to reposition the head and try again.

Troubleshooting ("If this happens...") for laypersons who lack experience

If there is still no breathing, give one breath every 5 seconds for an adult and one gentle puff every 3 seconds for an infant until breathing resumes.

If the victim's chest fails to expand, the problem may be an airway obstruction. Mouth-to-mouth respiration should be interrupted briefly to apply first aid for choking.

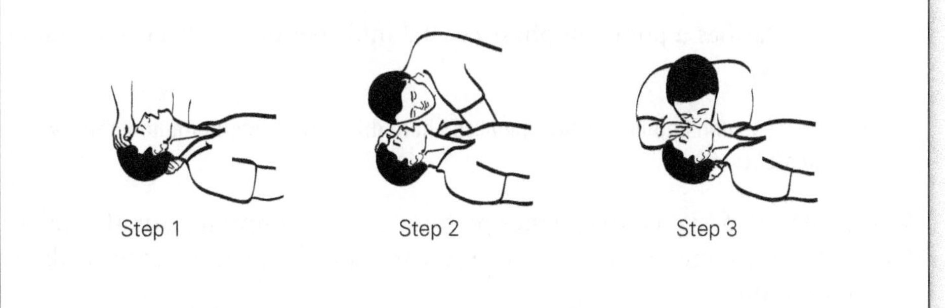

FIGURE 7 **Adequate Detail for Laypersons**

Source: From the book NEW YORK PUBLIC LIBRARY DESK REFERENCE. Copyright © 2002, 1998, 1993, 1989 by The New York Public Library and The Stonesong Press, Inc. Reprinted by permission of Hyperion. All rights reserved.

Give plenty of examples

3. Offer Examples. Instructions require specific examples (how to load a program, how to order a part) to help people follow the steps correctly:

> To load your program, type this command:
>
> Load "Style Editor"
>
> Then press RETURN.

Like visuals, examples *show* users what to do. Examples, in fact, often appear as visuals.

Include Troubleshooting Advice. Anticipate things that commonly go wrong when this task is performed—the paper jams in the printer, the tray of the DVD drive won't open, or some other malfunction. Explain the probable cause(s) and offer solutions.

Explain what to do when things go wrong

> NOTE: IF *X* doesn't work, first check *Y* and then do *Z*.

Logically Ordered Steps

Instructions are almost always arranged in chronological order, with warnings and precautions inserted for specific steps.

Show how the steps are connected

> You can't splice two wires to make an electrical connection until you have removed the insulation. To remove the insulation, you will need. . . .

Notes and Hazard Notices

Alert readers to special considerations

Following are the only items that normally should interrupt the steps in a set of instructions (Van Pelt 3):

- A *note* clarifies a point, emphasizes vital information, or describes options or alternatives.

> NOTE: If you don't name a newly initialized hard drive, the computer automatically names it "Untitled."

While a note is designed to enhance performance and prevent error, the following hazard notices—ranked in order of severity—are designed to prevent damage, injury, or death.

- A *caution* prevents possible mistakes that could result in injury or equipment damage:

The least forceful notice

> CAUTION: A momentary electrical surge or power failure may erase or damage the contents of an internal hard drive. To avoid losing your work, save your files to a backup disk on a regular basis.

- A *warning* alerts users to potential hazards to life or limb:

> WARNING: To prevent electrical shock, always disconnect your printer from its power source before cleaning internal parts.

A moderately forceful notice

- A *danger* notice identifies an immediate hazard to life or limb:

> DANGER: The red canister contains DEADLY radioactive material. **Do not break the safety seal** under any circumstances.

The most forceful notice

Inadequate notices of warning, caution, or danger are a common cause of lawsuits. Each hazard notice is legally required to (1) describe the specific hazard, (2) spell out the consequences of ignoring the hazard, and (3) offer instruction for avoiding the hazard (Manning 15).

Content requirements for hazard notices

Even the most emphatic verbal notice might be overlooked by an impatient or inattentive reader. Direct attention with symbols, or icons, as a visual signal (Bedford and Stearns 128):

Use hazard symbols

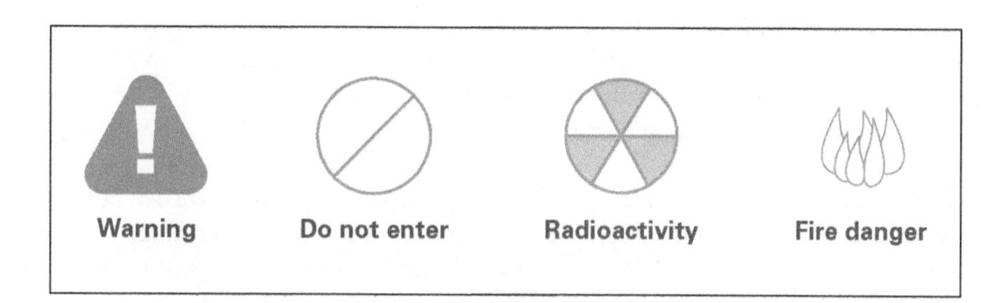

Keep the hazard notices prominent: Preview the hazards in your introduction and place each notice, *clearly highlighted* (by a ruled box, a distinct typeface, larger typesize, or color), immediately before the respective step.

> **NOTE** *Use hazard notices only when needed; overuse will dull their effect, and readers may overlook their importance.*

Readability

Instructions must be understood on the first reading because people want to take *immediate* action.

Write instructions that are easy to read quickly

Like descriptions, instructions name parts, use location and position words, and state exact measurements, weights, and dimensions. Instructions additionally require your strict attention to phrasing, sentence structure, and paragraph structure.

Use Direct Address, Active Voice, and Imperative Mood. Write instructions in the second person, as direct address, in order to emphasize the role of the reader.

In general, begin all steps and substeps with action verbs, using the *active voice* and *imperative mood* ("Insert the disk" instead of "The disk should be inserted" or "You should insert the disk").

Indirect or confusing

- The user keys in his or her access code.
- You should key in your access code.
- It is important to key in the access code.
- The access code is keyed in.

In this next version, the opening verb announces the specific action required.

Clear and direct

Key in your access code.

In certain cases, you may want to provide a clarifying word or phrase that precedes the verb (*Read Me* 130):

Information that might precede the verb

- [To log on,] **key in** your access code.
- [If your screen displays an error message,] **restart** the computer.
- [Slowly] **scan** the seal for gamma ray leakage.
- [In the Edit menu,] **click** on Paste.

NOTE *Certain cultures consider the direct imperative bossy and offensive. For cross-cultural audiences, you might rephrase an instruction as a declarative statement: from "Key in your access code" to "The access code should be keyed in." Or you might use an indirect imperative such as "Be sure to key in your access code" (Coe, "Writing" 18).*

Use Short and Logically Shaped Sentences. Use shorter sentences than usual, but never "telegraph" your message by omitting articles (*a*, *an*, *the*). Use one sentence for each step, so that people can perform one step at a time.

If a single step covers two related actions, describe these actions in their required sequence:

Confusing

Before switching on the computer, insert the DVD in the drive.

Logical

Insert the DVD in the drive; then switch on the computer.

Simplify explanations by using a familiar-to-unfamiliar sequence:

Hard

You must initialize a blank CD before you can store information on it.

Easier

Before you can store information on a blank CD, you must initialize the CD.

Use Parallel Phrasing. Parallelism is important in all writing but especially so in instructions, because repeating grammatical forms emphasizes the step-by-step organization. Parallelism also increases readability and lends continuity to the instructions.

To connect to the file server, follow these steps:

1. Switch the terminal to "on."
2. The CONTROL key and C key are pressed simultaneously.
3. Typing LOGON, and pressing the ESCAPE key.
4. Type your user number, and then press the ESCAPE key.

Not parallel

All steps should be in identical grammatical form:

To connect to the file server, follow these steps:

1. Switch the terminal to "on."
2. Press the CONTROL key and C key simultaneously.
3. Type LOGON, and then press the ESCAPE key.
4. Type your user number, and then press the ESCAPE key.

Parallel

Phrase Instructions Affirmatively. Research shows that people respond more quickly and efficiently to instructions phrased affirmatively rather than negatively (Spyridakis and Wenger 205).

Verify that your camera lens is not contaminated with dust.

Negative

Examine your camera lens for dust.

Affirmative

Use Transitions to Mark Time and Sequence. Transitional expressions provide a bridge between related ideas. Some transitions ("first," "next," "meanwhile," "finally," "ten minutes later," "the next day," "immediately afterward") mark time and sequence. They help users understand the step-by-step process, as in the next example.

PREPARING THE GROUND FOR A TENT

Begin by clearing and smoothing the area that will be under the tent. This step will prevent damage to the tent floor and eliminate the discomfort of sleeping on uneven ground. **First,** remove all large stones, branches, or other debris within a level area roughly 10 × 10 feet. Use your camping shovel to remove half-buried rocks that cannot easily be moved by hand. **Next,** fill in any large holes with soil or leaves. **Finally,** make several light surface passes with the shovel or a large, leafy branch to smooth the area.

Transitions enhance continuity

Effective Design

Instructions rarely get undivided attention. The reader, in fact, is doing two things more or less at once: interpreting the instructions and performing the task. An effective instructional design conveys the sense that the task is within a qualified person's range of abilities. The more accessible and inviting the design, the more likely your readers will follow the instructions.

GUIDELINES for Designing Instructions

- **Use informative headings.** Tell readers what to expect; emphasize what is most important; provide cues for navigation. A heading such as "How to Initialize Your Compact Disk" is more informative than "Compact Disk Initializing."
- **Arrange all steps in a numbered list.** Unless the procedure consists of simple steps (as in "Preparing the Ground for a Tent," above), list and number each step. Numbered steps not only announce the sequence of steps, but also help readers remember where they left off.
- **Separate each step visually.** Single-space within steps and double-space between.
- **Double-space to signal a new paragraph, instead of indenting.**
- **Make warning, caution, and danger notices highly visible.** Use ruled boxes or highlighting, and plenty of white space.
- **Make visual and verbal information redundant.** Let the visual repeat, restate, or reinforce the prose.
- **Keep the visual and the step close together.** If room allows, place the visual right beside the step; if not, right after the step. Set off the visual with plenty of white space.
- **Consider a multicolumn design.** If steps are brief and straightforward and require back-and-forth reference from prose to visuals, consider multiple columns.
- **Keep it simple.** Readers can be overwhelmed by a page with excessive or inconsistent designs.
- **For lengthy instructions, consider a layered approach.** In a complex manual, for instance, you might add a "Quick-Use Guide" for getting started, with cross-references to pages containing more detailed and technical information.

NOTE *Online instructions have their own design requirements. Also, despite the increasing popularity of online documentation, many people continue to find printed manuals more convenient and easier to navigate (Foster 10).*

AN OUTLINE FOR INSTRUCTIONS

You can adapt the following outline to any instructions. Here are the possible components to include:

- **I. Introduction**
  - A. Definition, Benefits, and Purpose of the Procedure
  - B. Intended Audience (often omitted for workplace audiences)
  - C. Prior Knowledge and Skills Needed by the Audience
  - D. Brief Overall Description of the Procedure
  - E. Principle of Operation
  - F. Materials, Equipment (in order of use), and Special Conditions
  - G. Working Definitions (always in the introduction)
  - H. Warnings, Cautions, Dangers (previewed here and spelled out at steps)
  - I. List of Major Steps
- **II. Required Steps**
  - A. First Major Step
    - 1. Definition and purpose
    - 2. Materials, equipment, and special conditions for this step
    - 3. Substeps (if applicable)
      - a. First substep
      - b. Second substep (and so on)
  - B. Second Major Step (and so on)
- **III. Conclusion**
  - A. Review of Major Steps (for a complex procedure only)
  - B. Interrelation of Steps
  - C. Troubleshooting or Follow-up Advice (as needed)

This outline is only tentative; you might modify, delete, or combine some components, depending on your subject, purpose, and audience.

Introduction

The introduction should help readers to begin "doing" as soon as they are able to proceed safely, effectively, and confidently (van der Meij and Carroll 245–46). Most people are interested primarily in "how to use it or fix it," and will require only a general understanding of "how it works." You don't want to bury your readers in a long introduction, nor do you want to set them loose on the procedure without adequate preparation. Know your audience—what they need and don't need.

Body: Required Steps

In the body section (labeled Required Steps), give each step and substep in order. Insert warnings, cautions, and notes as needed. Begin each step with its definition or purpose or both. Users who understand the reasons for a step will do a better job. A numbered list is an excellent way to segment the steps. Or, begin each sentence in a complex stage on a new line.

Conclusion

The conclusion of a set of instructions has several possible functions:

- Summarize the major steps in a long and complex procedure, to help people review their performance.
- Describe the results of the procedure.
- Offer follow-up advice about what could be done next or refer the reader to further sources of documentation.
- Give advice about troubleshooting if anything goes wrong.

You might do all these things—or none of them. If your procedural section has provided all that is needed, omit the conclusion altogether.

A SITUATION REQUIRING INSTRUCTIONS

Figure 8 shows a complete set of instructions written for a nontechnical audience. These instructions follow the basic outline by offering an overview, a list of equipment needed, and simple numbered instructions. The design, which uses informative headings, numbered steps, and simple visual diagrams, is easy to use.

A Complete Set of Instructions for a Nontechnical Audience

The Situation. The owner of your town's local hardware store tells you that he often is asked the same questions by customers who want to make simple home repairs. One common question is about how to replace a worn faucet washer. He decides to hire a technical writing student (you) to help him write and design a simple, yet effective, set of instructions.

Audience and Use Profile. These customers come from a wide range of backgrounds, but most of them are not engineers or plumbers. They are just regular homeowners who are confident in their ability to work with basic tools and comfortable trying a new task. They don't want a lot of detail about the history of faucets or the various types of faucets. They just want to know how to fix the problem. These people are busy—they have lots of chores to do on the weekend, and they want instructions that are easy to follow and use.

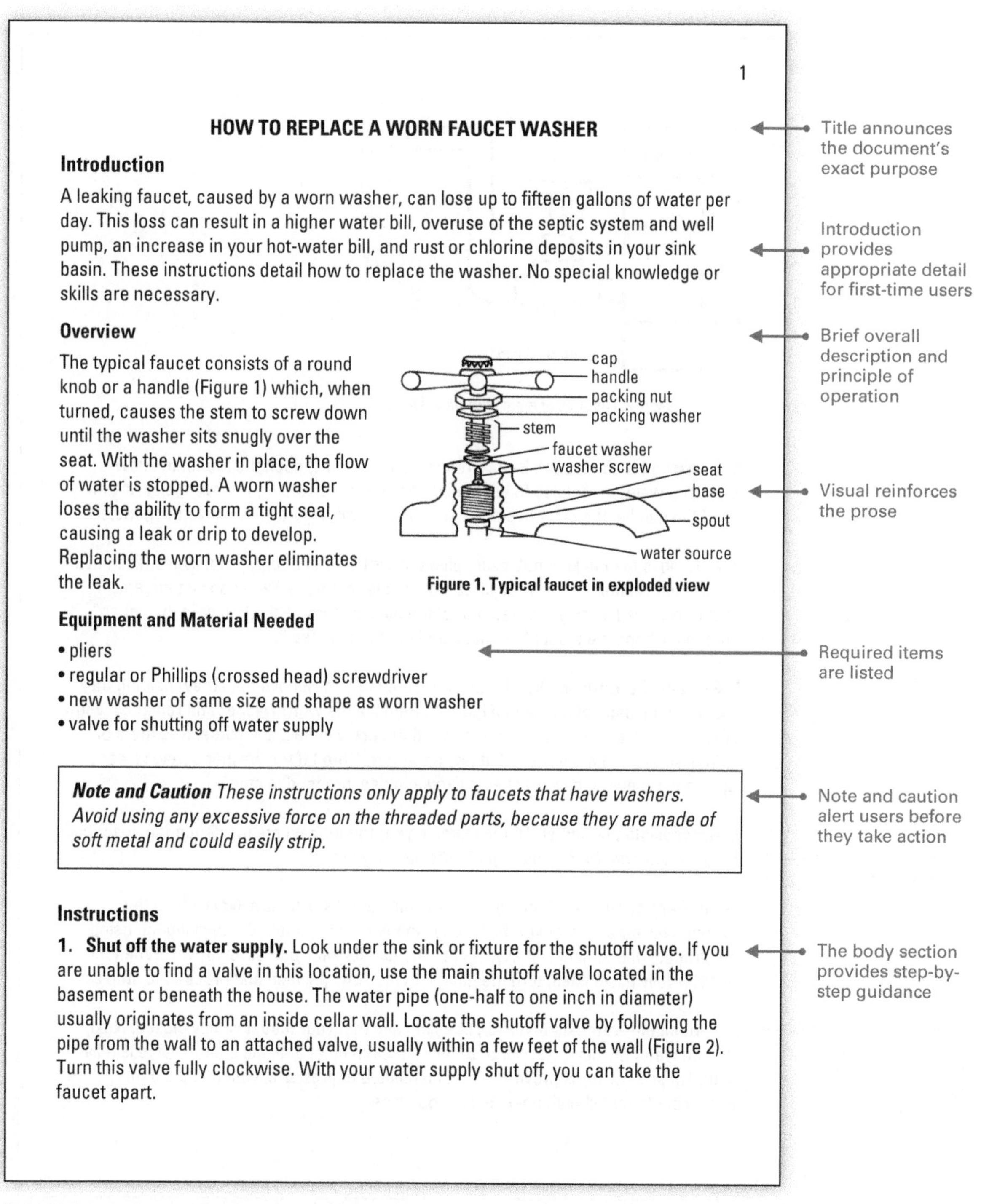

1

HOW TO REPLACE A WORN FAUCET WASHER

Introduction

A leaking faucet, caused by a worn washer, can lose up to fifteen gallons of water per day. This loss can result in a higher water bill, overuse of the septic system and well pump, an increase in your hot-water bill, and rust or chlorine deposits in your sink basin. These instructions detail how to replace the washer. No special knowledge or skills are necessary.

Overview

The typical faucet consists of a round knob or a handle (Figure 1) which, when turned, causes the stem to screw down until the washer sits snugly over the seat. With the washer in place, the flow of water is stopped. A worn washer loses the ability to form a tight seal, causing a leak or drip to develop. Replacing the worn washer eliminates the leak.

Figure 1. Typical faucet in exploded view

Equipment and Material Needed

- pliers
- regular or Phillips (crossed head) screwdriver
- new washer of same size and shape as worn washer
- valve for shutting off water supply

> ***Note and Caution*** *These instructions only apply to faucets that have washers. Avoid using any excessive force on the threaded parts, because they are made of soft metal and could easily strip.*

Instructions

1. Shut off the water supply. Look under the sink or fixture for the shutoff valve. If you are unable to find a valve in this location, use the main shutoff valve located in the basement or beneath the house. The water pipe (one-half to one inch in diameter) usually originates from an inside cellar wall. Locate the shutoff valve by following the pipe from the wall to an attached valve, usually within a few feet of the wall (Figure 2). Turn this valve fully clockwise. With your water supply shut off, you can take the faucet apart.

FIGURE 8 **A Complete Set of Instructions**

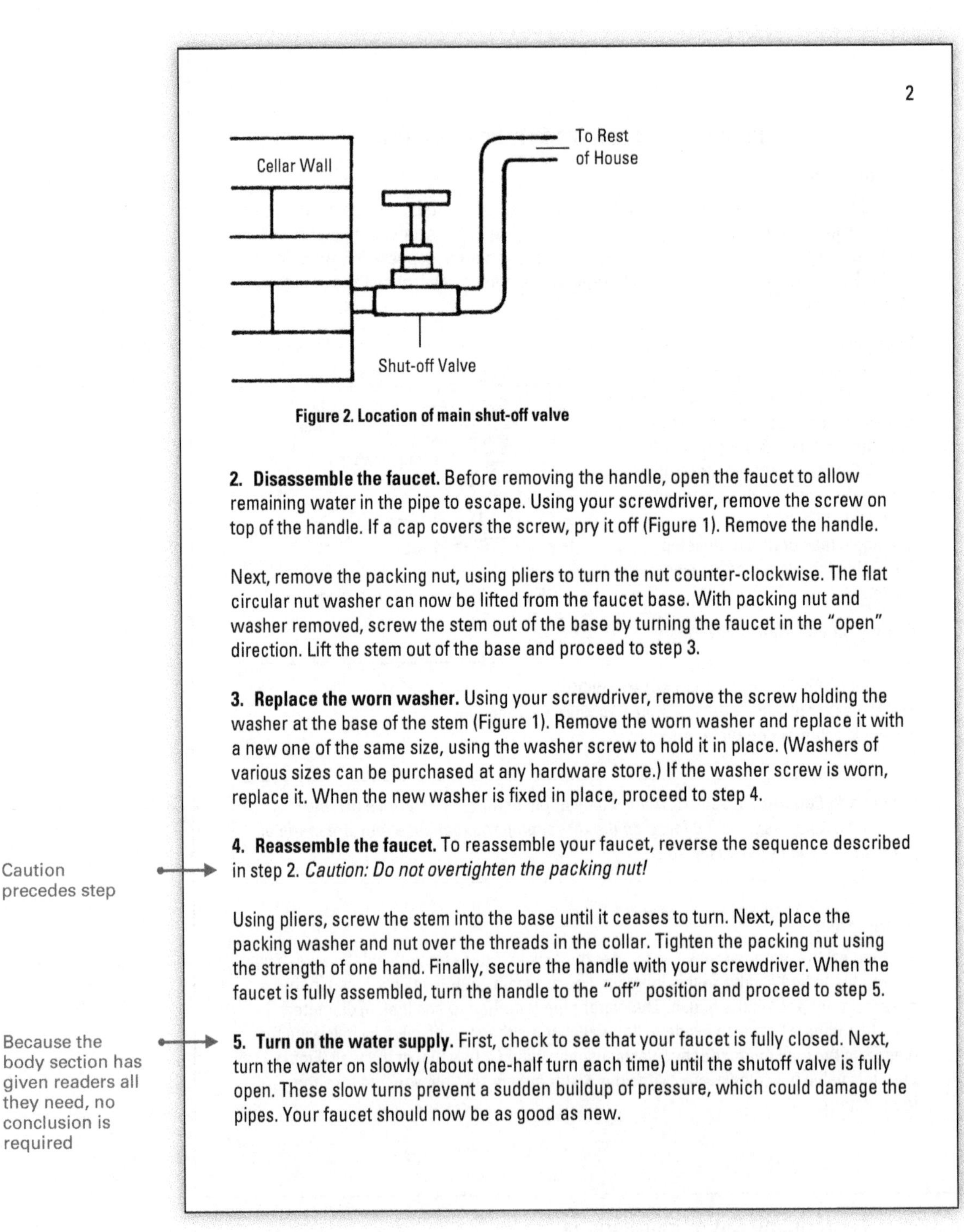

2

Figure 2. Location of main shut-off valve

2. Disassemble the faucet. Before removing the handle, open the faucet to allow remaining water in the pipe to escape. Using your screwdriver, remove the screw on top of the handle. If a cap covers the screw, pry it off (Figure 1). Remove the handle.

Next, remove the packing nut, using pliers to turn the nut counter-clockwise. The flat circular nut washer can now be lifted from the faucet base. With packing nut and washer removed, screw the stem out of the base by turning the faucet in the "open" direction. Lift the stem out of the base and proceed to step 3.

3. Replace the worn washer. Using your screwdriver, remove the screw holding the washer at the base of the stem (Figure 1). Remove the worn washer and replace it with a new one of the same size, using the washer screw to hold it in place. (Washers of various sizes can be purchased at any hardware store.) If the washer screw is worn, replace it. When the new washer is fixed in place, proceed to step 4.

Caution precedes step

4. Reassemble the faucet. To reassemble your faucet, reverse the sequence described in step 2. *Caution: Do not overtighten the packing nut!*

Using pliers, screw the stem into the base until it ceases to turn. Next, place the packing washer and nut over the threads in the collar. Tighten the packing nut using the strength of one hand. Finally, secure the handle with your screwdriver. When the faucet is fully assembled, turn the handle to the "off" position and proceed to step 5.

Because the body section has given readers all they need, no conclusion is required

5. Turn on the water supply. First, check to see that your faucet is fully closed. Next, turn the water on slowly (about one-half turn each time) until the shutoff valve is fully open. These slow turns prevent a sudden buildup of pressure, which could damage the pipes. Your faucet should now be as good as new.

FIGURE 8 *(Continued)*

DIGITAL AND ONLINE INSTRUCTIONS

PDF documents allow instructions to be accessed online

The rising cost of printing and updating instructions, particularly instructions that can be accessed easily online, has shifted much instructional material to digital formats. A common method of placing instructional material online is to use Portable Document Format, or PDF. These files retain their original formatting, so they look identical in print or on the screen. Figure 8, the instructions for replacing a worn faucet washer, would be easy to convert to a PDF file (using *Adobe Acrobat*, *Apple Pages*, or similar software). These instructions could then be posted on the hardware store's Web site.

Some instructions come on a CD

For some products, printed manuals have been replaced with CD versions. For example, when you buy new computer software, such as *Microsoft Word* or *Adobe Illustrator*, the program may come with a brief, printed, installation guide. These small guides are often titled "Getting Started" and look like small brochures. But the full-scale user manual will be available on the accompanying CD that you can download to your computer.

Some instructions are built into the program

Most software also provides the "help" information within the program itself. Online instructions (Figure 9) can be updated through the computer's "automatic update" feature, and they are designed to provide the following information:

Examples of online documentation

- error messages and troubleshooting advice
- reference guides to additional information or instructions
- tutorial lessons that include interactive exercises with immediate feedback
- help and review options to accommodate different learning styles
- link to software manufacturer's Web site

Instead of leafing through a printed manual or searching a digital version, people find what they need by typing a simple command, clicking a mouse button, using a help menu, or following an electronic prompt.

Special software such as *RoboHelp* or *Doc-to-Help* can convert print material into online help files that appear as dialog boxes that ask the person to input a response or click on an option, or as pop-up or balloon help that appears when the person clicks on an icon or points to an item on the screen for more information. (Explore, for example, the online help resources on your own computer.)

Like Web pages, online information should be written in well-organized chunks. It should never be paper documentation merely converted into an electronic file because some tasks that people perform with the paper document may not be possible with the online version without substantial modifications. In short, creating effective online documentation requires much training and practice.

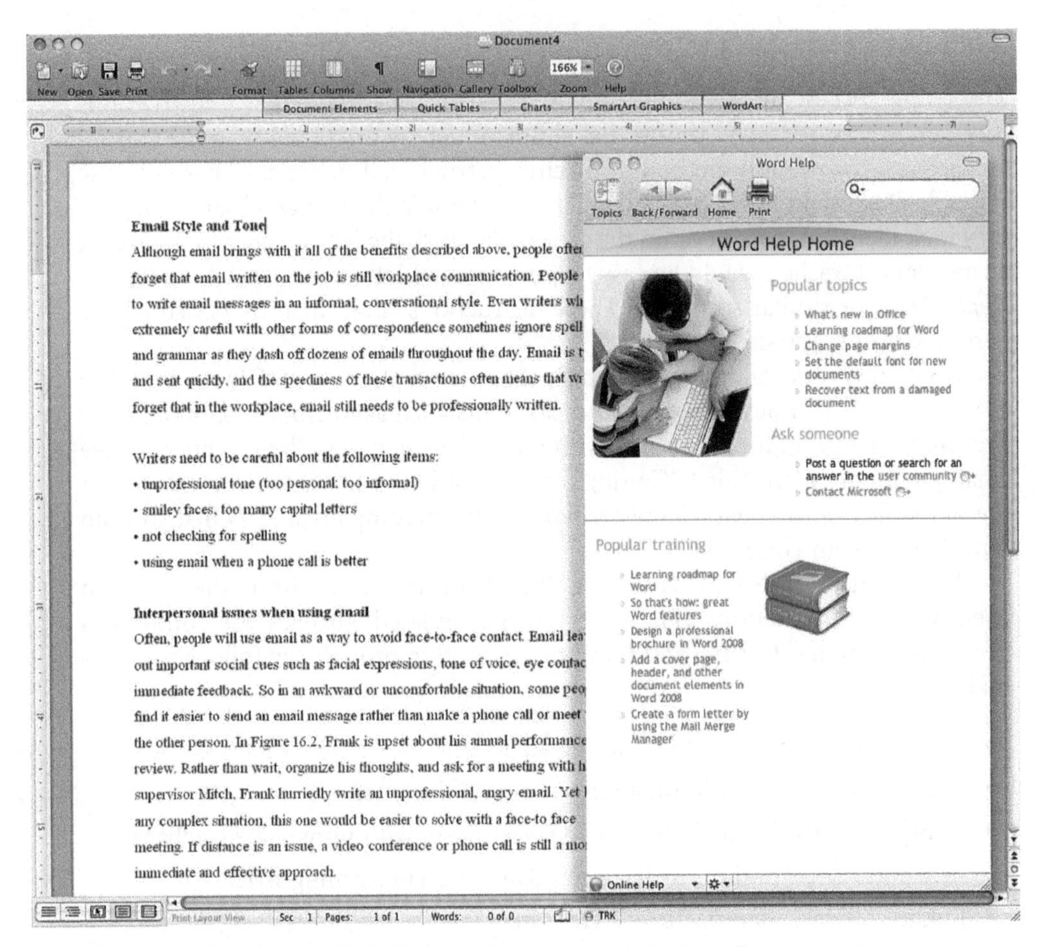

FIGURE 9 **An Online Help Screen** This electronic index offers instant access to any of the topics in the entire online manual.
Source: Used with permission from Microsoft.

VIDEO INSTRUCTIONS

Along with providing CDs and online instructions, many organizations are creating instructions in video format and posting them on a video-sharing site (such as YouTube) or on the company Web site. By combining sound, movement, color, speech, narration, and text, video instructions can show the full range of actions required to assemble the product or perform the task. *Showing* is a powerful teaching technique. People like to *see* how something is done and often will ask a friend or neighbor for advice about a given task before even reading the instruction manual.

Scripting Online Videos

Start by creating an outline

For a video, the outline takes the form of a script but serves the same function—to plan and sketch what you intend to create. The script outlines the narration, images, motion, and other features that will comprise the complete video. For an instructional video, begin by writing a printed set of instructions. Then adapt the print instructions to a video format: decide on background and foreground details, determine camera placement, decide where and when to include music or text, and write out the full narrative to be delivered.

Script the video (and then edit) to provide separate segments that orient the viewer, give a list of parts, supply step-by-step instructions, and offer a conclusion (such as a shot of the assembled product in action and a closing remark). Remove any unnecessary background or foreground clutter. Position the camera to keep the object or procedure at the center of the frame, at a distance that allows viewers to see clearly. Keep music to a minimum, usually only at the beginning and end. If text is included, make it easy-to-read on the screen—concise, clear, and to the point. Finally, accompany each step with narration, spoken clearly and slowly, with transitions between each step, and concise information.

Figure 10 features selected stills from an instructional video on how to properly apply insecticides, known as ant baits, to control fire ants. This video combines text, sound, images and narration. The script for these four slides would resemble the example shown on the next page.

FIGURE 10 Stills from a Set of Video Instructions

Source: 4 stills from How to Apply Fire Ant Baits video, found at http://www.extension.org/pages/Fire_Ant_Control_Made_Easy_Video:_How_to_Apply_Fire_Ant_Baits. Used with permission of eXtension Initiative.

Sample script for Figure 10 Usability in relation to instructions

- **Video still 1:** After opening music and slide, begin with video footage demonstrating how to use the hand seed spreader. Narration: "The most effective way to apply bait is to broadcast it."
- **Video still 2:** Close shot of a person wearing a seeder. Follow the person as he walks across the yard, toward camera.
- **Video still 3:** Still shot of three types of push spreaders. Narration: "Bait can be applied with the same spreader you use for fertilizer."
- **Video still 4:** Combine text and visual shot of how to calculate the amount of ant bait.

EVALUATING THE USABILITY OF INSTRUCTIONAL DOCUMENTS

A usable document is one that enables people to perform a task or do something effectively. Although usability is an important feature of all documents, it is critical with instructions and procedures because of safety and liability concerns (see Faulty Instructions and Legal Liability).

Conducting usability evaluations on instructional documents

Once you have written and designed a first draft, you can conduct some simple yet effective usability evaluations to help you see how people use your document and to determine whether you need to revise the instructional material. Obtaining this feedback in the early stages of document preparation enables you to correct any errors or problems before the instructions are finalized.

Two Approaches to Evaluating an Instructional Document's Usability

In general, you can evaluate a document's usability by observing how people read, respond to, and work with your document. For instructional documents in particular, try the following two approaches with people who represent the typical audience for your instructions.

Focus Groups. Based on a targeted list of questions about the document's content, organization, style, and design, people in a focus group are asked to describe (out loud) what information they think is missing or excessive, what they like or dislike, and what they find easy or hard to understand. They may also suggest revisions for graphics, format, or level of technicality.

Think-aloud Evaluation. In this approach, a small group (3–4) of people are provided with both your instructions and a way they can actually test this document. For instance, if your instructions explain how to connect a digital camera to a computer, provide a camera, cable, and laptop. Ask people to talk out loud as they try to follow your instructions. Note those places where people are successful and where they get stuck. Don't coach them, but do remind them to describe their thinking.

If members of your document's intended audience are unavailable, one alternative for testing usability is to consult the Checklist for Instructions.

Revise your document based on what you learn from the usability evaluations.

PROCEDURES

How instructions and procedures differ

Instructions show an uninitiated person how to perform a task. *Procedures,* on the other hand, provide rules and guidance for people who usually know how to perform the task but who are required to follow accepted practice. To ensure that everyone does something in exactly the same way, procedures typically are aimed at groups of people who need to coordinate their activities so that everyone's performance meets a certain standard. Consider, for example, police procedures for properly gathering evidence from a crime scene: Strict rules stipulate how evidence should be collected and labeled and how it should be preserved, transported, and stored. Evidence shown to have been improperly handled is routinely discredited in a courtroom.

Policy documents models and template (Go to *Student Resources>Chapter 21> Models and Templates*)

Procedures help keep everyone "on the same page"

Organizations need to follow strict safety procedures, say, as defined by the U.S. Occupational Safety and Health Administration (OSHA). As laws and policies change, such procedures are often updated. The written procedures must be posted for employees to read. Figure 11 shows one page outlining OSHA regulations for evacuating high-rise buildings.

Procedures help ensure safety

Procedures are also useful in situations in which certain tasks need to be standardized. For example, if different people in your organization perform the same task at different times (say, monitoring groundwater pollution) with different equipment, or under different circumstances, this procedure may need to be standardized to ensure that all work is done with the same accuracy and precision. A document known as a *Standard Operating Procedure (SOP)* becomes the official guideline for that task, as shown in Figure 12.

The steps in a procedure may or may not need to be numbered. This choice will depend on whether or not steps must be performed in strict sequence. Compare for example, Figure 11 versus Figure 12.

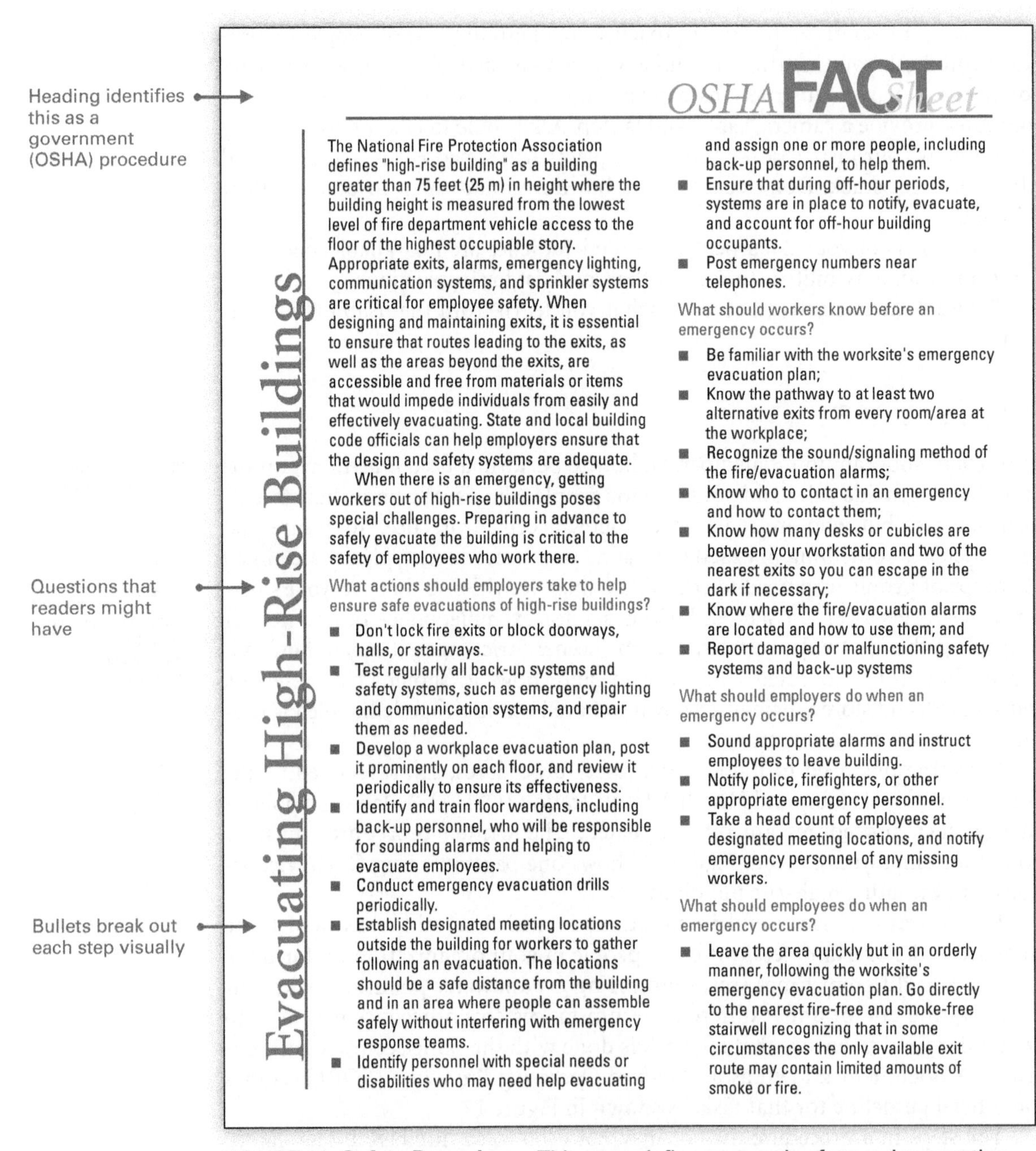

OSHA **FACT** Sheet

Evacuating High-Rise Buildings

The National Fire Protection Association defines "high-rise building" as a building greater than 75 feet (25 m) in height where the building height is measured from the lowest level of fire department vehicle access to the floor of the highest occupiable story. Appropriate exits, alarms, emergency lighting, communication systems, and sprinkler systems are critical for employee safety. When designing and maintaining exits, it is essential to ensure that routes leading to the exits, as well as the areas beyond the exits, are accessible and free from materials or items that would impede individuals from easily and effectively evacuating. State and local building code officials can help employers ensure that the design and safety systems are adequate.

When there is an emergency, getting workers out of high-rise buildings poses special challenges. Preparing in advance to safely evacuate the building is critical to the safety of employees who work there.

What actions should employers take to help ensure safe evacuations of high-rise buildings?

- Don't lock fire exits or block doorways, halls, or stairways.
- Test regularly all back-up systems and safety systems, such as emergency lighting and communication systems, and repair them as needed.
- Develop a workplace evacuation plan, post it prominently on each floor, and review it periodically to ensure its effectiveness.
- Identify and train floor wardens, including back-up personnel, who will be responsible for sounding alarms and helping to evacuate employees.
- Conduct emergency evacuation drills periodically.
- Establish designated meeting locations outside the building for workers to gather following an evacuation. The locations should be a safe distance from the building and in an area where people can assemble safely without interfering with emergency response teams.
- Identify personnel with special needs or disabilities who may need help evacuating and assign one or more people, including back-up personnel, to help them.
- Ensure that during off-hour periods, systems are in place to notify, evacuate, and account for off-hour building occupants.
- Post emergency numbers near telephones.

What should workers know before an emergency occurs?

- Be familiar with the worksite's emergency evacuation plan;
- Know the pathway to at least two alternative exits from every room/area at the workplace;
- Recognize the sound/signaling method of the fire/evacuation alarms;
- Know who to contact in an emergency and how to contact them;
- Know how many desks or cubicles are between your workstation and two of the nearest exits so you can escape in the dark if necessary;
- Know where the fire/evacuation alarms are located and how to use them; and
- Report damaged or malfunctioning safety systems and back-up systems

What should employers do when an emergency occurs?

- Sound appropriate alarms and instruct employees to leave building.
- Notify police, firefighters, or other appropriate emergency personnel.
- Take a head count of employees at designated meeting locations, and notify emergency personnel of any missing workers.

What should employees do when an emergency occurs?

- Leave the area quickly but in an orderly manner, following the worksite's emergency evacuation plan. Go directly to the nearest fire-free and smoke-free stairwell recognizing that in some circumstances the only available exit route may contain limited amounts of smoke or fire.

FIGURE 11 **Safety Procedures** This page defines general safety and evacuation procedures to be followed by employers and employees. Each building in turn is required to have its own specific procedures, based on such variables as location, design, and state law.

Source: U.S. Occupational Safety and Health Administration, 2007 <www.osha.gov>.

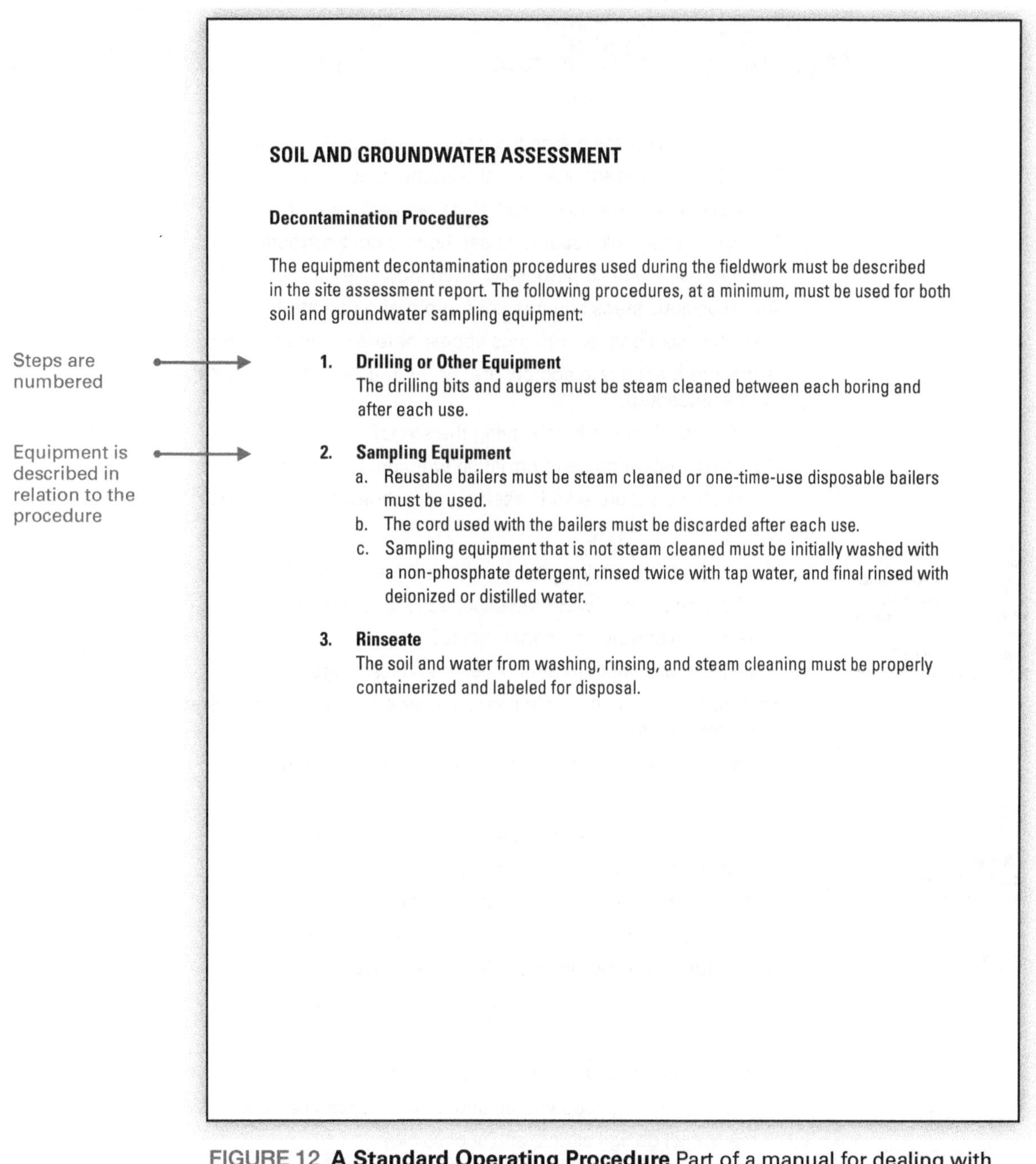

FIGURE 12 **A Standard Operating Procedure** Part of a manual for dealing with leaking underground fuel tanks, this SOP is aimed at technicians already familiar with techniques such as "steam cleaning" and "containerizing." However, to prevent contamination of testing equipment, each technician needs to follow that strict sequence of steps.

Source: Ventura County LUFT Guidance Manual. Ventura, CA. April 2001. Used with permission.

CHECKLIST: Instructions and Procedures

Content

- ☐ Does the title promise exactly what the instructions deliver?
- ☐ Is the background adequate for the intended audience?
- ☐ Do explanations enable readers to understand what to do?
- ☐ Do examples enable readers to see how to do it correctly?
- ☐ Are the definition and purpose of each step given as needed?
- ☐ Are all obvious steps and needless information omitted?
- ☐ Do notes, cautions, or warnings appear before or with the step?
- ☐ Is the information rate appropriate for the reader's abilities and the difficulty of this procedure?
- ☐ Are visuals adequate for clarifying the steps?
- ☐ Do visuals repeat prose information whenever necessary?
- ☐ Is everything accurate and based on your thorough knowledge?

Organization

- ☐ Is the introduction adequate without being excessive?
- ☐ Do the instructions follow the exact sequence of steps?
- ☐ Is each step numbered, if appropriate?
- ☐ Is all the information for a particular step close together?
- ☐ For lengthy instructions, is a layered approach, with a brief reference card, more appropriate?
- ☐ Is the conclusion necessary and, if necessary, adequate?

Style

- ☐ Does the familiar material appear *first* in each sentence?
- ☐ Do steps generally have short sentences?
- ☐ Does each step begin with an action verb?
- ☐ Are all steps in the active voice and imperative mood?
- ☐ Do all steps have parallel and affirmative phrasing?
- ☐ Are transitions adequate for marking time and sequence?

Page Design

- ☐ Does each heading clearly tell readers what to expect?
- ☐ Are steps single-spaced within, and double-spaced between?
- ☐ Is the overall design simple and accessible?
- ☐ Are notes, cautions, or warnings set off or highlighted?
- ☐ Are visuals beside or near the step, and set off by white space?

TC WEB **Chapter quiz, Exercises, Web links, and Flashcards** (Go to *Student Resources>Chapter 21*) **Instructions/procedure**

s Activities, Case studies, Model documents, and Quiz (Go to *Technical Communication Documents*)

Brochures/manuals Activities, Case studies, and Model documents (Go to *Technical Communication Documents*)

Projects

GENERAL

1. Improve readability by revising the style and design of these instructions.

> **What to Do Before Jacking Up Your Car**
>
> Whenever the misfortune of a flat tire occurs, some basic procedures should be followed before the car is jacked up. If possible, your car should be positioned on as firm and level a surface as is available. The engine has to be turned off; the parking brake should be set; and the automatic transmission shift lever must be placed in "park" or the manual transmission lever in "reverse." The wheel diagonally opposite the one to be removed should have a piece of wood placed beneath it to prevent the wheel from rolling. The spare wheel, jack, and lug wrench should be removed from the luggage compartment.

2. Select part of a technical manual in your field or instructions for a general audience and make a copy of the material. Using the checklist on the previous page, evaluate the sample's usability. In a memo to your instructor, discuss the strong and weak points of the instructions. Or explain your evaluation in class.

3. Assume that colleagues or classmates will be serving six months as volunteers in agriculture, education, or a similar capacity in a developing country. Do the research and create a set of procedures that will prepare individuals for avoiding diseases and dealing with medical issues in that specific country. Topics might include safe food and water, insect protection, vaccinations, medical emergencies, and the like. Be sure to provide background on the specific health risks travelers will face. Design your instructions as a two-sided brief reference card, as a chapter to be included in a longer manual, or in some other format suggested by your instructor.

   Hint: Begin your research for this project by checking out the National Centers for Disease Control's Web site at <www.cdc.gov/travel/>.

4. Choose a topic from your major, or an area of interest. Using the general outline in this chapter as a model, prepare instructions for a task that requires at least three major steps. Address a general audience, and begin by completing an audience and use profile. Include (a) all necessary visuals, or, (b) an "art brief" and a rough diagram for each visual, or (c) a "reference visual" (a copy of a visual published elsewhere) with instructions for adapting your visual from that one. (If you borrow visuals from other sources, provide full documentation.)

5. Select any one of the instructional visuals in Figure 5 and write a prose version of those instructions—without using visual illustrations or special page design. Bring your version to class and be prepared to discuss the conclusions you've derived from this exercise.

6. Find a set of instructions or some other technical document that is easy-to-use. Assume that you are Associate Director of Communications for the company that produced this document and you are doing a final review before the document is released. With the Checklist for Instructions and Procedures as a guide, identify those features that make the document usable and prepare a memo to your boss that justifies your decision to release the document.

   Following the identical scenario, find a document that is hard to use, and identify the features that need improving. Prepare a memo to your boss that spells out the needed improvements. Submit both memos and the examples to your instructor.

TEAM

1. Draw a map of the route from your classroom to your dorm, apartment, or home—whichever is closest.

Be sure to include identifying landmarks. When your map is completed, write instructions for a classmate who will try to duplicate your map from the information given in your written instructions. Be sure your classmate does not see your map! Exchange your instructions and try to duplicate your classmate's map. Compare your results with the original map. Discuss your conclusions about the usability of these instructions.

2. Divide into small groups and visit your computer center, library, or any place on campus or at work where you can find operating manuals for computers, lab or office equipment, or the like. (Or look through the documentation for your own computer hardware or software.) Locate fairly brief instructions that could use revision for improved content, organization, style, or format. Choose instructions for a procedure you are able to perform. Make a copy of the instructions, test them for usability, and revise as needed. Submit all materials to your instructor, along with a memo explaining the improvements. Or be prepared to discuss your revision in class.

3. Test the usability of a document prepared for this course.

   Revise the document based on your findings. Obtain your data through focus group discussions and/or think-aloud evaluation.

   Appoint a group member to explain the usability testing procedure and the results to the class.

DIGITAL

Do the research and prepare a set of instructions that will show general readers how to become more environmentally informed consumers and how to find, identify, evaluate, and compare environmentally friendly consumer goods such as appliances, building materials, and household products. Design your instructions as a foldout brochure or a one-page (double-sided) handout, or in a format requested by your instructor. *Hint:* Begin your research by checking out the following Web sites:

- *The Environment at MIT* at <http://web.mit.edu/environment/reduce/env_living.html/>
- The U.S. Environmental Protection Agency's *Energy Star* site at <www.energystar.gov>
- *Buyer's Guide for the Ethical consumer* site at <www.ethicalconsumer.org/FreeBuyersGuides.aspx>

GLOBAL

In many cultures, the use of imperative mood is considered impolite or too direct. For instance, instructions that state "Place the disk into the disk drive" may sound bossy and inconsiderate. Find a set of instructions that use imperative mood (for example, Figure 8 in this chapter) and rewrite these for a cross-cultural audience where the imperative mood would be offensive. For instance, you might use an indirect imperative ("Be sure to insert the disk into the drive").

For more support in mastering the objectives of this chapter, go to **www.mytechcommlab.com**

Formal Analytical Reports

Considering Audience and Purpose

Typical Analytical Problems

Elements of an Effective Analysis

An Outline and Model for Analytical Reports

Front Matter and End Matter Supplements

A Situation Requiring an Analytical Report

Guidelines for Reasoning through an Analytical Problem

Checklist: Analytical Reports

Projects

Stefanie Aulmann/Getty Images

"Our clients make investment decisions based on feasibility and strategy for marketing new products. Our job is to research consumer interest in these potential products (say, a new brand of low-calorie chocolate). In designing surveys, I have to translate the client's information needs into precise questions. I have to be certain that the respondents are answering exactly the question I had in mind, and not inventing their own version of the question. Then I have to analyze these data and translate them into accurate interpretations and recommendations for our clients."

—James North, Senior Project Manager, market research firm

LEARNING OBJECTIVES FORTHIS CHAPTER

- Appreciate the role of formal analytical reports in the workplace
- Understand the role of audience and purpose for such reports
- Identify three major types of analyses: casual, comparative, and feasibility
- Know the criteria for sound analytical reasoning
- Identify the parts that typically accompany a long report (front matter and end matter)
- Write a formal analytical report

Chapter overview
(Go to *Student Resources>Chapter 23*)

The formal analytical report usually leads to recommendations. The formal report replaces the memo when the topic requires lengthy discussion. Formal reports generally include a title page, table of contents, a system of headings, a list of references or works cited, and other front-matter and end-matter supplements.

An essential component of workplace problem solving, analytical reports are designed to answer these questions:

What readers of an analytical report want to know

- Based on the information gathered about this issue, what do we know?
- What conclusions can we draw?
- What should we do or not do?

Assume, for example, that you receive this assignment from your supervisor:

A typical analytical problem

> Recommend the best method for removing the heavy-metal contamination from our company dump site.

Recommendations have legal and ethical implications

First, you will have to learn all you can about the problem. Then you will compare the advantages and disadvantages of various options based on the criteria you are using to assess feasibility: say, cost-effectiveness, time required versus time available for completion, potential risk to the public and the environment. For example, the cheapest option might also pose the greatest environmental risk and could result in heavy fines or criminal charges. But the safest option might simply be too expensive for this struggling company to afford. Or perhaps the Environmental Protection Agency has imposed a legal deadline for the cleanup. In making your recommendation, you will need to weigh all the criteria (cost, safety, time) very carefully, or you could land in jail.

The above situation calls for critical thinking and research. Besides interviewing legal and environmental experts, you might search the literature and the Web. From these sources you can discover whether anyone has been able to solve a problem like yours, or learn about the newest technologies for toxic waste cleanup. Then you will have to decide how much, if any, of what others have done applies to your situation.

CONSIDERING AUDIENCE AND PURPOSE

Using analysis on the job

On the job, you may be assigned to evaluate a new assembly technique on the production line, or to locate and purchase the best equipment at the best price. You might have to identify the cause behind a monthly drop in sales, the reasons for low employee morale, the causes of an accident, or the reasons for equipment failure. You might need to assess the feasibility of a proposal for a company's expansion or merger or investment. You will present your findings in a formal report.

Audience considerations

Because of their major impact on the decision-making process, formal reports are almost always written for an audience of decision makers such as government officials or corporate managers. You need to know whom you are writing for and whether the report will be read primarily by an individual, a team, or a series of individuals with differing roles in the company.

Purpose considerations

To determine the purpose of the report, consider what question or questions it will ultimately answer. Also, consider why this particular topic is timely and useful to the intended audience. Use an Audience and Use Profile Sheet to begin mapping out your audience and purpose for the report.

TYPICAL ANALYTICAL PROBLEMS

Report models and template
(Go to *Student Resources>Chapter 23> Models and Templates*)

Far more than an encyclopedia presentation of information, the analytical report traces your inquiry, your evidence, and your reasoning to show exactly how you arrived at your conclusions and recommendations.

Workplace problem solving calls for skills in three broad categories: *causal analysis*, *comparative analysis*, and *feasibility analysis*. Each approach relies on its own type of reasoning.

Causal Analysis: "Why Does *X* Happen?"

Designed to reveal a problem at its source, the causal analysis answers questions such as this: *Why do so many apparently healthy people have sudden heart attacks?*

CASE **The Reasoning Process in Causal Analysis**

Identify the problem

Medical researchers at the world-renowned Hanford Health Institute recently found that 20 to 30 percent of deaths from sudden heart attacks occur in people who have none of the established risk factors (weight gain, smoking, diabetes, lack of exercise, high blood pressure, or family history).

Examine possible causes

To better identify people at risk, researchers are now tracking down new and powerful risk factors such as bacteria, viruses, genes, stress, anger, and depression.

Recommend solutions

Once researchers identify these factors and their mechanisms, they can recommend preventive steps such as careful monitoring, lifestyle and diet changes, drug treatment, or psychotherapy (H. Lewis 39–43).

A different version of causal analysis employs reasoning from effect to cause, to answer questions such as this: *What are the health effects of exposure to electromagnetic radiation?*

NOTE *Keep in mind that faulty causal reasoning is extremely common, especially when we ignore other possible causes or we confuse correlation with causation.*

Comparative Analysis: "Is *X* OR *Y* Better for Our Needs?"

Designed to rate competing items on the basis of specific criteria, the comparative analysis answers questions such as this: *Which type of security (firewall/encryption) program should we install on our company's computer system?*

CASE **The Reasoning Process in Comparative Analysis**

Identify the criteria

XYZ Corporation needs to identify exactly what information (personnel files, financial records) or functions (in-house communication, file transfer) it wants to protect from whom. Does it need both virus and tamper protection? Does it wish to restrict network access or encrypt email and computer files so they become unreadable to unauthorized persons? Does it wish to restrict access to or from the Web? In addition to the level of protection, how important are ease of maintenance and user-friendliness?

Rank the criteria

After identifying their specific criteria, XYZ decision makers need to rank them in order of importance (for example, 1. tamper protection, 2. user-friendliness, 3. secure financial records, and so on).

Compare items according to the criteria, and recommend the best one

On the basis of these ranked criteria, XYZ will assess relative strengths and weaknesses of competing security programs and recommend the best one (Schafer 93–94).

Feasibility Analysis: "Is This a Good Idea?"

Designed to assess the practicality of an idea or a plan, the feasibility analysis answers questions such as this: *Should healthy young adults be encouraged to receive genetic testing to measure their susceptibility to various diseases?*

TC WEB **Feasibility Studies models and template** (Go to *Student Resources>Chapter 23> Models and Templates*)

CASE The Reasoning Process in Feasibility Analysis

As a step toward "[translating] genetic research into health care," a National Institutes of Health (NIH) study is investigating the feasibility of offering genetic testing to healthy young adults at little or no cost. The testing focuses on diseases such as melanoma, diabetes, heart disease, and lung cancer. This study will measure not only the target audience's interest but also how those people tested "will interpret and use the results in making their own health care decisions in the future."

Arguments in favor of testing include the following:

Consider the strength of supporting reasons

- Young people with a higher risk for a particular disorder might consider preventive treatments.
- Early diagnosis and treatment could be "personalized," tailored to an individual's genetic profile.
- Low-risk test results might "inspire healthy people to stay healthy" by taking precautions such as limiting sun exposure or changing their dietary, exercise, and smoking habits.

Arguments against testing include the following:

Consider the strength of opposing reasons

- The benefits of early diagnosis and treatment for a small population might not justify the expense of testing the population at large.
- False positive results are always traumatic, and false negative results could be disastrous.
- Any positive result could subject a currently healthy young person to biased treatment from employers or disqualification for health and life insurance (National Institutes of Health; Notkins 74, 79).

Weigh the pros and cons, and recommend a course of action

After assessing the benefits and drawbacks of testing in this situation, NIH decision makers can make the appropriate recommendations.

Combining Types of Analysis

Analytical categories overlap considerably. Any one study may in fact require answers to two or more of the previous questions. The sample report later in this chapter is both a feasibility analysis and a comparative analysis. It is designed to answer these questions: *Is technical marketing the right career for me? If so, which is my best option for entering the field?*

ELEMENTS OF AN EFFECTIVE ANALYSIS

Reports project
(Go to *Student Resources>Chapter 23> Projects and Case Studies>Monsanto Case Research*)

The formal analytical report incorporates many elements from documents along with the suggestions that follow.

Clearly Identified Problem or Purpose

Define your purpose

To solve any problem or achieve any goal, you must first identify the issues precisely. Always begin by defining the main questions and thinking through any subordinate questions they may imply. Only then can you determine what to look for, where to look, and how much information you will need.

Your employer, for example, might pose this question: Will a low-impact aerobics program significantly reduce stress among my employees? The aerobics question obviously requires answers to three other questions: What are the therapeutic claims for aerobics? Are they valid? Will aerobics work in this situation? With the main questions identified, you can formulate an audience and purpose statement:

Audience and purpose statement

> My goal is to examine and evaluate claims about the therapeutic benefits of low-impact aerobic exercise and to recommend a course of action to my employer.

Words such as *examine* and *evaluate* (or *compare, identify, determine, measure, describe,* and so on) help readers understand the specific analytical activity that forms the subject of the report.

Adequate But Not Excessive Data

Decide how much is enough

A superficial analysis is basically worthless. Worthwhile analysis, in contrast, examines an issue in depth. In reporting on your analysis, however, you filter that material for the audience's understanding, deciding what to include and what to leave out. "Do decision makers in this situation need a closer look or am I presenting excessive detail when only general information is needed?" Is it possible to have too much information? In some cases, yes—as behavioral expert Dietrich Dorner explains:

Excessive information hampers decision making

> The more we know, the more clearly we realize what we don't know. This probably explains why . . . organizations tend to [separate] their information-gathering and decision-making branches. A business executive has an office manager; presidents have . . . advisers; military commanders have chiefs of staff. The point of this separation may well be to provide decision makers with only the bare outlines of all the available information so they will not be hobbled by excessive detail when they are obliged to render decisions. Anyone who is fully informed will see much more than the bare outlines and will therefore find it extremely difficult to reach a clear decision. (99)

Confusing the issue with excessive information is no better than recommending hasty action on the basis of inadequate information (Dorner 104).

As you research the issue you may want to filter material for your own understanding as well. Your decision about whether to rely on the abstract or summary or to read the complete text of a specialized article or report depends on the question you're trying to answer and the level of technical detail your readers expect. If you are an expert in the field, writing for other experts, you probably want to read the entire document in order to assess the methods and reasoning behind a given study. But if you are less than expert, a summary or abstract of this study's findings might suffice. The fact sheet in Figure 1, for example, summarizes a detailed feasibility study for a general reading audience. Readers seeking more details, including nonclassified elements of the complete report, could visit the Transportation Security Administration's Web site at <www.tsa.gov>.

When you might consult an abstract or summary instead of the complete work

NOTE *If you have relied merely on the abstract or summary instead of the full article, be sure to indicate this ("Abstract," "Press Release" or the like) when you cite the source in your report.*

Accurate and Balanced Data

Avoid stacking the evidence to support a preconceived point of view. Assume, for example, that you are asked to recommend the best chainsaw brand for a logging company. Reviewing test reports, you come across this information:

Give readers all they need to make an informed judgment

> Of all six brands tested, the Bomarc chainsaw proved easiest to operate. However, this brand also offers the fewest safety features.

In citing these equivocal findings, you need to present both of them accurately, and not simply the first—even though the Bomarc brand may be your favorite. Then argue for the feature (ease of use or safety) you think should receive priority.

Fully Interpreted Data

Interpretation shows the audience "what is important and what is unimportant, what belongs together and what does not" (Dorner 44). For example, you might interpret the above chainsaw data in this way:

Explain the significance of your data

> Our logging crews often work suspended by harness, high above the ground. Also, much work is in remote areas. Safety features therefore should be our first requirement in a chainsaw. Despite its ease of operation, the Bomarc saw does not meet our safety needs.

Explain the meaning of your evidence

FACT SHEET: Train and Rail Inspection Pilot, Phase I

U.S. DEPARTMENT OF HOMELAND SECURITY
Transportation Security Administration
FOR IMMEDIATE RELEASE – June 7, 20xx
TSA Press Office: (571) 227-2829

Objective:
Implement a pilot program to determine the feasibility of screening passengers, luggage and carry-on bags for explosives in the rail environment.

TRIP I Background:

- Homeland Security Secretary announced TRIP on March 22, 20xx, to test new technologies and screening concepts.
- The program is conducted in partnership with the Department of Transportation, Amtrak, Maryland Rail Commuter, and Washington D.C.'s Metro.
- The New Carrollton, Md. station was selected because it serves multiple types of rail operations and is located close to Washington, D.C.

TRIP I Facts:

- Screening for Phase I of TRIP began on May 4 and was completed on May 26, 20xx.
- A total of 8,835 passengers and 9,875 pieces of baggage were screened during the test.
- The average time to wait in line and move through the screening process was less than 2 minutes.
- Customer Feedback cards reflect a 93 percent satisfaction rate with both the screening process and the professional demeanor of TSA personnel.

Lessons Learned:

- Results indicate efficient checkpoints throughout with minimal customer inconvenience.
- Passengers were overwhelmingly receptive to the screening process.
- Providing a customer service representative on-site during all screening operations helped Amtrak ensure passengers received outstanding customer service.
- Skilled TSA screeners from the agency's National Screening Force were able to quickly transition to screening in the rail environment.
- Most importantly, Phase I showed that currently available technology could be utilized to screen for explosives in the rail environment.

FIGURE 1 **A Summary Description of a Feasibility Study** Notice that the criteria for assessing feasibility include passenger wait times, passenger receptiveness to screening, and—most important—effectiveness of screening equipment in this environment.

Source: Transportation Security Administration. Press Release.

By saying "therefore" you engage in analysis—not just information sharing. Don't merely list your findings, explain what they mean.

Subordination of Personal Bias

To arrive at the *truth* of the matter, you need to see clearly. Don't let your biases fog up the real picture. Each stage of analysis requires decisions about what to record, what to exclude, and where to go next. You must evaluate your data (Is this reliable and important?), interpret your evidence (What does it mean?), and make recommendations (What action is needed?). An ethically sound analysis presents a balanced and reasonable assessment of the evidence. Do not force viewpoints that are not supported by dependable evidence.

Evaluate and interpret evidence impartially

Appropriate Visuals

Graphs are especially useful in an analysis of trends (rising or falling sales, radiation levels). Tables, charts, photographs, and diagrams work well in comparative analyses. Be sure to accompany each visual with a fully interpreted "story."

Use visuals generously

NOTE *As the simplicity of Figure 2 and its brief caption illustrate, a powerful visual does not need to be complex and fancy, nor its accompanying story long and involved. Sometimes, less can be more.*

Valid Conclusions and Recommendations

Along with the informative abstract, conclusions and recommendations are the sections of a long report that receive the most audience attention. The goal of analysis is to reach a valid conclusion—an overall judgment about what all the material means (that *X* is better than *Y*, that *B* failed because of *C*, that *A* is a good plan of action). The following example shows the conclusion of a report on the feasibility of installing an active solar heating system in a large building.

Be clear about what the audience should think and do

1. Active solar space heating for our new research building is technically feasible because the site orientation will allow for a sloping roof facing due south, with plenty of unshaded space.
2. It is legally feasible because we are able to obtain an access easement on the adjoining property, to ensure that no buildings or trees will be permitted to shade the solar collectors once they are installed.
3. It is economically feasible because our sunny, cold climate means high fuel savings and faster payback (fifteen years maximum) with solar heating. The long-term fuel savings justify our short-term installation costs (already minimal because the solar system can be incorporated during the building's construction—without renovations).

Offer a final judgment

Conclusions are valid when they are logically derived from accurate interpretations.

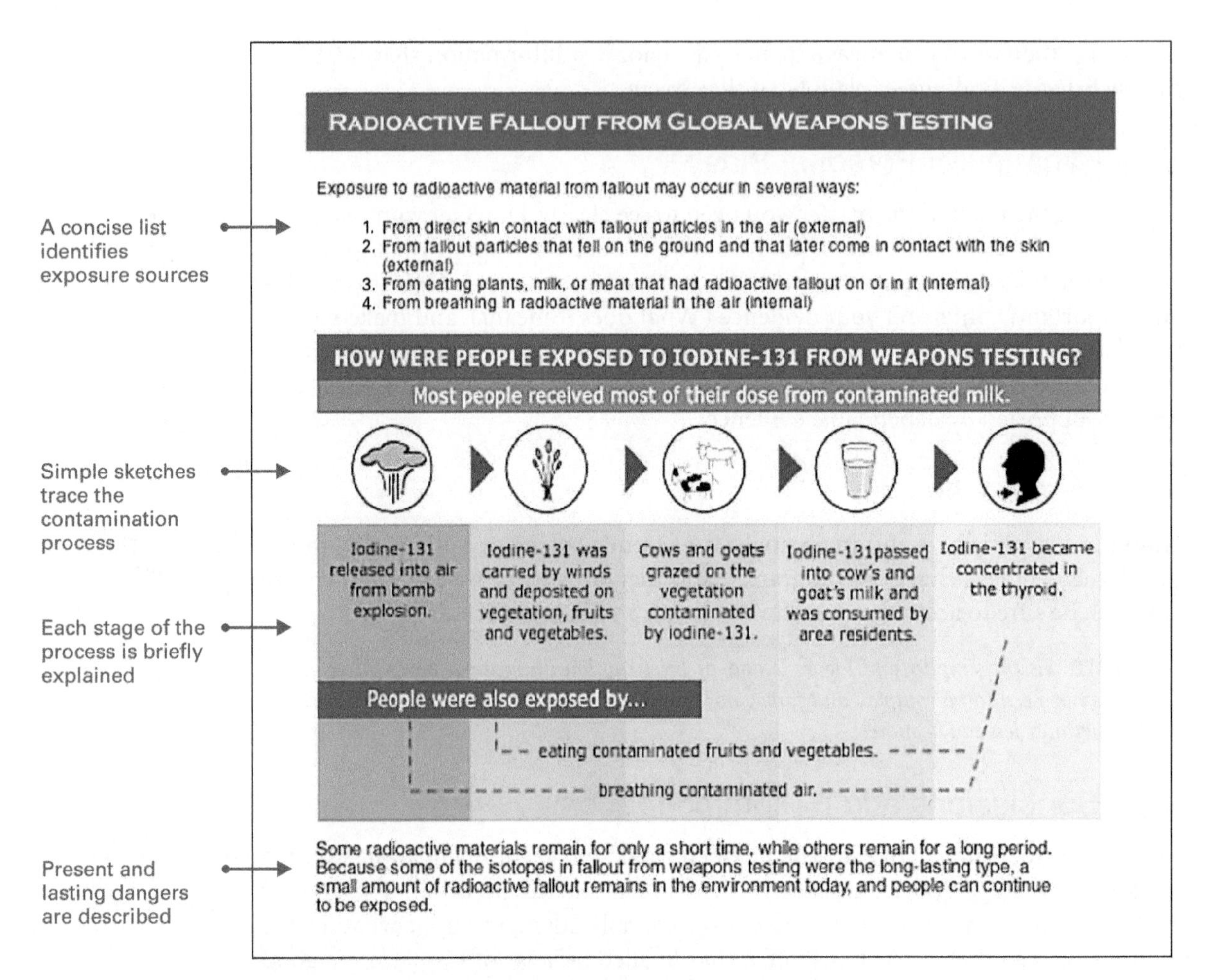

FIGURE 2 **A Simple but Highly Informative Visual**

Source: Adapted from *Radiation Studies*, Centers for Disease Control (CDC) <www.cdc.gov/nceh/radiation/fallout/RF-GWT_exposure.htm>.

Having explained *what it all means,* you then recommend *what should be done.* Taking all possible alternatives into account, your recommendations urge the most feasible option (to invest in *A* instead of *B,* to replace *C* immediately, to follow plan *A,* or the like). Here are the recommendations based on the previous conclusions:

Tell what should be done

1. I recommend that we install an active solar heating system in our new research building.
2. We should arrange an immediate meeting with our architect, building contractor, and solar heating contractor. In this way, we can make all necessary design changes before construction begins in two weeks.
3. We should instruct our legal department to obtain the appropriate permits and easements immediately.

Recommendations are valid when they propose an appropriate response to the problem or question.

Because they culminate your research and analysis, recommendations challenge your imagination, your creativity, and—above all—your critical thinking skills. What strikes one person as a brilliant suggestion might be seen by others as irresponsible, offensive, or dangerous. (Figure 3 depicts the kinds of decisions writers encounter in formulating, evaluating, and refining their recommendations.)

> **NOTE** *Keep in mind that solving one problem might create new and worse problems—or unintended consequences. For example, to prevent crop damage by rodents, an agriculture specialist might recommend trapping and poisoning. While rodent eradication may increase crop yield temporarily, it also increases the insects these rodents feed on—leading eventually to even greater crop damage. In short, before settling on any recommendation, try to anticipate its "side effects and long-term repercussions" (Dorner 15).*

Use a confident tone to state your conclusions

When you do achieve definite conclusions and recommendations, express them with assurance and authority. Unless you have reason to be unsure, avoid noncommittal statements ("It would seem that" or "It looks as if"). Be direct and assertive ("The earthquake danger at the reactor site is acute," or "I recommend an immediate investment"). Announce where you stand.

If, however, your analysis yields nothing definite, do not force a simplistic conclusion on your material. Instead, explain the limitations ("The contradictory responses to our consumer survey prevent me from reaching a definite conclusion. Before we make any decision about this product, I recommend a full-scale market analysis"). The wrong recommendation is far worse than no recommendation at all.

Self-Assessment

Assess your analysis continuously

The more we are involved in a project, the larger our stake is in its outcome—making self-criticism less likely just when it is needed most! For example, it is hard to admit that we might need to backtrack, or even start over, in instances like these (Dorner 46):

Things that might go wrong with your analysis

- During research you find that your goal isn't clear enough to indicate exactly what information you need.
- As you review your findings, you discover that the information you have is not the information you need.
- After making a recommendation, you discover that what seemed like the right course of action turns out to be the wrong one.

If you meet such obstacles, acknowledge them immediately, and revise your approach as needed.

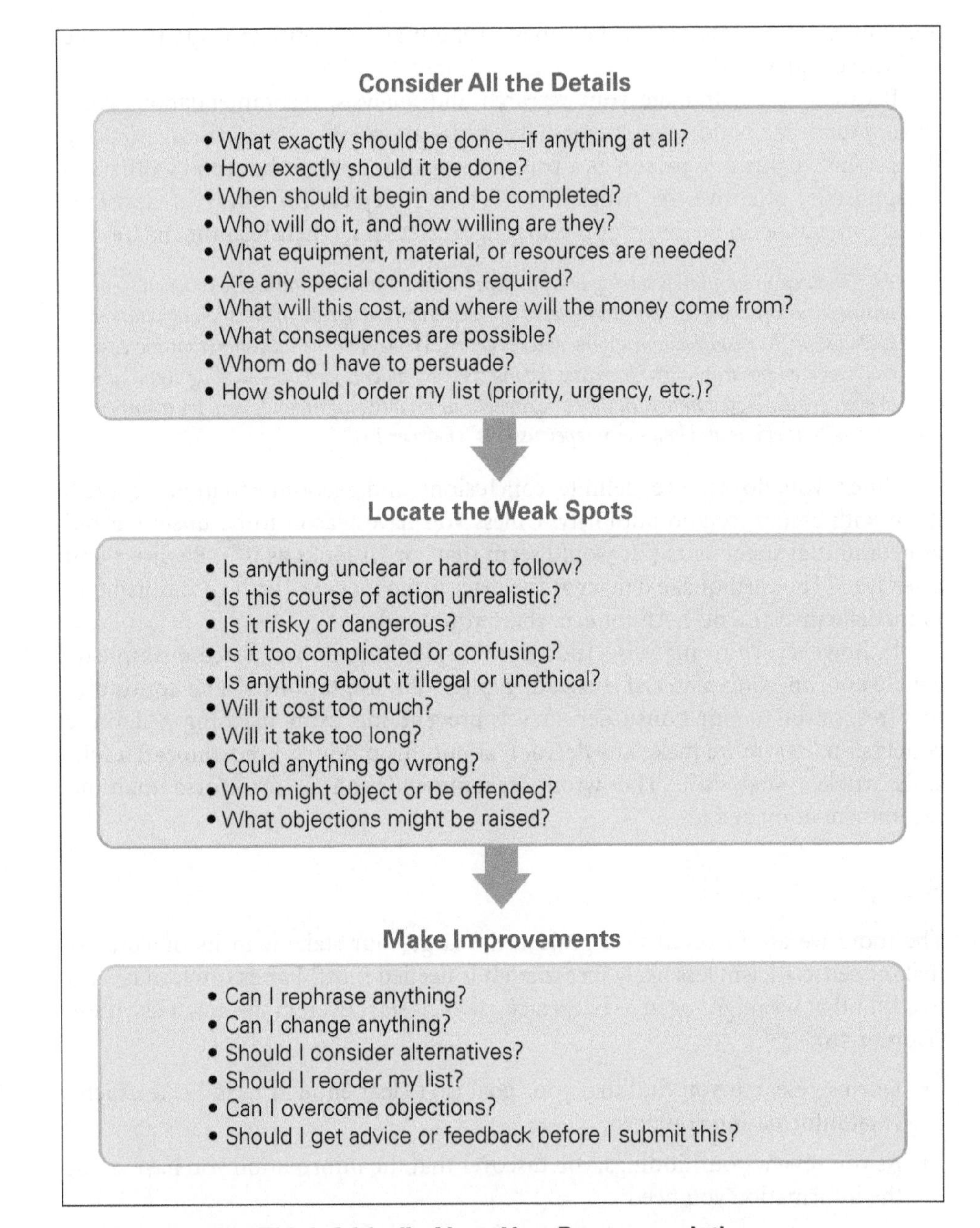

FIGURE 3 **How to Think Critically About Your Recommendations**
Source: Adapted from Vincent R. Ruggiero, *The Art of Thinking*, 8th ed. Longman, 2006, pp. 188-189. Used with permission.

AN OUTLINE AND MODEL FOR ANALYTICAL REPORTS

Whether you outline earlier or later, the finished report depends on a good outline. This model outline can be adapted to most analytical reports.

- **I. Introduction**
  - A. Definition, Description, and Background
  - B. Purpose of the Report, and Intended Audience
  - C. Method of Inquiry
  - D. Limitations of the Study
  - E. Working Definitions (here or in a glossary)
  - F. Scope of the Inquiry (topics listed in logical order)
  - G. Conclusion(s) of the Inquiry (briefly stated)
- **II. Collected Data**
  - A. First Topic for Investigation
    - 1. Definition
    - 2. Findings
    - 3. Interpretation of findings
  - B. Second Topic for Investigation
    - 1. First subtopic
      - a. Definition
      - b. Findings
      - c. Interpretation of findings
    - 2. Second subtopic (and so on)
- **III. Conclusion**
  - A. Summary of Findings
  - B. Overall Interpretation of Findings (as needed)
  - C. Recommendations (as needed and feasible)

(This outline is only tentative. Modify the components as necessary.)

Two sample reports in this chapter follow the model outline. The first one, "Children Exposed to Electromagnetic Radiation: A Risk Assessment" (minus the front matter and end matter that ordinarily accompany a long report), begins on the next page. The second report, "Feasibility Analysis of a Career in Technical Marketing," appears in Figure 4.

Each report responds to slightly different questions. The first tackles these questions: *What are the effects of* X *and what should we do about them?* The second tackles two questions: *Is* X *feasible, and which version of* X *is better for my purposes?* At least one of these reports should serve as a model for your own analysis.

Introduction

The introduction engages and orients the audience, and provides background as briefly as possible for the situation. Often, writers are tempted to write long introductions because they have a lot of background knowledge. But readers generally don't need long history lessons on the subject.

Identify your topic's origin and significance, define or describe the problem or issue, and explain the report's purpose. (Generally, stipulate your audience only in the version your instructor will read and only if you don't attach an audience and use profile.) Briefly identify your research methods (interviews, literature searches, and so on) and explain any limitations or omissions (person unavailable for interview, research still in progress, and so on). List working definitions, but if you have more than two or three, use a glossary. List the topics you have researched. Finally, briefly preview your conclusion; don't make readers wade through the entire report to find out what you recommend or advise.

NOTE *Not all reports require every component. Give readers only what they need and expect.*

As you read the following introduction, think about the elements designed to engage and orient the audience (i.e., local citizens), and evaluate their effectiveness.

**CHILDREN EXPOSED TO ELECTROMAGNETIC RADIATION:
A RISK ASSESSMENT**

LAURIE A. SIMONEAU

INTRODUCTION

Definition and background of the problem

Wherever electricity flows—through the largest transmission line or the smallest appliance—it emits varying intensities of charged waves: an *electromagnetic field* (EMF). Some medical studies have linked human exposure to EMFs with definite physiologic changes and possible illness including cancer, miscarriage, and depression.

Experts disagree over the health risk, if any, from EMFs. Some question whether EMF risk is greater from high-voltage transmission lines, the smaller distribution lines strung on utility poles, or household appliances. Conclusive research may take years; meanwhile, concerned citizens worry about avoiding potential risks.

Description of the problem

In Bocaville, four sets of transmission lines—two at 115 Kilovolts (kV) and two at 500 kV —cross residential neighborhoods and public property. The Adams elementary school is less than 100 feet from this power line corridor. EMF risks—whatever they may be—are thought to increase with proximity.

Based on examination of recent research and interviews with local authorities, this report assesses whether potential health risks from EMFs seem significant enough for Bocaville to (a) increase public awareness, (b) divert the transmission lines that run adjacent to the elementary school, and (c) implement widespread precautions in the transmission and distribution of electrical power throughout Bocaville.

Purpose and methods of this inquiry

This report covers five major topics: what we know about various EMF sources, what research indicates about physiologic and health effects, how experts differ in evaluating the research, what the power industry and the public have to say, and what actions are being taken locally and nationwide to avoid risk.

Scope of this inquiry

The report concludes by acknowledging the ongoing conflict among EMF research findings and by recommending immediate and inexpensive precautionary steps for our community.

Conclusions of the inquiry (briefly stated)

Body

The body section (or data section) describes and explains your findings. Present a clear and detailed picture of the evidence, interpretations, and reasoning on which you will base your conclusion. Divide topics into subtopics, and use informative headings as aids to navigation.

NOTE *Remember your ethical responsibility for presenting a fair and balanced treatment of the material, instead of "loading" the report with only those findings that support your viewpoint. Also, keep in mind the body section can have many variations, depending on the audience, topic, purpose, and situation.*

As you read the following section, evaluate how effectively it informs readers, keeps them on track, reveals a clear line of reasoning, and presents an impartial analysis.

DATA SECTION

Sources of EMF Exposure

First major topic

Electromagnetic intensity is measured in *milligauss* (mG), a unit of electrical measurement. The higher the mG reading, the stronger the field. Studies suggest that consistent exposure above 1–2 mG may increase cancer risk significantly, but no scientific evidence concludes that exposure even below 2.5 mG is safe.

Definition

Table 1 gives the EMF intensities from electric power lines at varying distances during average and peak usage.

Findings

As Table 1 indicates, EMF intensity drops substantially as distance from the power lines increases.

Interpretation

Although the EMF controversy has focused on 2 million miles of power lines criss-crossing the country, potentially harmful waves are also emitted by household wiring, appliances, computer terminals—and even from the earth's natural magnetic field. The background magnetic field (at a safe distance from any electrical appliance) in

Table 1 EMF Emissions from Power Lines (in milligauss)

Types of Transmission Lines	Maximum on Right-of-Way	Distance from lines			
		50'	100'	200'	300'
115 Kilovolts (kV)					
Average usage	30	7	2	0.4	0.2
Peak usage	63	14	4	0.9	0.4
230 Kilovolts (kV)					
Average usage	58	20	7	1.8	0.8
Peak usage	118	40	15	3.6	1.6
500 Kilovolts (kV)					
Average usage	87	29	13	3.2	1.4
Peak usage	183	62	27	6.7	3.0

Source: United States Environmental Protection Agency. *EMF in Your Environment.* Washington: GPO, 1992. Data from Bonneville Power Administration.

the average American home varies from 0.5 to 4.0 mG (United States Environmental 10). Table 2 compares intensities of various sources.

Interpretation

EMF intensity from certain appliances tends to be higher than from transmission lines because of the amount of current involved.

Table 2 EMF Emissions from Selected Sources (in milligauss)

Source	*Range*[a,b]
Earth's magnetic field	0.1–2.5
Blowdryer	60–1400
Four in. from TV screen	40–100
Four ft from TV screen	0.7–9
Fluorescent lights	10–12
Electric razor	1200–1600
Electric blanket	2–25
Computer terminal (12 inches away)	3–15
Toaster	10–60

[a]Data from Miltane, John. Interview 5 Apr. 2010; National Institute of Environmental Health. *EMF Electric and Magnetic Fields Associated with the Use of Electric Power.* Washington: GPO, 2002: 32-35.

[b]Readings are made with a gaussmeter, and vary with technique, proximity of gaussmeter to source, its direction of aim, and other random factors.

Definitions

Voltage measures the speed and pressure of electricity in wires, but *current* measures the volume of electricity passing through wires. Current (measured in *amperage*) is what produces electromagnetic fields. The current flowing through a transmission line typically ranges from 200 to 400 amps. Most homes have a 200-amp service. This means that if every electrical item in the house were turned on at the same time, the house could run about 200 amps—almost as high as the transmission line. Consumers then have the ability to put 200 amps of current-flow into their homes, while transmission lines carrying 200 to 400 amps are at least 50 feet away (Miltane).

Finding

Proximity and duration of exposure, however, are other risk factors. People are exposed to EMFs from home appliances at close proximity, but appliances run only periodically: exposure is therefore sporadic, and intensity diminishes sharply within a few feet (Figure 1).

As Figure 1 indicates, EMF intensity drops dramatically over very short distances from the typical appliance.

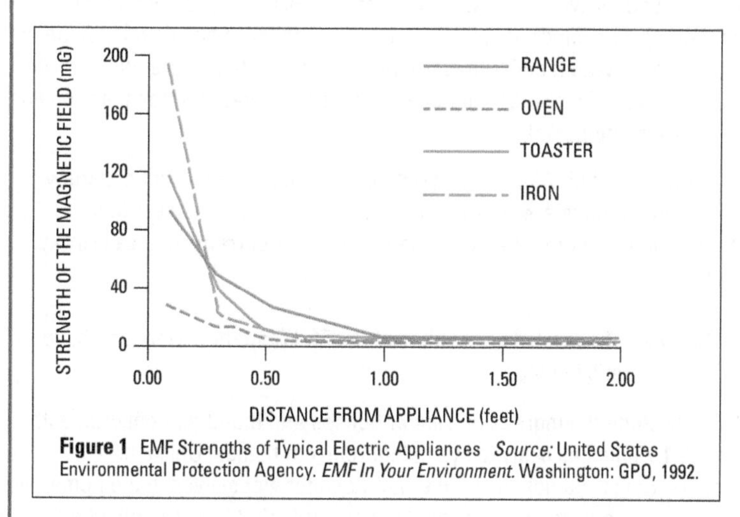

Figure 1 EMF Strengths of Typical Electric Appliances *Source:* United States Environmental Protection Agency. *EMF In Your Environment.* Washington: GPO, 1992.

Power line exposure, on the other hand, is at a greater distance (usually 50 feet or more), but it is constant. Moreover, its intensity can remain strong well beyond 100 feet (Miltane).

Finding

Research has yet to determine which type of exposure might be more harmful: briefly, to higher intensities or constantly, to lower intensities. In any case, proximity seems most significant because EMF intensity drops rapidly with distance.

Interpretation

Physiologic Effects and Health Risks from EMF Exposure

Second major topic

Research on EMF exposure falls into two categories: epidemiologic studies and laboratory studies. The findings are sometimes controversial and inconclusive, but also disturbing.

Epidemiologic Studies. Epidemiologic studies look for statistical correlations between EMF exposure and human illness or disorders. Of 77 such studies in recent

First subtopic

Definition

decades, over 70 percent suggest that EMF exposure increases the incidence of the following conditions (Pinsky 155–215):

General findings

- cancer, especially leukemia and brain tumors
- miscarriage
- stress and depression
- learning disabilities
- heart attacks

Following, for example, are summaries of several noted epidemiologic studies implicating EMFs in occurrences of cancer.

Detailed findings

A Landmark Study of the EMF/Cancer Connection. A 1979 Denver study by Wertheimer and Leeper was the first to implicate EMFs as a cause of cancer. Researchers compared hundreds of homes in which children had developed cancer with similar homes in which children were cancer free. Victims were two to three times as likely to live in "high-current homes" (within 130 feet of a transmission line or 50 feet of a distribution line).

Critiques of findings

This study has been criticized because (1) it was not "blind" (researchers knew which homes cancer victims were living in), and (2) researchers never took gaussmeter readings to verify their designation of "high-current" homes (Pinsky 160–62; Taubes 96).

Detailed findings

Follow-up Studies. Several major studies of the EMF/cancer connection have confirmed Wertheimer's findings:

- In 1988, Savitz studied hundreds of Denver houses and found that children with cancer were 1.7 times as likely to live in high-current homes. Unlike his predecessors, Savitz did not know whether a cancer victim lived in the home being measured, and he took gaussmeter readings to verify that houses could be designated "high-current" (Pinsky 162–63).
- In 1990, London and Peters found that Los Angeles children had 2.5 times more risk of leukemia if they lived near power lines (Brodeur 115).
- In 1992, a massive Swedish study found that children in houses with average intensities greater than 1 mG had twice the normal leukemia risk; at greater than 2 mG, the risk nearly tripled; at greater than 3 mG, it nearly quadrupled (Brodeur 115).
- In 2002, British researchers evaluated findings from 34 studies of power line EMF effects (a *meta-analysis*). This study found "a degree of consistency in the evidence suggesting adverse health effects of living near high voltage power lines" (Henshaw et al. 1).

Workplace Studies. More than 80 percent of 51 studies from 1981 to 1994—most notably a 1992 Swedish study—concluded that electricians, electrical engineers, and power line workers constantly exposed to an average of 1.5 to 4.0 mG had a significantly elevated cancer risk (Brodeur 115; Pinsky 177–209).

Two additional workplace studies seem to support or even amplify the above findings.

- A 1995 University of North Carolina study of 138,905 electric utility workers concluded that occupational EMF exposure roughly doubles brain cancer risk. This study, however, found no increased leukemia risk (Cavanaugh 8; Moore 16).
- A Canadian study of electrical-power employees published in 2000 indicates that those who had worked in strong electric fields for more than 20 years had "an eight- to tenfold increase in the risk of leukemia," along with a significantly elevated risk of lymphoma ("Strong Electric Fields" 1–2).

Although none of the above studies can be said to "prove" a direct cause-effect relationship, their strikingly similar results suggest a conceivable link between prolonged EMF exposure and illness.

Interpretation

Laboratory Studies. Laboratory studies assess cellular, metabolic, and behavioral effects of EMFs on humans and animals. EMFs directly cause the following physiologic changes (Brodeur 88; Pinsky 24–29; Raloff, "EMFs'" 30):

Second subtopic

General findings

- reduced heart rate
- altered brain waves
- impaired immune system
- interference with the synthesis of genetic material
- disrupted regulation of cell growth
- interaction with the biochemistry of cancer cells
- altered hormonal activity
- disrupted sleep patterns

These changes are documented in the following summaries of several significant laboratory studies.

EMF Effects on Cell Chemistry. Other studies have demonstrated previously unrecognized effects on cell growth and division. Most notably, a 2000 study by Michigan State University found that EMFs equal to the intensity that occurs "within a few feet" of outdoor power lines caused cells with cancer-related genetic mutations to multiply rapidly (Sivitz 196).

Detailed findings

EMF Effects on Hormones. Studies have found that EMF exposure (say, from an electric blanket) inhibits production of melatonin, a hormone that fights cancer and depression, stimulates the immune system, and regulates bodily rhythms. A 1997 study at the Lawrence National Laboratory found that EMF exposure can suppress both melatonin and the hormone-like, anticancer drug Tamoxifen (Raloff, "EMFs' " 30). In 1996, physiologist Charles Graham found that EMFs elevate female estrogen levels and depress male testosterone levels—hormone alterations associated with risk of breast or testicular cancer, respectively (Raloff, "EMFs' " 30).

Interpretation

Although laboratory studies seem more conclusive than the epidemiologic studies, what these findings *mean* is debatable.

Third major topic

Debate over Quality, Cost, and Status of EMF Research

Experts differ over the meaning of EMF research findings largely because of the following limitations attributed to various studies.

First subtopic

Critiques of population studies

Limitations of Various EMF Studies. Epidemiologic studies are criticized for overstating evidence. For example, some critics claim that so-called EMF-cancer links are produced by "data dredging" (making countless comparisons between cancers and EMF sources until random correlations appear) (Taubes 99). Other critics argue that news media distort the issue by publicizing positive findings while often ignoring negative or ambiguous findings (N. Goodman). Some studies are also accused of mistaking *coincidence* for *correlation,* without exploring "confounding factors" (e.g., exposure to toxins or to other adverse conditions—including the earth's natural magnetic field) (Moore 16).

Response to critiques

Supporters of EMF research respond that the sheer volume of epidemiologic evidence seems overwhelming (Kirkpatrick 81, 83). Moreover, the Swedish studies cited earlier seem to invalidate the above criticisms (Brodeur 115).

Critiques of lab studies

Laboratory studies are criticized—even by scientists who conduct them—because effects on an isolated culture of cells or on experimental animals do not always equal effects on the total human organism (Jauchem 190–94).

Response to critiques

Until recently critics argued that no scientist had offered a reasonable hypothesis to explain the possible health effects of EMFs (Palfreman 26). However, a 2004 University of Washington study showed that a weak electromagnetic field can break DNA strands and lead to brain cell death in rats, presumably because of cell-damaging agents known as free radicals (Lai and Singh).

Cost objections

Costs of EMF Research. Critics claim that research and publicity about EMFs are becoming a profit venture, spawning "a new growth industry among researchers, as well as marketers of EMF monitors" ("Electrophobia" I). Environmental expert Keith Florig identifies adverse economic effects of the EMF debate that include decreased property values, frivolous lawsuits, expensive but needless "low field" consumer appliances, and costly modifications to schools and public buildings (Monmonier 190).

Conflicting scientific opinions

Present Status of EMF Research. In July 1998, an editor at the *New England Journal of Medicine* called for the ending of EMF/cancer research. He cited studies from the National Cancer Institute and other respected sources that showed "little evidence" of any causal connection. In a parallel development, federal and industry funding for EMF research has been reduced drastically (Stix 33). But, in August 1998, experts from the Energy Department and the National Institute of Environmental Health Sciences (NIEHS) proposed that EMFs should be officially designated a "possible human carcinogen" (Gross 30).

However, one year later, in a report based on its seven-year review of EMF research, NIEHS concluded that "the scientific evidence suggesting that . . . EMF exposures pose any health risk is weak." But the report also conceded that such exposure "cannot be recognized at this time as entirely safe" (National Inst., *Health* 1–2). In 2005, the National Cancer Institute fueled the controversy, concluding that the EMF–cancer connection is supported by only "limited evidence" and "inconsistent associations" (1). In a 2009 update, NIEHS announced "that the overall pattern of results suggests a weak association between exposure to EMFs and increased risk of childhood leukemia" (National Inst., *Electric* 1). Recently, noted epidemiologist Daniel Wartenberg has testified in support of the "Precautionary Principle," arguing that policy decisions should be based on "the possibility of risk." Specifically, Wartenberg advocates "prudently lowering exposures of greatest concern [i.e., of children] in case the possible risk is shown eventually to be true" (6).

Interpretation

In short, after more than twenty-five years of study, the EMF/illness debate continues, even among respected experts. While most scientists agree that EMFs exert measurable effects on the human body, they disagree about whether a real hazard exists. Given the drastic cuts in research funding, definite answers are unlikely to appear any time soon.

Fourth major topic

Views from the Power Industry and the Public

While the experts continue their debate, other viewpoints are worth considering as well.

First subtopic

The Power Industry's Views. The Electrical Power Research Institute (EPRI), the research arm of the nation's electric utilities, claims that recent EMF studies have provided valuable but inconclusive data that warrant further study (Moore 17). What does our local power company think about the alleged EMF risk? Marianne Halloran-Barney, Energy Service Advisor for County Electric, expressed this view in an email correspondence:

Findings

> There are definitely some links, but we don't know, really, what the effects are or what to do about them. . . . There are so many variables in EMF research that it's a question of whether the studies were even done correctly. . . . Maybe in a few years there will be really definite answers.

Echoing Halloran-Barney's views, John Miltane, Chief Engineer for County Electric, added this political insight:

> The public needs and demands electricity, but in regard to the negative effects of generation and transmission, the pervasive attitude seems to be "not in my back yard!" Utilities in general are scared to death of the EMF issue, but at County Electric we're trying to do the best job we can while providing reliable electricity to 24,000 customers.

Miltane stresses that County Electric takes the EMF issue very seriously: Whenever possible, new distribution lines are run underground and configured to diminish EMF intensity.

Second subtopic

Public Perception. Industry views seem to parallel the national perspective among the broader population: Informed people are genuinely concerned, but remain unsure about what level of anxiety is warranted or what exactly should be done. A survey by the Edison Electric Institute did reveal that EMFs are considered a serious health threat by 33 percent of the American public (Stix 33).

Fifth major topic

Risk-Avoidance Measures Being Taken

Although conclusive answers may require decades of research, concerned citizens are already taking action against potential EMF hazards.

First subtopic

Risk Avoidance Nationwide. Following are examples of steps taken by various communities to protect schoolchildren from EMF exposure:

Findings

- Hundreds of individuals and community groups have taken legal action to block proposed construction of new power lines. A single Washington law firm has defended roughly 140 utilities in cases related to EMFs (Dana and Turner 32).
- Houston schools "forced a utility company to remove a transmission line that ran within 300 feet of three schools. Cost: $8 million" (Kirkpatrick 85).
- California parents and teachers are pressuring reluctant school and public health officials to investigate cancer rates in the roughly 1,000 schools located within 300 feet of transmission lines, and to close at least one school (within 100 feet) in which cancer rates far exceed normal (Brodeur 118).

Although critics argue that the questionable risks fail to justify the costs of such measures, widespread concern about EMF exposure continues to grow.

Second subtopic

Risk Avoidance Locally. Local awareness of the EMF issue seems low. The main public concern seems to be with property values. According to Halloran-Barney, County Electric receives one or two calls monthly from concerned customers, including people buying homes near power lines. The lack of public awareness adds another dimension to the EMF problem: People can't avoid a health threat that they don't know exists.

Interpretation

Before risk avoidance can be considered on a broader community level, the public must first be informed about EMFs and the associated risks of exposure.

Conclusion

The conclusion is likely to interest readers most because it answers the questions that originally sparked the analysis.

NOTE *Many workplace reports are submitted with the conclusion preceding the introduction and body sections.*

In the conclusion, you summarize, interpret, and recommend. Although you have interpreted evidence at each stage of your analysis, your conclusion presents a broad interpretation and suggests a course of action, where appropriate. The summary and interpretations should lead logically to your recommendations.

Elements of a logical conclusion

- The summary accurately reflects the body of the report.
- The overall interpretation is consistent with the findings in the summary.
- The recommendations are consistent with the purpose of the report, the evidence presented, and the interpretations given.

NOTE *Don't introduce any new facts, ideas, or statistics in the conclusion.*

As you read the following conclusion, evaluate how effectively it provides a clear and consistent perspective on the whole document.

CONCLUSION

Summary and Overall Interpretation of Findings

Review of major findings

Electromagnetic fields exist wherever electricity flows; the stronger the current, the higher the EMF intensity. While no "safe" EMF level has been identified, long-term exposure to intensities greater than 2.5 milligauss is considered dangerous. Although home appliances can generate high EMFs during use, power lines can generate constant EMFs, typically at 2 to 3 milligauss in buildings within 150 feet. Our elementary school is less than 100 feet from a high-voltage power line corridor. Notable epidemiologic studies implicate EMFs in increased rates of medical disorders such as cancer, miscarriage, stress, depression, and learning disabilities—all directly related to intensity and duration of exposure. Laboratory studies show that EMFs cause the kinds of cellular and metabolic changes that could produce these disorders.

An overall judgment about what the findings mean

Though still controversial and inconclusive, most of the various findings are strikingly similar and they underscore the need for more research and for risk avoidance, especially as far as children are concerned.

Concerned citizens nationwide have begun to prevail over resistant school and health officials and utility companies in reducing EMF risk to schoolchildren. And even though our local power company is taking reasonable risk-avoidance steps, our community can do more to learn about the issues and diminish potential risk.

Recommendations

In light of the conflicting evidence and interpretations, any type of government regulation any time soon seems unlikely. Also, considering the limitations of what we know, drastic and enormously expensive actions (such as burying all the town's power lines or increasing the height of utility towers) seem inadvisable. In fact, these might turn out to be the wrong actions.

Despite this climate of uncertainty, however, our community still can take some immediate and inexpensive steps to address possible EMF risk. Please consider the following recommendations:

Feasible and realistic course of action

- Relocate the school playground to the side of the school most distant from the power lines.
- Discourage children from playing near any power lines.
- Distribute a version of this report to all Bocaville residents.
- Ask our school board to hire a licensed contractor to take milligauss readings throughout the elementary school, to determine the extent of the problem, and to suggest reasonable corrective measures.
- Ask our Town Council to meet with County Electric Company representatives to explore options and costs for rerouting or burying the segment of the power lines near the school.
- Hold a town meeting to answer citizens' questions and to solicit opinions.
- Appoint a committee (consisting of at least one physician, one engineer, and other experts) to review emerging research as it relates to our school and town.

A call to action

As we await conclusive answers, we need to learn all we can about the EMF issue, and to do all we can to diminish this potentially significant health issue.

FRONT MATTER AND END MATTER SUPPLEMENTS

Most formal reports or proposals consist of the front matter, the text of the report or proposal, and the end matter. (Some parts of the front and end matter may be optional.) Submit your completed document with these supplements, in this order:

Front matter precedes the report

- letter of transmittal
- title page
- table of contents
- list of tables and figures
- abstract
- **text of the report** (introduction, body, conclusion)

- glossary (as needed)
- appendices (as needed)
- Works Cited page (or alphabetical or numbered list of references)

End matter follows the report

For discussion of the above supplements, see below. For examples in a formal report or proposal, see Figure 4.

Front Matter

Preceding the text of the report is the front matter: letter of transmittal, title page, table of contents, list of tables and figures (if appropriate), and abstract or executive summary.

Letter of Transmittal

Many formal reports or proposals include a letter of transmittal, addressed to a specific reader or readers, which precedes the document. This letter might acknowledge people that helped with the document, refer readers to sections of special interest, discuss any limitations of the study or any problems in gathering data, offer personal (or off-the-record) observations, or urge readers to take immediate action.

Title Page. The title page provides the document title, the names of all authors and their affiliations (and/or the name of the organization that commissioned the report), and the date the report was submitted. The title announces the report's purpose and subject by using descriptive words such as *analysis, comparison, feasibility,* or *recommendation.* Be sure the title fully describes your report, but avoid an overly long and involved title. Make the title the most prominent item, highest on the page, followed by the name of the recipient(s), the author(s), and the date of submission.

Table of Contents. For any long document, the table of contents helps readers by listing the page number for each major section, including any front matter that falls after the table of contents. (Do not include the letter of transmittal, title page, or the table of contents itself, but do include the list of tables and figures, along with the abstract or executive summary.)

Indicate page numbers for front matter in lowercase Roman numerals (i, ii, iii). Note that the title page, though not numbered itself or listed on the table of contents, is counted as page i. Number the report text pages using Arabic numerals (1, 2, 3), starting with the first page of the report. Number end matter using Arabic numerals continuing from the end of the report's text.

Make sure headings and subheadings in the table of contents match exactly the headings and subheadings in the document. Indicate headings of different levels (a-level, b-level, c-level) using different type styles or indentations. Use *leader lines* (........) to connect headings with their page numbers.

List of Tables and Figures. On a separate page following the table of contents (or at the end of the table of contents, if it fits), list the tables and figures in the report. If the report contains only one or two tables and figures, you may skip this list.

Abstract or Executive Summary. Instead of reading an entire formal report, readers interested only in the big picture may consult the abstract or executive summary that commonly precedes the report proper. The purpose of this summary is to explain the issue, describe how you researched it, and state your conclusions (and, in the case of an executive summary, indicate what action the conclusions suggest). Busy readers can then flip through the document to locate sections important to them.

Make the abstract or executive summary as brief as possible. Summarize the report without adding new information or leaving out crucial information. Write for a general audience and follow a sequence that moves from the reason the report was written to the report's major findings, to conclusions and recommendations.

Text of the Report

The text of the report consists of the introduction, the body, and the conclusion.

End Matter

Following the report text (as needed) is the end matter, which may include a glossary, appendices, and/or a list of references cited in your report. Readers can refer to any of these supplements or skip them altogether, according to their needs.

Glossary. Use a glossary if your report contains more than five technical terms that may not be understood by all intended readers. If five or fewer terms need defining, place them in the report's introduction as working definitions, or use footnote definitions. If you do include a separate glossary, announce its location when you introduce technical terms defined there ("see the glossary at the end of this report").

Appendices. If you have large blocks of material or other documents that are relevant but will bog readers down, place these in an appendix. For example, if your report on the cost of electricity at your company refers to another report issued by the local utility company, you may wish to include this second report as an appendix. Other items that belong in an appendix include complex formulas, interview questions and responses, maps, photographs, questionnaires and tabulated responses, and texts of laws and regulations.

Do not stuff appendices with needless information or use them to bury bad or embarrassing news that belongs in the report itself. Title each appendix clearly: "Projected Costs." Mention the appendixes early in the introduction, and refer to them at appropriate points in the report: ("see Appendix A").

References or Works Cited List. If you have used outside sources in your report (and typically you should), you must provide a list of References (per APA style) or of Works Cited (per MLA style).

A SITUATION REQUIRING AN ANALYTICAL REPORT

The formal report that follows, patterned after the model outline, combines a feasibility analysis with a comparative analysis.

A Formal Report

The Situation. Richard Larkin, author of the following report, has a work-study job fifteen hours weekly in his school's placement office. His boss, John Fitton (placement director), likes to keep up with trends in various fields. Larkin, an engineering major, has developed an interest in technical marketing and sales. Needing a report topic for his writing course, Larkin offers to analyze the feasibility of a technical marketing and sales career, both for his own decision making and for technical and science graduates in general. Fitton accepts Larkin's offer, looking forward to having the final report in his reference file for use by students choosing careers. Larkin wants his report to be useful in three ways: (1) to satisfy a course requirement, (2) to help him in choosing his own career, and (3) to help other students with their career choices.

With his topic approved, Larkin begins gathering his primary data, using interviews, letters of inquiry, telephone inquiries, and lecture notes. He supplements these primary sources with articles in recent publications. He will document his findings in APA (author-date) style.

As a guide for designing his final report (Figure 4), Larkin completes the following audience and use profile.

Audience and Use Profile. The primary audience consists of John Fitton, Placement Director, and the students who will refer to the report. The secondary audience is the writing instructor.

Because he is familiar with the marketing field, Fitton will need very little background to understand the report. Many student readers, however, will have questions like these:

- What, exactly, is technical marketing and sales?
- What are the requirements for this career?
- What are the pros and cons of this career?
- Could this be the right career for me?
- How do I enter the field?

Readers affected by this document are primarily students making career choices. Readers' attitudes likely will vary:

- Some readers should have a good deal of interest, especially those seeking a people-oriented career.
- Others might be only casually interested as they investigate a range of possible careers.
- Some readers might be skeptical about something written by a fellow student instead of by some expert. To connect with all these people, this report needs to persuade them that its conclusions are based on reliable information and careful reasoning.

All readers expect things spelled out, but concisely. Visuals will help compress and emphasize material throughout.

Essential information will include an expanded definition of technical marketing and sales, the skills and attitudes needed for success, the career's advantages and drawbacks, and a description of various paths for entering the career.

This report combines feasibility and comparative analysis, so the structure of the report must reveal a clear line of reasoning: in the feasibility section, reasons for and reasons against; in the comparison section, a block structure and a table that compares the four entry paths point by point. The report will close with recommendations based on solid conclusions.

For various readers who might not wish to read the entire report, an informative abstract will be included.

165 Hammond Way
Hyannis, MA 02457
April 29, 20XX

John Fitton
Placement Director
University of Massachusetts
North Dartmouth, MA 02747

Dear Mr. Fitton:

Here is my report, Feasibility Analysis of a Career in Technical Marketing. In preparing this report, I've learned a great deal about the requirements and modes of access to this career, and I believe my information will help other students as well. Thank you for your guidance and encouragement throughout this process.

Letter of transmittal targets and thanks specific reader and provides additional context

Although committed to their specialties, some technical and science graduates seem interested in careers in which they can apply their technical knowledge to customer and business problems. Technical marketing may be an attractive choice of career for those who know their field, who can relate to different personalities, and who communicate well.

Technical marketing is competitive and demanding, but highly rewarding. In fact, it is an excellent route to upper-management and executive positions. Specifically, marketing work enables one to develop a sound technical knowledge of a company's products, to understand how these products fit into the marketplace, and to perfect sales techniques and interpersonal skills. This is precisely the kind of background that paves the way to top-level jobs.

I've enjoyed my work on this project, and would be happy to answer any questions. Please phone at 690-555-1122 or email at larkin@com.net anytime.

Sincerely,

Richard B. Larkin, Jr.

FIGURE 4 **A Formal Report**

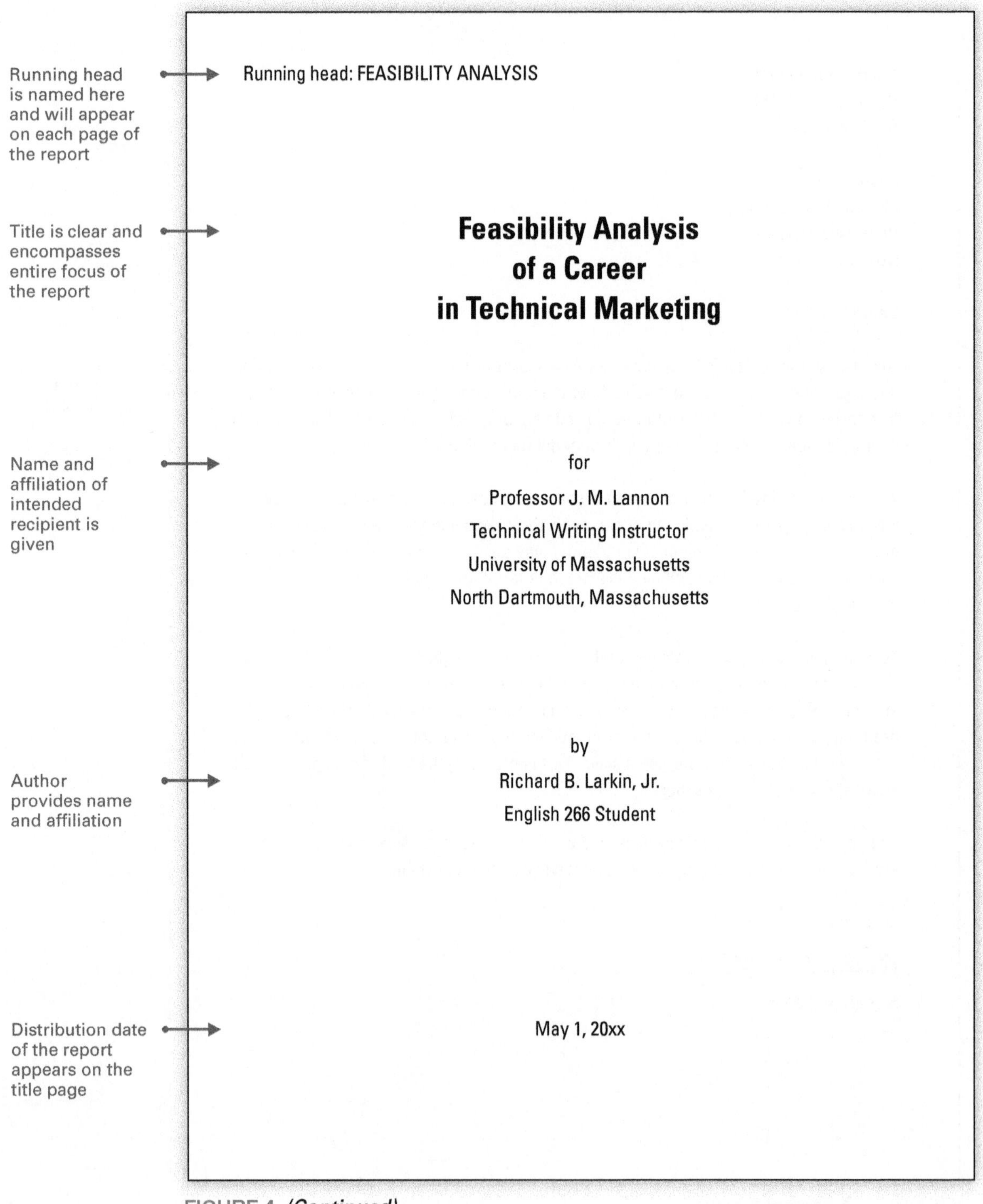

FIGURE 4 *(Continued)*

FEASIBILITY ANALYSIS

Table of Contents

Table of contents helps readers find information and visualize the structure of the report

Figures and Tables

This section makes visuals easy to locate

FIGURE 4 *(Continued)*

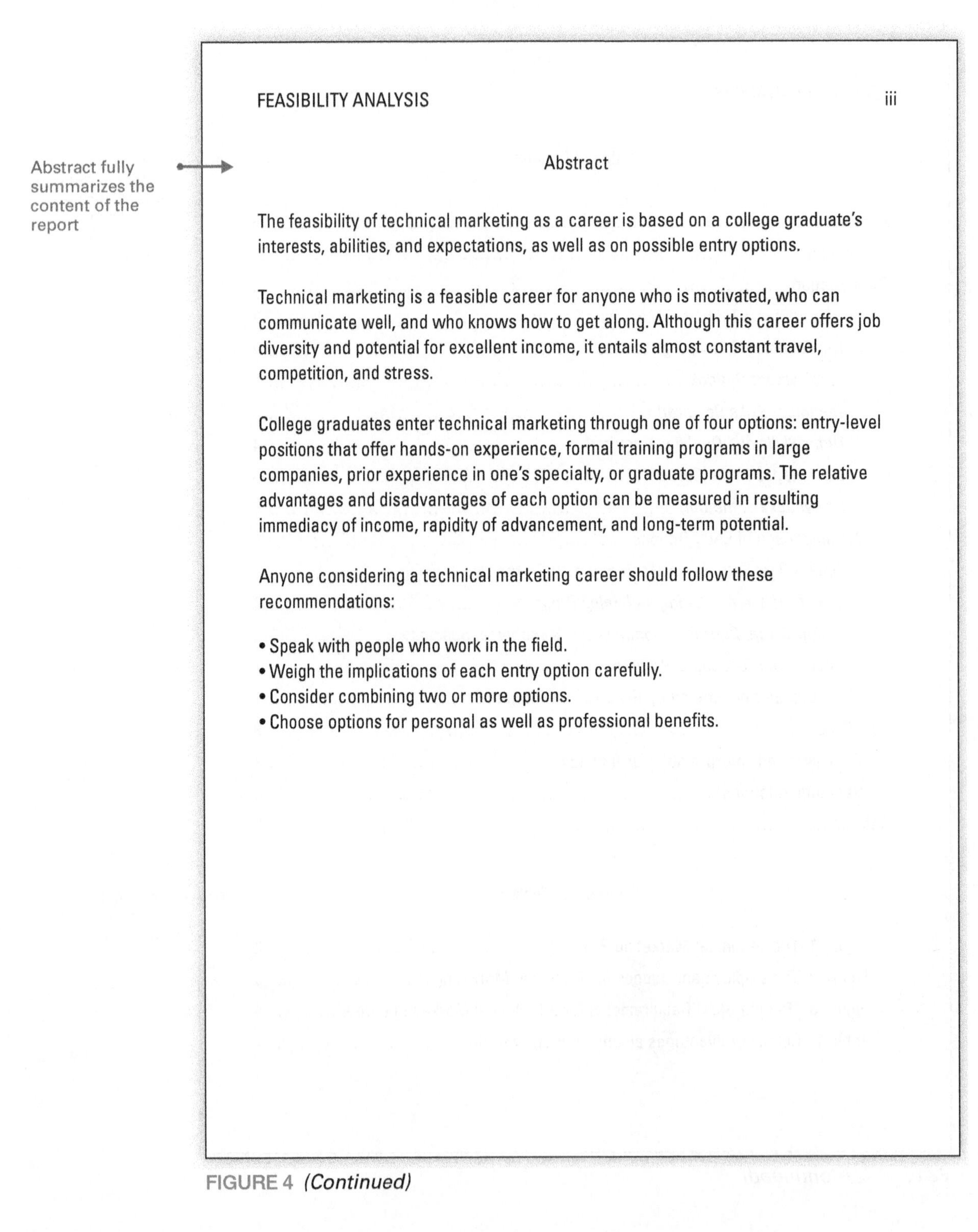

Abstract fully summarizes the content of the report

FEASIBILITY ANALYSIS iii

Abstract

The feasibility of technical marketing as a career is based on a college graduate's interests, abilities, and expectations, as well as on possible entry options.

Technical marketing is a feasible career for anyone who is motivated, who can communicate well, and who knows how to get along. Although this career offers job diversity and potential for excellent income, it entails almost constant travel, competition, and stress.

College graduates enter technical marketing through one of four options: entry-level positions that offer hands-on experience, formal training programs in large companies, prior experience in one's specialty, or graduate programs. The relative advantages and disadvantages of each option can be measured in resulting immediacy of income, rapidity of advancement, and long-term potential.

Anyone considering a technical marketing career should follow these recommendations:

- Speak with people who work in the field.
- Weigh the implications of each entry option carefully.
- Consider combining two or more options.
- Choose options for personal as well as professional benefits.

FIGURE 4 *(Continued)*

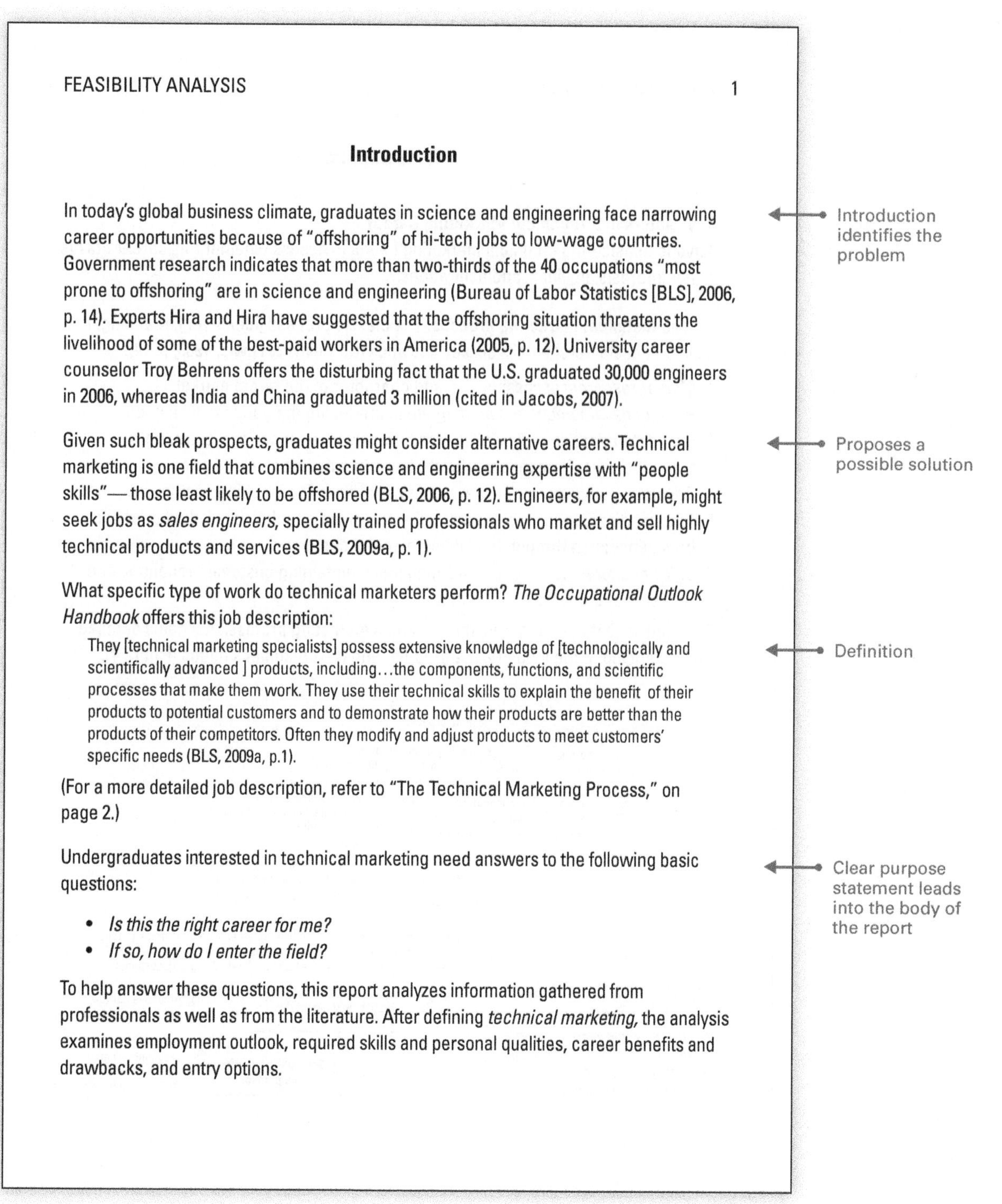

FEASIBILITY ANALYSIS 1

Introduction

In today's global business climate, graduates in science and engineering face narrowing career opportunities because of "offshoring" of hi-tech jobs to low-wage countries. Government research indicates that more than two-thirds of the 40 occupations "most prone to offshoring" are in science and engineering (Bureau of Labor Statistics [BLS], 2006, p. 14). Experts Hira and Hira have suggested that the offshoring situation threatens the livelihood of some of the best-paid workers in America (2005, p. 12). University career counselor Troy Behrens offers the disturbing fact that the U.S. graduated 30,000 engineers in 2006, whereas India and China graduated 3 million (cited in Jacobs, 2007).

Introduction identifies the problem

Given such bleak prospects, graduates might consider alternative careers. Technical marketing is one field that combines science and engineering expertise with "people skills"—those least likely to be offshored (BLS, 2006, p. 12). Engineers, for example, might seek jobs as *sales engineers,* specially trained professionals who market and sell highly technical products and services (BLS, 2009a, p. 1).

Proposes a possible solution

What specific type of work do technical marketers perform? *The Occupational Outlook Handbook* offers this job description:

> They [technical marketing specialists] possess extensive knowledge of [technologically and scientifically advanced] products, including...the components, functions, and scientific processes that make them work. They use their technical skills to explain the benefit of their products to potential customers and to demonstrate how their products are better than the products of their competitors. Often they modify and adjust products to meet customers' specific needs (BLS, 2009a, p.1).

Definition

(For a more detailed job description, refer to "The Technical Marketing Process," on page 2.)

Undergraduates interested in technical marketing need answers to the following basic questions:

Clear purpose statement leads into the body of the report

- *Is this the right career for me?*
- *If so, how do I enter the field?*

To help answer these questions, this report analyzes information gathered from professionals as well as from the literature. After defining *technical marketing,* the analysis examines employment outlook, required skills and personal qualities, career benefits and drawbacks, and entry options.

FIGURE 4 *(Continued)*

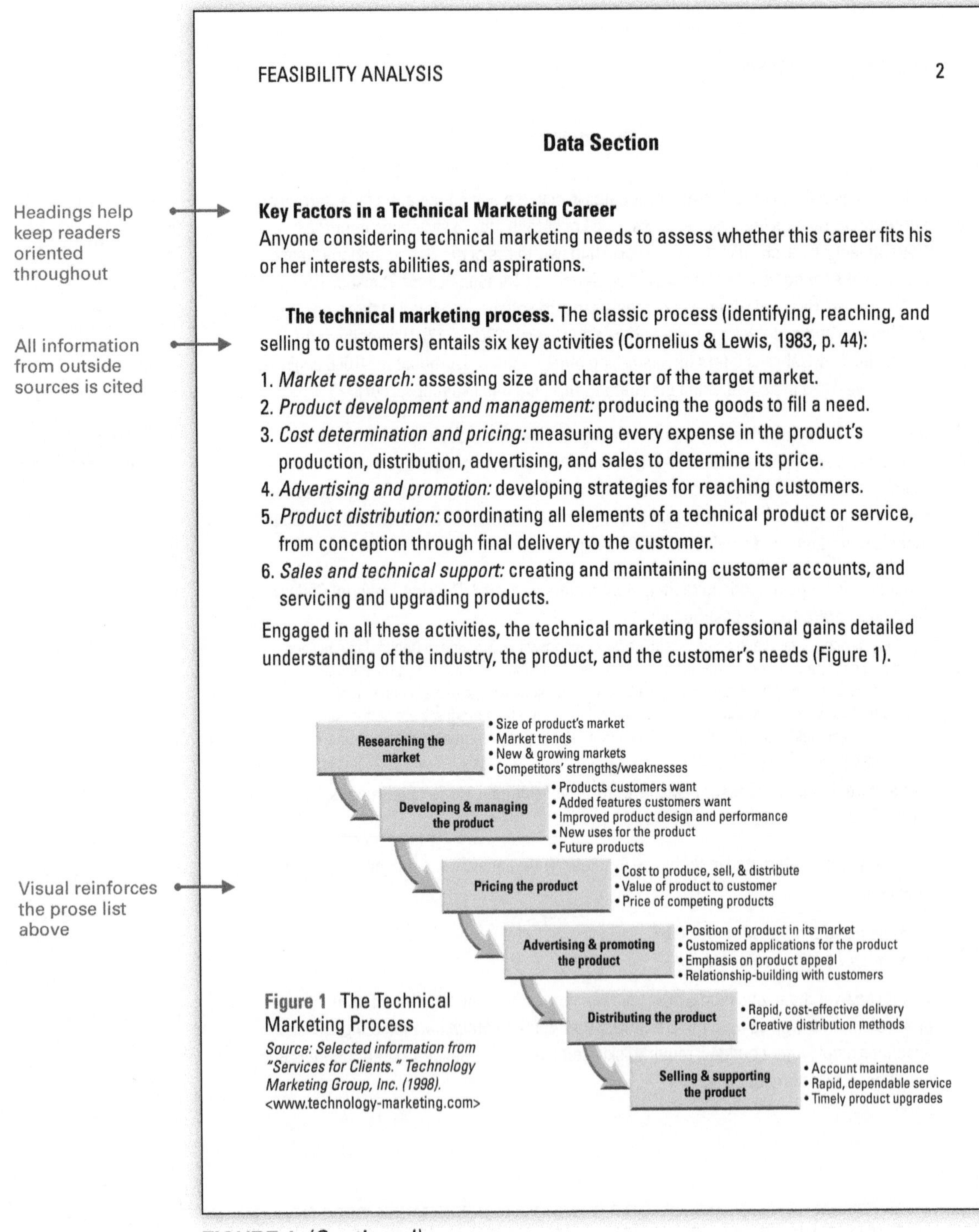

FEASIBILITY ANALYSIS 2

Data Section

Key Factors in a Technical Marketing Career
Anyone considering technical marketing needs to assess whether this career fits his or her interests, abilities, and aspirations.

The technical marketing process. The classic process (identifying, reaching, and selling to customers) entails six key activities (Cornelius & Lewis, 1983, p. 44):

1. *Market research:* assessing size and character of the target market.
2. *Product development and management:* producing the goods to fill a need.
3. *Cost determination and pricing:* measuring every expense in the product's production, distribution, advertising, and sales to determine its price.
4. *Advertising and promotion:* developing strategies for reaching customers.
5. *Product distribution:* coordinating all elements of a technical product or service, from conception through final delivery to the customer.
6. *Sales and technical support:* creating and maintaining customer accounts, and servicing and upgrading products.

Engaged in all these activities, the technical marketing professional gains detailed understanding of the industry, the product, and the customer's needs (Figure 1).

Figure 1 The Technical Marketing Process
Source: Selected information from "Services for Clients." Technology Marketing Group, Inc. (1998). <www.technology-marketing.com>

FIGURE 4 *(Continued)*

FEASIBILITY ANALYSIS 3

Employment outlook. For graduates with the right combination of technical and personal qualifications, the outlook for technical marketing (and management) is excellent. Most engineering jobs will increase at less than average for jobs requiring a Bachelor's degree, while marketing and marketing management jobs will exceed the average rate (Figure 2).

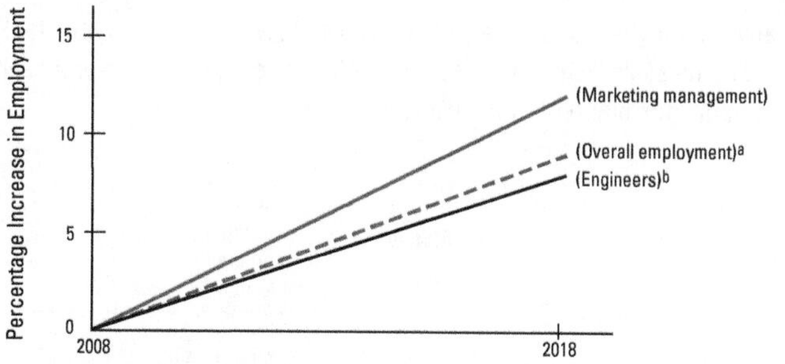

Percentage Increase in Employment
15
10
5
0
2008
2018
(Marketing management)
(Overall employment)[a]
(Engineers)[b]

Visual provides instant comparison

Figure 2 The Employment Outlook for Technical Marketing

[a]Jobs requiring a Bachelor's degree.

[b]Excluding outlying rates for specialties at the positive end of the spectrum (environmental engineers: +31%; biomedical: +72%; civil: +24%; petroleum: +18%).

Source: Data from U.S. Department of Labor. Bureau of Labor Statistics. (2009). http://www.bls.gov/oco/ocos027.htm

Although highly competitive, these marketing positions call for the very kinds of technical, analytical, and problem-solving skills that engineers can offer—especially in an automated environment.

Technical skills required. Interactive Web sites and social media marketing will increasingly influence the way products are advertised and sold. Also marketing representatives increasingly work from a "virtual office." Using laptops, smartphones, and other such devices, representatives out in the field have real-time access to digital catalogs of product lines, multimedia presentations, pricing for customized products, inventory data, product distribution channels, and sales contacts (Tolland, 2010).

With their rich background in computer, technical, and problem-solving skills, engineering graduates are ideally suited for (a) working in automated environments, and (b) implementing and troubleshooting these complex and often sensitive electronic systems.

FIGURE 4 *(Continued)*

For emphasis, select sources are quoted directly

Report is based on primary as well as secondary research

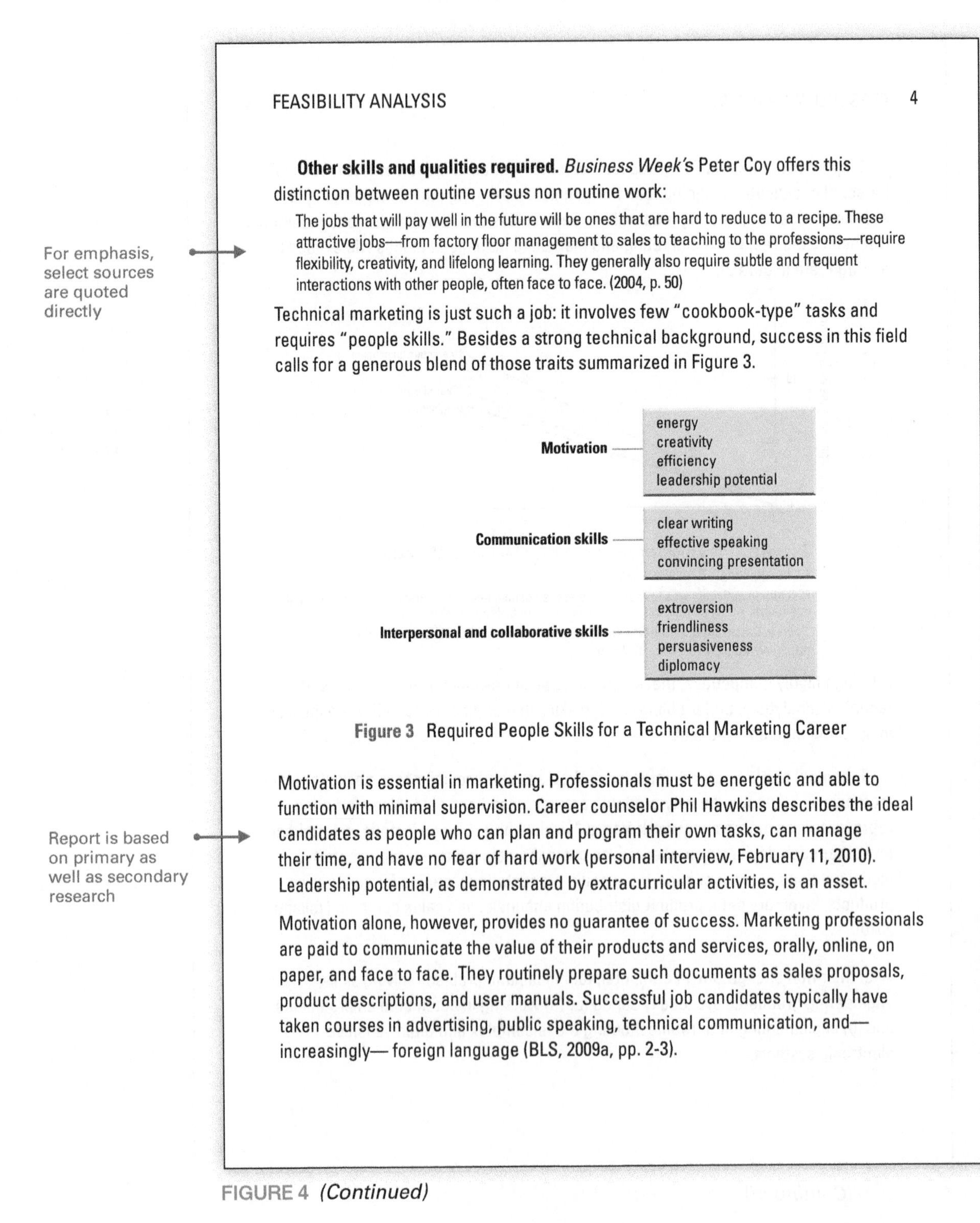
FEASIBILITY ANALYSIS 4

Other skills and qualities required. *Business Week's* Peter Coy offers this distinction between routine versus non routine work:

> The jobs that will pay well in the future will be ones that are hard to reduce to a recipe. These attractive jobs—from factory floor management to sales to teaching to the professions—require flexibility, creativity, and lifelong learning. They generally also require subtle and frequent interactions with other people, often face to face. (2004, p. 50)

Technical marketing is just such a job: it involves few "cookbook-type" tasks and requires "people skills." Besides a strong technical background, success in this field calls for a generous blend of those traits summarized in Figure 3.

Figure 3 Required People Skills for a Technical Marketing Career

Motivation is essential in marketing. Professionals must be energetic and able to function with minimal supervision. Career counselor Phil Hawkins describes the ideal candidates as people who can plan and program their own tasks, can manage their time, and have no fear of hard work (personal interview, February 11, 2010). Leadership potential, as demonstrated by extracurricular activities, is an asset.

Motivation alone, however, provides no guarantee of success. Marketing professionals are paid to communicate the value of their products and services, orally, online, on paper, and face to face. They routinely prepare such documents as sales proposals, product descriptions, and user manuals. Successful job candidates typically have taken courses in advertising, public speaking, technical communication, and—increasingly— foreign language (BLS, 2009a, pp. 2-3).

FIGURE 4 *(Continued)*

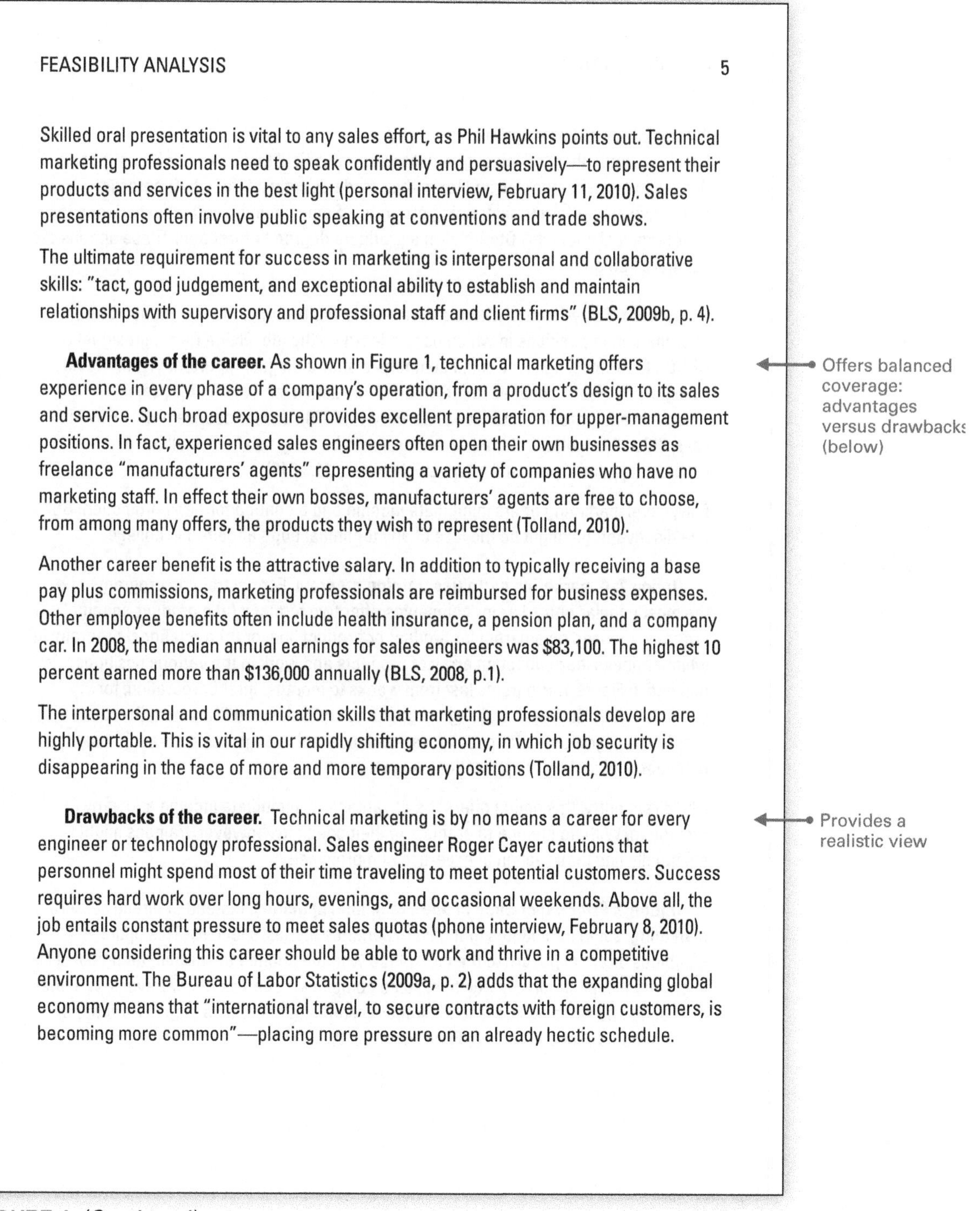

FEASIBILITY ANALYSIS 5

Skilled oral presentation is vital to any sales effort, as Phil Hawkins points out. Technical marketing professionals need to speak confidently and persuasively—to represent their products and services in the best light (personal interview, February 11, 2010). Sales presentations often involve public speaking at conventions and trade shows.

The ultimate requirement for success in marketing is interpersonal and collaborative skills: "tact, good judgement, and exceptional ability to establish and maintain relationships with supervisory and professional staff and client firms" (BLS, 2009b, p. 4).

Advantages of the career. As shown in Figure 1, technical marketing offers experience in every phase of a company's operation, from a product's design to its sales and service. Such broad exposure provides excellent preparation for upper-management positions. In fact, experienced sales engineers often open their own businesses as freelance "manufacturers' agents" representing a variety of companies who have no marketing staff. In effect their own bosses, manufacturers' agents are free to choose, from among many offers, the products they wish to represent (Tolland, 2010).

Another career benefit is the attractive salary. In addition to typically receiving a base pay plus commissions, marketing professionals are reimbursed for business expenses. Other employee benefits often include health insurance, a pension plan, and a company car. In 2008, the median annual earnings for sales engineers was $83,100. The highest 10 percent earned more than $136,000 annually (BLS, 2008, p.1).

The interpersonal and communication skills that marketing professionals develop are highly portable. This is vital in our rapidly shifting economy, in which job security is disappearing in the face of more and more temporary positions (Tolland, 2010).

Drawbacks of the career. Technical marketing is by no means a career for every engineer or technology professional. Sales engineer Roger Cayer cautions that personnel might spend most of their time traveling to meet potential customers. Success requires hard work over long hours, evenings, and occasional weekends. Above all, the job entails constant pressure to meet sales quotas (phone interview, February 8, 2010). Anyone considering this career should be able to work and thrive in a competitive environment. The Bureau of Labor Statistics (2009a, p. 2) adds that the expanding global economy means that "international travel, to secure contracts with foreign customers, is becoming more common"—placing more pressure on an already hectic schedule.

FIGURE 4 *(Continued)*

Each option in the comparison is previewed

Here and below, interpretations clarify the pros and cons of each entry option

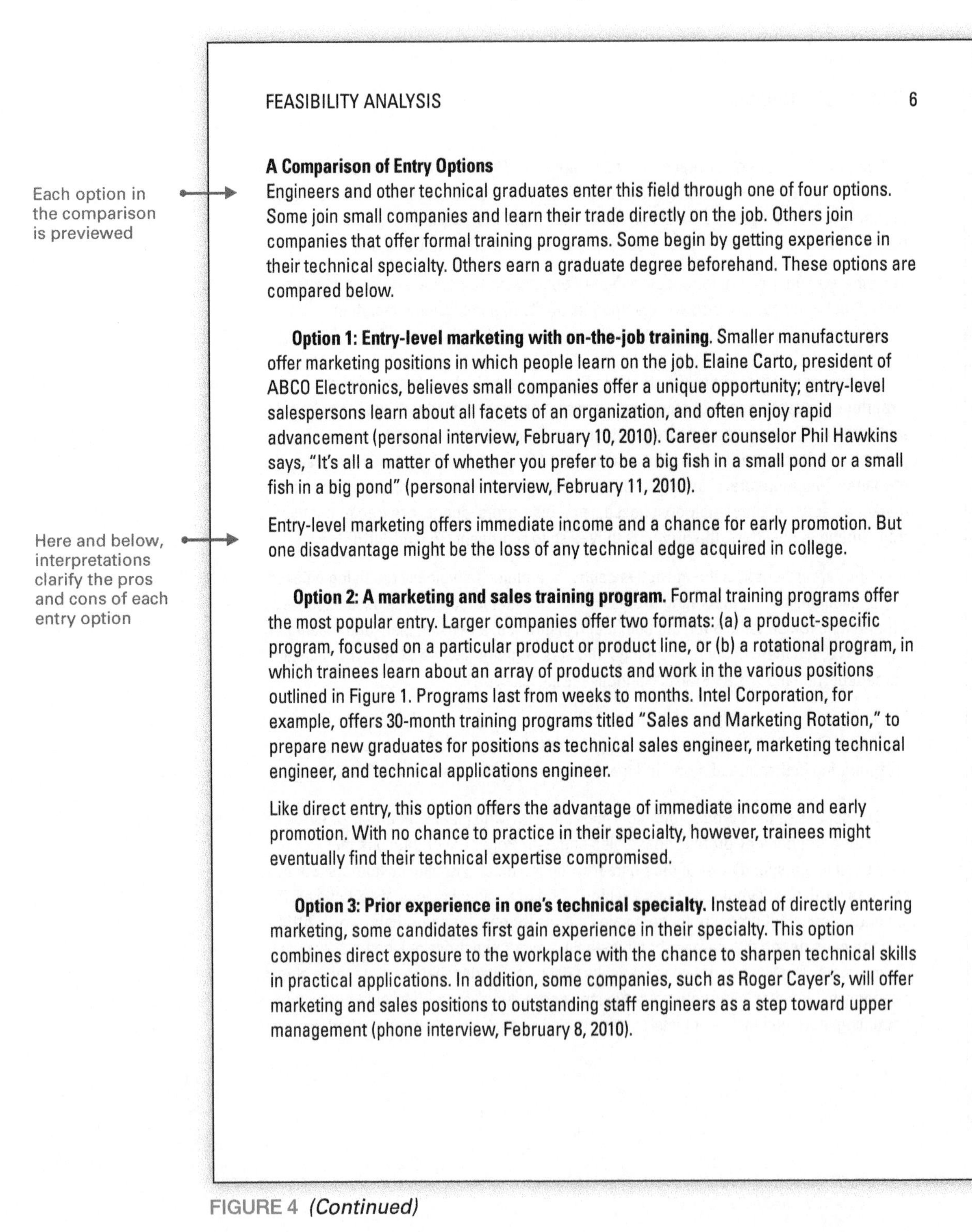

FEASIBILITY ANALYSIS 6

A Comparison of Entry Options

Engineers and other technical graduates enter this field through one of four options. Some join small companies and learn their trade directly on the job. Others join companies that offer formal training programs. Some begin by getting experience in their technical specialty. Others earn a graduate degree beforehand. These options are compared below.

Option 1: Entry-level marketing with on-the-job training. Smaller manufacturers offer marketing positions in which people learn on the job. Elaine Carto, president of ABCO Electronics, believes small companies offer a unique opportunity; entry-level salespersons learn about all facets of an organization, and often enjoy rapid advancement (personal interview, February 10, 2010). Career counselor Phil Hawkins says, "It's all a matter of whether you prefer to be a big fish in a small pond or a small fish in a big pond" (personal interview, February 11, 2010).

Entry-level marketing offers immediate income and a chance for early promotion. But one disadvantage might be the loss of any technical edge acquired in college.

Option 2: A marketing and sales training program. Formal training programs offer the most popular entry. Larger companies offer two formats: (a) a product-specific program, focused on a particular product or product line, or (b) a rotational program, in which trainees learn about an array of products and work in the various positions outlined in Figure 1. Programs last from weeks to months. Intel Corporation, for example, offers 30-month training programs titled "Sales and Marketing Rotation," to prepare new graduates for positions as technical sales engineer, marketing technical engineer, and technical applications engineer.

Like direct entry, this option offers the advantage of immediate income and early promotion. With no chance to practice in their specialty, however, trainees might eventually find their technical expertise compromised.

Option 3: Prior experience in one's technical specialty. Instead of directly entering marketing, some candidates first gain experience in their specialty. This option combines direct exposure to the workplace with the chance to sharpen technical skills in practical applications. In addition, some companies, such as Roger Cayer's, will offer marketing and sales positions to outstanding staff engineers as a step toward upper management (phone interview, February 8, 2010).

FIGURE 4 *(Continued)*

FEASIBILITY ANALYSIS 7

Although the prior-experience option delays entry into technical marketing, industry experts consider direct workplace and technical experience key assets for career growth in any field. Also, work experience becomes an asset for applicants to top MBA programs (Shelley, 1997, pp. 30–31).

Option 4: Graduate program. Instead of direct entry, some people choose to pursue an MS in their specialty or an MBA. According to engineering professor Mary McClane, MS degrees are usually unnecessary for technical marketing unless the particular products are highly complex (personal interview, April 2, 210).

In general, jobseekers with an MBA have a competitive advantage. Also, new MBAs with a technical bachelor's degree and one to two years of experience command salaries from 10 to 30 percent higher than MBAs who lack work experience and a technical bachelor's degree. In fact, no more than 3 percent of candidates offer a "techno-MBA" specialty, making this unique group highly desirable to employers (Shelley, 1997, p. 30). A motivated student might combine graduate degrees. Dora Anson, president of Susimo Systems, sees the MS/MBA combination as ideal preparation for technical marketing (2010).

One disadvantage of a full-time graduate program is lost salary, compounded by school expenses. These costs must be weighed against the prospect of promotion and monetary rewards later in one's career.

Interprets evidence impartially

An overall comparison by relative advantage. Table 1 compares the four entry options on the basis of three criteria: immediate income, rate of advancement, and long-term potential.

Table 1 Relative Advantages Among Four Technical-Marketing Entry Options

Table summarizes the prior information, for instant comparisons

	Relative Advantages		
Option	Early, immediate income	Greatest advancement in marketing	Long-term potential
Entry level, no experience	yes	yes	no
Training program	yes	yes	no
Practical experience	yes	no	yes
Graduate program	no	no	yes

FIGURE 4 *(Continued)*

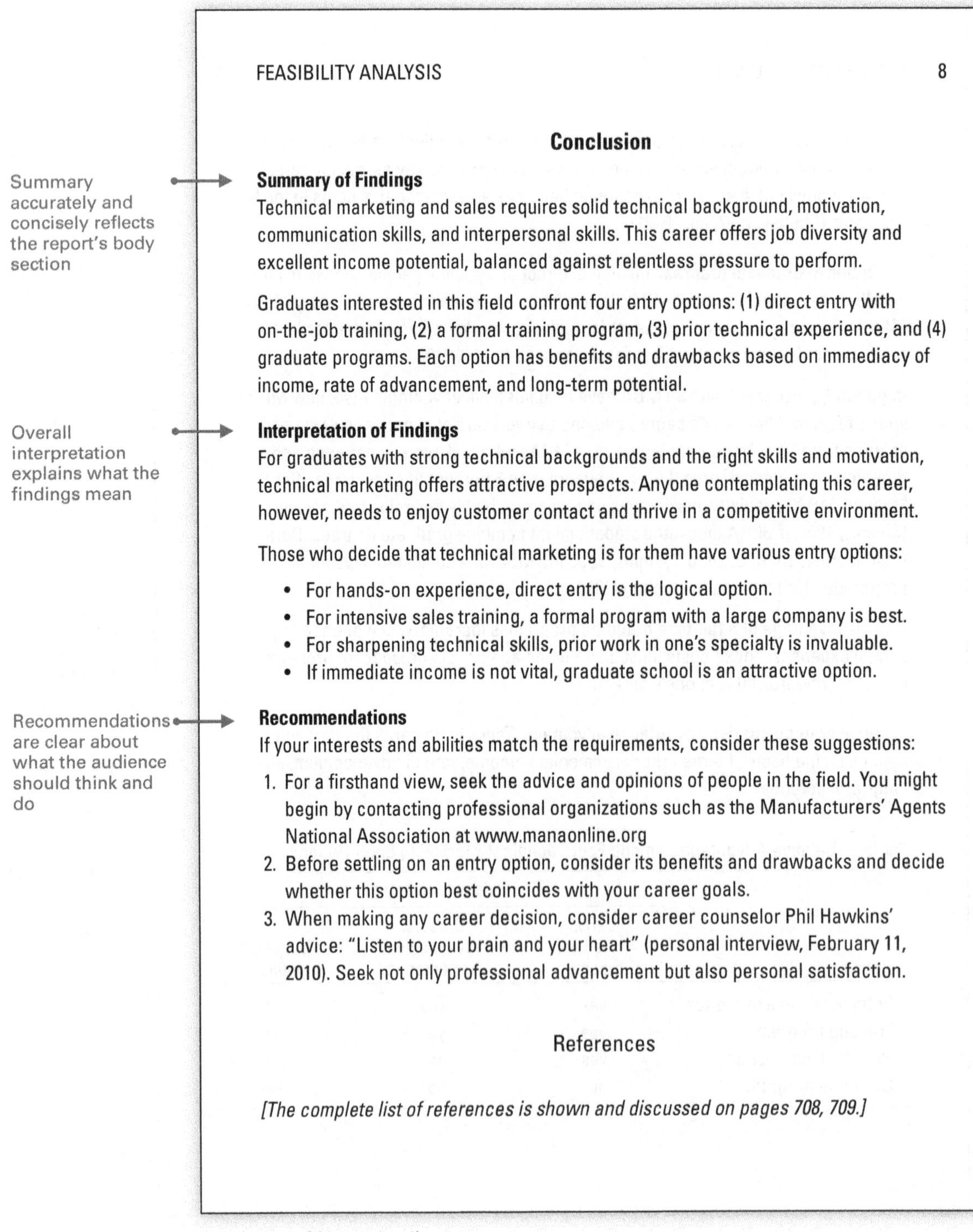

FEASIBILITY ANALYSIS 8

Conclusion

Summary of Findings

Technical marketing and sales requires solid technical background, motivation, communication skills, and interpersonal skills. This career offers job diversity and excellent income potential, balanced against relentless pressure to perform.

Graduates interested in this field confront four entry options: (1) direct entry with on-the-job training, (2) a formal training program, (3) prior technical experience, and (4) graduate programs. Each option has benefits and drawbacks based on immediacy of income, rate of advancement, and long-term potential.

Interpretation of Findings

For graduates with strong technical backgrounds and the right skills and motivation, technical marketing offers attractive prospects. Anyone contemplating this career, however, needs to enjoy customer contact and thrive in a competitive environment.

Those who decide that technical marketing is for them have various entry options:

- For hands-on experience, direct entry is the logical option.
- For intensive sales training, a formal program with a large company is best.
- For sharpening technical skills, prior work in one's specialty is invaluable.
- If immediate income is not vital, graduate school is an attractive option.

Recommendations

If your interests and abilities match the requirements, consider these suggestions:

1. For a firsthand view, seek the advice and opinions of people in the field. You might begin by contacting professional organizations such as the Manufacturers' Agents National Association at www.manaonline.org
2. Before settling on an entry option, consider its benefits and drawbacks and decide whether this option best coincides with your career goals.
3. When making any career decision, consider career counselor Phil Hawkins' advice: "Listen to your brain and your heart" (personal interview, February 11, 2010). Seek not only professional advancement but also personal satisfaction.

References

[The complete list of references is shown and discussed on pages 708, 709.]

FIGURE 4 *(Continued)*

GUIDELINES for Reasoning through an Analytical Problem

Audiences approach an analytical report with this basic question:

> *Is this analysis based on sound reasoning?*

Whether your report documents a causal, comparative, or feasibility analysis (or some combination) you need to trace your line of reasoning so that readers can follow it clearly.

As you prepare your report, refer to the usability checklist and observe the following guidelines:

For Causal Analysis

1. **Be sure the cause fits the effect.** Keep in mind that faulty causal reasoning is extremely common, especially when we ignore other possible causes or when we confuse mere coincidence with causation.
2. **Make the links between effect and cause clear.** Identify the immediate cause (the one most closely related to the effect) as well as the distant cause(s) (the ones that often precede the immediate cause). For example, the immediate cause of a particular airplane crash might be a fuel-tank explosion, caused by a short circuit in frayed wiring, caused by faulty design or poor quality control by the airplane manufacturer. Discussing only the immediate cause often just scratches the surface of the problem.
3. **Clearly distinguish between possible, probable, and definite causes.** Unless the cause is obvious, limit your assertions by using *perhaps, probably, maybe, most likely, could, seems to, appears to,* or similar qualifiers that prevent you from making an insupportable claim. Keep in mind that "certainty" is elusive, especially in causal relationships.

For Comparative Analysis

1. **Rest the comparison on clear and definite criteria: costs, uses, benefits/ drawbacks, appearance, results.** In evaluating the merits of competing items, identify your specific criteria (cost, ease of use, durability, and so on) and rank these criteria in order of importance.
2. **Give each item balanced treatment.** Discuss points of comparison for each item in identical order.
3. **Support and clarify the comparison or contrast through credible examples.** Use research, if necessary, for examples that readers can visualize.
4. **Follow either a block pattern or a point-by-point pattern.** In the block pattern, first one item is discussed fully, then the next. Choose a block pattern when the overall picture is more important than the individual points.

▶▶

GUIDELINES *continued*

In the point-by-point pattern, one point about both items is discussed, then the next point, and so on. Choose a point-by-point pattern when specific points might be hard to remember unless placed side by side.

Block pattern	**Point-by-point pattern**
Item A	first point of A/first point of B, etc.
first point second point, etc.	
Item B	second point of A/second point of B, etc.
first point second point, etc.	

5. **Order your points for greatest emphasis.** Try ordering your points from least to most important or dramatic or useful or reasonable. Placing the most striking point last emphasizes it best.
6. **In an evaluative comparison ("X is better than Y"),** offer your final judgment. Base your judgment squarely on the criteria presented.

For Feasibility Analysis

1. **Consider the strength of supporting reasons.** Choose the best reasons for supporting the action or decision being considered—based on your collected evidence.
2. **Consider the strength of opposing reasons.** Remember that people—including ourselves—usually see only what they want to see. Avoid the temptation to overlook or downplay opposing reasons, especially for an action or decision that you have been promoting. Consider alternate points of view; examine and evaluate all the evidence.
3. **Recommend a realistic course of action.** After weighing all the pros and cons, make your recommendation—but be prepared to reconsider if you discover that what seemed like the right course of action turns out to be the wrong one.

CHECKLIST: Analytical Reports

Content

- ☐ Does the report address a clearly identified problem or purpose?
- ☐ Is the report's length and detail appropriate for the subject?
- ☐ Is there enough information for readers to make an informed decision?
- ☐ Are all limitations of the analysis clearly acknowledged?
- ☐ Is the information accurate, unbiased, and complete?
- ☐ Are visuals used whenever possible to aid communication?
- ☐ Are all data fully interpreted?
- ☐ Are the conclusions logically derived from accurate interpretation?
- ☐ Do the recommendations constitute an appropriate and reasonable response to the question or problem?
- ☐ Is each source and contribution properly cited?
- ☐ Are all needed front and end matter supplements included?

Arrangement

- ☐ Is there a distinct introduction, body, and conclusion?
- ☐ Does the introduction provide sufficient orientation to the issue or problem?
- ☐ Does the body section present a clear picture of the evidence and reasoning?
- ☐ Does the conclusion answer the question that originally sparked the analysis?
- ☐ Are there clear transitions between related ideas?

Style and Page Design

- ☐ Is the level of technicality appropriate for the primary audience?
- ☐ Are headings informative and adequate?
- ☐ Is the writing clear, concise, and fluent?
- ☐ Is the language precise, and informative?
- ☐ Is the report grammatical?
- ☐ Is the page design inviting and accessible?

Chapter quiz, Exercises, Web links, and Flashcards
(Go to *Student Resources>Chapter 23*)
Informal/formal

reports Activities, Case studies, Model documents, and Quiz
(Go to *Technical Communication Documents*)

Projects

GENERAL

Prepare an analytical report, using this procedure:

a. Choose a problem or question for analysis from your major or a subject of interest.
b. Restate the main question as a declarative sentence in your audience and purpose statement.
c. Identify an audience—other than your instructor—who will use your information for a specific purpose.
d. Hold a private brainstorming session to generate major topics and subtopics.
e. Use the topics to make a working outline based on the model outline in this chapter.
f. Make a tentative list of all sources (primary and secondary) that you will investigate. Verify that adequate sources are available.
g. In a proposal memo to your instructor, describe the problem or question and your plan for analysis. Attach a tentative bibliography.
h. Use your working outline as a guide to research.
i. Submit a progress report to your instructor describing work completed, problems encountered, and work remaining.
j. Compose an audience and use profile.
k. Write the report for your stated audience. Work from a clear statement of audience and purpose, and be sure that your reasoning is shown clearly. Verify that your evidence, conclusions, and recommendations are consistent. Be especially careful that your recommendations observe the critical-thinking guidelines in Figure 3.
l. After writing your first draft, make any needed changes in the outline and revise your report according to the revision checklist. Include front matter and end matter.
m. Exchange reports with a classmate for further suggestions for revision.
n. Prepare an oral report of your findings for the class as a whole.

TEAM

1. Divide into small groups. Choose a topic for group analysis—preferably, a campus issue—and brainstorm. Draw up a working outline that could be used as an analytical report on this subject.
2. In the workplace, it is common for reports to be written in teams. Think of an idea for a report for this class that might be a team project. How would you divide the tasks and ensure that the work was being done fairly? What are the advantages and disadvantages of a team approach to a report? In groups of 2–3, discuss these issues. If your instructor indicates that your report is to be team-based, write a memo (as a team) to your instructor indicating the role of each team member and the timeline.

DIGITAL

Many reports, particularly government reports, are turned into PDF documents and are available on the Web. When you have a draft of your report, experiment with turning it into a PDF document or uploading it to a file sharing site (such as *Google Docs* or *iWork.com*) and sending it to others on your team (or to your instructor).

GLOBAL

Use the Internet to look for reports written in English by government agencies of different countries. Look for similarities to the reports you are familiar with in the United States (or the one you are preparing for class), as well as differences in features such as organization, word choice, formatting, use of visuals, levels of politeness, and so on.

For more support in mastering the objectives of this chapter, go to **www.mytechcommlab.com**

dex

references followed by "f" indicate illustrated
s or photographs; followed by "t" indicates a

G

H

I

J

K

L

M

N

O

P

S

T

U

V

W

Y